The Cambridge Companion to Global Rap

Rap has remapped the way we think about music. For more than fifty years its poetics, performance, and political power have resonated across the globe. This Companion offers an array of perspectives on the form, from the fields of sociology, musicology, psychology, criminology, linguistics, literary studies, and education, unpacking how this versatile form of oral communication has permeated nearly every aspect of daily life. Taking a decidedly global perspective, these accounts draw from practice in Australia, China, France, Germany, Jamaica, India, and Tanzania, exploring how the form has taken hold in particular contexts, and what this can tell us about the medium itself and the environments in which it was repurposed. An indispensable resource for students and researchers, the collection provides an introduction to global rap studies as well as insights into some of the most important and exciting new developments in this field.

RICHARD BRAMWELL is Lecturer in Communication and Media Studies at Loughborough University and Senior Member, Wolfson College, University of Cambridge. He is the author of *UK Hip Hop, Grime and the City* (2015). His research has been published in *Popular Music*, *Ethnic and Racial Studies*, and *Identities: Global Studies in Culture and Power*.

ALEX DE LACEY is Assistant Professor in Popular Music, University of Groningen. He is the author of *Level Up: Live Performance and Creative Process in Grime Music* (2023). His research on rap has appeared in *Popular Music*, *Popular Music History*, and *Global Hip Hop Studies*.

Cambridge Companions to Music

Topics

The Cambridge Companion to Ballet
Edited by Marion Kant

The Cambridge Companion to Blues and Gospel Music
Edited by Allan Moore

The Cambridge Companion to Caribbean Music
Edited by Nanette de Jong

The Cambridge Companion to Choral Music
Edited by André de Quadros

The Cambridge Companion to Composition
Edited by Toby Young

The Cambridge Companion to the Concerto
Edited by Simon P. Keefe

The Cambridge Companion to Conducting
Edited by José Antonio Bowen

The Cambridge Companion to Eighteenth-Century Opera
Edited by Anthony R. DelDonna and Pierpaolo Polzonetti

The Cambridge Companion to Electronic Music second edition,
Edited by Nick Collins and Julio D'Escriván

The Cambridge Companion to the 'Eroica' Symphony
Edited by Nancy November

The Cambridge Companion to Film Music
Edited by Mervyn Cooke and Fiona Ford

The Cambridge Companion to French Art Song
Edited by Stephen Rumph

The Cambridge Companion to French Music
Edited by Simon Trezise

The Cambridge Companion to Global Rap
Edited by Richard Bramwell and Alex de Lacey

The Cambridge Companion to Grand Opera
Edited by David Charlton

The Cambridge Companion to Hip-Hop
Edited by Justin A. Williams

The Cambridge Companion to Jazz
Edited by Mervyn Cooke and David Horn

The Cambridge Companion to Jewish Music
Edited by Joshua S. Walden

The Cambridge Companion to K-Pop
Edited by Suk-Young Kim

The Cambridge Companion to Krautrock
Edited by Uwe Schütte

The Cambridge Companion to the Lied
Edited by James Parsons

The Cambridge Companion to *The Magic Flute*
Edited by Jessica Waldoff

The Cambridge Companion to Medieval Music
Edited by Mark Everist

The Cambridge Companion to Metal Music
Edited by Jan-Peter Herbst

The Cambridge Companion to Music and Romanticism
Edited by Benedict Taylor

The Cambridge Companion to Music in Australia
Edited by Amanda Harris and Clint Bracknell

The Cambridge Companion to Music in Digital Culture
Edited by Nicholas Cook, Monique Ingalls and David Trippett

The Cambridge Companion to the Musical, third edition
Edited by William Everett and Paul Laird

The Cambridge Companion to Opera Studies
Edited by Nicholas Till

The Cambridge Companion to Operetta
Edited by Anastasia Belina and Derek B. Scott

The Cambridge Companion to the Orchestra
Edited by Colin Lawson

The Cambridge Companion to Pop and Rock
Edited by Simon Frith, Will Straw and John Street

The Cambridge Companion to Recorded Music
Edited by Eric Clarke, Nicholas Cook, Daniel Leech-Wilkinson and John Rink

The Cambridge Companion to Rhythm
Edited by Russell Hartenberger and Ryan McClelland

The Cambridge Companion to *The Rite of Spring*
Edited by Davinia Caddy

The Cambridge Companion to Schubert's 'Winterreise'
Edited by Marjorie W. Hirsch and Lisa Feurzeig

The Cambridge Companion to Serialism
Edited by Martin Iddon

The Cambridge Companion to Seventeenth-Century Opera
Edited by Jacqueline Waeber

The Cambridge Companion to the Singer-Songwriter
Edited by Katherine Williams and Justin A. Williams

The Cambridge Companion to the String Quartet
Edited by Robin Stowell

The Cambridge Companion to the Symphony
Edited by Julian Horton

The Cambridge Companion to Tango
Edited by Kristin Wendland and Kacey Link

The Cambridge Companion to Twentieth-Century Opera
Edited by Mervyn Cooke

The Cambridge Companion to Video Game Music
Edited by Melanie Fritsch and Tim Summers

The Cambridge Companion to Wagner's *Der Ring des Nibelungen*
Edited by Mark Berry and Nicholas Vazsonyi

The Cambridge Companion to *West Side Story*
Edited by Paul R. Laird and Elizabeth A. Wells

The Cambridge Companion to Women Composers
Edited by Matthew Head and Susan Wollenberg

The Cambridge Companion to Women in Music since 1900
Edited by Laura Hamer

Composers

The Cambridge Companion to Bach
Edited by John Butt

The Cambridge Companion to Bartók
Edited by Amanda Bayley

The Cambridge Companion to Amy Beach
Edited by E. Douglas Bomberger

The Cambridge Companion to the Beatles
Edited by Kenneth Womack

The Cambridge Companion to Beethoven
Edited by Glenn Stanley

The Cambridge Companion to Berg
Edited by Anthony Pople

The Cambridge Companion to Berlioz
Edited by Peter Bloom

The Cambridge Companion to Brahms
Edited by Michael Musgrave

The Cambridge Companion to Benjamin Britten
Edited by Mervyn Cooke

The Cambridge Companion to Bruckner
Edited by John Williamson

The Cambridge Companion to John Cage
Edited by David Nicholls

The Cambridge Companion to Chopin
Edited by Jim Samson

The Cambridge Companion to Debussy
Edited by Simon Trezise

The Cambridge Companion to Elgar
Edited by Daniel M. Grimley and Julian Rushton

The Cambridge Companion to Duke Ellington
Edited by Edward Green

The Cambridge Companion to Gershwin
Edited by Anna Celenza

The Cambridge Companion to Gilbert and Sullivan
Edited by David Eden and Meinhard Saremba

The Cambridge Companion to Handel
Edited by Donald Burrows

The Cambridge Companion to Haydn
Edited by Caryl Clark

The Cambridge Companion to Liszt
Edited by Kenneth Hamilton

The Cambridge Companion to Mahler
Edited by Jeremy Barham

The Cambridge Companion to Mendelssohn
Edited by Peter Mercer-Taylor

The Cambridge Companion to Monteverdi
Edited by John Whenham and Richard Wistreich

The Cambridge Companion to Mozart
Edited by Simon P. Keefe

The Cambridge Companion to Arvo Pärt
Edited by Andrew Shenton

The Cambridge Companion to Ravel
Edited by Deborah Mawer

The Cambridge Companion to the Rolling Stones
Edited by Victor Coelho and John Covach

The Cambridge Companion to Rossini
Edited by Emanuele Senici

The Cambridge Companion to Schoenberg
Edited by Jennifer Shaw and Joseph Auner

The Cambridge Companion to Schubert
Edited by Christopher Gibbs

The Cambridge Companion to Schumann
Edited by Beate Perrey

The Cambridge Companion to Shostakovich
Edited by Pauline Fairclough and David Fanning

The Cambridge Companion to Sibelius
Edited by Daniel M. Grimley

The Cambridge Companion to Richard Strauss
Edited by Charles Youmans

The Cambridge Companion to Stravinsky
Edited by Jonathan Cross

The Cambridge Companion to Michael Tippett
Edited by Kenneth Gloag and Nicholas Jones

The Cambridge Companion to Vaughan Williams
Edited by Alain Frogley and Aiden J. Thomson

The Cambridge Companion to Verdi
Edited by Scott L. Balthazar

The Cambridge Companion to Wagner
Edited by Thomas S. Grey

Instruments

The Cambridge Companion to Brass Instruments
Edited by Trevor Herbert and John Wallace

The Cambridge Companion to the Cello
Edited by Robin Stowell

The Cambridge Companion to the Clarinet
Edited by Colin Lawson

The Cambridge Companion to the Drum Kit
Edited by Matt Brennan, Joseph Michael Pignato and Daniel Akira Stadnicki

The Cambridge Companion to the Electric Guitar
Edited by Jan-Peter Herbst and Steve Waksman

The Cambridge Companion to the Guitar
Edited by Victor Coelho

The Cambridge Companion to the Harpsichord
Edited by Mark Kroll

The Cambridge Companion to the Organ
Edited by Nicholas Thistlethwaite and Geoffrey Webber

The Cambridge Companion to Percussion
Edited by Russell Hartenberger

The Cambridge Companion to the Piano
Edited by David Rowland

The Cambridge Companion to the Saxophone
Edited by Richard Ingham

The Cambridge Companion to Singing
Edited by John Potter

The Cambridge Companion to the Violin
Edited by Robin Stowell

The Cambridge Companion to Global Rap

Edited by

RICHARD BRAMWELL
Loughborough University

ALEX DE LACEY
University of Groningen

Shaftesbury Road, Cambridge CB2 8EA, United Kingdom

One Liberty Plaza, 20th Floor, New York, NY 10006, USA

477 Williamstown Road, Port Melbourne, VIC 3207, Australia

314–321, 3rd Floor, Plot 3, Splendor Forum, Jasola District Centre, New Delhi – 110025, India

103 Penang Road, #05–06/07, Visioncrest Commercial, Singapore 238467

Cambridge University Press is part of Cambridge University Press & Assessment, a department of the University of Cambridge.

We share the University's mission to contribute to society through the pursuit of education, learning and research at the highest international levels of excellence.

www.cambridge.org
Information on this title: www.cambridge.org/9781316515266

DOI: 10.1017/9781009099738

© Cambridge University Press & Assessment 2025

This publication is in copyright. Subject to statutory exception and to the provisions of relevant collective licensing agreements, no reproduction of any part may take place without the written permission of Cambridge University Press & Assessment.

When citing this work, please include a reference to the DOI 10.1017/9781009099738

First published 2025

A catalogue record for this publication is available from the British Library

Library of Congress Cataloging-in-Publication Data
Names: Bramwell, Richard, 1977– editor. | De Lacey, Alex, editor.
Title: The Cambridge companion to global rap / edited by Richard Bramwell, Alex de Lacey.
Description: [1.] | Cambridge, United Kingdom ; New York, NY : Cambridge University Press, 2025. | Series: Cambridge companions to music | Includes bibliographical references and index.
Identifiers: LCCN 2024058998 (print) | LCCN 2024058999 (ebook) | ISBN 9781316515266 (hardback) | ISBN 9781009096553 (paperback) | ISBN 9781009099738 (ebook)
Subjects: LCSH: Rap (Music) – History and criticism. | Rap (Music) – Social aspects. | Hip-hop.
Classification: LCC ML3531 .C355 2025 (print) | LCC ML3531 (ebook) | DDC 782.421649–dc23/eng/20241209
LC record available at https://lccn.loc.gov/2024058998
LC ebook record available at https://lccn.loc.gov/2024058999

ISBN 978-1-316-51526-6 Hardback
ISBN 978-1-009-09655-3 Paperback

Cambridge University Press & Assessment has no responsibility for the persistence or accuracy of URLs for external or third-party internet websites referred to in this publication and does not guarantee that any content on such websites is, or will remain, accurate or appropriate.

For EU product safety concerns, contact us at Calle de José Abascal, 56, 1°, 28003 Madrid, Spain, or email eugpsr@cambridge.org

Dedicated to the memory of Benedict Okwuchukwu Godwin Chijioke, also known as Ty (1972–2020)

Contents

List of Figures [*page* xiii]
Notes on Contributors [xiv]

Introduction
RICHARD BRAMWELL AND ALEX DE LACEY [1]

PART I HISTORICAL AND CULTURAL PERSPECTIVES [15]

1   Travelling Sounds: Tracing the Global Origins of Rhythm
    And Poetry
    PAROMA GHOSE [17]
2   A History of Sound System and Emcee Culture
    MARVIN SPARKS [34]

PART II APPROACHES TO RAP [47]

3   *Beats, Rhymes and Life*: Connecting the Sonic and the Social
    in Hip-Hop Music Studies
    J. GRIFFITH ROLLEFSON [49]
4   'Listen When I Flip the Linguistics': Linguistic Approaches to Rap
    and the Case of 2Pac
    STEVEN GILBERS [72]
5   Pioneers, Postmodernisms and Aesthetic Experience: A Brief
    History of Aesthetic Approaches to Rap Music
    MAX RYYNÄNEN AND PETTERI ENROTH [88]
6   The Literary Singularity of Roots Manuva's *Awfully Deep*
    RICHARD BRAMWELL [100]
7   The French (Hip-Hop) Revolution Is Yet to Come: A Sociology
    of Rap Music in France
    KARIM HAMMOU AND MARIE SONNETTE-
    MANOUGUIAN [113]

PART III APPLICATIONS OF RAP [125]

8   Lords of the Mic: Live Collective Performance in Grime Music
    ALEX DE LACEY   [127]
9   Hip-Hop and Mental Health: Perspectives from Psychiatry, Psychology, Public Health, and Neuroscience
    AKEEM SULE AND BECKY INKSTER   [144]
10 The Beat of the Gavel: Rap, 'Race', and Criminal Injustice
    LAMBROS FATSIS   [158]
11 Express Yourself: Education and Wellbeing in Australian Applied Hip-Hop Workshops
    DIANNE RODGER   [168]
12 Rap to Skool: Hip-Hop in the Classroom
    PATRICK TURNER   [181]

PART IV CONTEXTS FOR RAP [195]

13 Honoring the Honorable: Tanzanian Hip-Hop Artists, Award Shows, and the Power of Popular Song
    ALEX PERULLO   [197]
14 'It Will Never Go Away': Re-imagining Black German Identity in 'Ich Bin Schwarz'
    SINA A. NITZSCHE AND LAURA I. K. SPILKER   [211]
15 The Art of Capping: Exploring Digital Cloutchasing Strategy of Black Male Youth in Chicago's Drill Rap Scene
    JABARI EVANS   [225]
16 Drill as Cultural Form: Video-Music, Chromatism, War and the Alternative
    MALCOLM JAMES   [236]
17 English Rap in India and the Fault Lines of Sociolinguistic Politics
    ELLOIT CARDOZO AND JASPAL NAVEEL SINGH   [249]
18 Television and the Janus Face of Chinese Hip-Hop: Style, Ideology, and Precarious Syncretization in *The Rap of China*
    SHENG ZOU   [261]

Selected Bibliography   [273]
Index   [282]

Figures

3.1 Musical transcription of the opening groove of 'Fight the Power'. (Courtesy of Robert Walser) [*page* 58]
3.2 Flow map of Poor Righteous Teachers' 'Ghetto We Love'. (Courtesy of Felicia Miyakawa) [61]
3.3 Flow map for 'Wu Gambinos' showing rhythmic patterning as well as rhyme schemes (color coded). (Courtesy of Kyle Adams) [63]
3.4 Notation of a basic reggaeton beat using DAW-style tick boxes. (Courtesy of Wayne Marshall) [65]
3.5 Screenshot of Solareye's hip-hop 'literature review' from the lyric video 'Rap Academics', 2022. (Courtesy of Solareye) [66]
3.6 Hand-drawn visual analysis of Lisa 'Left Eye' Lopes on 'Waterfalls', 1994. (Courtesy of Kjell Oddekalv) [67]
4.1a Sixty-fourth note heat map baselines for West Coast and East Coast rap. Transcription by Author. [83]
4.1b Sixty-fourth note heat map averages for 2Pac's pre-Death Row era and his Death Row era. Transcription by Author. [83]
8.1 Chipmunk on F**k Radio. Transcription by Author. [135]
8.2 Lil Nasty on F**k Radio. Transcription by Author. [135]
8.3 Griminal on F**k Radio. Transcription by Author. [137]
8.4 Ghetts on F**k Radio. Transcription by Author. [137]
13.1 Tanzanian rap artists who won TMAs in multiple years 2002–2015, 2022. Compiled by Author. [207]

Notes on Contributors

RICHARD BRAMWELL is Lecturer in Media and Communication at Loughborough University. Richard's research interests are focused around the areas of black British vernacular and popular cultures. His research has been published in *Popular Music*, *Ethnic and Racial Studies*, and *Identities: Global Studies in Culture and Power*. He is the author of *UK Hip Hop, Grime and the City* (Routledge, 2015).

ELLOIT CARDOZO is a fellow at Maulana Abul Kalam Azad Institute of Asian Studies (MAKAIAS) and teaches the module on hip-hop and research for the University of Mumbai's certificate in 'Introduction to Hip-Hop Studies' course. His research interests include Indian hip-hop studies, film studies, and popular culture.

ALEX DE LACEY is Assistant Professor in Popular Music at the University of Groningen. He is the author of *Level Up: Live Performance and Creative Process in Grime Music* (Routledge, 2023). His research on rap music has been published in *Popular Music*, *Popular Music History*, and *Global Hip Hop Studies*, among other volumes. He is also a practicing DJ and a live performer with grime collective Over the Edge.

PETTERI ENROTH is a freelance critic, writer, and independent academic with interests in popular culture, everyday aesthetics, sound and media art, and critical theory. He graduated from the University of Helsinki's Aesthetics Department in 2011 with a thesis on Theodor W. Adorno's aesthetics.

JABARI EVANS is Assistant Professor of Race and Media at the University of South Carolina in the School of Journalism and Mass Communication (SJMC). His research focuses on the digital subcultures that urban youth and young adults of colour develop and inhabit to understand their social environments, promote their identity development, and pursue their professional aspirations. His forthcoming book project, *Hip-Hop Civics* (University of Michigan Press) centres on a hip-hop–based education programme in Chicago Public Schools and argues for rap song making's utility for fostering connected learning in the formal classroom. Outside of academia, Dr Evans has enjoyed a decorated career spanning two decades as a hip-hop performer, songwriter, and producer performing and collaborating with Grammy-award-winning artists under the moniker of 'Naledge' in the rap group Kidz in the Hall.

LAMBROS FATSIS is Senior Lecturer in Criminology at City, University of London. Fusing cultural criminology and Black radical thought, his research focuses on police racism and the criminalisation of Black/Afro-diasporic music(s) from the era of colonial slavery to the present day. Lambros is also a member of the Prosecuting Rap experts' network, the Art, Not Evidence campaign, and an advisor at the youth-music charity, AudioActive.

PAROMA GHOSE is a sociocultural historian, currently working with the CONDE project at the Leibniz Institute for Contemporary History, Munich, as a postdoctoral researcher. Her work predominantly looks at music as political expression and consequence, on both national and global levels. Her PhD used the lyrics of French rap to write a history of the 'Other' in France (1981–2012). Her postdoctoral work looks at postcolonial voices in music and the shaping of the modern world, using South Korean popular music (1987–present) as its principal lens.

STEVEN GILBERS is Assistant Professor in the field of hip-hop linguistics at the University of Groningen who specialises in the connection between language and music in a hip-hop context as well as regional variation in African-American English and rap flows from the American West Coast and East Coast. In 2021, he successfully defended his doctoral dissertation on 2Pac's changing accent and flow. Gilbers is a former Fulbright Visiting Scholar at New York University and the University of California, Los Angeles where he worked with Renée Blake and H. Samy Alim. Aside from his academic endeavours, he is also active as a rapper and producer, and is involved with Dutch hip-hop platform Homebase.

KARIM HAMMOU is Research Fellow at the CNRS, and a member of the Centre for Sociological and Political Research of Paris (CRESPPA-CSU). He authored *Une histoire du rap en France* (*A History of French Rap Music*, 2022) and co-authored with Cara Zina *Fear of a Female Planet. Straight Royeur: un son punk, rap et féministe* (a punk, rap, and feminist sound, 2021).

BECKY INKSTER has spent over twenty years in academia running multimillion-pound projects across a wide range of topics including neuroscience and mental health. She obtained her DPhil in psychiatry at Oxford University and is currently affiliated with the Department of Psychiatry at Cambridge University. Becky has sat on the International Advisory Board for Lancet Digital Health for over five years. She is a co-founder of Hip Hop Psych with over ten years' experience merging her lifelong passions of hip-hop and mental health. She has further broadened her skills to include artificial intelligence, creative computing, and responsible technological innovation through her more recent work and has since worked with numerous international universities, over 100 companies, and different governments. She is Head of Science at Arts ARKADE, a new store in the heart of London, dedicated to supporting youth in forward-thinking ways.

MALCOLM JAMES is Senior Lecturer in Media and Cultural Studies, and Co-director of Sussex Centre for Cultural Studies, at the University of Sussex. He is interested in how minor keys of freedom and liberation are sustained in popular culture. He has explored this in his writing on everyday life, sound and music, and race and postcoloniality; and, through his collaborations with youth clubs, activist and community groups. He is author of *Sonic Intimacy: Reggae Sound Systems, Jungle Pirate Radio and Grime YouTube Music Videos* (Bloomsbury, 2021) and *Urban Multiculture: Youth, Politics and Cultural Transformation* (Palgrave, 2015); and co-editor of *Regeneration Songs: Sounds of Investment and Loss in East London* (Repeater, 2018). He has written for *The Guardian*, *Tribune*, *Salvage*, *Red Pepper*, *Open Democracy* and has contributed to BBC Radio 4 *The Listening Project* and BBC Asian Network.

SINA A. NITZSCHE is Honorary Research Fellow of Hip Hop Studies in the Department of Music at the University of Bristol. Her research focuses on mediated knowledge practices in Afro-diasporic rap music as well as discourses around institutionalisation and legitimisation of hip-hop culture in Europe and beyond. She founded the European Hiphop Studies Network and is editor of the journal *Global Hip Hop Studies*. Her books include *Poetic Resurrection: The Bronx in American Popular Culture* (transcript, 2020), *Popular Music and Public Diplomacy: Transnational and Transdisciplinary Perspectives* (transcript, 2018), and *Hip-Hop in Europe: Cultural Identities and Transnational Flows* (LIT, 2013).

ALEX PERULLO is Professor of Anthropology at Bryant University in Rhode Island. He has a variety of publications including an ethnography *Live from Dar es Salaam: Popular Music and Tanzania's Music Economy* and a box set of 1940s and 1950s African music titled 'Listen All Around'. He is currently writing a series of articles studying post-pandemic life in Tanzania that focuses on the ways that different populations, including street sellers, transport drivers, and artists, attempt to earn a living in highly competitive and overcrowded urban environments.

DIANNE RODGER is Senior Lecturer in Anthropology at the University of Adelaide. Her research primarily focuses on hip-hop culture in Australia including: processes of localisation and authentication, hip-hop education, and, the experiences of First Nations practitioners. She is currently researching 'Australian' histories of hip-hop, work that also informs her book *The Calling* (2023). She is co-editor of the first edited book to explore hip-hop in Australia (*Representing Hip Hop Histories, Politics and Practices in Australia*, 2024).

J. GRIFFITH ROLLEFSON is Professor of Music at University College Cork, National University of Ireland. He is the author of the award-winning *Flip the Script: European Hip Hop and the Politics of Postcoloniality* (University of Chicago Press, 2017) and *Critical Excess: Watch the Throne and the New Gilded Age* (University of Michigan Press, 2021). Rollefson is Principal Investigator of the ERC hip-hop knowledge mapping project, CIPHER: Hip Hop Interpellation, and founding co-editor (with University of Cape Town's Adam Haupt) of the journal *Global Hip Hop Studies*.

MAX RYYNÄNEN is Principal University Lecturer at Aalto University in Finland, and Adjunct Professor at the Universities of Helsinki, Jyväskylä, and Eastern Finland. His research interests include popular culture, body culture, and cultural scenes. Webpage: http://maxryynanen.net.

JASPAL NAVEEL SINGH is a hip-hop head and critical knowledge producer, who has lived and worked in Germany, Wales, India, and Hong Kong. He currently works as Lecturer in Applied Linguistics and English Language at the Open University. Jaspal has widely published on the intersections of language and global hip-hop, including his linguistic-ethnographic monograph *Transcultural Voices: Narrating Hip Hop Culture in Complex Delhi* (Multilingual Matters, 2022) and the cutting-edge anthology *Global Hiphopography* (Palgrave Macmillan, 2023), which he co-edited with Quentin Williams from the University of the Western Cape.

MARIE SONNETTE-MANOUGUIAN is Associate Professor at the University of Angers, attached to the ESO laboratory (CNRS, France). As a sociologist of culture, her work focuses on hip-hop music. With Karim Hammou, she co-edited and co-authored *40 ans de musiques hip-hop en France* (*40 Years of Hip-Hop Music in France*) published in 2022 by Presses de Sciences Po.

MARVIN SPARKS is the author of the critically acclaimed *Run the Riddim: The Untold Story of 90s Dancehall to the World*, podcaster and lifelong student of various musical genres, specialising in Jamaican dancehall and the fruits of sound system culture. As a London-born, second-generation Jamaican, much of his writing reflects the cultural melting pot he was raised in.

LAURA I. K. SPILKER is an editorial assistant at TU Dortmund University. Her research interests include hip-hop femininities and LGBTQ+ young adult literature. She studies Gender Studies at the Ruhr University Bochum and British and Postcolonial Studies at the University of Duisburg-Essen.

AKEEM SULE is a co-founder of Hiphoppsych and a locum consultant psychiatrist at Essex Partnership University NHS Foundation Trust. He has interests in hip-hop, psychotherapies, film, and TV shows. Akeem is a college research associate at Wolfson College and Honorary Clinical Research Associate in the Department of Psychiatry at the University of Cambridge.

PATRICK TURNER is Senior Lecturer in Sociology at Bath Spa University. He researches and teaches on culture, class, race, and the politics of identity. Theoretically, his work is informed by cultural materialism, critical realism, and phenomenology, and he has employed a range of qualitative research methodologies. He is the author of the book *Hip Hop versus Rap: The Politics of Droppin' Knowledge*, published by Routledge.

SHENG ZOU (PhD, Stanford University) is Assistant Professor at the School of Communication, Hong Kong Baptist University, and concurrently a center associate of the Lieberthal-Rogel Center for Chinese Studies at the University of Michigan. He is broadly interested in critical theory, political aesthetics, digital media and society, cultural industries, and global communication. Through comparative and transnational perspectives, his current work explores the politics of cultural production (e.g., musical and digital screen cultures) and aesthetic approaches to popular propaganda.

Introduction

RICHARD BRAMWELL AND ALEX DE LACEY

On Sunday, June 25, 2023, Busta Rhymes received a lifetime achievement award at the 23rd BET Awards held in Los Angeles, California. After a fiery rendition of M.O.P. classic 'Ante Up', East Flatbush's finest worked through the classics, bringing along a star-studded line-up of guests that included Massachusetts-born BIA – for the single 'Beach Ball' – and fast-rising Coi Leray for their track 'Players'. Halfway through, the music cuts, and the cameras focus on Busta, clad in his gleaming white suit. *'Be clear, we be celebrating Hip Hop 50'* said Busta. *'[but] Kool Herc, the founding father of hip-hop, he's a bloodclaat Jamaican. Make sure you know that. So as much as we going to represent hip-hop tonight, we're going to represent this dancehall culture. All Caribbean people haffi get up, haffi tun up.'* The LED wall behind the performers suddenly lights up, with twenty-foot-tall graphics of bassbins and tweeters doused in red, yellow and green, widely recognised as the colours of Rastafari. Dexta Daps launches himself onto the stage to perform 'Shabba Madda Pot', before dancehall royalty Super Cat, Cutty Ranks, the 'Queen of the Dancehall' Spice and man-of-the-moment Skillibeng take to the stage.

Although only afforded ten minutes to acknowledge this heritage, Busta's honouring of the Caribbean points to the myriad intersections and overlaps between Caribbean and African-American cultural practice: a timely reminder that origin stories, while useful and important, often smooth over the complex and multifaceted histories that result in approaches to practice today.

Aims of the Volume

As we write this introduction, Hip Hop 50 celebrations are in full swing across the United States and the world. The Yankee stadium was turned inside out by a star-studded cast on August 11, 2023; *Men's Health* magazine ran a feature with 50 Cent and Method Man to celebrate; while KRS-ONE could be seen sidling up to controversial New York mayor Eric Adams to launch the '5X5 Block Party Series', celebrating five decades of rap across the five boroughs, Brooklyn, Queens, Staten Island, the Bronx and Harlem.[1] At this important juncture in the history of hip-hop, this volume calls for both a deepening and a widening of our gaze. First, it calls for a deepening, through a focus on rap – a distinct component of hip-hop – to appreciate the rich history of this culture. Second, it calls for a widening, to bring into focus the global significance of this verbal art form. Rap has travelled far from hip-hop's origins in deindustrialised New York, to Europe, Asia, Oceania, Africa and beyond. While this oral form made an important contribution to the culture fashioned by African-American, Latin-American, and Caribbean youths, during the 1970s, hip-hop itself has become a multi-billion-dollar world-wide industry and plays a significant role in cultural diplomacy, with figures such as Toni Blackman acting as hip-hop ambassador to the US State Department, and Def Jam mogul Russell Simmons working as a Goodwill Ambassador to the UN since 2009. These global developments highlight the importance of a musical culture that remains vitally important and relevant to the lives of people across the planet.

Our call for an acknowledgement of the significance of global rap does not diminish the importance of hip-hop's other elements, breakdancing, DJing and graffiti. All of them deserve recognition, both in their own right and as fundamental components of hip-hop culture. Nor does it devalue the organic ties that hip-hop has to the communities from which it emerged. In this volume we attempt to provide space for a consideration of the distinctive contribution that rap has made to contemporary culture, both within hip-hop and beyond it. Rap has become more and more ubiquitous as the decades pass. Rap music is a mainstream commercial genre. Recordings are used in film, television and video-game soundtracks and rap artists have become ambassadors for organisations such as the US State Department, the British Council and numerous charities. Alongside this mainstream recognition, rap is deeply embedded in the everyday lives of ordinary citizens and denizens. It forms a vibrant aspect of many youth cultures, and the performance, circulation and viewing of rap songs and music videos via social media, radio and television plays an influential role in the social and cultural development of young people across the globe.

Reflecting its social, political and cultural importance, rap has become a common topic for study in university courses. There is a plethora of scholarly works on rap, which approach this verbal art form from a variety of perspectives. This volume provides an introduction to global rap. It begins with a cultural history, before exploring some of the key disciplinary approaches to the study of rap. We then highlight how rap is used beyond academia, in areas such as public health, the criminal justice system and education. Finally the book turns to the varied contexts in which rap is produced, circulated, received and interpreted. Throughout the book the distinct influences of the national, transnational, or diasporic contexts for rap culture and those who participate in it are shown to be vitally apparent. Busta Rhymes's call for recognition of dancehall is prudent, but this story should encompass the full spectrum of rap as a verbal art. While the *Companion* opens with a consideration of rap's history as an oral practice and the shaping of emcee culture through the sound system, it closes with an examination of mediated performances of rap on television and social media, as well as within the recording industry in contrasting contexts.

In closing the collection with these divergent arenas (including Germany, China, India, Tanzania and the United States), we hope to make the case for a continuation of the conversation around rap in a global context: the ways in which transnational, translocal and glocal versionings of this practice fold in autochthonous elements, *alongside* received histories of practice (be it of hip-hop or rap more generally), while remaining contingent on particular social and political contexts. In Sheng Zou's chapter on talent shows in China, he makes clear that it is quite simply impossible to offer a comprehensive history of rap's emergence in the country, owing to varying underground tributaries across multiple cities. Instead, Zou prefers to see this history as rhizomatic, with a proliferation domestically through different nodes at different points in time. While we are not here to engage in ahistorical revisionism, we might extend this provocation to August 11, 1973, and – in particular – question what uncritical lionising of particular moments, and moreover people, entails.

In a provocative piece for the Wall Street Journal a week ahead of the fabled anniversary, Dan Charnas – author of *The Big Payback* and *Dilla Time* – refers to the inaugural party in the Bronx as 'engendered [with] embellishments, emphasising one figure ... erasing those who came before and after'.[2] He goes on to highlight DJ Hollywood's parties in Harlem back in 1968 where he talked over records. Charnas also notes that many of the innovations attributed to Herc cannot be fully validated, with DJ Rob Swift quoted as saying that the 'merry-go round technique' attributed to Herc might have more accurately been credited to Grandmaster Flash. Elsewhere, Arusha Quershi's vital intervention *Flip The Script: How Women Came to Rule Hip Hop* (2021) strongly advocates for the women who get written out of rap histories in favour of their male counterparts: from Debbie D of the Juice Crew to Pebblee Poo of the Herculoids and Lisa Lee of the Universal Zulu Nation.[3]

The strategy of centring particular individuals in the writing of the cultural history of rap inevitably marginalises others within those narratives. More pertinently, the centring of these key figures can, unfortunately, mean that serious wrongdoings are erased or overlooked in a bid to maintain the mysticism around these formative moments. Afrika Bambaataa, a celebrated figure within hip-hop culture, was appointed to a visiting scholarship at Cornell University, in 2012. To our knowledge, no scholarly work on hip-hop has addressed the multiple allegations that he has faced since 2016, regarding sexual abuse and trafficking of young men dating back to the 1990s.[4] The Zulu Nation, which was founded by Bambaataa, holds particular weight in the global rap community. Notably in France, where the Zulu Nation's activities stretch back as far as 1982, with their visit to Paris with assistance from rock personalities Bernard Zekri and Jean Karakos. While Bambaataa stepped down from the organisation following the first wave of allegations in 2016, the Universal Hip Hop Museum in the Bronx has since come under fire for its executive director Rocky Bucano's alleged ties to the Zulu Nation. A 2023 protest organised by the advocacy organisation 'Hip Hop Stands with Survivors' pushed back against public funding of the venture, with co-founder Leila Wills citing the 're-traumatizing [of] survivors'.[5] The risks of lionising key figures is not limited to those seen to pioneer the form at its outset. Russell Simmons has faced multiple allegations of sexual assault. A $10 million lawsuit against Simmons raised in 2018 was eventually dropped because it fell outside the statute of limitations, as it related to a case from 1988.[6] At the time of writing, Simmons remains in his role for the UN. A great deal of hip-hop scholarship highlights the agency of those who are marginalised within wider society. However, the silence regarding these hidden histories within (academic) accounts of hip-hop raises questions about hip-hop studies and the position that scholars take in relation to those that have been marginalised, exploited or abused within hip-hop.

These concerns, as with this volume's scope, are of course not limited to rap in a North American context. A number of this *Companion*'s chapters – notably de Lacey and James – explore grime music, the hybrid of dancehall, ragga, hip-hop and UK garage that emerged from the United Kingdom at the turn of the millennium. Its key figures include Wiley, Dizzee Rascal and Skepta. In recent years, grime's 'godfather' Wiley has been criticised strongly for a string of antisemitic tweets, one of which likened Jewish people to the Ku Klux Klan.[7] Notably for this volume's consideration of key moments, twentieth-anniversary celebrations of Dizzee Rascal's landmark album *Boy in Da Corner* have eclipsed his domestic violence conviction, in

April 2022, which resulted from a violent confrontation with his ex-partner.[8] Of course, denying Bambaataa's contributions to hip-hop or minimising Dizzee Rascal's to grime would be ahistorical, but choosing to speak about their role in the histories of rap and grime without reckoning with such serious allegations risks placing figures who have caused significant harm in positions where they are beyond criticism.

We hope that by highlighting the breadth and complexity of the history of this verbal art form as well as the significance of its global proliferation, this volume will make a critical intervention in how rap is studied. Thus, we call to exercise a level of caution when celebrating foundational figures. Rather than be beholden to origin narratives, we must interrogate and uncover why a history is remembered in a particular way, and what mythologised histories afford and omit.

We are, though, living in a vibrant time of rap scholarship, and this volume is, of course, not without important forebears. After the pioneering first wave of writers who took dancehall, reggae, and rap seriously – from Greg Tate to Joan Morgan; Paul Gilroy to Carolyn Cooper – we now have a welter of tools and compendiums that chronicle hip-hop, and oral poetics more broadly. Murray Forman and Mark Anthony Neal's *That's the Joint*, originally published in 2004, celebrated its third edition in 2023, with Southern hip-hop expert Regina N. Bradley joining the editorial team. Tony Mitchell's turn-of-the-millennium collection *Global Noise* remains pertinent, convincingly arguing for an understanding of rap practice outside of the United States, while *Reggaeton (Refiguring American Music)* from Wayne Marshall, Raquel Z. Rivera and Deborah Pacini Hernandez looks at the enormously popular musical hybrid that leans on Caribbean aesthetics and is read through a Latin-American lens. In more recent times, Justin Williams's *Cambridge Companion to Hip-Hop* acts as a substantial contribution, one which saw importance in having 'US and non-US hip-hop sharing space in the same volume'[9], with chapters from Noriko Manabe on Japanese rap, and Ali Colleen Neff on Senegal. The *Companion to Global Rap*, however, offers a considered move from the US / non-US binary to an understanding and appreciation of craft which is predicated on exchange, simultaneity, intertwined colonial histories, and the fundamentally polysemous and flexible method of oral poetics shared among many communities and cultures worldwide.

Beginning with 'Historical and Cultural Perspectives', Part I offers two interventions from contrasting positions. Paroma Ghose's extensive history tracks developments from the enforced movement of people under seventeenth-century chattel slavery through to the emergence of hip-hop in the United States, before attending to global manifestations, with a particular focus on France, the second biggest rap market in the world. After mapping out the emergence of the French underground rap scene during the 1980s, Ghose shows how legislation designed to ensure that radio stations broadcast a substantial proportion of French language material invigorated the French rap music scene. As this scene grew, increasing numbers of rappers used their position to draw attention to racism and inequality in French society. Ghose indicates how prominent politicians have used political and legal means to censure rappers (a theme which is picked up by Karim Hammou and Marie Sonnette-Manouguian in Chapter 7) before exploring some of the characteristics that distinguish French rap. French rappers can, perhaps, be seen to articulate a future in which their complex identities and France's history are recognised by the Republic.

In Chapter 2, Dancehall expert Marvin Sparks speaks to the fundamental importance of the sound system, as a vessel for public communion, musical alchemy and its capacity to disseminate the words and wisdom of vital deejays such as King Stitt and U-Roy. Leaning upon American-imported jukeboxes and Japanese technologies, Jamaican sounds flourished throughout the 70s – almost concurrently with innovations from Kool Herc and others – resulting in a heyday for both Jamaican and British deejays in the 1980s with Yellowman, Super Cat, and Sister Nancy flying the flag for Kingston, with Saxon Sound's Tippa Irie, Maxi Priest, and Smiley Culture pioneering styles and sounds in South London. Travel back and forth between the Caribbean, the United States and the United Kingdom, by sound-system owners and entrepreneurs, rappers, and deejays, alongside the use of technology to produce innovations, such as toasting, dubplates and riddims, played an important role in the development of emcee culture. Sparks shows, through his cultural history of the sound system, how global rap has been fostered through innovation, circulation and exchange. (Malcolm James, in Chapter 16, returns us to the significance of technology in shaping rap music cultures through a focus on music videos.) The two contrasting perspectives on the history of global rap in these chapters highlight the importance of the movement of people, technologies and cultural practices around the world to the formation of both dancehall and hip-hop. We suggest that an understanding of the complex circuits through which global rap historically developed is crucial for an appreciation of the significance of contemporary rap cultures.

Part II of the *Companion* addresses key disciplinary approaches that have contributed to the field of global rap studies. Rap music's vitality and political punch has often been met with resistance from above. Karim Hammou (author of *Une Histoire de Rap En France*) and Marie Sonnette-Manouguian outline how sociology can bring into focus the social relationships which give meaning to rap as a cultural practice. In their examination of French hip-hop culture, Hammou and Sonnette-Manouguian develop further insights into the political issues introduced by Ghose, highlighting the power relations at play in French popular music culture. After critically interrogating the association between rap and postcolonial minorities in France, they address the criminalisation of rappers by politicians, through prosecution in the courts, calls for censorship in parliament, and far-right media campaigns, which construe rap as a threat to the state.

These issues regarding power and culture can also be seen at work in the United Kingdom. In Chapter 10, Lambros Fatsis adopts a criminological lens through which to engage with the use of rap in court. He examines the use of ancillary orders imposed by courts to regulate the social relations and cultural production of UK drill artists as well as the use of lyrics and music videos as evidence criminal trials. Fatsis's critique of the strategies adopted by the police and prosecutors, in the use of rap as evidence, draws attention to how the generic conventions employed in drill music to elicit emotional responses from the audience can be misinterpreted within court proceedings. Fatsis argues forcefully against attempts to use rap as a record of actual events or as evidence of character, highlighting the lack of literacy that judges and prosecutors possess in relation to the drill genre. The fact that courts continue to admit the use of rap as evidence in this way, raises questions about the status of lyrics and music videos, and perhaps the importance of attending to the features that constitute rap as a verbal art form.

In contrast to the focus on social, political, legal and cultural issues raised by Fatsis, Hammou, Sonnette-Manouguian, Ghose and Sparks, Bramwell argues for an orientation towards the literary value of rap lyrics. Through a focus on Stockwell soundman Roots Manuva, Richard Bramwell suggests that the study of poetry would be enriched by embracing the oral poetics of rap. Through a close analysis of rap lyrics, Bramwell draws attention to Roots Manuva's literary inventiveness. The dominance of cultural studies has perhaps left the formal qualities produced within emcee cultures underappreciated in academic debates. Indeed in Chapter 5, Max Ryynänen and Petteri Enroth look outside this dominant gaze towards elaborate – yet often forgotten – aesthetic approaches to rap, from as early as 1984 by Finnish philosopher Esa Sironen (notably published in the same year as David Toop's lauded *Rap Attack*). In their historical overview of the aesthetics of rap, Ryynänen and Enroth tantalisingly point towards the numerous 'rap-like practices' that can be found in oral poetic forms across the globe, before turning to rap as a modern phenomenon. In its sound system–enabled form, rap could be seen as not just a new style of music, but a new art form. After showing how David Toop constructed an aesthetic history of rap, they examine Richard Shusterman's substantial contribution to philosophical aesthetics, through his work on rap. In a departure from Kantian aesthetics, Shusterman adopted an engaged approach to the aesthetic experience of rap, through listening and dance. Ryynänen and Enroth highlight how insights from philosophical aesthetics have been lost in recent academic debates on rap, and argue that rap and hip-hop call for and deserve serious consideration as art. They conclude their contribution to this volume with an indication of how the study of rap could be advanced through environmental aesthetics and phenomenological approaches.

Part III departs from a focus on disciplinary considerations, turning towards the 'Applications for Rap' outside academia. In addition to the study of the genre, rap itself can be mobilised for educational and therapeutic purposes. Indeed, there has been a concerted effort across educational initiatives (both within formal schooling and outside) and wellbeing, towards greater integration. Three chapters in this volume look to how rap can be employed to facilitate a better tomorrow.

Hip-hop education's changing face is addressed by Patrick Turner. Historically the role of rap in the classroom has been nostalgic and secessionist, trying to cling to core values of hip-hop without necessarily engaging pragmatically with practice in its current form. The UK-based initiative Roadworks, however, seeks to meet young people 'where they are', using drill as a means to evocatively engage with their experiences – however troubling they may be – as a means to actually deal with trauma, rather than require the genre to act as restorative balm. Turner documents participants' experiences, which resulted in the recording of a drill song, noting how a deliberate attempt to leave moralising at the door allows a bridge to be made between the quotidian and the classroom, helping us to 'learn about the world through music'.

Rap's role in settler colonial states was first chronicled at length in the 1990s, one example being Ian Maxwell's examination of practice on Sydney's westside.[10] Dianne Rodger explores the benefits of applied hip-hop for young First Nations people in Kaurna Yerta, with a focus on the therapeutic affordances of self-expression. While the more institutional work can replicate existing power relationships between First Nations people and non-indigenous stakeholders, Rodger focuses on hip-hop workshops in Adelaide, presenting conversations with mentors on the program, many of whom are artists in their own right, such as MCs Eskatology and Social Change. The capacity to equip young people with skills to work through their emotions is acknowledged, with an appreciation of the particular importance for indigenous peoples whose everyday existence is entangled with political and social violence from above.

Akeem Sule and Becky Inkster also attend to the therapeutic capacity of rap, calling for more pertinent interventions in healthcare. Rather than be relegated to secondary and tertiary interventions, they see hip-hop as central to wellbeing, calling for primary, preventative work that is culturally relevant and increasingly relatable, owing to rap's position on the world stage. Rappers are 'street epidemiologists' chronicling everyday woes that are pronounced – and exacerbated – by proximity to the carceral system, over-policing, housing troubles and other ailments. Their work, on many occasions, has had a tangible benefit on public health: Logic's partnership with the Suicide Prevention Hotline in the United States saw a noted increase in calls to the line from those in need; and in keeping with Turner's notion of appreciation rap as a challenging, multivalent form, Angel Haze's retelling of childhood sexual abuse on 'Cleaning out My Closet', while upsetting for some, can help others process their own trauma.

Sule and Inkster also note that we can learn about societal change and the zeitgeist through paying close attention to artists' subject matter. In a similar manner to the method adopted by Gilbers in Chapter 4, their examination of how rappers changed tack following the 2008 global financial crisis – away from glossy materialism to a more muted engagement with 'bling' – demonstrates how public health trends (and impending crises) can be caught early by listening to artists working at street level.

Part IV of the *Companion* turns towards contrasting contexts in which global rap has flourished. Sina A. Nitzsche and Laura Spilker, in Chapter 14, adopt an intersectional approach to the analysis of race, class, gender and nationality in German hip-hop. By situating their analysis of SXTN's music video, 'Ich bin Schwarz', within the context of the global circulation of US hip-hop culture, Nitzsche and Spilker show how US-American understandings of race are received and reinterpreted within the German hip-hop scene. They argue that Nura's performance of female sexuality addresses racial stereotypes and expands our understanding of black womanhood. Through a focus on the black body and bodily functions, rappers Juju and Nura can be seen to mock symbols of white supremacy and German nationalism.

Complexities around language are explored by Elloit Cardozo and Jaspal Singh (Chapter 17), who examine rap in India, and how decisions on whether to use English or not have multiple implications in a multilingual society. They place these contemporary questions firmly within the historical context of British colonial rule and the Indian independence movement. English, Cardozo and Singh argue, can be thought of as both a language of *decolonisation* – a lingua franca, a levelling of the playing field / upward mobility – as well as a sign of 'psychological conquest'; the colonial past rearing its head once again. Cardozo and Singh's genealogy of rap in India highlights that artists' negotiation of language is indicative of how the means by which you deliver your experiences are never neutral. They show how rapping in any of India's languages, including Hindi, English, Kannada, Punjabi, or combining multiple languages in rap lyrics, are influenced by aesthetic, political, and biographical considerations. Their contribution concludes with an examination of the politics of rapping in English. Whereas Manmeet Kaur uses English to position herself as a cosmopolitan woman capable of moving between India's patriarchal structures and her international connections across the world, Sumeet Samos draws on a combination of languages (including English) to draw attention to caste-based atrocities. The broad range of issues that Indian rappers are concerned with, has produced a complex, multilingual environment, in which these artists articulate their present conditions and negotiate transformative relations with the global rap community.

Alex Perullo, whose contribution opens the section, explores the Tanzanian music recording industry, with a focus on award shows. Perullo charts the growth of the Tanzanian music industry, from a post-independence cultural landscape that was strictly government-controlled and subject to state censorship towards an environment in which freedom of expression is more widely practised. This transition did not take place smoothly and Perullo shows how appropriate the metaphor of 'army' was in the characterisation of young Tanzanian rap fans. While rappers in a number of African countries entered formal politics, the struggle within Tanzania's cultural economy also led to artists being imprisoned. The censoring of lyrics and criminalisation of musical expression, that Perullo describes in Chapter 13, recalls the criminalisation of rap in France, Britain and the United States described by Ghose, Hammou, Sonnette-Manouguian, and Fatsis. However, Perullo also shows how rap has now gained recognition at the highest levels of Tanzanian politics, as vital to the country's social, cultural, and economic wellbeing.

Rap's relationship with the state is also explored in Sheng Zou's chapter on *The Rap of China*. TV has been fundamental to rap and its dissemination within an (increasingly) global audience. While terrestrial presentations of rap – and rappers – in the United States have shifted from music-focused products such as *Yo MTV Raps!* to hip-hop–adjacent reality and lifestyle shows, such as *Pimp My Ride* and *Snoop Dogg's Father Hood*, talent shows have become a promising ground in East Asia for new artists and budding stars. Yet, this platform comes with its own particular set of complications. After the ferocious success of the television series *The Rap of China*, rap music faces an identity crisis, with its 'televisual remediation' coming into conflict with authenticity narratives, favouring 'sanitization, domestication, and commercialization'. Sheng Zhou argues that this 'precarious cultural formation' has resulted in grassroots, mainstream and state coming together in complex ways, with television reinforcing dominant values regarding masculinity, nationality and decorum while stifling innovative practice.

Perhaps more amorphous and flexible in its representations of practice is social media. Malcolm James's chapter on drill music videos firstly explores how notoriety in its predecessor grime really came post-YouTube when legendary moments – once restricted to out-of-print DVDs – became accessible to the wider populace. To listen to heralded grime station DejaVu FM in the 2000s you had to be within the radius of its east London transmitters, otherwise your best hope was that a friend had taped the 'set' so you could listen back. In the genre's much-chronicled 'second wave' during the 2010s (with luminaries such as Stormzy, Skepta and Lady Leshurr taking center stage), YouTube – and social media more generally – became du jour. Soon, channels such as Mixtape Madness and PressPlay began incubating what would become known as UK Drill: a hybrid of grime and sounds from Chicago's South Side. Rather than address its complex alignments with criminality (explored by Fatsis in Chapter 10), James argues for drill as a cultural form, his particular theoretical gambit being that drill music videos are contradictory and multivalent. Drill functions as an 'alternative', as per Raymond Williams's definition, in that it is generative and vital, sitting outside simple binaries of oppression and resistance. These visual representations are chromatic: they're 'austere and opulent', boastful. They depict council estates without eschewing glamour, with artists such as 67 and Harlem Spartans maximising the medium in effect of language, affect and style.

These strategies are remarkably successful. Indeed, having an affinity with apps such as Instagram and TikTok is almost a pre-requisite for success for drill artists. In Chapter 15, Jabari Evans looks at how societal fears around rap are turned on their heads by innovative 'cloutchasing' strategies of young drillers on Chicago's South Side. Through aggrandising their proximity to violence, with social media posts that refer to guns and illicit drugs, these artists leverage a level of authenticity while also building notoriety through a 'shock factor'. Employing strategies not too dissimilar to NWA in the 1980s, artists play the fearmongers at their own game, consequently elevating their status in the scene.

As hip-hop studies continues to move forward as an interdisciplinary field, with the genre itself becoming ever more present in society, perhaps the most pressing question one could pose is, 'What is it to study rap?' What tools do we have at our disposal to make sense of and contextualise this form? These questions are attended to by two chapters in the volume that anchor the 'Approaches to Rap' section.

Steven Gilbers addresses linguistic approaches to rap, and the (understandable) fascination with linguistic innovations within the genre. He notes at the outset that artists have always been self-aware and reflexive regarding phonology, ethnolects, and their own positionality in relation to their craft, but sociolinguistic research over the last two decades has done its best to catch up. With a special focus on 2Pac's deployment of African-American English (AAE), Gilbers maps how the artist altered his approach to rap as he moved westwards: born on the East Coast, the rapper came of age in the Bay Area before moving to Los Angeles. This final move, before his fateful death, saw him adopt a more West Coast lilt as part of dialect acquisition through immersion in the City of Angels.

J. Griffith Rollefson's searing chapter, entitled 'Beats, Rhymes and Life', argues for the pre-eminence of the sonic and its intersection with the social. The chapter reckons with the conservativist 'white racial frame' of musicology, and how we might employ the tools of musicology without falling into unhelpful habits. There exists a crisis of representation, wherein etic methods get imposed on a form that resists such an approach. With the academic theorising of 'flow' for example, an analytical prioritising of virtuosity and technicality, shown through either staff notation or computational methods, can get us close, but we remain distant from truly capturing – as Kjell Oddekalv asks – what makes this 'shit dope'? As Paul Gilroy famously wrote, music *is* music, and its physical enactment, social context and setting all build into its vitality. Thus, when we study rap, it's important to not forget all of the components that make it what it is. de

Lacey, in particular, in this volume spends time addressing creative process, looking at communal creation of new music in grime, with a focus on DJing as well as the craft of MCs as part of a unified whole (see Chapter 8).

What these chapters have at their centre, though, is an acknowledgement of community and lived experience. Rollefson asks us to foreground the intimate relationship between the sonic and social; meanwhile Gilbers points us to how language in rap – often positioned under the umbrella of H. Samy Alim's 'Hip Hop Nation Language' – is co-constituted by both an imagined community of 'heads' and on-the-ground experience.

As our field continues to move forward, then, it's important not to lose sight of the practice of scholarship in relation to these realities. In both our theoretical and empirical endeavours, we enter into communion with artists, their work, and their lives. Rap's status as a global force therefore demands appreciation of myriad cultural contexts, approaches to performance, and means by which this art form is sustained. This volume's goal, then, is to introduce the tools, approaches, and perspectives through which to get to grips with this vital area of artistic practice.

Notes

1. 'Mayor Adams, 'ITSALLBLACKMUSIC Presents,' and Hip Hop Legend KRS-One Announce Series of Block Party'. 2023. The Official Website of the City of New York. 20 July 2023. www.nyc.gov/office-of-the-mayor/news/528-23/mayor-adams-itsallblackmusic-presents-hip-hop-legend-krs-one-series-block-party.
2. Charnas, Dan. 2023. 'Essay | Was Hip-Hop Really Invented 50 Years Ago?' *Wall Street Journal*, 4 August 2023, sec. Life. www.wsj.com/articles/was-hip-hop-really-invented-50-years-ago-1dd40947.
3. Qureshi, Arusa. 2021. *Flip the Script: How Women Came to Rule Hip Hop*. 404 Ink, 9.
4. Beaumont-Thomas, Ben. 2021. 'Afrika Bambaataa Sued for Alleged Child Sexual Abuse'. *The Guardian*, 10 September 2021, sec. Music. www.theguardian.com/music/2021/sep/10/afrika-bambaataa-sued.
5. Gee, Andre. 2023. 'Afrika Bambaataa's Abuse Allegations Cast a Cloud over The Universal Hip-Hop Museum'. *Rolling Stone* (blog). 28 March 2023. www.rollingstone.com/music/music-features/afrika-bambaataa-abuse-allegations-bronx-universal-hip-hop-museum-1234705041/.
6. Ryzik, Melena. 2020. 'Suit Accusing Russell Simmons of Rape Was Filed Too Late, Judge Rules'. Accessed 1 May 2024. www.nytimes.com/2020/11/17/arts/suit-russell-simmons-rape-too-late-judge-rules.html.

7. Beaumont-Thomas, Ben. 2020. 'Wiley Posts Antisemitic Tweets, Likening Jews to Ku Klux Klan | Music | The Guardian'. Accessed 7 August 2023. www.theguardian.com/music/2020/jul/24/wiley-accused-of-antisemitism-after-likening-jews-to-ku-klux-klan.
8. Thomas, Tobi. 2022. 'Dizzee Rascal's Ex-Fiancee Left Rapper over 'Domestic Abuse', Court Hears'. *The Guardian*, 18 February 2022, sec. UK news. www.theguardian.com/uk-news/2022/feb/18/dizzee-rascal-ex-fiancee-left-rapper-over-domestic-abuse-court-hears; 'Dizzee Rascal Appeal – Sentence Upheld | The Crown Prosecution Service'. n.d. Accessed 7 August 2023. www.cps.gov.uk/london-south/news/dizzee-rascal-appeal-sentence-upheld.
9. Williams, Justin (ed.) *The Cambridge Companion to Hip-Hop* (Cambridge University Press, 2015), 5.
10. Maxwell, Ian *Phat Beats, Dope Rhymes: Hip Hop Down Under Comin' Upper*, (Middletown, CT: Wesleyan University Press, 2003)

PART I

Historical and Cultural Perspectives

1 | Travelling Sounds

Tracing the Global Origins of Rhythm And Poetry

PAROMA GHOSE

'Rap is Rhythm and Poetry, cuts create sound effects'.[1] In one succinct line, American rapper Rakim (from New York City) captures the essence of the art of rapping and inaugurates the use of the acronym 'r-a-p' as rhythm and poetry. Although the word's association with beat and rhyme may already have been in wide circulation in the hip-hop underground, this was its first traceable utterance and has become emblematic in the history of rap. In fact, the second half of his sentence also delineates rap's relationship with hip-hop, two terms that have increasingly been used interchangeably to the detriment of the nuances of both. Rap is one element of what is known as the hip-hop square, which includes DJ-ing (the 'cuts' and 'sound effects' referred to by Rakim), breakdancing, and graffiti. Each of these provides a different contribution, which, when brought together, become a hip-hop ensemble: the DJ provides the musical element, graffiti the visual, break-dancing the moving or physical, and rap the lyrical. Beatboxing is also often included, bringing the fifth, instrumental element into the mix. The sixth element of 'knowledge' was an addition made by Afrika Bambaataa, considered one of the founding fathers of hip-hop. Knowledge, as a fundamental part of hip-hop, refers to the origins and meaning of the word 'hip', which is explored in the history that follows.

Each of these terms and practices has its own history. Moreover, these discrete but related cultural practices have each evolved in meaning and implication over time, and continue to do so, as much on their own as under the aegis of the hip-hop movement. This chapter provides a historical grounding and introduction to rap, the lyrical element of hip-hop, detailing its origins and the multicultural nature of its roots as well as its subsequent development. It will begin with a succinct overview of the deep history that rap carries in its words and rhythms, then examine rap's complicated relationship with politics, followed by a short case study of rap in France (a very short introduction to themes that are explored in Chapter 7 by Karim Hammou and Marie Sonnette-Manouguian).

'Old School' Flows

Globally, the history of rap and hip-hop is usually traced to 1973, when Cindy Campbell began throwing parties where her brother, DJ Kool Herc (also known as Kool DJ Herc), deejayed and introduced the concept of the 'break', already a familiar feature of the musical culture of Jamaican dance halls, into what became hip-hop.[2] Originally from Kingston, Jamaica, both brother and sister were likely familiar with 'the break' prior to its proliferation in the Bronx, New York, where they were raised, and repurposed a 'drum break' from funk/soul rhythms. A 'break' involved the isolation of a particular passage of music on a two-turntable set-up, a familiar technical set in the disco clubs of the time. DJ Kool Herc's experimental variation was in using the break on funk and soul records, contrary to the disco music that was the usual sound of parties at the time,[3] and assembling his speakers in a style most common in the sound system set-up originating in the Caribbean. Favouring passages with stronger beats, DJ Kool Herc would isolate and use these beats to create a different rhythm favourable to the dancers in the crowd. Sampling disco music, which was very much at its zenith at the time, turntables became the central pivot of the hip-hop movement. Taking inspiration from the role and practice of the 'selector' in Jamaican dancehall, the hip-hop DJ provided the musical atmosphere, while the rappers or MCs took on a function similar to that of the dancehall deejay, which was to use their voice to keep the crowd engaged with the music. This began with occasional injunctions to test the atmosphere and push it where it needed to go, and over time evolved into a more rhymed, verbal delivery, which eventually became recognised as rap.

The Weight of Words: How Rap Came to Be

A medley of different cultural influences and practices blended together to form what is identified as rap today, some stretching as far back as the seventeenth century at the height of the transatlantic slave trade. Enslaved people first carried these musical forms and traditions, originating in their many different communities and geographic origins, out of the African continent and into the many spaces to which they were taken in the Caribbean, Brazil, and the United States. Due to ocean currents and wind paths, the resultant trade routes developed around two centres: enslaved peoples from West Africa (principally the islands and regions surrounding the countries of Nigeria, Benin, Togo, and Ghana today) were carried to North America and the Caribbean; while enslaved peoples from the area of modern-day Angola, and Southeast Africa more generally, were taken to Brazil.[4] The musical traditions carried by these enslaved peoples were therefore already a concord of multicultural origins. This enforced cultural exchange continued amongst the different populations within each area in which they were sold and relocated, and as these musical forms intermingled over time, they developed their own set of cultural traditions in situ. Moreover, the blend of cultures and identities that enslaved peoples carried with them from the African continent, the Caribbean, or Brazil, to the American South where they laboured, coalesced over time with the cultures of white indentured labourers, and sometimes their masters, of European origin.[5]

There was a strong interdependency between communities in the plantations, particularly the smaller ones where slaves and white, indentured labourers, and even masters on occasion, were all working the fields together and thus interacting on a regular basis through shared work and spaces, complexifying the dynamics of an oppressive relationship. Both black and white communities in the United States were further distanced from their connections to Africa and Europe with every new generation, while their ties – both enforced and inadvertent – to each other became more definitive. These led to important developments of vernacular language and wordplay that are still in use today. Reciprocity evolved the English of these areas to include its own vernacular, injunctions, and rhythms from different African languages, imbuing it with new inflections. Concurrently, coded words and language developed amongst enslaved people to allow them to communicate within the presence of the master without the latter understanding what was actually being said. An example of this is the reversal of the meanings of the words 'good' and 'bad'. If an enslaved person had escaped, another might comment that it was 'bad'; the master would take the word at its literal meaning, while those who were enslaved would take it at its actual implication, which implied the opposite: that it was *good*. Bad became good, good became bad, a coded move away from the literal meaning of words that has stayed with rap still today, evident in the contextual interchangeability of technical antonyms like 'hot' and 'cool', and so on. Indeed, 'Words from various African languages entered the olio of the new land, becoming *hip, dig, jive, juke, banjo, jazz* and *honky* ... [emphasis added]'.[6] This historical, cultural connection has been linked to the foundation of all that is encapsulated in the word 'hip', which is itself an evolution of the Wolof[7] word 'hepi' meaning 'to see' or 'open one's eyes'.[8] In his song 'Hip Hop Lives (I Come Back)', rapper KRS-One refers to the origins of this word when he says 'Hip means to know / It's a form of intelligence / To be hip is to be up-date and relevant'.[9]

The imprints of the blending of identities and the harrowing histories that brought them together are therefore evident in the weight of the words that form the lexicon of contemporary rap. These then further absorbed influences that travelled from other geographies with traditions of their own, for example, the Jamaican tradition of 'toasting' or 'chatting', which involved speaking in rhyme over a beat, and is also part of the calypso music tradition that has many different national iterations across the many islands of the French and English-speaking Caribbean. These practices travelled with migrants from the Caribbean islands to the United States of America, where they encountered musical features like jazz scat – improvised, rhythmic wordplay, an example of which can be seen in the famous musical sequence in the 1941 film *Hellzapoppin'* – and spoken word, all of which were circulating across cultural sectors in the United States in the decades prior to 1973. Once in the United States, these musical forms became localised in the growing hip-hop scene of the Bronx, New York City, in the 1960s and 1970s, evolving into the now familiar form of 'rap'.[10]

Toasting and chatting were derived from the griot traditions in West Africa and travelled with the slaves brought to islands across the Caribbean. The figure of the griot has been seen by some academics as the antecedent to the MC, or 'Mic Controller', in rap today. The griot is often evoked figuratively in American rap lyrics, particularly in homage to the African roots of the many musical genres that had their origins in African-American and Afro-Caribbean populations in the Americas, between whom there was a great deal of cultural interpolation, driven by diasporic movements. However, as rap globalised and grew out of the United States and back into the spaces from which it derived its ancestry, the conceptual griot contrasted with the modern-day griots who still practice traditions of orality in West Africa. The tradition of the griot is still strongly embedded in many societies and has had its own role in nurturing the local hip-hop scenes in certain countries, like Senegal. Within those societies 'while rappers depict "ancient" griots as storytellers, genealogists, and topical commentators, they generally are critical of modern griots'.[11] Historically, the role of the West African griots has been to preserve culture and history, while also accompanying royalty and singing their songs of praise. In fact, the latter feature constitutes a form of social conservatism and is at odds with the general lyrical drift and spatial environment of rap in the form in which it has become known today, in West Africa itself, as much as anywhere else that rap has taken seed. This distinction also serves to draw the line between the griot tradition as it continues to be carried out in West African countries still today, a distinct genre of music to rap – a modern genre that arrived from the United States – in which the griot stands as an original or ancestral inspiration and influence.

While it is important to acknowledge the historical influence that the griot traditions in their travelled forms have had in creating a cultural space within which rap could emerge, this can easily wander into the tendency, prevalent in hip-hop studies in general, to reach towards a constructed 'African imaginary'. This results in a lack of analysis of the dissimilarities between certain traditions, with an overt focus only on the similitudes, creating a compelling myth that is somewhat distanced from history. It is critical, therefore, to find a balance between the role of the African imaginary in nurturing notions of identity within hip-hop and rap, and the historical influence that various African, Caribbean, European, and American traditions exercised, blending to create the many rap music genres with which we are familiar today.

Indeed, the debate surrounding the racial and ethnic origins of rap, even within the more contemporary frame, is a discussion that is still ongoing in academia. Some academics, such as Tricia Rose and Denise Herd, explicitly identify rap music as a 'Black Art', while others, such as Nelson George, emphasise the diversity of ownership of the art form and the important contributions made by Latino youth. The predominant identification of rap has remained very strongly tied to African-American (in particular) and black (in general) identities. Nevertheless, both the community 'represented' and the target audience are often more all-encompassing and multicultural, particularly when rap moves out of its cultural context of the United States, but continues to carry a lot of cultural attributes that are tied to the African-American community.

Rap (and hip-hop more largely) is inextricably and historically tied to transnational black communities, and more specifically to the African-American experience. An identitarian link that has been replicated first by the American, and then global, music industries, it has carried many cultural traits and features that are particular to this combined legacy. Whether through music, dance, fashion, style (hair, etc.), or vernacular, African-American identity has been, and continues to be, the main point of return for global hip-hop culture. Within the American context, where hip-hop forms part of a larger discussion around racial discrimination, cultural appropriation, and the long minority struggle of the community, these cultural features associated with rap exist within a framework that is conscious of this complexity, and where the community participates in the development and debate around rap and the social issues it addresses.

Even here, controversies court white rappers whenever they enter the cultural space of hip-hop given the long history of white artists appropriating black music in the United States and claiming intellectual and cultural ownership of this art. Rapper Vanilla Ice became synonymous with reproducing tropes of African-American life as depicted in hip-hop, and capitalising on his social capital as a white man to accrue a far wider audience than his African-American peers in the industry were able to reach. The fact that his song 'Ice Ice Baby' (1990) became the first rap single to reach no. 1 on the pop chart in the United States is symptomatic of this shift from a genre-specific or community-specific audience to a mass public.[12] Vanilla Ice has a tarnished reputation within the rap community because of his musical and cultural antics, while other white rappers, most notably The Beastie Boys and Eminem, have been conscious and careful of the line between rap as a musical genre that can technically become the mode of expression for any musician, and paying homage to the deep cultural roots of the African-American community to which it continues to be tied. This issue becomes even more complex when carried outside the United States to countries that do not have the same history of racial discrimination or relations, nor necessarily any connection with the debates around identity and appropriation within hip-hop.

This is an issue that repeatedly surfaces in countries where rap has taken root, and local or national identities are combined with African-American cultural norms. The degree to which this is performed or problematic varies from country to country, as much as from artist to artist. Yet, there continue to be episodic instances of blackface and performative 'blackness', which many artists, devoid of the historical and cultural context of the United States or black racial politics, see as an admiring homage to hip-hop culture, but which may be considered closer to appropriation. Nonetheless, the spectrum of appropriation varies greatly depending on the national space and cultural scene within which it is performed. In some countries, this debate has not emerged at all because of the completely different set of racial and ethnic politics that are dominant within them. In France, as we shall see later in this chapter, rap crosses lines of ethnicity and race, and instead converges along a slightly different nexus of identity, hinged on issues related to socioeconomic, migratory, and national origins of rappers, with race remaining a crucial part of their discourse, but in a manner very different to that of the United States.

Rap Goes Global

Attributes from a wide spectrum of geographies, traditions, and origins came together and variously exercised influence (tangible, ephemeral, or intentionally evoked) over what eventually emerged as rap. This made for a long historical and multicultural contribution that preceded its traceable development in the Bronx. By 1979, within six years of DJ Kool Herc's experimental introduction of the 'break' into hip-hop culture, The Sugarhill Gang released their now classic single 'Rapper's Delight'. The song sampled R&B band Chic's disco-funk inspired song 'Good Times' and turned it into a more rhythmic bassline for the Sugarhill MCs to rap over. Its opening lines, originally composed by the uncredited Grandmaster Caz, are some of the most referenced and repeated in hip-hop history. The song climbed the charts, becoming a regional hit on the east coast of the United States, and travelled across the Atlantic to Western Europe and beyond, becoming a regular feature of the club scene in Tokyo, Japan within the same year. Nevertheless, it was still uncertain whether the success of 'Rapper's Delight' had been an anomaly to the musical norm of the times. As rap began to be more widely practiced and circulated, moving from street ciphers to battle rap scenarios, its commercial potential became apparent. Its link to African-American culture and history then became a more considered curation on the part of the American recording industry, which fanned the flames of a stereotypical image around hip-hop culture that was separate from the political and social realities of the communities on the ground, and often those expressed in the lyrics themselves.

Alongside its gradual entry into the mainstream cultural scene, the hip-hop underground continued to thrive and nurture the rhythmic and lyrical experimentation that became a permanent feature of rap. Meanwhile, many other contiguous art and musical scenes were developing in and around New York City. Fab Five Freddy, who was principally a graffiti artist, provided the bridge between two of these worlds – the hip-hop underground, and the No Wave movement[13] – through his friendship with Debbie Harry, best known for being the lead singer of the American rock band Blondie. Using lyrical wordplay tricks particular to Fab Five Freddy's style, Debbie Harry recorded a rap verse as part of Blondie's 1981 song 'Rapture'. 'Rapture' effectively allowed the still marginalised rap to enter the mainstream charts housed within the more popular and familiar genre of pop-rock. It allowed rap's market potential to be tested without a huge risk on the part of the record label, an experiment that proved rap's commercial viability. The song went on to become the first video clip with a rapped verse to be shown on MTV.[14]

Within a year of 'Rapture', Grandmaster Flash and the Furious Five, then led by rapper Melle Mel, released their single 'The Message' (July 1, 1982). Although the group had been previously associated largely with playful and boastful rapped deliveries on the party scene, they burst onto the popular culture stage with a much more sombre version of everyday reality. This shift fundamentally changed the way in which rappers considered the potential of their burgeoning art form, and the ways in which their lyrics could resonate and be harnessed towards depicting real struggles, establishing what has since become known as 'reality rap'. This took an outrightly politicised turn with the advent of groups like Public Enemy, with iconic songs 'Bring the Noise' (1988) and 'Fight the Power' (1989), which had a strong political manifesto tied not just to the notion of equality in social justice, but particularly to the long history of the civil rights movement and its importance to African-American identity. Unusually for the time, Public Enemy's founders hailed from middle-class families in Long Island, New York, and their studied and more concerted approach to the social issues that faced the black community were different from what had been heard thus far. Nonetheless, their version of reality was as unfamiliar in 'white America' (to borrow rapper Eminem's term) as previous rap lyrical narratives had been; but it was also distinct – in approach if not in social theme – to the turbulent violence that California natives such as Schooly D, Ice T, and N.W.A. would describe in their music.[15] N.W.A's 1988 tracks 'Straight Outta Compton' and 'Fuck Tha Police' cemented the place of 'gangsta rap' in the mix, bringing the violent, distorted realities of law and order in the streets of Los Angeles, California to the eyes and ears of the world. 'You are now about to witness the strength of street knowledge'[16] echoed the haunting words of Dr. Dre.

The advent of Grandmaster Flash and the Furious Five's 'The Message' in 1982 and its powerful warning, 'Don't push me 'cause I'm close to the edge / I'm trying not to lose my head' effectively kick-started rap's active and engaged political expression. This has resulted in the bifurcation of rap into what is often labelled as 'real' or 'authentic', that is, rap which is political, and what is considered to be its adulterated offshoot. The latter association is usually attributed to those artists and songs who demonstrate an unbridled embrace of capitalism that proliferates a great deal of mainstream rap, and is accused of parading senseless lyricism without social or political agenda, and often replete with casual misogyny, homophobia, and other forms of bigotry. This binary has been generated not just by the media and public, but also by rappers themselves, sometimes allying with certain caricatures of the genre. Yet, as a genre of music that places a unique importance on words, rap has been, and continues to be, written and performed by a plethora of rappers of different backgrounds, ideas, political opinions, and, increasingly, nationalities, each producing a lyrical repository that might reflect any, all, or none of the stereotypes associated with it. Indeed, early rap performances (live and recorded) were aimed at dancers and partying, defying the logic of this binary. Tupac Shakur, one of the most iconic rappers of all time, is perhaps the best example of a significant shift in lyrical themes, moving from political statements on the state of the wider world and deploring of the place of women in society, to features typically associated with (US) West Coast gangsta rap and a more open embrace of violence in gang warfare. Yet, his fight against the racism and injustice wrought within the American system is a continuous thread through all his musical phases and personas. Thus, not only can these multiple discourses be contained within the lyrical repository of a rapper's overall discography, but can sometimes shift several times within the same song. When analysed through this more complex lens, other (in)famous artists like Snoop Dogg, Notorious B.I.G., Nas, 50 Cent, and Jay Z, to name a few, are afforded a more holistic platform upon which to be seen and understood. Therefore, the division of rap into this kind of binary is neither useful nor reflective of its vast spectrum of expression. Though rap has been courted by controversy for its creatively harsh and sometimes vitriolic vocabulary, and its unrestrained treatment of topics commonly perceived as illicit, this has allowed the predominant prejudices of the societies and communities of rappers to surface, often inadvertently, through their lyrics as a blueprint of the larger social conscience of its time. Thus, the avarice, misogyny, and homophobia that pervade a great deal of rap are arguably a mark of the societies that produce them, with rap providing a vocal expression that requests challenge and subversion. Those discourses are also challenged by many female rappers, including Queen Latifah, Salt-N-Pepa, Lauryn Hill, and Missy Elliott, to name a few.

Indeed, these complicated dynamics of a media-generated rap 'binary' and the proverbial absence of a large numerical base of female rappers to balance the male-dominated voice were replicated in variations in countries around the world where hip-hop (with its multiple elements) travelled, and was adopted. Hip-hop left its American incubator soon after its inception, and throughout the late 1980s and early 1990s, while it was still finding its voice in its country of origin, rap found its way to national spaces across the world, mostly through youthful enthusiasm and illegal means. This includes the import and distribution of undeclared mixtapes (France),[17] the salvaging of broken CDs (mainland China),[18] pirate radio stations (France and the UK),[19] the cultural exchanges between countries and their diaspora (Algeria),[20] by shared (black) identity movements (Brazil),[21] or indeed through the continued and burgeoning dominance of American cultural influence in newly open markets (South Korea, Morocco), to cite a few examples.[22]

In the globalising and digitalising world of music, the influence and integration of rap into the popular norm has proliferated and established rap as a truly global genre, recognisable everywhere. Although rap scenes outside the United States initially 'borrowed' from and emulated the commercialised American form, rap music's voyage to other national spaces allowed it to develop into local and national iterations with distinctive identities for two important reasons: first, the significance of words and diction in the genre meant that in its new local and national spaces, it would find its feet in the spoken language or languages particular to those contexts; second, diverging historical experiences and resultant legal and political regimes meant that lyrical themes were adapted to address local issues and audiences. Moreover, there is a plethora of local or regional histories of rhythmic wordplay resembling rap that preceded its American avatar in the areas to which it travelled.[23] This allowed for a natural, national musical integration and innovation. It also enabled the larger national publics to be more receptive of the adapted artform marketed as something intrinsically local, a blending of the foreign and the familiar that was more palatable to those who were sceptical of American imports or fearful of anglophone cultural dominance, as was the case in France. Meanwhile, in spaces like the UK, aspects of MC culture found their voices outside the genre parameters of hip-hop per se, with rap becoming an integral part of other genres including grime, jungle and garage. Overall, there was an inherent 'cultural hybridity' that evolved in all of these national spaces, and the development of local rap music genres was not the product of a one-way influence.

The slight temporal lag in rap's travels outside its national ambit of origin meant that multiple versions of rap's politicism were heard simultaneously with its concurrent thematic of 'having fun'. In other words, youth in countries beyond the United States were able to make a conscious choice about what kind of lyricism they wanted to use as the basis for their local rap scenes, making rap a space of constant and continuing international cultural dialectical exchange. Effectively, just as rap was a controversial and marginalised form of emerging music in the US, associated with a minority political voice at the point of production, and youth rebellion at its point of reception, this association with the political undercurrent, or indeed counter-current, was a large part of the reputation that came with rap as it travelled to other geographies, easily tapping into a similar dynamic of subverting the polemical status quo. Rap therefore became a form of political expression in many of the places where it arrived. This brought some controversy, and resultant marginalisation, to rap in many different national contexts, giving it a global reputation as a music that had the potential to be politically salient and discursive, an element of the musical genre that is particularly relevant in the case of France, as we shall explore in more detail in the following section.

France: Rhythm and Politics

France is the second largest producer and consumer of rap in the world today. Rap, and the other elements of hip-hop, came across the Atlantic along two distinct, concurrent, and equally important streams, which eventually bound together. The first was through a handful of convinced and young individuals who used every possible opportunity to make a space for hip-hop on radio and TV stations in France. The second was the simultaneous underground movement, which brought the sounds and rhythms of the streets of the East Coast straight into the basements and backyards of the urban French youth by means of amateur mixtapes, individual trips back and forth between the two geographies, and snippets of influence that stayed amongst those individuals who had a desire to replicate the art.

The first stream brought rap and hip-hop to the television screens and radios in people's homes across the country, propelled by a few particularly convinced and influential individuals. These included radio and television presenters / DJs like Sidney Duteil, who pioneered a radio show dedicated exclusively to hip-hop on *Radio Libre 7* (predecessor to *Radio France*) in 1981, and then the TV show 'H.I.P.-H.O.P.', the first programme in the world to be dedicated exclusively to rap and breakdancing. There were also journalists like Olivier Cachin, who was discerningly quick to push for the recognition of this new musical form. Here, Fab Five Freddy makes an appearance again, as he enabled a dialogue between the world of American and French rap (or more specifically between New York City and Paris) when rap was still underground in both spaces. At the same time that he was working with Blondie, Fab Five Freddy collaborated with Sophie Bramly and Bernard Zékri, who produced his track 'Change the Beat' (1982) in which he rapped in both English and French. The track has since become one of the most sampled hip-hop tunes of all time. This was followed by DJ Dee Nasty's 1984 release of the now iconic mixtape *Paname City Rappin'* ('Paname' being an argotic term for Paris), produced entirely in France.

Dedicated magazines promoted the spread of hip-hop culture, while general newspapers and magazines had a more deleteriously sceptical approach. Ultimately, however, it was the audio-visual mediums that really triumphed. Mixtapes, cassette recordings, and the illegal borrowing of airwave time and space all had their roles to play in the dispersal of rap, as much as the more official channels of the media. As an 'imported' musical genre, hip-hop raised initial suspicion and was treated with trepidation by mainstream media outlets. Once provided with an inlet, however, rap in France took on a momentum of its own. The 1980s saw the selective showcasing of a ballooning underground rap scene through a handful of radio and television outlets, bringing to the fore the first musical iterations of rappers such as Jhony Go, Lionel D, Destroy Man, Assassin, and Timide Sans Complexe, all of whom would eventually be regarded as some of the founding pillars of French rap. Not unlike its American counterpart, it was the end of the 1980s and the early 1990s that saw French rap break into the mainstream and experience what has since been labelled as its 'golden age'. It took until 1990 for the first episode of 'Rapline' (channel M6) to air, the first radio or TV show to host an entire episode dedicated to *French* rap.[24] The first ever rap compilation *Rapattitude* was also released in 1990 and sold more than 100,000 copies and was certified gold (according to the French classification standards of the time). Soon thereafter, the advent of IAM's album ... *De la planète Mars* (1991), NTM's *Authenthik* (1991), MC Solaar's *Qui sème le vent récolte le tempo* (1991), and Ministère A.M.E.R.'s *Pourquoi tant de haine?* (1992) within a year of each other, saw French rap flourish and proliferate. It quickly became a favourite topic of debate and controversy in the mainstream media, which often misrepresented this cultural form. French rap also found itself a subject of common currency amongst politicians, who used political and legal means to critique what they considered an illicit, cultural representation of the marginalised youth of France, often alluding to their extra-French origins and/or descent as a political weapon. This would set the scene for what would become a continual back and forth between French rappers and various authorities (including the French state, the police, individual politicians, and the media) about their incendiary lyricism in the decades to come. The most infamous example is that of former French President Nicolas Sarkozy, who became embroiled in a legal altercation with the rap group La Rumeur in 2002 that lasted eight years and which he eventually lost.

'Free' radio stations, like Radio Nova and Skyrock, greatly aided the growth and popularity of rap in France throughout this period, as licensed radio stations were not always at liberty to make their own musical choices. Ironically, the control and micro-management of the French cultural space by the French state eventually helped to elevate rap from a marginal genre in the 1990s to the 'new norm' of popular music (by the mid 2010s). This shift was helped, however inadvertently, by the restrictions placed on 'culture' and its dispersal within the French state. From 1 January 1996, France saw the enforcement of a law drafted in 1994 that required 40 per cent of all material played on air by private radio stations to be in the French language, with preference accorded to newer musical acts.[25] The effects of this law were resounding, particularly for the French rap community. By promoting a form of protectionism and shielding the interior French musical market from external, and particularly Anglophone, competition, it marked a watershed in the spectrum of opportunities available for French artists and coincided with the heyday of French rap. Meanwhile, between the mid 1990s and mid 2000s, the number of independent rappers hugely increased, and French rap established its seat on the French music stage in spite of the marginalising tendencies of both the music industry and the French state. Karim Hammou estimates that around 450 albums of French rap were produced and distributed in and amongst French territories between 1990 and 2005 alone.[26] By the mid 2000s, rappers such as Booba, Youssoupha, Sinik, Diam's, Psy 4 de la Rime, Keny Arkana, Kery James, Sniper, and Orelsan, amongst others, had established themselves as central to the French music scene at large, and rap had become the definition of popular music for the French youth.

Many rappers in France wanted to express themselves politically through their art, but initially in the 1980s, the volume of music produced that centred around the 'festive' dimension was greater and proved more popular. Very quickly, however, rappers in France began to intentionally carry the onus of *representing* the communities from which they came. This played a key role in bringing definition to the character of rap that was particular to France: the communities that were being provided a voice and platform by the rappers they produced were a medley of linguistic, cultural, and religious groups, brought together by their shared experience of marginalisation in France. This ostracism was commonly the result of these communities not being considered to be 'French' by both the French state and society, though the definition of what 'being French' meant remained largely undefined and officially untied to any racial or ethnic make-up. Given that the French nation-state is officially 'colour-blind' and therefore does not 'see' race, it has historically been challenging to raise the question of racism in any discursive format or in any public sphere, including within academia.[27] Rap therefore emerged as a contrasting discourse to this state-enabled reluctance to acknowledge and address the racial and ethnic discrimination faced by its minority populations. The French universalism that promises liberty, equality, and fraternity (amongst other aspects of justice and human rights) to all those who reside within its geographical and legal boundaries has therefore been a favourite subject of French rap, demonstrating how universalism has failed in practice.[28] In fact, the sheer volume of rappers in France who have directed their lyrical critiques to the Republic, or engaged with politicians, often within the ambit of the judicial court, demonstrates that beyond being a leitmotif of French rap polemics, the issues of poverty, violence, racism, discrimination, and the unequal distribution or attribution of justice that afflicts minority communities in France, have remained largely unchanged and unaddressed between 1981 and the present day.[29]

These issues are the result of the realities, both past and present, faced by rappers in France. These can be summarised by three imaginaries of French rap that are, statistically, often reflective of their lived experiences: their straitened socioeconomic circumstances; their geographical marginalisation in *banlieues*[30] located in urban peripheries; and their societal ostracism based on their categorisation as 'outsiders' or 'the other' because of their race, ethnicity, origin, religion, or a combination of any or all of these.[31] In fact, rap in France has come to represent in microcosm all those who wish to belong to the nation-state, 'but to whom the Republic does not reciprocate this loyalty'.[32] In their songs, rappers tend to display their multi-national, multi-partisan, or multiplicitous origins with pride, despite often being ostracised by society or rebuked by the state of France for so doing. French rappers continue to advocate for the possibility of complicated national identities, and recognition that this is the reality of a modern France in a postcolonial world. This signals something that is very apparent in their diction: that there is a duality of belonging, but that this need not connote a contradiction. They argue for an acceptance of these complexities rather than a blindness to history. This kind of 'multi-partisanship' is reflected in their music, through rapped injunctions in Arabic, Lingala, Spanish, and Portuguese (etc.), as much as in the content of their lyrics. These themes and struggles are particular to French rap and gave it the national characteristics that distinguished it from its American roots.

This demonstrates very effectively how the global and national necessarily coexist in French rap and continue to bring the larger French identity into question. The French example brings together the two separate strands that we have discussed in this chapter: on the one hand, the continued prevalence of the origin story of rap, still defined against the history and aesthetic standards of the United States, and on the other, France's own national, historical, and linguistic framework within which rap becomes very much a *French* musical form with its own distinctive discourse and audience. Verses rapped in various languages proliferate amongst musical instrumentation from all corners of the world. A recent and continued relationship with the countries from which rappers have originally come, or from which they can claim their ancestry, results in a very current dialogue with transnational musical genres (like raï from Algeria[33] or rumba from both Congos[34]) and traditions (like griot[35]) that we have examined historically, with very different results to what emerged in the United States. France is a living musical space where different traditions, histories, languages, and cultures continue to meet and become part of the evolution of rap.

Notes

1. Rakim and Eric B., *Follow the Leader* (Uni Records, 1988); lyrics as seen on genius.com (last updated 15 April 2022).
2. Sha Be Allah, 'Today in Hip Hop History: Kool Herc's Party at 1520 Sedgwick Avenue 45 Years Ago Marks the Foundation of the Culture Known as Hip Hop', *The Source* (2018). https://thesource.com/2018/08/11/today-in-hip-hop-history-kool-hercs-party-at-1520-sedgewick-avenue-45-years-ago-marks-the-foundation-of-the-culture-known-as-hip-hop.
3. David Upshal, *The Hip Hop Years – Part 1: Close to the Edge*, Documentary, Channel 4, 1999.
4. David Eltis, 'A Brief Overview of the Trans-Atlantic Slave Trade', *Voyages: The Transatlantic Slave Trade Database* (2007): 1700–1810.
5. John Leland, *Hip: The History* (New York: HarperCollins, 2004).
6. Leland, *Hip: The History*, p. 23.
7. One of the languages of the Senegambia region in Western Africa.

8. Leland, *Hip: The History*, p. 5. Also see Clarence Major (ed.), *Juba to Jive: A Dictionary of African American Slang*.
9. KRS-One, 'Hip Hop Lives (I Come Back)', *Hip Hop Lives* (Koch Records, 2007).
10. Heather Augustyn, 'Spinning Wheels: The Circular Evolution of Jive, Toasting, and Rap', *Caribbean Quarterly* 61/1 (2015): 60–74.
11. Catherine Appert, 'On Hybridity in African Popular Music: The Case of Senegalese Hip Hop', *Ethnomusicology* 60/2 (2016): 279-299.
12. James Bernard, *The New York Times*, 3 February 1991, Section 2, Page 1 of the National edition with the headline 'Why the World is after Vanilla Ice'.
13. Marc Masters, 'NO!: The Origins of No Wave', *Pitchfork* (15 January 2008).
14. Thomas Gaetner, *Hip-Hop: Le rap français des années 1990* (Paris : Editions Fetjaine, 2012) pp. 20–21.
15. Felicia A. Viator, 'West Coast Originals: A Case for Reassessing the "Bronx West" Story of Black Youth Culture in 1980s Los Angeles', *American Studies* 58/3 (2019): 87–105.
16. NWA, 'Straight Outta Compton', *Straight Outta Compton* (Ruthless Records, Priority Records, 1988).
17. Karim Hammou, *Une histoire du rap en France* (la Découverte, 2014).
18. Nathanel Amar, '"Do You Freestyle?" The Roots of Censorship in Chinese Hip-Hop', *China Perspectives* 1–2 (2018): 107–113.
19. Hammou, *Une histoire du rap en France*; Richard Bramwell, *UK Hip-Hop, Grime and the City: The Aesthetics and Ethics of London's Rap Scenes* (London: Routledge, 2015).
20. Felix Wiedemann, 'The Local and the Global in Networks of Lebanese and Algerian Rappers', *Open Library of Humanities* 5/1 (2019): 26.
21. Jaqueline Lima Santos, 'Hip-Hop and the Reconfiguration of Blackness in Sao Paulo: The Influence of African American Political and Musical Movements in the Twentieth Century', *Social Identities* 22/2 (2016): 160–177.
22. Eun-Young Jun, 'Seo Taiji Syndrome: Rise of Korean Youth and Cultural Transformation through Global Pop Culture Music Styles in the Early 1990s', in Shin, Hyunjoon, and S. Lee. *Made in Korea* (London: Routledge, 2017) p. 145; Kendra Salois, *The Networked Self: Hip Hop Musicking and Muslim Identities in Neoliberal Morocco* (University of California, Berkeley, 2013).
23. References have variously been made, for example, to *Raï* in Algeria, *Shulaibao* in China, *Bol* in North India, and *Konnakol* in South India.
24. Hammou, *Une Histoire du Rap en France*, p. 78.
25. Article 'Entrée en vigueur du quota de 40% de chansons francophones à la radio', *Conseil Supérieur d'Audiovisuel (CSA)*, République Française, published on 19 January 1996, as seen on 1 November 2017.
26. Hammou, *Une Histoire du Rap en France*, pp. 240–242.
27. Karim Hammou and Patrick Simon, 'Rap en français et racialisation', *Mouvements* 96/4 (2018): 29–35.

28. Paroma Raya Ghose, 'Silence ... on est en France': a rap history of the 'other' in France (1981–2012). PhD thesis (Graduate Institute of International and Development Studies, 2020).
29. Paroma Raya Ghose, 'Rap Speaks, But Who Listens? The Musical "Other" in France'. Histories of the Present. *History Workshop Journal Online*, 4 January 2021.
30. The term *banlieue* has been mistranslated into English as 'suburb'. Although it technically occupies the same geographic spaces as a suburb, that is, the urban periphery of large cities, in France the term has socioeconomic connotations that are usually associated with government or social housing and its occupants, often from a working-class background [Author's definition].
31. Marie Sonnette 'Des mises en scène du "nous" contre le "eux" dans le rap français'. *Sociologie de l'Art* 1 (2015): 153–177.
32. Ghose, 'Rap Speaks, But Who Listens?'
33. Nouri Gana, 'Rap and Revolt in the Arab World'. *Social Text* 30/4 (2012): 25–53.
34. Rapper Youssoupha, who is half Senegalese and half Congolese, is the son of Tabu Ley Rochereau, who was a famous singer of African rumba from the Democratic Republic of Congo. Youssoupha, who made his career in France, has sampled his father's music in his rap song, for example 'Les Disques de mon père', *Noir Désir* (2012).
35. The song 'Diaraby' by French rapper Kaaris (2017) uses references to the African continent, including mention of griot; he characterises himself as singing/expressing himself as a griot.

2 | A History of Sound System and Emcee Culture

MARVIN SPARKS

The old adage says 'the revolution will not be televised', but while it isn't a traditional instrument, the sound system has empowered countless revolutions in sound. It has spawned multiple billion-dollar-generating genres and changed not only the way we make music but also the way we interact with music. With its origins tied to the Caribbean island of Jamaica, the huge speaker boxes, series of amplifiers, and microphones provide a space for everything from innovative record producers and engineers to improvising microphone controllers (or emcees).

Commonly associated with clubs, warehouses, and open-air lawns, a sound system's main job is to ensure the music fills the space and entertains according to expectation. However, there is a culture and history behind the system's functionality which includes numerous moving factors beyond the sound and the system. At its core, a sound system is more than a 'mobile disco'. It is an organisation, central to a community, with its own followers, and it helps to generate income for persons beyond those directly involved in providing the music selection.

Through firstly tracing the history of the sound system and Jamaica's nascent recording industry, this chapter will then unpack how this instrument has become fundamental for understanding rap music in the twenty-first century. Musical links between Jamaica, the United States and the United Kingdom are underpinned by approaches and agendas that have emerged from sound system practice in forms such as hip-hop, UK garage, and grime. It will also detail core techniques tied to sound system culture more broadly (such as toasting, clashing, and the production of riddims), and how these elements have been incorporated into this variety of diasporic rap styles.

Sound System Culture: The Origins of Toasting

Travelling back to 1940s Jamaica, American-imported jukeboxes and loudspeaker cabinets amplifying the radio or record player ran the town. Bar owners employed these machines to entice punters to their establishments. Not only did they entertain customers with the latest jazz and rhythm & blues records, jukeboxes also earned venues extra money as listeners paid to hear their requests or bought more drinks the longer they stayed. But a new vehicle for sound approached the horizon in the 1950s: the sound system–powered events. Makeshift dancehalls on open-air lawns were where people from lower working-class, or ghetto communities would put on their best clothes, drink alcohol, and gather to hear their favourite songs.[1] In pre-independent Jamaica, the sound systems (or 'sounds' as they were called) garnered tribal support from the area they dominated or represented. They gave people an identity, hope, and purpose, as well as respite from the working week and stresses of life.

Pioneers like Tom the Great Sebastian, King Edwards, and Count Smith the Blues Blaster each had their own section of Kingston and devoted supporters to boot. Together they inadvertently laid the foundations for the highly revered second wave of sound-system practitioners who would eventually be heralded for changing the landscape of Jamaican music and the world with it. Clement 'Coxsone' Dodd's Downbeat, Arthur 'Duke' Reid's Trojan, and Prince Buster's Voice of the People have come to be recognised as the Big Three, and with three people come three characters, stories, and stages of entry.

Clement Dodd, a carpenter from Kingston, could regularly be seen entertaining patrons with his dance moves at his parents' bar. The jazz and R&B lover soon moved to America for work, where he honed in on record collecting. Upon his return to Jamaica, those carpentry skills enabled his first steps into the sound-system world, as he would regularly be asked to build speaker boxes. He eventually formed the Downbeat sound system. Duke Reid or 'Duke the Mighty Trojan', a retired policeman, did much to change the complexion of the live entertainment space. Upon leaving the police force, Reid set up sound at the Treasure Isle Grocery and Liquor Store, which he owned with his wife. To survive in the island's police force, it was commonly thought you had to be badder than the baddest of criminals, and both his reputation and connections followed him into the music space. To make headway within what he saw as a competitive environment, Duke chose brute force, with his strong-armed friends using intimidation and physical strength to overrun other local sound systems, a tactic he tried to employ against Coxsone. Cecile Bustamante Campbell, better known as Prince Buster, then an amateur boxer, was employed by Coxsone as a form of security against Duke Reid. Buster was also tasked with standing outside their rival's parties and paid $5 to identify exclusive songs. But while he was an astute businessman,

Coxsone's cash flow didn't always trickle down to his employees. Payment was often withheld, causing a rift between the two and an eventual split. In the early 1960s Buster founded his own sound system, named the Voice of the People.

Prince Buster brought along with him another disgruntled member of Coxsone's outfit, Count Machuki. Inspired by American radio jockeys' jive talking and 'chku-chku' vocal accompaniments, Machuki built a solid reputation for toasting on records (not just talking in between them) at parties on lawns across the island.[2] Alongside peers such as King Stitt, toasting became a vital component to ensuring the crowds were entertained and would later evolve into what is now known as deejaying or emceeing, Jamaican parlance for rapping.[3]

Both the personal stories and legacies of 'Coxsone' Dodd and 'Duke' Reid are tied to being the two powerhouses behind Jamaica's first wave of global popular music. Exclusive imports could only last for a limited time before the competitor identified a particular anthem. Therefore, the duo began recording exclusive songs for their sound systems, before eventually recording and releasing 45 rpm vinyl records for retail. Coxsone's Studio One was the breeding ground for the island's early superstars such as Bob Marley, John Holt, Marcia Griffiths, Toots and the Maytals, Lee 'Scratch' Perry and its house band, the Skatalites. Reid founded the Treasure Isle record label, named after the shop he ran with his wife. The label released popular ska records and was pivotal in the rocksteady era. Crucially, Treasure Isle produced Jamaica's first three hits by toasting pioneer U-Roy.

Regularly cited as the originator or godfather of deejaying, the Kingston-born U-Roy honed his craft on a few sound systems before making his name on Coxsone's Downbeat as an understudy to King Stitt. U-Roy etched his name in history when he achieved an unthinkable feat with 'Wake the Town', 'Rule the Nation', and 'Wear You to the Ball' occupying numbers 1, 2, and 3 on the Jamaican music chart for six weeks in 1970. In putting the artform on the record and reaching unquestionable popularity, U-Roy helped legitimise the craft, spread the word internationally, and inspired successive generations.[4] Due to the success of those records, Duke Reid also compiled and produced the debut album *Version Galore* in 1971 before U-Roy was signed by Virgin Records and relocated to England.

Producers were initially resistant to the new delivery style, often refusing to record toasters' tracks. Singers' hits were easier to gain placement on radio which was owned by and geared towards the tastes of the middle-class, making them safer investments for the independent record labels. What played on the sound systems appealed to the working-class communities, something the Jamaican middle class didn't want to be associated with or promote. So, the sound system provided a home for deejays to sharpen their skills. With many radio stations ignoring their appeal, sound systems also amplified their voices.

Outernational Sound

For the most part, during the 1970s, Jamaican deejays were still gate crashing four- and eight-bar instrumental breaks on singers' hit recordings or over the dubbed-out instrumental version. Meanwhile, over the ocean in Britain and the United States, Caribbean migrants and first-generation Caribbean youths were adopting similar practices over music from their surroundings. One such person was a New York resident, born Clive Campbell in Kingston, Jamaica. Campbell, better known as DJ Kool Herc, began hosting what has become known as the first hip-hop parties at 1520 Sedgwick Avenue on 11 August 1973 and is widely credited as a founding father of hip-hop.[5] Kool Herc's journey began with a sound system called the Herculords. This was a continuation of his father's PA system, bought as a contribution to a music band he was a member of. Upon seeing another crew playing turntables through the same equipment, Herc found a way to wire the speakers into channel one in a Bogen preamplifier and the two turntables into channel two. Herc played funk and disco club-oriented rockers. But what made the crowd return week after week was what Herc calls the 'Merry-go-round', extending the riffs or instrumental breaks for the dancers, starting with the Incredible Bongo Band's 'Apache'. Other mainstay records include The Whole Darn Band's '7 Minutes of Funk', Eastside Connect's 'Frisco Disco', and James Brown hits. Through his girlfriend at the time, Herc met the man who would become recognised as the first hip-hop MC, Coke La Rock. Coke gained traction firstly through shout-outs to friends who were in the party, before graduating to improvised rhymes over the breaks. The short, catchy lines complemented rather than dominated the music. As the rappers enjoyed more freedom and appreciation from the partygoers, lyrics grew in complexity with groups like Cold Crush Brothers, Melle Mel, and Kid Creole, emerging as stand-outs in that era. Like King Stitt and Count Machuki before him, Coke La Rock's contribution is less well known because he didn't record his songs. Another son of Caribbean immigrants devised an ingenious way to extend the instrumental break. As a youth, Grandmaster Flash watched his Barbadian father play vinyl records, which intrigued him. Fascinated by music and electronics, he searched for scrap parts in neighbours' gardens to build a sound system: amplifiers, turntables, receivers, taking capacitors, and diodes, whilst finding speakers in the back of cars.

Moving into the 1980s, deejays began dominating the Jamaican musical landscape. Where reggae singers were previously the major pull, 1982 marked deejay Yellowman's ascension. Yellowman's initial steps began at the Alpha Boys school, a vocational residential school operated by Roman Catholic nuns in Kingston, Jamaica. Famous musical attendees of the school include trombonist Rico Rodriguez, singer Johnny Osbourne, and members of the Skatalites. The school's sound system, owned by Sister Mary Ignatius Davies (known as Sister Ignatius) was where Yellowman, born Winston Foster, learnt his trade before causing waves across the country with an Aces International sound system.

In the 'mother country', England, first-generation black British teenagers and young adults began establishing their own start-ups, following the blueprints heard through cassette tape recordings of events held at places like Skateland Park and Prison Oval with the likes of Gemini, Stereo Mars, and Volcano sound systems. Up to four sound systems would gather at those spaces with a crew of star deejays and singers along with their apprentices to entertain masses who had travelled island-wide to bear witness. Oftentimes, these places were referenced in songs, like Barrington Levy's 'Prison Oval Rock'. The running order would be an apprentice deejay to warm up for the headliners, the selector (Disc Jockey) would play the 'vocal' side before flipping to the instrumental version for the deejay to chat lyrics. Saying the right words at the right moment on the right riddim track would trigger loud cheers from the feverish crowd, encouraging the selector to play the record from the beginning, so they could hear the moment again. This became known as a forward, wheel-up, rewind, or reload.

British 'Yout' man sounds', as sound systems in the UK became known, plied their trade at birthday parties or held functions in houses or church halls, charging a small entrance fee. Teenagers who had studied a trade in college could lend their electrician or carpentry skills to build systems, while stronger friends transported equipment from storage to trucks and into the venue, otherwise known as 'box boys'.[6] Unity, Wassifa, and Sir Coxsone (a UK sound led by Lloydie Coxsone, named after Coxsone Dodd) made headway, while a group formed in Lewisham, southeast London broke into the mainstream. Saxon Sound International, organised by Lloyd 'Musclehead' Francis and Dennis Rowe, recruited an elite cast of microphone-handling entertainers including Smiley Culture, Tippa Irie, Papa Levi, Asher Senator, and Maxi Priest.

In 1984, Papa Levi landed a number one in Jamaica with 'Mi God, Mi King', and Smiley Culture hit UK top 20 with the racial profiling 'Police Officer'.[7] Singer Maxi Priest claimed a number one in the United States of America with 'Close to You' and numerous other hits across the world. Upon visiting Jamaica for the first time to perform, Tippa Irie recalled hearing Peter Metro, Yellowman, and Pinchers borrowing parts of their lyrics to entertain the audience. The innovative sound from London also developed a 'fast chat' style that inspired a generation. In the process, they inspired various rappers in diverse genres, ranging from reggae deejay General Levy and jungle MC Skibadee to the pioneering UK hip-hop outfit London Posse and Mercury Music Prize nominee Roots Manuva.

During the 1980s, Jamaican deejays were influencing rappers such as KRS-One, Heavy D, Smif-N-Wessun, and Busta Rhymes. In the 1990s the Notorious B.I.G. regularly travelled to the island. Biggie landed his first big feature on the remix for Super Cat's 'Dolly My Baby', an opportunity afforded to him by visionary music executive Sean 'Puffy' Combs. Combs saw merging dancehall with hip-hop as an opportunity to grow Biggie's presence in the market through dancehall's popularity, especially with Super Cat, who was arguably hip-hop's favourite Jamaican deejay. Busta Rhymes, another Brooklyn native also born to Jamaican parents, credits dancehall deejays for inspiring both his rapping prowess, presence, and performance style. 'There's two artists that I first ever seen do a million words in like two seconds: Papa San and Lieutenant Stitchie. Them two dudes were crazy', he said on the *Drink Champs* podcast, before referring to their clash at Sting 1986. 'They would rehearse their battles. One man do speed rap, then the other, then they'll do a verse together saying the same thing line for line, to see who gonna keep up or mess up. I saw that one day at a party when I was cutting school and I was in such amazement I wanted to do it too. At the time I wasn't hearing rappers do it.'[8] Perhaps the finest examples of Busta's dancehall influence are seen in both his breakthrough feature on A Tribe Called Quest's 'Scenario' and breakout single 'Woo-Hah!!! Got You All In Check'. The former sees Busta's vocal presence and delivery overshadow everybody else as if he were holding the microphone on a sound system, years beyond his experience as he calls for a 'Wheel-up, bring it back, come rewind!'. But on 'Woo-Hah!', the rapper dons a dancehall-inflected timing on the hard-hitting hip-hop instrumental, explicitly bridging his two worlds. His vocals can easily be lifted and placed onto a 1980s riddim track like Sleng Teng without missing a beat. A Jamaican-born New Yorker, Heavy D did much to inject his home country's flavours into hip hop, whether covering Third World's version of 'Now That We Found Love' for his most successful global charting hit to working with Super Cat on their cross-cultural collaboration 'Dem No Worry We'. 'The idea of two turntables and a microphone with a deejay chanting – or toasting – is Jamaican',[9] he said on BBC Radio 1Xtra whilst paying homage to the 'Godfather of Hip-Hop' DJ Kool Herc.

Clash

One approach that remains core to sound system practice is clashing. However, clashing has existed as a sport within sound system culture since the days of the Big Three in the '50s and '60s. Whereas sounds would spar with exclusive American imports and sound clarity, as time progressed deejays and singers traded lyrics to see who was the best crew. As some deejays rose in prominence, clashing became more synonymous with them. Prince Jazzbo and I-Roy warred on wax in the '70s, sounds like People's Choice (with Charlie Chaplin and Josey Wales) and Volcano battled on the lawn in the '80s, and Ninja Man and Super Cat verbally jousted on stage at landmark concert Sting in the '90s.

A competitive spirit has been present in the UK since the 1950s, when early Windrush Generation sound men, Count Suckle and Duke Vin, brought over what they had experienced back home in the Caribbean. This spirit grew in notoriety in the '80s with Saxon versus Coxsone being a much talked-about and referenced battle. 'The relationship was good. We had the clashes where if the dance was built as a clash, you'll clash but there was no fighting or arguing afterwards. We just clash and everything was nice after that', Flinty Badman said of clashes with Coxsone, Saxon, and Java when he was in east London's Unity Sound. Saxon Sounds' Tippa Irie had varied experiences, including ones that mirrored the Duke Reid days. 'There were sounds who would be gunning for us because we're the number one sound. And when you are at the top, then you've got people who want to bring you down and target you. We used to go to dances and there's [people] there and they want to turn over your sound and come with knives . . . There were sounds that took it to another level . . . When we went to New York, there was gunshots. We had to hide behind sounds [sound system equipment]!'

Sound systems offered artists direct contact with their audiences, who gave instant approval or indifference to their sometimes pre-written, or often freestyled lyrics. Without laying lyrics on the record, deejays could chop and change parts to maximise the potential for a reload. The trial-and-error nature invited artists to invent styles, timing, and vocal inflections that would catch on and begin a fresh approach. The evolution from an artist in the dancehall to a recording artist took many stages of development. A crucial step involved dubplates; testing lyrics in the dance led to cutting the lyrics on a riddim (instrumental of a popular vocal record), which were then pressed to a dubplate (an acetate plate) before being tested in the dancehall by the sound systems. Sometimes known as the test press, as a sign of their functionality, record labels would often release the best-performing songs based on popularity in the '70s and '80s dancehalls. The dubplate special, often simplified to the dubplate, became better known in the '90s onwards as a weapon in sound clashes where warring sounds would compete with customised versions of popular songs tagged with the sound's name.

Wyclef Jean, from rap trio the Fugees, recalled the dubplate background to their UK number one 'Killing Me Softly'.[10] Frequent Fugees collaborator Jerry 'Wonda' Duplessis had introduced him to the Stone Love sound system through cassette tapes, otherwise known as 'sound tapes'. Inspired by soundclashes, the Roberta Flack cover was recorded as a 'sound killing' tune, much to the original singer's dismay. Deciding to re-record the lyrics to match the original, the motivation became one of usurping the original – again with a sound clash mentality. The group became known for combining dancehall and hip-hop, frequently merging hip-hop and reggae, a concept ignited by the Salaam Remi-produced 'Fu-Gee-La'.

Likewise, UK garage's first number one started life as a dubplate. 'We initially made [Bound 4 Da] Reload as a dubplate for the pirate radio show', the track's producer DJ Oxide said, 'but my brother's £2,000 redundancy money paid for the first 1,000 white-label singles'. Initially known as the 'Casualty tune', it grew organically through the pirate radio and rave channels. 'When Oxide first played me the beginnings of "Bound 4 Da Reload", it was mainly the beat and the Casualty theme', Neutrino said. 'He wanted me to add some lyrics. "Bound for da reload" was something I said on pirate radio, meaning: "DJ, reload the track."'[11] The hours upon hours of practising in those environments enabled the MC to record it in one take even though it was his first time in a recording studio. UK sound system culture began to take on a different shape in the 1990s by operating in a different setting. Makeshift radio studios, such as Supreme and Delight FM, in council flats housed the two mics and a mixer set-up, while aerials sat on the tower block buildings' roofs broadcasting to the local geographical area.[12] The practice of MCs passing a mic while the DJ mixed vinyl records wasn't confined to the in-the-dance experience any longer.

By the time the UK moved to grime, getting a reload had become paramount. 'It's like euphoria', says Wiley, the Godfather of grime: 'When you're saying them to yourself you can realise the fans are going to get it. What you say has to be what other people want to say . . . When you're writing the bar, you can tell what's going to get a reload'.[13] The Heartless Crew are the best-known UK garage crew from north London, who operated in a similar fashion to Jamaican sound systems. Their performances catered to a female audience, which contrasted to the hyper-masculine lyrics by their peers Pay As U Go and So Solid Crew, playing everything from dancehall and hip-hop to R&B.[14] In 2001, on the bridge between UK garage and grime, they were involved in a historical clash with east London's Pay As U Go Cartel at Destiny's nightclub in Watford. Heartless Crew's Bushkin had an issue with Pay As U Go's Major Ace, because he felt Ace was copying his lyrics – an accusation Ace refuted. HLC were meant to clash south London's So Solid at the Camden Palace, but that failed to materialise due to So Solid's absence from the stage. Bushkin counteracted PAUG's anthem 'Know We', rewording the chorus from 'Know we, them no know we' to 'Nowhere, you're going nowhere' much to the crowd's delight. 'We could clash in a way where Pay As U Go couldn't handle it', Bushkin recalled. The Heartless Crew won the crowd over on the day as proven by the party-goers and Bushkin's interaction: 'When I say Pays As U Go, you say: "Dead"'. 'People kinda say we patterned up grime because there wasn't any clashing in garage prior to us', the MC said, 'but because we had come from a sound system ting, clashing was normal to us'. So Solid's Asher D versus Roll Deep's Dizzee Rascal clash on Choice FM's Night Flight show, hosted by Commander B, helped solidify the changing of the guards. 'Clashing is a sport', Bushkin said. 'It's just like watching two of your best boxers fight. You want to see who is the best and who does what on the day. Competition builds champions. It's definitely an important part of reggae and sound system culture'.

Whilst clashing wasn't prevalent in the genres of jungle or UK garage, London's next generation of youths were consuming all the previously referenced moments. Primarily known for champagne, Patrick Cox loafers, and high-fashion brands, UK garage signified optimism and good times. As the 2000s approached, a darker sound with a more confrontational attitude began its ascendancy.[15] Grime, as it would become known, embraced many of the sound system culture elements, perhaps more than any of its predecessors. Microphone relays over instrumentals to get a wheel-up and recording songs as dubplates carried over, but clashing became a pillar for the competitive spirit. Any grime MC worth something clashed, be it in the school playground, youth clubs, on radio, or on stage. 'The reason why I'm the warlord of this country – I'm not Bounty Killer – but the reason why I war is because I'm a sportsman about it. I do it because it helps raise my level. I feel like if I didn't battle, I wouldn't have got better as a person', said Wiley.[16] Not only did Wiley grow the genre by making instrumental riddims pushing the fresh sound and helping to usher in young talents, he clashed many other MC's and built an arena for clashing with the Eskimo Dance series of events.

Riddim

Riddims are also a pillar of sound system culture. Artists offering different interpretations of the same instrumental can be drawn back to the times on the lawns. Back in 1972 Jamaica, an accident provided a gateway to the next stage. It is said a disc cutter named Smithy forgot to attach the vocals to the Paragons' song 'On the Beach', thus leaving an instrumental version.[17] The first notable riddim project came via the Uniques' recording 'My Conversation'; one of the three group members, singer Jimmy Riley, offered to sell the rhythm track ('riddim') to a producer named Rupie Edwards. Without a grand plan, but a series of song ideas, the producer recorded a few songs packaging them as the Yamaha Skank. As Jamaica's recording industry began to form, riddims made by producers were pressed with numerous vocal options for DJs to play and listeners to debate. Althea & Donna's 'Uptown Top Ranking' topped the UK singles chart in 1978; its origins are on an older recording. The original song is Alton Ellis' 'I'm Still In Love', which was re-versioned by Marcia Aitken who offered a female perspective. However, there was a gear shift when deejay Trinity got a hold of it for 'Three Piece Suit', detailing his romantic experience with a woman in the spaces between Marcia Aitken's vocals. 'Uptown Top Ranking' responded to that.

The culture prevailed and similar movements happened in hip-hop, whether by economy or inspiration. Sugarhill Gang's 'Rapper's Delight' works in a similar fashion to the aforementioned songs, starting life as a disco record, Chic 'Good Times', before being repurposed to provide an instrumental for rappers' lyrics. New York rapper 50 Cent scored street hits from beat-jackin' on mixtapes. The Jamaica, Queens native and his G-Unit members were able to demonstrate their own song-crafting ability compared to the original version. If theirs was better, they automatically elevated themselves to the same talent level as those with bigger investment budgets, smash hits, and longer careers. Road rap, a sub-genre which emerged in London during the late 2000s, had a strong base amongst those living in similar environments. To break beyond the community constraints, a sound system–friendly track broke ranks and set the pace for the underground sound of the 2010s. Giggs, a rapper from south London, traced early steps as an entertainer to DJing reggae and dancehall records for locals on his Peckham housing estate. After a short stint in prison, he built a steady following through mixtapes; however, 'Talking the Hardest' from the 'Ard Bodied mixtape with Dubz sent shockwaves through clubs. Now considered to be the unofficial national anthem, in black British music circles, 'Talking the Hardest' started out abroad as the Dr. Dre–produced 'Here We Go' by West Coast rapper Stat Quo. Detailing road tales and exploits, Giggs channels the spirit of the '90s dancehall songs he played in the community in his setup of punchlines and landing his words on the beat. In Giggs' footsteps came a number of rappers who applied their words to other established artists' work, many of which were dancehall. J Hus recorded one of his first songs, 'Vacation', on the Dark Skies Riddim; Ratlin remixed Mavado's 'Messiah'; and Dr Vades ft. Yxng Bane, Kojo Funds & Don Elito 'Balenciaga' is on the 'Messiah' riddim and most notably, Sneakbo on Vybz Kartel's 'Touch a Button', which featured on the Sprite Riddim. These early songs in the careers of rising artists formed the basis of the afro-swing movement, thus affirming the fundamentality of the sound system for understanding present manifestations of rap.

Conclusion

Sound system's spirit in the 2020s is far wider reaching than its pioneers could have imagined. In its purest form, there are crews of DJs and MCs directly inspired by their Jamaican heroes who have formed their own organisations across the world. World-renowned Englishman David Rodigan MBE, Japanese sound Mighty Crown, Germany's One Love, and South Sudanese refugee Dynamq have clashed and sometimes beaten Jamaican heavyweights. Award-winning electronic dance music (EDM) group Major Lazer took the spirit of sound systems to the world's charts and festivals with their unique fusion of Jamaican music with EDM culminating in their 2015 global smash-hit 'Lean On'. On stage, they utilise the

DJ (Diplo) and MC (Walshy Fire, formerly of Miami-Jamaican sound system Black Chiney) combination that rose to the fore in the 1990s, which saw MCs adopt a style more geared towards introducing records and interacting with the audience with speeches than chatting lyrics for a rewind.

The most explicit living example of sound-system culture in its thrilling performance form lives on through grime. While a DJ plays instrumentals, crews of MCs still pass a microphone and wait their turn in silently competitive environments to showcase their most interactive lyrics for crowd approval and a rewind. But mostly the sound systems' legacy today is linked to depths in sound it opened the door for. Before the hand-built Jamaican sound systems, speaker boxes weren't capable of handling such a wide range of top-end and deep bass line frequencies whilst maintaining high power output without distortion. Numerous multi-billion-dollar genres, including genres like hip-hop, reggaeton, and electronic dance music, and UK bass genres, benefit from the capabilities offered by this revolutionary instrument as a result.

Notes

1. Sonjah Stanley Niaah, *Dancehall: From Slave Ship to Ghetto* (Ottawa: University of Ottawa Press, 2010).
2. Heather Augustyn, 'Spinning Wheels: The Circular Evolution of Jive, Toasting, and Rap', *Caribbean Quarterly* 61/1 (2015): 60–74.
3. Dick Hebdige, *Cut 'n' Mix* (Abingdon: Routledge, 1987).
4. Ibid., pp. 84–85.
5. Jeff Chang, *Can't Stop, Won't Stop: A History of the Hip Hop Generation* (London: Ebury Press, 2007).
6. Julian Henriques, *Sonic Bodies: Reggae Sound Systems, Performance Techniques, and Ways of Knowing* (New York: Continuum, 2011).
7. Paul Gilroy, *There Ain't no Black in the Union Jack: The Cultural Politics of Race and Nation* (London: Routledge, 1987).
8. www.youtube.com/watch?v=i7nieCNVbE4&t=7498s [Date accessed: 11 October 2023].
9. www.youtube.com/watch?v=_5Gdr9fA-1M&t=598s [Date accessed: 11 October 2023].
10. www.youtube.com/watch?v=eyM4NwLY5rs [Date accessed: 10 October 2023].
11. Dave Simpson, 'Oxide & Neutrino: How We Made Bound 4 Da Reload (Casualty)', *The Guardian* (2019). www.theguardian.com/culture/2019/jan/

29/oxide-neutrino-how-we-made-bound-4-da-reload-casualty [Date accessed: 10 October 2023].

12. Dan Hancox, *Inner City Pressure* (London: William Collins, 2018); White, J. *Urban Music and Entrepreneurship: Beats, Rhymes and Young People's Enterprise* (London: Routledge, 2017).
13. Marvin Sparks, 'Now Things: Talking Grime and Bashment with Wiley', *Large Up* (2012). www.largeup.com/2012/02/23/now-things-talking-grime-and-bashment-with-wiley/ [Date accessed: 10 October 2023].
14. Marvin Sparks, 'Without the Windrush Generation, British MC Culture Would Be Non-Existent', *Complex* (2019). www.complex.com/music/a/marvin-sparks/without-the-windrush-generation-british-mc-culture-would-be-non-existent [Date accessed: 10 October 23].
15. Richard Bramwell, *UK Hip-Hop, Grime and the City* (London: Routledge, 2015).
16. Sparks (2012).
17. Marvin Sparks, *Run The Riddim: The Untold Story of '90s Dancehall to the World* (London: No Long Stories, 2021).

PART II

Approaches to Rap

3 | *Beats, Rhymes and Life*

Connecting the Sonic and the Social in Hip-Hop Music Studies

J. GRIFFITH ROLLEFSON

In his 1994 article for *Public Culture*, 'After the Love Has Gone: Bio-Politics and Etho-Poetics in the Black Public Sphere', Paul Gilroy issued a strongly worded caution against critics and scholars reducing rap music to text. Writing at the dawn of the dynamically interdisciplinary constellation of critics, scholars, activists, and artists that would become hip-hop studies, Gilroy offered an early course correction, urging us to remember that this music *is music*.

> The first adjustment involves querying the hold that this outlaw form exerts on critical writers who see in it a quiet endorsement of their own desire that the world can be readily transformed into text – that nothing resists the power of language. This is a familiar problem that Michel Foucault has stated succinctly in his famous cautioning against reducing the bloody "open hazardous reality of conflict" to the "calm Platonic form of language and dialogue". It bites sharply in this area especially when the phenomenology of musical forms is dismissed in favour of analysing lyrics, the video images that supplement them and the technology of Hip hop production.[1]

Gilroy's proposed 'adjustment' was an important and prescient one, as the academic study of rap music flourished in comparative literature and media studies departments long before notoriously conservative university music departments were forced to play catch-up (there's a reason for the term 'conservatory' after all) and offer a way forward in dealing with rap music and musicking as sonic phenomena and praxis.[2]

Like most African-American musics in university music departments, hip-hop was caught in a typically racialized double bind at this time. In addition to being at the fraught center of the infamous culture wars of the 1990s, rap music was *too Other* to be of concern to the musicologists of the time and *too Western* to be of concern to ethnomusicologists. A telling index of this odd past is that the first monograph on hip-hop by a music scholar was Cheryl Keyes's 2002 *Rap Music and Street Consciousness*, which took the subtitle: *The Roots and Rhythms of Rap from Its Early Origins to the Twenty-First Century*. Before Keyes's ethnomusicological study, the most sonically attentive academic study of hip-hop was Adam Krims's 2000 *Rap*

Music and the Poetics of Identity – a book on the musicology/music theory side but authored by a cultural theorist. In short, it took two decades after hip-hop blew up for the academy's music scholars to take the world-changing musical sound of hip-hop seriously.

This is not to downplay the contributions of those journalists, cultural theorists, sociologists, linguists, African Americanists, Latin Americanists, and others – foremost among them, the artists, activists, and culture bearers themselves – who laid the basis for hip-hop studies. Those first writers and scholars to take up the banner of hip-hop studies laid an invaluable foundation, documenting musical language and discourses about the sound of hip-hop recordings and live performances as well as ear-to-the-ground emic perspectives on the artistry of MCs, DJs, producers, turntablists, beatboxers, singers, instrumentalists, and other hip-hop musicians – Tricia Rose, Greg Tate, Joan Morgan, Juan Flores, and James G. Spady, in particular, come to mind. Because of the severely myopic and limiting ways that university music departments have historically taught music, a look at musical approaches to hip-hop – this chapter's focus – must necessarily think critically about situating rap music within the state of the academic field that we call 'music'.[3]

Because 'music' remains such a conservative frame in the university – and a fraught cultural concept when regarded in planetary perspective, where music is often inseparable from dance, poetry, ritual, culture, and cultural identity – this chapter will approach the topic with a broadly decolonial, practical, and sound-centred approach to rap music. Such an approach will open us up to the important sonically minded contributions of arts practitioners, journalists, and scholars outside of music departments and conservatories, while focusing in on the recent contributions of scholars bringing to bear methods developed in the increasingly interdisciplinary – and thankfully now less insular – fields of musicology, ethnomusicology, music theory, popular music studies, and sound studies. The discussion will take a chronological tack, attending to the historical emergence of sound-centred approaches – refiguring received histories as necessary – and commenting on the place of those approaches in contemporary hip-hop scholarship.

While this critical survey will not (indeed, cannot) attend to every landmark study, author, or approach, I hope to provide examples from the field to broadly outline historical developments and contemporary approaches and help hip-hop scholars enrich their thinking about how they might make their research and writing more musical. And as a second disclaimer, I have attempted to include scholarship on hip-hop outside of the United States and discussion of some non-English publications, but because of the history of the music and the field and due to the readership of this collection, I've taken off my global hip-hop scholar hat here to look more closely at the particularly musical approaches that are well-developed in the Anglophone scholarship. I do hope that these approaches will be taken up, further developed, and localized around the world as this manifestly global music enters its second half-century.

'So What?': Connecting the Sonic and the Social

I remember first-hand the 'debates' about whether rap was even *music* as hip-hop blew up in the early 1980s.[4] This discourse is famously lampooned in a skit from De La Soul's 1996 *Stakes Is High*, wherein the voice of a Southern white man offers his two cents: 'Rap? ... There's no *music* in it. It's just, you know, [plural racist slur] talking' as honky-tonk music plays in the background.[5] As such, we might say that Gilroy's 1994 intervention not only calls out the academic discourse around hip-hop as insufficiently sound and praxis-centred but says something more foundational about how we hear and represent this music and its critical power. To be sure, 'music', as applied to hip hop, is a field of human creativity that encompasses everything from rapping, singing, making beats, and playing instruments to writing lyrics, thinking about word shape and diction, creating choreographies, staging shows, recording tracks, designing album art and fashion, and even marketing music and musicians. Music is not *just* sonic phenomena. But sometimes we need to be reminded that sonic practice – crafting sounds, listening to sounds, and moving to sounds – is at the core of rap music and hip-hop culture more broadly.

Thus spawned the title of this chapter: as A Tribe Called Quest put it almost thirty years ago, when you strip everything else away, rap music is *Beats, Rhymes, and Life*.[6] The title of that 1996 album has helped me sharpen my own thinking about the mutual constitution of music and life over the course of the past decades. The title also speaks to something of the magic in a Ralph Ellison line that I fell in love with twenty years ago: 'the real secret of the game is to make life swing' (1970). I may be preaching to the converted here, but in the next few pages I want to convince you that in taking musical sound seriously and developing our toolkits around how to approach it, we can tear down the wall between art and life a bit and gain insight into how the study of rap music and/as hip-hop culture might hold some new keys to unlocking those 'secrets'.

This brings us to (what I argue should be) a core tenet of musical enquiry – and a guiding principle for the present chapter: any musical approach to hip-hop should seek to connect the sonic and the social.[7] That is, if you're gonna tell us about musical sound, you'd better also tell us why it matters. As Jeff Chang recalled in his 2014 'new foreword' to the revised edition of Joe Schloss's landmark, *Making Beats*, 'choosing to write critically about hip-hop meant confronting "So what?" every day' for hip-hop heads like himself and Schloss (ix). This gets to the crux of Gilroy's early suggestion that hip-hop studies needed a better focus on the 'phenomenology of musical forms' that might help us not only take hip-hop's structures seriously, but understand how rap music's meaning and value is not (only) to be found on the page and in the abstract, but in the booming and bumping auditory experiences of clubs, ciphers, streetcorners, studios, the binaural headspace between L and R, and the affective (and propulsive) space between mind and heart (and ass).

So, if you're unsure about how to write about hip-hop's musical sound and practice or want to develop further your toolkit, please read on. If you're not sure musical sound matters, get sure.

Music Writing: Hip-Hop Journalism

Before hip-hop entered the academy, a new generation of culturally savvy and plugged-in music journalists established what hip-hop sounded like on the written page. Essays like those from Nelson George, Tracii McGregor, Joan Morgan, and the late, great Greg Tate, put into writing the connections between hip-hop music and its social bonds.[8] As just one example, in his 1988 review essay, 'Eric B. & Rakim: Titty Boom-A-Rooney', Tate introduces us to the sound of *Follow the Leader* thus:

The music on "Follow the Leader" is spooky, a science-fiction score that sounds straight out of the Tangerine Dream songbook. Rakim's on an elocutionary speed-trip, a black bullet train slitting through hyperspace. The rhymes are telemetric, tracking sucker-soft targets with a monomania more relentless than anybody's Terminator. In rap's ongoing war for poetic supremacy, Rakim has metaphoric space he can call his own, though for others it's a danger zone.[9]

The language not only captures the sound of the album and connects it to its communities, but encodes the linguistic swag, dope rhymes, and ill flows of hip-hop performance within its very arguments. Indeed, Tate epitomizes a sort of gold standard for hip-hop writing that we might render as 'hip-hop (studies)'. That is, his work performed for us why this music mattered, implicitly recognizing the mutual implications of the sonic and the social by uniting form and content in his writing, practicing a hip-hop studies that is always already within hip-hop's questing organic intellectual ethos.[10]

The best of hip-hop studies today takes the lead from the honesty and urgency of those early writers, simultaneously keeping 'the bloody "open hazardous reality"' of hip-hop's subject matter in focus and reminding us that *this music is music*. From decolonial scholarship that reminds us of the power of the musician in her role as storyteller, historian, griot, and 'Black CNN',[11] to political economy research that notes the sonically disruptive potential of hip-hop and its destabilizing and remixing cultural practices,[12] hip-hop studies that centre musical sound open up broader vistas and more elemental soundscapes, reminding us that *stakes is high*.

Black Noise: Sound Studies

Speaking of the griots, it is an oft-forgotten fact that Rose's conceptual frame in *Black Noise* was sparked by an interest in Jacques Attali's *Noise: The Political Economy of Music*. Attali's 1977 book theorized the prophetic role that music has played throughout history, from shamanic ritual practice to free improvisation. His theory that prophecy comes in the form of sonic disruptions to the social status quo provided Rose with the blueprint for thinking about how hip-hop changed everything – from music, media, and remix culture, to social protest and identity, to language and politics. Notably, his book also paved the way for the field of sound studies.

While the field of sound studies is relatively new compared with the approaches that I outline here, it is important to recognize that Rose's 1994 *Black Noise* elaborated that nascent field at a similarly important moment for hip-hop studies. While a primary target of Gilroy's critique of 'bio-politics' and the essentialization of hip-hop, it also anticipated Gilroy's musical challenge and set a new standard in taking sound and sonic praxis seriously. The book perfectly captured the 'Bring the Noise' militancy of Public Enemy's 1988 track and hip-hop's broader interest in sonic disruption *as* political action. Further, it kicked the 'noise' theme from the apex of hip-hop's lauded 'Golden Age' into the future, inspiring the landmark collection, *Global Noise* (Mitchell, 2001), and the new *Nordic Noise* (2024) – both of which interrogate the disruptive power of hip-hop in social contexts outside of the United States in sonically attentive ways.

While sound studies approaches are by definition interdisciplinary and generatively ambiguous in scope and method, the field's expanded view of music *and/as* sound *and/as* politics provided the big tent necessary for imagining a thing called hip-hop studies. In this regard it is worth noting that a decade before *Black Noise*, the musician and writer David Toop published one of the first books on hip-hop under the title *Rap Attack: African Jive to New York Hip Hop* (1984). While Toop did not define his work as sound studies in this era before the field's codification, he, like Attali, presaged the broadened view of environmental sound and soundscapes that would become central to the field's expansion beyond the potentially limiting frame of 'music'. It was a fitting frame. If conservative commentators were going to dismiss hip-hop as 'not even music', then rap artists would 'bring the noise'. Along with its influential framing of rap music as a political 'attack' – what he theorized as a 'resistance vernacular' – the book also captured hip-hop's command of public space with a sonically attuned imagination of boom boxes on street corners and sound systems wired up to park lampposts.

Today, scholars like Jennifer Lynn Stoever expand the wide-ranging quotidian and environmental approaches of sound studies to examine untold stories about rap musicking and hip-hop social and cultural production. Her article, 'Crate Digging Begins at Home', examines the listening, collecting, and selecting praxis of Black and Latinx women in the era leading up to the dawn of hip-hop's genesis in the South Bronx. Most notably, her *sound* studies approaches attend to *silences* in hip-hop studies – from correcting hip-hop's often dangerously masculinist hagiography to rethinking and enlivening the spaces in which hip-hop was *birthed*. Stoever nicely summarizes what sound studies can bring to hip-hop studies in a 2010 post to her acclaimed blog, *Sounding Out!* Commenting on the continued deficit of attentive sonic approaches in hip-hop studies, she writes:

> sound in hip hop studies seems to be taken for granted in the same way that vision is just about everywhere else. Although hip hop is understood to be an audio-visual art, its organizing metaphors are sonic: remixing, sampling, scratching, and Dj-ing all describe sonic phenomena as well as aural frameworks for understanding the world. The way in which hip hop studies take sound for granted presents both a lesson and an opportunity for sound studies.[13]

Stoever's intervention in her thoughtful conclusion is that sound studies can bring to hip-hop studies a methodology that highlights rap music not as cultural product but as process, focusing on 'the way in which sound is treated as an active process, a way of thinking and being, rather than solely an object of study'. As Shortie No Mass and De La Soul put it thirty years ago: 'I am / I be'.[14]

Hiphopography: Ethnomusicology and Anthropology

Stoever's processual focus recalls Christopher Small's active frame of 'musicking' to highlight musical praxis as well as product. It should also remind us that the fields of cultural anthropology and ethnomusicology have long stressed just such a focus on music and/as cultural production. While a historian and journalist by trade, James G. Spady's development of a community-engaged, culture-bearer focused, and ethnographically rich method of 'hiphopography' set an early standard for culture-centred hip-hop research in his 1991 *Nation Conscious Rap*. As Alim et al. elaborate in *Global Linguistic Flows*, Spady's hiphopography insists on 'direct engagement with the "culture creators"' as critics and scholars in their own right as part of an aim 'to reinvigorate cultural studies' commitment to the people and put into practice what cultural anthropology (and, by extension, ethnomusicology) espouses, that is, a nonhierarchical, anticolonial approach that humanizes its subject'.[15]

Importantly, ethnographic musical approaches help us to contextualize musical sound and cultural praxis, attending to sonic phenomena and musical forms while offering rich detail about how and why people engage in these sounding and listening practices. In short, hiphopography implicitly asks us to connect the sonic and the social. Keyes's landmark ethnomusicological hip-hop monograph, *Rap Music and Street Consciousness* (2002), for instance, helps us situate the music of hip-hop's African storytelling inheritances in the 'street feeling' and call-and-response musical structures of hip-hop – and does so using Western musical notation to help freeze in time and examine salient structural details of hip-hop's syncopated swing and swag (a set of methods we will investigate shortly).[16] Schloss's ethnographic study of sample-based hip-hop, *Making Beats* (2004), uses participant observation to study the art and life of beat makers from inside these communities of practice, examining and privileging hip-hop's own 'elaborate theoretical frameworks' along the way.[17] Marcyliena Morgan's, *The Real Hip Hop* (2009), explores the music and motivations of artists through detailed ethnographic writing from her fieldwork with LA's Project Blowed.[18] More recently, in her 2018 *In Hip Hop Time*, Catherine

Appert combines analyses of historical musical flows and contemporary sociocultural meaning with ethnographic thick description of hip-hop storytelling in Dakar, Senegal to better understand 'music's intersections with speech'.[19]

Hiphopographic approaches, broadly defined, help us contextualize musical recordings, music making, music listening, and musical communities in their cultural and historical realities. They keep us honest. Such 'direct engagement' with artists and communities forces researchers to struggle through complexity, resist abstraction and overtheorizing, and represent with nuance. That is, hiphopographic methods help us resist reducing hip-hop to the 'calm Platonic form of language and dialogue' and avoid flattening the diverse flips and flows of DJs and MCs into facile tropes that suit our own agendas.[20] Perhaps most importantly, ethnographic methods – especially sustained, trust building, and slow research methods – help open us up to hip-hop's organic intellectual ethos and worldviews.

Sounding Race in Popular Music Studies: Musicology and Cultural Studies

Something of a mainline practice today, musicological and cultural studies approaches that centre sound and musical practice take up and broaden the field of popular music studies to connect the sonic and the social. Where the field of popular music studies began with a sociological interest in musical subcultures, it soon began turning towards the primary artefacts of those communities: records. The musicology side of hip-hop studies best typifies this interest in the recorded sonic artefacts of hip-hop culture, the musical 'works' of hip-hop artists, and the production, industry, and commerce of hip-hop.

Emerging from the Leftist scholarship of British cultural studies, in its early days popular music studies centered on white artists and subcultural communities. But even a cursory look at organizations like the International Association for the Study of Popular Music (IASPM) and gatherings like the Pop Conference (formerly Experience Music Project) will attest to the rise of research that focuses on music and race – especially in the realm of hip hop – given the centrality of Black music to the popular music industries. Taking their cues from critical race theory, political economy, gender studies, queer studies, and other social justice–centred theoretical frames, hip-hop scholars in this very active research space have examined a vast array of ways that music making and listening are central to who we are (and who we are becoming). Importantly, like sound studies (with which these fields overlap regularly), the broadly defined field of popular music studies finds in music an alternative space for self-making, not just in the sociopolitical terms of sub-cultural affiliation and solidarity, but in the music's liminal, artistic, and non-logocentric worlds of listening, dancing, concertgoing, and musicking.

While certainly not the first book to examine hip-hop and race (see Tate, Rose, Keyes, and others listed earlier), Loren Kajikawa's *Sounding Race in Rap Songs* (2015) is emblematic of sonically attentive close reading work that helps us better understand how hip-hop tracks and their breakbeats sound racial formations, 'providing an understanding of the aesthetic grounds from which rap's projections of race emerge'.[21] Importantly, approaches like Kajikawa's situate those aesthetics in the complex, often fraught, interplay between cultural expressions from the street and the capitalist imperatives and niche marketing practices of the culture industries.

As the undeniable artistry of hip-hop's much lauded 'golden age' artists started to sink in by the mid 1990s, articles like Robert Walser's 'Rhythm, Rhyme, and Rhetoric in the Music of Public Enemy' (1995) began to set the standard for academic studies of hip-hop tracks.[22] By taking musical sound seriously, connecting it to social meanings and functions, and applying a type of academic rigor heretofore reserved for the 'masterworks' of the Western art music (aka 'classical') canon, Walser theorized 'the intentionality of hip hop's "noise"' through a close reading of PE's 'Fight the Power'. Like Keyes before him, Walser's article (notably published in *Ethnomusicology*, not a musicology journal) used musical transcriptions in Western notation (see Figure 3.1) to represent the carefully layered and densely textured productions – creating something akin to orchestral scores. He uses this notational analysis not only to establish the artistry of this street form, but to examine the sampling, layering, and production techniques which turned these samples and other sounds into the dense, noisy, and destabilizing textures that earned the Bomb Squad its name. This noisy music, Walser suggests, was crafted to propel similarly disruptive lyrics as an immanent critique of the culture industries (see also: 'Burn Hollywood Burn'). Indeed, he then goes on to notate Chuck D and Flavor Flav's polyrhythmic flows and call-and-response lines.

As Walser is quick to point out, using classical music notation to examine hip-hop music 'requires some justification' as a classic 'etic' or 'outsider' analytical approach. Classical music aesthetics centre on pitches and tonal environments, therefore the systems developed to notate (and analyse) this

Figure 3.1 Musical transcription of the opening groove of 'Fight the Power'. (Courtesy of Robert Walser).[23]

music do their best work in these areas.[24] Rap music aesthetics, by contrast, tend to focus on timbres, textures, and – most notably – rhythms. That said, this set of notational systems is a widely used one and has the potential to let us freeze and visually represent not only pitch, but rhythm, tempo, texture, instrumentation (and therefore timbre in a way), and other features of musical form and praxis. As such, Walser suggests, 'if notation conceals, it also reveals. Rhythms and certain other kinds of relationships can be sketched with some amount of accuracy, if we keep in mind that we are looking at static representations of dynamic relationships'.[25]

We'll come back to these caveats and related pitfalls – examining visual notation systems that have been developed from more emic perspectives – but for non-music specialists it is important to underscore the concluding point here. Musical notation is not 'the music'. If anything is 'the music' it is the musical sound – or our hearing and conceptualization thereof. Instead, musical notation is simply an analytical tool that can help us symbolize and freeze musical sounds (make a 'static representation') to give us a new angle of consideration of our often slippery and ephemeral sonic experiences. Notice too, that I didn't use the word 'objective' in this explanation. Musical notation is no less subjective than our writing about personal experiences of boom bap on the dancefloor, for it too is an analytical practice – the result of human decisions around what questions we're asking and what we're looking to represent. While we might rightly question the strategy of *proving* hip-hop's complexity, artistry, and therefore value through the 'white racial frame' and ideological baggage of Western notation (to which we'll return shortly), as Walser suggested some thirty years ago, such approaches reveal just as they conceal. As such, notation can be a useful addition to our scholarly toolboxes.

Over the past twenty years, scholars like Kajikawa, Mark Katz, and Justin Williams have performed insightful close readings armed with musicological and sound-centered cultural studies tools that help connect the sonic to the social and centre the question, 'so what?' Like Stoever, Justin Burton, Lauron Kehrer, Elliott Powell, and others have built on these tools to theorize how hip-hop sounds intersectionality and in many ways *is* critical race theory, opening up new vistas on rap music's sound-borne solidarities, affective economies, and much more. While my own scholarship often deploys hiphopographic methods such as interviews and community engagement – and looks to incorporate all of the methods described in this overview – this realm of musicological close reading is my home base. And while the handle 'close reading' does the best work at communicating the method, what we're usually talking about is, of course, 'close listening' – a scholarly practice that I call 'ear work' in describing this praxis to students. Ear work requires that we listen in and around our subject of study until, as I've suggested earlier, we 'get sure' that we know how the sound that we're investigating matters.

Of course, close listening practices encompass not only academic research, but our ethical responsibilities to the artists we're working on or with and the postcolonial Black and Brown communities who birthed this culture and its music.[26] As such, in this discussion of close listening to beats and rhymes I must stress the need to listen too for the lives represented on hip-hop tracks – and (re)commit to listening not just for data that supports our respective theses, but to enact an ethics of close listening that might open us up to new worlds and unimagined perspectives – the type of ethically sensitive ear work that Pauline Oliveros dubbed 'Deep Listening'.[27]

Flow Studies: Music Theory and Graphic Notation Approaches

While Keyes and Walser used notation as part of their respective ethnomusicological and musicological studies, the creation of such 'static representations' is at the very core of another academic discipline: music theory. It is this field of musical analysis that has developed the most detailed methods and techniques for examining the sonic details and musical forms of hip-hop – if sometimes at the expense of the social, 'so what?' question.

A model for hip-hop scholarship that connects the sonic and the social is the work of Noriko Manabe, a scholar whose work on Japanese hip-hop is centred in music theory but augmented by sustained ethnographic work and cultural studies methodologies. Her 2013 article 'Representing Japan: "National" Style among Japanese Hip-Hop DJs' is emblematic of this approach, using notation to examine and elaborate how DJs rep Japan sonically while situating those artists in their national and international contexts and highlighting ideas that came up in her ethnographic interviews with the artists.[28] As even a cursory overview of the literature will show, however, the DJ, producer, and turntablist remain badly underrepresented in hip-hop scholarship – a fact that suggests: (1) how hard and time-consuming ear work is to do, (2) how difficult it is to represent the slipperiness, multivalence, and ephemerality of sonic phenomena, and (3) how much easier it is to focus on and interpret hip-hop's eye-catching lyric and video 'texts' that Gilroy noted. There are wonderful studies that situate the art of the DJ and producer within the broader context of hip-hop arts practice and social life, but it is curious to note the small handful of influential monographs that delve into hip-hop production – a line running from Joe Schloss's groundbreaking *Making Beats* (2004), to Mark Katz's *Groove Music* (2012), to Dan Charnas's *Dilla Time* (2022). It is true that books are less common in the field of music theory (indeed, neither Schloss, Katz, nor Charnas are theorists per se), but the continuing dearth of beat-centered monographs in the field is nonetheless remarkable. With a few exceptions, these books remain the exceptions that prove the rule.

An area that has gotten increased attention from music theorists in recent years is the sound of rapping – the sonic substance and phenomenology of performed lyrics and rhymes. This impressively active field of 'flow studies' has mounted an impressive intervention into the racist discourses that devalue hip-hop production by suggesting it is 'noise' and MCs are 'just … talking'. Further, through their nuanced sonic analyses, the field of flow studies also issues a potentially powerful corrective against, to refigure Gilroy, 'reducing the bloody "open hazardous reality of"' sound to text. At their best, flow studies can remind us that rappers are not just writers, reporters, authors, and poets, but storytellers, griots, and musicians. Indeed, the very need for this corrective is ironic considering that written lyrics are something of a historical aberration – the exception to millennia of poetic praxis, not the rule.

Two scholars that laid the groundwork for this area of research are Adam Krims and Felicia Miyakawa. In his 2000 *Rap Music and the Poetics of Identity*, Krims expertly details and theorizes the need for us to pay closer attention to sound in hip-hop studies (and popular music studies more broadly) before laying out his 'Genre System for Rap Music' – a 'vocabulary of flow' schema that helps us think more systematically about how rappers rap. In her 2005 *Five Percenter Rap*, Miyakawa builds on Krims's schema, offering numerous musical examples in both standard Western notation and a new bespoke form of 'flow maps' (see Figure 3.2) developed for notating hip-hop rhythms and emphases.

	1	–	*	–	2	–	*	–	3	–	*	–	4	–	*	–	
m 88													x	x	x	x	Then they give us
m 89	*x*		x	x	x	x	x		x		x	x	x	x	*church*, a trick to try to *ease* this, thought I'd check
m 90	*x*		x	x	x	x			x		x		x	x	x	x	it *out*, had to learn about *Jesus*. Told them he was
m 91	*x*		x	x	x			x	x	x	x		x	x	x	x	*black* and they called me a *hater*, then he's on a
m 92	*x*			x	x	x	x			x	x						church *wall*, yeah like a slave *trader*.

Poor Righteous Teachers, "Ghetto We Love," mm. 88–92.

Figure 3.2 Flow map of Poor Righteous Teachers' 'Ghetto We Love'. (Courtesy of Felicia Miyakawa). The map shows measure numbers at left (y-axis), subdivisions of beats at top (x-axis), x-marks within the resultant grid, and the lyrics under consideration (with stressed syllables in italics) at right.[29]

Most notably, both of these landmark monographs in flow studies are keen to underscore how their detailed sonic analyses help us better understand how musical form is of central import to lyrical content.

In his influential 2009 article 'On the Metrical Techniques of Flow in Rap Music', music theorist Kyle Adams built on Krims and Miyakawa's work to codify a new standard in flow mapping. Using a modified form of Time Unit Box System (TUBS) – developed by ethnomusicologist Mantel Hood – the system sidestepped standard notation's focus on pitch, instead highlighting rhythm and rhyme. Developing Miyakawa's side-by-side system, this now standard mapping technique doesn't require familiarity with standard music notation and uses spreadsheet software to map rhythmic patterning with the words right in the grid. Further, this notation system based on widely available software allowed researchers to colour code, bold, or italicize other salient details such as rhyme (as in Figure 3.3).

In addition to showing us the rhythm and rhyme schemes at play, Adams's publication of this article in the journal *Music Theory Online* allowed him the game-changing option to include a digital musical excerpt with the visual notation – here a 41-second clip of 'Wu-Gambinos'. This type of notation with sound will be a key aid in foregrounding the sonic substance of hip-hop music as we enter a multimodal digital publishing environment. Today, such work in flow studies is also beginning to use computational analytical methods, extending our understanding of rhythm, meter, and groove through corpus techniques that augment our own ear work. The landmark monograph in this area is Mitchell Ohriner's 2019, *Flow: The Rhythmic Voice in Rap Music*.

While hip-hop researchers like Adams and Ohriner are breaking important new ground in this emergent area of 'flow studies', here we also run into the inherited traps of armchair 'etic' (non-insider) approaches and their structural myopia. As such, I want to issue a caution that such music theory and computational approaches also need to be grounded in the lives and cultures of the hip-hop community lest they risk misrepresentation, flaneurism, cultural appropriation, implicit bias, or 'reducing the bloody "open hazardous reality"' of rap musicking (from bedroom producers to 'THUG LIFE' in full bloom) to academic exercise (from humanistic overtheorizing to dehumanizing algorithms, graphs, and charts).

As music theorist Ewell has eloquently and forcefully argued, the discipline has both passively and actively sustained and promoted a 'white racial frame' through its construction of the Western art music canon and its (dead, white,

Example 1d. Lyric chart for "Wu-Gambinos," third verse, showing accented and rhyming syllables

	1				2				3				4			
	x	y	z		x	y	z		x	y	z		x	y	z	
1	CROWN	is	SHIN-			we're	BLIND-					Sol-	id	gold	I'm	re-
2	CLI-	nin'	the		SKY	on	a	cloud		din'	like	some	DIA-	monds	dou-	ble
3	BREAST-	ed			Bul-	let-	proof	VEST-	ed	with	sil-	ver	LIN-	ings		
4	The	heart	the		CAGE	the	chest			and	well	pro-	TEC-	ted	cast-	in'
5	STONES		rib-		crack-	in'	two	hun-	dred-	and	so-	lar	PLE-	xus	and	watch
6	yo'	ass	get		blown	to	a	sea	of	six	and	BONES				
7	How	dare	you		'proach	with	DIM		FIRE	poems	and	brim-		STONE		
8	like	no-	ah		bean	green			souls		with	a	the	ov-	fiend	
9	the	grand	ex-		qui-	im-	pe-		a	ri-	al	wiz-	sol-	dier	mean	
10	za	rec-	come		site	your	ass			vi-	sit	ard	is	it	the	R[i]-
11	chem-	i-	cal		pay	sal	gi-		ant	the	black	oh	Lo-	cal	bi-	o
12	shots	to	Da-		un-	ver-			on	the	bi-		ge-	ne-	Lick-	in'
13	i-	mil-	vy		CROCK	ett	sand		mic-	ro-	chips	cen-	tenn-	ral	Hap-	py
14		cli-	len-	i-	thou-	a-	dre-		lin	son	it's	time	two	i-	shots	of
15	It's	a	um		out	sem-	na-		nig-	gaz	who	like	for	al	bou-	pen-
16	Trapped	in-	burst		re-	like	blin'		ge-	nie	side	the	fol-	shots	low-	tin'
17			age	you're	duct		a				in-		bot-		in'	and...
			your										tle			

Figure 3.3 Flow map for 'Wu Gambinos' showing rhythmic patterning as well as rhyme schemes (color coded). (Courtesy of Kyle Adams). Note that the system here also includes the musical excerpt under consideration.[30]

male) 'masters' – and through myriad other institutional, pedagogical, and intellectual structures. For our purposes here, it is music theory's positivist inheritance and claims to empirical objectivity that pose the most immediate danger (claims not unique to music theory, but to musicology, ethnomusicology, and beyond, as well). Indeed, the flip side to the much-needed focus on hip-hop's musical sound that I'm stressing here is a lost-in-the-weeds myopia that smuggles in a tautological art-for-art's-sake ideological bent inherited from the Western art music tradition. Valuing and studying hip-hop for its complexity and artistry can be a fruitful and transformative exercise, but not without the context and perspectives of hip-hop communities of practice – and definitely not using the master's ~~tools~~ terms.

Indeed, I'll point the finger at myself in the 'humanistic overtheorizing' category, and it must be noted that many of the approaches to hip-hop studies emanating from music departments I've outlined here have been pioneered by white cis male scholars. In the interest of decolonization, my aim here is thus to foreground where we're at – noting all the important progress in the field along with all the dangerous and potentially violent pitfalls. Apropos of this aim, it is worth pointing out that such work is important and paradigm-changing, but that we need to have a robust and honest conversation about what these empirical, quantitative, and computational advances mean vis-à-vis questions of perspective and community legibility regarding hip-hop arts, practice, process, content, and form – just as we need to interrogate established cultural studies and ethnographic approaches like my own.

Judging from Adams's 2019 'Hip Hop in the Golden Age' and Sina Nitzsche's recent European Hip Hop Studies Network conferences that are bringing artists into sustained conversation with scholars, this conversation already seems well underway – and increasingly open about the politics of representation.[31] Indeed, practitioner-based music theory approaches like those of Kjell Andreas Oddekalv are emerging, and are indebted to the analytical rigor of Adams, Ohriner, Oliver Kautny, and others, suggesting that sound-centred and performative approaches to hip-hop are in the midst of an exciting and generative diversification. As just one exemplary case in point, ethnomusicologist Wayne Marshall has found common ground between music theory and hip-hop musicking perspectives in his analytical work in 'technomusicology', composing emically satisfying audiovisual analyses[32] and using the very DAW visual interfaces that hip-hop producers use to craft his visual examples (see Figure 3.4).

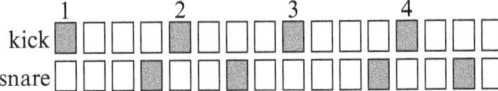

1. A skeletal sketch of reggaeton's boom-ch-boom-chick.

Figure 3.4 Notation of a basic reggaeton beat using DAW-style tick boxes. (Courtesy of Wayne Marshall).[33]

Arts Practice Approaches: *Owning My Masters* to *What Makes It Dope?*

This brings us to the leading-edge approaches to hip-hop in the burgeoning area of arts practice research. At the vanguard of this movement is A. D. Carson, the MC and Professor of Hip Hop and the Global South at the University of Virginia who also performs and records under the name Aydee the Great. Carson set a new standard in hip-hop studies when, in proposing his PhD dissertation in Rhetoric at Clemson, he insisted on submitting the document, not as a traditional written document, but as a recording in itself. While it is increasingly common for hip-hop artist-scholars to augment written scholarship with artistic outputs, Carson's move inverted the relationship in submitting his thirty-four-track album, *Owning My Masters: The Rhetorics of Rhymes and Revolutions* as the dissertation. The move proved a conceptually and artistically savvy one, earning Carson a great deal of media coverage and, more importantly, establishing hip-hop as a form of scholarship in its own right in the hallowed halls of academia.[34]

In 2020, Carson went on to publish the first academically peer-reviewed hip-hop album, *i used to love to dream*, with University of Michigan Press. This album, that Carson dubs a 'mixtap/e/ssay,' 'performs hip-hop scholarship using sampled and live instrumentation; repurposed music, film, and news clips; and original rap lyrics' – a set of organic scholarly processes grounded in hip-hop's own 'emic' ethos, ethics, concepts, and citational practices.[35] Furthering this hip-hop mode of scholarship, the mixtap/e/ssay is open access, like the freely circulating hip-hop 'mixtapes' that give the hybrid arts practice research form its name.

Today, hip-hop artists, like DJ Spooky (That Subliminal Kid), 9th Wonder, and others, increasingly teach and lecture in university departments and a new generation of artist-scholars are earning doctorates in their respective creative fields. Just two with whom I am personally familiar are the MC, Dave Hook, who performs and records as Solareye and the DJ, Michail Exarchos, who performs and records as Stereo Mike. The Scottish

MC, Solareye, earned an international reputation for his witty and honest raps with the live hip-hop band Stanley Odd before writing an autoethnographic analysis of his work for the PhD.[36] His arts practice work took a page from Carson's rap as research methodology, recently resulting in the track 'Rap Academics' – a literature review of hip-hop studies in the form of a rhythmically animated YouTube lyric video (see Figure 3.5).

On the DJ side of things, the Greek hip-hop producer, Stereo Mike, has recently published his PhD research as a book on hip-hop music production and the techniques that beatmakers use to avoid running afoul of copyright laws. Notably, his book *Reimagining Sample-Based Hip Hop: Making Records within Records* (2024) includes a companion album that essentially *is the research* in recorded form.

Such ingenious and generative arts practice research methods inspired my own PhD supervisee, the established Irish MC, vocalist, and producer, 0phelia (Ophelia McCabe), who is exploring hip-hop freestyle ciphers as healing spaces in her PhD study, *Healing in the Cipher: From Ego to Knowledge of Self*.[37] That study uses audiovisual recordings and filmmaking methods to document the musical magic that happens when MCs come together to 'show and prove', making themselves vulnerable to become part of something greater. There are even arts practice research methods grounded in music

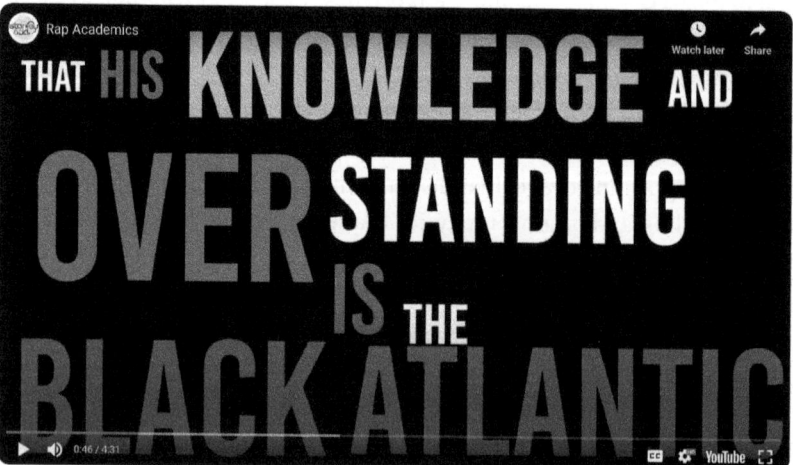

Figure 3.5 Screenshot of Solareye's hip-hop 'literature review' from the lyric video 'Rap Academics', 2022. (Courtesy of Solareye). The line here links hip-hop's Afrodiasporic 'knowledge of self' discourses to Rasta 'overstanding' and Paul Gilroy's landmark, *The Black Atlantic: Modernity and Double Consciousness* (1993).[38]

Figure 3.6 Hand-drawn visual analysis of Lisa 'Left Eye' Lopes on 'Waterfalls', 1994. (Courtesy of Kjell Oddekalv). For a more detailed version of this figure please visit www.cambridge.org/9781316515266 and navigate to the Resources tab.

theory and cognition, as spearheaded by the Norwegian MC and instrumentalist, Kjell Andreas Oddekalv, who performs with the Oslo crew, Sinsenfist. Oddekalv's PhD dissertation put the 'so what?' question front and center in flow studies with the emically titled 'What Makes the Shit Dope? The Techniques and Analysis of Rap Flows', not only developing new theory and methods for the field, but doing so with the performative flair of a hip-hop artist and student of the culture who both understands and cares deeply about how MCs develop their art. As just one illustrative case in point, the static representations developed by Oddekalv's music theory run the gamut from flow boxes and waveform sonographs to hand-drawn visual analyses (see Figure 3.6) that call to mind doodles in an MC's lyric book.

Conclusions: 'Thinking of a Master Plan'

Suffice it to say, hip-hop studies has come a long way since Gilroy issued his 1994 corrective imploring scholars to take musical sound seriously. I hope the overview of the preceding pages has given readers with less experience in thinking and writing about musical sound some workable tools to take their research to the next level. For just as those first hip-hop writers like Morgan, George, and Tate brought the swing and swag of hip-hop music alive on the written page, our current generation of arts practice scholars like Aydee, Solareye, Mike, 0phelia, and Kjell are breaking new ground and exposing us to whole new worlds of possibility – not just for hip-hop studies, but for university scholarship and creative and intellectual life more broadly. Indeed, by starting with the basics of journalism, sound studies, and music studies and then getting into some of the newer and more niche fields like music theory and arts practice research, my hope is that we might take the lid off the current conditions of possibility and imagine what's next. How can we develop even more radical and community-centred ways to explore and understand how the sonic and the social are intertwined, mutually constituted, and inextricable?

I think we can start by working collaboratively *on the regular*, learning from each other's methods by researching, co-creating, and co-authoring on topics of shared interest. This way, we can build hip-hop's own multi-disciplinary, multi-element culture into a truly interdisciplinary academic arts field that sees the connections, not only between the sonic and the social, but beyond, into the kinetic and the visual and so on. So, of course we can't do all this alone. We can't all be expert DJs, MCs, *and* scholars, *and* breakers, *and* graf writers, *and* beatboxers, *and* fashion designers. We need to rely on the cipher – our fellow hip-hop headz.

If we as hip-hop scholars – whether artists, activists, fans, or academics – can take on Gilroy's suggestion that we think and feel beyond our own desires and comfort zones, not only will we be able to see, hear, and understand hip-hop in all its manifestations, we will be a model – a 'blueprint', as Tricia Rose put it back in 1994 – for the decolonial, organic intellectual university – the 'pluriversity' as Achille Mbembe put it.[39] As I suggest, it all starts by connecting the sonic and the social – taking sound seriously. As A Tribe Called Quest put it on the title of their fourth album, when you boil it down, hip-hop is about *Beats, Rhymes, and Life*. Let's start there, build our cipher, and see where we can take it in the next fifty years.

Notes

1. Paul Gilroy, 'After the Love Has Gone: Bio-Politics and Etho-Poetics in the Black Public Sphere', *Public Culture* 7 (1994) p. 52.
2. To learn more about the entrenched eurocentrism and white supremacy of the conservatory/music department model, see Philip A. Ewell, 'Music Theory and the White Racial Frame', *Music Theory Online* Vol. 26, No. 2 (September 2020). https://mtosmt.org/issues/mto.20.26.2/mto.20.26.2.ewell.html [Date accessed: 10 November 2023].

3. Deborah Wong, 'Sound, Silence, Music: Power', *Ethnomusicology* 58/2 (2014); Loren Kajikawa, 'The Possessive Investment in Classical Music' in *Seeing Race Again: Countering Colorblindness across the Disciplines*, edited by Kimberlé Williams Crenshaw (Berkeley: University of California Press, 2019). Ewell, 'Music Theory and the White Racial Frame'.
4. Tricia Rose, *The Hip Hop Wars: What We Talk about when We Talk About Hip Hop – and Why It Matters* (New York: Basic Books, 2008).
5. De La Soul, 'Long Island Degrees' on *Stakes is High* (Tommy Boy 1996).
6. A Tribe Called Quest, *Beats, Rhymes, and Life* (Jive 1996).
7. In my construction, 'connecting the sonic and the social', I'm extending and refiguring an approach I first learned from Wayne Marshall. See Wayne Marshall, 'From Música Negra to Reggaeton Latino: The Cultural Politics of Nation, Migration, and Commercialization' in *Reggaeton*, edited by Raquel Z. Rivera, Wayne Marshall, and Deborah Pacini Hernandez (Durham, NC: Duke University Press, 2009), pp. 19–76.
8. See Dean Van Nguyen, 'How a Group of Journalists Turned Hip-Hop into a Literary Movement: Looking Back at the Golden Era of Rap Writing', *Pitchfork* (12 March 2018). https://pitchfork.com/features/article/how-a-group-of-journalists-turned-hip-hop-into-a-literary-movement/.
9. Greg Tate, 'Eric B. & Rakim: Titty Boom-A-Rooney', *Village Voice* (3 September 1988). www.villagevoice.com/2020/11/20/eric-b-rakim-titty-boom-a-rooney/ [Date accessed: 1 May 2024].
10. Indeed, it's worth noting here that in addition to Tate and other journalists' work prefiguring scholarship *about* hip-hop, rap artists like Phife of A Tribe Called Quest ('hip hop scholar since being knee-high to a duck'), Large Professor, and PE's Professor Griff had imagined themselves as 'hip hop scholars'. The naming practice should help remind us and our university research machines that arts practice is also a form of research and scholarship.
11. Halifu Osumare, *The Africanist Aesthetic in Global Hip-Hop: Power Moves* (New York: Palgrave MacMillan, 2007); Cheryl Keyes, *Rap Music and Street Consciousness* (Urbana: University of Illinois Press, 2002).
12. Tricia Rose, *Black Noise: Rap Music and Black Culture in Contemporary America* (Hanover, NH: Wesleyan University Press, 1994); Imani Perry, *Prophets of the Hood: Politics and Poetics in Hip Hop* (Durham, NC: Duke University Press, 2004).
13. Jennifer Lynn Stoever, 'Ill Communication: Hip Hop Studies & Sound Studies @ Show And Prove'. https://soundstudiesblog.com/2010/09/20/ill-communication/ [Date accessed: 1 May 2024].
14. De La Soul, 'I Am I Be' ft. Maceo Parker, Fred Wesley, and Pee Wee Ellis, *Buhloone Mindstate* (Tommy Boy 1993).
15. Samy Alim, Awad Ibrahim, and Alistair Pennycook, *Global Linguistic Flows: Hip Hop Cultures, Youth Identities, and the Politics of Language* (New York: Routledge, 2009), p. 18.

For more on hiphopography, see Quentin Williams and Jaspal Naveel Singh eds., *Global Hiphopography* (Cham, Switzerland: Palgrave Macmillan, 2023) and J. Griffith Rollefson et al., 'Networking Global Hip Hop Knowledges: The CIPHER Method', *Ethnomusicology* Vol. 67, No. 3 (Autumn 2023), pp. 430–464.

16. Keyes, *Rap Music and Street Consciousness*, p. 124.
17. Schloss, *Making Beats*, p. 6.
18. Marcyliena Morgan, *The Real Hip Hop* (Durham, NC: Duke University Press, 2009).
19. Catherine M. Appert, *In Hip Hop Time: Music, Memory, and Social Change in Urban Senegal* (New York: Oxford University Press, 2018), p. 19.
20. Michel Foucault, 'Truth and Power' in *PowerKnowledge*, edited by Colin Gordon (New York: 1980), p. 15.
21. Loren Kajikawa, *Sounding Race in Rap Songs* (Berkeley: University of California Press, 2015), p. 9.
22. Robert Walser, 'Rhythm, Rhyme, and Rhetoric in the Music of Public Enemy', *Ethnomusicology* Vol. 39, No. 2 (Spring – Summer, 1995), pp. 193–217.
23. Ibid., p. 201.
24. Ibid., p. 199. See also Kyle Adams, 'The Musical Analysis of Hip-Hop' in *The Cambridge Companion to Hip-Hop* (Cambridge: University of Cambridge Press, 2015).
25. Walser, p. 199.
26. See conclusion to Rollefson et al., 'Networking Global Hip Hop Knowledges', 457–459.
27. Pauline Oliveros, *Deep Listening: A Composer's Sound Practice* (Lincoln, NE: Deep Listening Publications, 2005).
28. Noriko Manabe, 'Representing Japan: "National" Style among Japanese Hip-Hop DJs', *Popular Music* 32, no. 1 (2013), pp. 35–50.
29. Felicia Miyakawa, *Five Percenter Rap: God Hop's Music, Message, and Black Muslim Mission* (Bloomington: Indiana University Press, 2005), p. 74.
30. Kyle Adams, 'On the Metrical Techniques of Flow in Rap Music', *Music Theory Online* Vol. 15, No. 5 (October 2009). www.mtosmt.org/issues/mto.09.15.5/mto.09.15.5.adams.html [Date accessed: 10 November 2023].
31. Kyle Adams (organizer), Hip-Hop in the Golden Age Conference (with Keynote Speaker Prince Paul (Paul Huston) of De La Soul), 16–17 February, 2019. https://intranet.music.indiana.edu/departments/academic/music-theory/hip-hop-golden-age.html; Sina Nitzsche (founder), European HipHop Studies Network Annual Meetings (2018–2024). https://europeanhiphopstudiesnetwork.wordpress.com/.
32. Wayne Marshall, 'The Dembow Variations' sonic visualisation mix on Vimeo. https://vimeo.com/69325906 [Date accessed: 1 May 2024].
33. Wayne Marshall, 'From Música Negra to Reggaeton Latino: The Cultural Politics of Nation, Migration, and Commercialization' in *Reggaeton*, edited by

Rivera, Raquel Z., Wayne Marshall, and Deborah Pacini Hernandez (Durham, NC: Duke University Press, 2009), p. 23.

34. Ashley Young and Michel Martin, 'After Rapping His Dissertation, A. D. Carson is UVa's New Hip-Hop Professor' on *All Things Considered* (15 July 2017). www.npr.org/2017/07/15/537274235/after-rapping-his-dissertation-a-d-carson-is-uvas-new-hip-hop-professor [Date accessed: 1 May 2024].
35. A. D. Carson, i used to love to dream (University of Michigan Press, 2020). www.press.umich.edu/11738372/i_used_to_love_to_dream.
36. Dave Hook, An Autoethnography of Scottish Hip-Hop: Identity, Locality, Outsiderdom and Social Commentary (PhD thesis, Edinburgh Napier University, June 2018). https://napier-repository.worktribe.com/OutputFile/1255225.
37. McCabe's study is previewed in excerpt in the last section of Rollefson et al., 'Networking Global Hip Hop Knowledges', pp. 453–457.
38. Solareye (Dave Hook), 'Rap Academics' (2020). www.solareye.co.uk/rapacademics.
39. Achille Mbembe, '"Decolonizing Knowledge and the Question of the Archive." Africa is a Country', contributed by Angela Okune, *Platform for Experimental Collaborative Ethnography,* 2015. Last modified 14 August 2018, accessed 17 November 2023. https://worldpece.org/content/mbembe-achille-2015-"decolonizing-knowledge-and-question-archive"-africa-country [Date accessed: 1 May 2024].

4 | 'Listen When I Flip the Linguistics': Linguistic Approaches to Rap and the Case of 2Pac

STEVEN GILBERS

From rap's dense lyrical content to its speech-like vocal delivery, it seems apparent that few (if any) genres of music and perhaps, in a broader sense, cultural movements have a greater focus on language than hip-hop. There are numerous instances of rappers showing a distinct interest in or awareness of language and linguistics. The most notable example of this might be Big L's song "Ebonics (Criminal slang),"[1] on which the rapper breaks down his street slang vocabulary, alluding to an alternative name for the language variety of African-American English (AAE) in the song's title. Regiolects and ethnolects are a frequent topic of conversation in many rap songs, too. 50 Cent, for instance, raps "I'm a New Yorker, but I sound Southern" on the song "Like my style,"[2] and on the song "The way I am," Eminem comments on his AAE-influenced accent: "I just do not got the patience / To deal with these cocky Caucasians who think I'm some / Wigger who just tries to be black 'cause I talk with an accent."[3] Rappers also display a strong awareness of phonology and articulatory phonetics, especially in relation to their own regional accents. For example, on "Shoot me down," Lil Wayne brilliantly raps "I'ma do it again, like 'nigga'[4] backwards."[5] Here, Lil Wayne is cleverly playing with the linguistic phenomenon that in AAE, the so-called PIN-PEN sound merger causes words like *pin* and *pen* to be homophonous, meaning that the AAE phonetic transcription of the word *again* (i.e., [əgɪn]) is identical to the AAE phonetic transcription of the n-word (i.e., [nɪgə]) in reverse. A similar awareness of phonology and phonetics can be attested in emcees like Eminem telling people to "listen when I flip the linguistics,"[6] who once broke down to Anderson Cooper how you can "bend" the phonology of words and phrases to make them rhyme with the word "*orange*", the classic example of a word in the English language that should not have any rhyming counterpart.[7]

As such, it should come as no surprise that hip-hop – both the music and the culture in a broader sense – has been the subject of a range of linguistics-oriented research. In this chapter, I discuss such linguistic approaches to hip-hop with a special focus on sociolinguistic research on AAE in the context of hip-hop, discourse analytical approaches to rap lyrics, and linguistic approaches to hip-hop musicology. It is important to note here that this chapter by no means offers an exhaustive literature review of linguistic research into hip-hop – that would be near impossible given how long the field of hip-hop linguistics has been around and how diverse it is – but it should serve as a starting point for those interested in diving deeper into hip-hop language. Following this literature review, I turn my focus to one of hip-hop's most prolific artists – Tupac "2Pac" Shakur – examining from several hip-hop linguistics perspectives how his lyrical content, speech, and style of rapping evolved throughout his career.

Sociolinguistic Approaches to Hip-Hop

The majority of hip-hop linguistics research finds its origins in the fields of (variationist) sociolinguistics and linguistic anthropology. As early as the 1990s already, scholars from these fields took an interest in hip-hop, oftentimes because they were investigating AAE and wanted to see how it operated in the context of hip-hop. Looking at AAE in the American hip-hop context, Morgan assessed that "in [hip-hop] culture, language is not simply a means of communication [...] but is viewed as a series of choices that represent beliefs and have consequences."[8] She also noted that the spread of hip-hop culture across the United States brought along with it hip-hop's urban language ideology, resulting in "new speech community formations and a drive to distinguish and articulate linguistic characteristics to represent major cities and regions on the East and West Coasts" as well as the emergence of a "locally marked lexicon" and a strong "awareness of the importance of phonology" in expressing these local identities.[9] For instance, research on AAE in a hip-hop context showed that vowels are significantly longer in the West Coast dialect of AAE than in the East Coast one,[10] and regarding intonation, West Coast AAE prosody was found to be more rhythmically and melodically variable than East Coast AAE in the speech of prominent African-American rappers.[11] Focusing on a different regional context than the East Coast or West Coast, Blake and Shousterman investigated the so-called URR variable (i.e., vowel centralization) of AAE as spoken in St. Louis, a staple of many rap lyrics from the region (for example, in the works of Chingy and Nelly) which was long thought to have been a product of hip-hop.[12] However, as Blake and Shousterman show, the variable had been around long before it was used in hip-hop, leading them to conclude that the "increased usage and acceptance of vowel centralization in local communities is supported by hip-hop language as opposed to innovated through it."[13]

H. Samy Alim, one of hip-hop linguistics' most prominent voices, takes it one step further, arguing that the language spoken by the (American) hip-hop community is a language variety in its own right: Hip-Hop Nation Language (HHNL).[14] Alim defines HHNL as "the language and language use within the [Hip-Hop] Nation [...], a diverse, imagined community whose members (known as *heads*) practice and/or appreciate [hip-hop]'s expressive culture."[15] He also outlines ten tenets by which the variety is characterized, demonstrating the complexity of HHNL through an examination of "[hip-hop] heads' unabated drive for stylistic distinction, creativity, manipulation of grammar and pronunciation, and the politics and pleasure involved in their use of the verbal art of slang."[16] Crucial to Alim's definition of HHNL is that it is "widely spoken across the [United States] and is adapted and transformed by various racial and ethnic groups inside and outside of the United States."[17] In other words, the variety is also spoken by people who are not African-American or who are not even based in America. In light of the former category, Cecelia Cutler's work on the language of white hip-hoppers is of particular interest, as she documents how white adolescents drawn to hip-hop culture may stylize their speech using features of AAE and/or HHNL, in the process crossing ethnolinguistic boundaries and listener expectations.[18] When analyzing HHNL's international dimension – which is explored in detail in edited volumes by, for instance, Alim, Ibrahim, and Pennycook,[19] Terkourafi,[20] and Ross and Rivers[21] – it becomes clear that we should start thinking "beyond a normative [HHNL] and move toward [HHNL varieties], including those that borrow from but are not necessarily derived from [AAE] and [African-American] culture,"[22] as HHNL has evolved in different ways around the world due to the simultaneous and competing processes of globalization and localization – or "glocalization".[23]

Hip-Hop Corpus Linguistics and Discourse Analysis

In recent years, several researchers have taken up a corpus linguistic approach to study hip-hop, a movement that was pioneered in the 2000s by multimedia artist and ethnolinguist Tahir Hemphill. He created a searchable online corpus of the lyrics to approximately one million rap songs,[24] and digital media company Genius took a similar approach with their Rap Stats tool, built around their immense database of rap lyrics.[25] The quantitative approach to rap lyricism has inspired several corpus linguistic studies on lyrical complexity in rap. Most notably, Matt Daniels took a token analysis approach, analyzing lyrics of 149 rappers/rap groups to see how their vocabulary sizes compared to each other.[26] Daniels also compared the rappers' vocabularies to the works of acclaimed authors William Shakespeare and Herman Melville, showing that some rappers' vocabulary sizes were actually larger than the authors'. Daniels's study quickly went viral and was soon replicated for other artists and contexts, for instance for Dutch hip-hop.[27]

Corpus linguistic approaches have also been applied to the study of hip-hop discourse in rap lyrics. Gilbers, for instance, investigated whether the 2008 financial crisis might have had an effect on how materialistic rappers were, given that the mid 2000s are generally considered hip-hop's hyper-materialistic "bling era" and that the (African-American) hip-hop community was among the biggest victims of the subprime mortgage crisis.[28] To this end, a corpus of American rap lyrics from before and after the onset of the financial crisis (2006–8 and 2009–11) was created, and the two periods were quantitatively compared with regard to how many materialistic terms they featured. It was found that on average, lyrics from before the onset of the crisis included significantly more materialistic words than lyrics from the latter period, suggesting the crisis might have affected rappers' lyrical choices.[29] Kreyer and Werner performed hip-hop corpus studies to investigate whether rap lyrics have their own linguistic register, concluding that 'street credibility' and 'authenticity' are hip-hop's key lyrical concepts, as evidenced by, for example, the comparatively high frequency of semantic domains related to street life and AAE grammatical features.[30]

Linguistic Approaches to Hip-Hop Musicology

While most of the research into hip-hop music takes a strictly musicological approach, recent years have seen a number of researchers engaging with the musical aspects of hip-hop from a linguistic perspective, specifically when it comes to the analysis of the concept of "flow."[31] Flow is generally defined as the melodic and rhythmic aspects of a rap performance,[32] and Gilbers et al. describe their motivation for investigating flow from a linguistic perspective as follows: "[flow] is to rap what prosody is to language; both are concerned with the rhythmic and melodic aspects of their respective domains."[33] Rhythm and melody are treated quite differently in rap compared to most other forms of music. As a result of this, most existing methodologies for studying musical rhythm and pitch are suboptimal for the study of flow, causing researchers to have to adapt them or even design entirely new approaches, several of which are rooted in the linguistic subfields of phonology and phonetics.

Rhythm

There is great variation when it comes to individual (and regional) rap flow rhythms. Two variables that are often considered to define what makes these flows distinct from each other are degrees of variation in note interval duration (i.e., the time between when two consecutive notes/syllables are performed) and the rappers' microtiming: whether rappers perform syllables right on the beat or slightly before or after the beat instead. Plenty of musicological work has engaged with rhythm in rap,[34] but these studies have mostly been qualitative in nature and/or highly impressionistic when it comes to the assessment of note interval duration and microtiming in flow. In other words, they do not offer a way of quantitatively comparing rappers' rhythms to each other. The reason for this initial gap in the literature is simple: no reliable method of quantitatively measuring rhythm in rap existed yet.

The answer to this problem appeared to lie in linguistic approaches to speech rhythm. Mitchell Ohriner, a music theorist by training, was inspired by linguistic methods when he constructed a corpus of rap flows to analyze their rhythmic characteristics,[35] and sharply identified the need for bridging the gap between musicological and linguistic approaches to rhythm in flow research: "While flow exists in a rhythmic space between music and speech, existing theories of rhythm in these two domains [...] are framed quite differently, [...] and an analysis of flow must reconcile these theories."[36] In line with this argument, Gilbers et al. set out to quantitatively study rhythm in rap flows from a phonetic perspective.[37] They investigated whether the rap flows of West Coast rappers were distinct from those of East Coast rappers in terms of rhythmic variability. To this end, the researchers devised a MIDI-based method of measuring note interval duration and microtiming, and interpreting their data using tools from the existing linguistic literature on rhythm in language and music, they concluded West Coast rap flows exhibited higher levels of rhythmic variation than East Coast rap flows.[38]

Melody

As a form of vocal musical expression, rap tends to be distinguished from singing based on its lack of melody. However, pitch contours are essential to our perception of flow.[39] Rappers indeed deviate from singers in that their performances are usually not melodic in the traditional sense of matching one's vocal pitch to the song's key or "hitting" precise notes on a scale,[40] but all rappers still manipulate pitch in some way, shape, or form.[41] While all researchers of flow would freely admit that melody and pitch play a role in rap, few have actually studied it, mostly focusing on rap's rhythmic characteristics instead, possibly because until just a few years ago, no methods for analyzing the pitch of the rapping voice existed yet.[42] As it turned out, a solution to this problem lay in the linguistic disciplines of phonetics and phonology.

One study that investigated melody in rap phonetically was the 2020 study by Gilbers et al., which analyzed the pitch contours in the rap flows of sixteen African-American rappers from the West and the East Coast.[43] They devised a method for this study that was based on phonetic approaches to speech prosody, measuring the pitch value in the selected performances on a semitone-based scale 100 times per second to measure the average rate of pitch variability in minute detail. The study's findings showed that West Coast rappers exhibited greater levels of pitch fluctuation in their rapping compared to East Coast rappers.[44] Another study that phonetically analyzed pitch in rap performances is a 2019 study by Ohriner.[45] Ohriner segmented several rappers' verses into separate intonational phrases, phonetically measured their pitch contours, annotated his measurements using the phonological "tones and break indexes" (ToBI) system, and then assessed how the intonation patterns of rap relate to singing and regular speech. Broadly speaking, Ohriner's conclusions suggest that rap occupies a unique space compared to the other two, as it appears to amplify the intonational characteristics of speech in some regards (e.g., more frequent peaks and larger slopes at the endings of intonational phrases), patterns more like singing in others (e.g., a relatively small pitch range within intonational phrases), and sometimes does something completely different (e.g., a lack of upward glissandi).[46]

The Language–Music Connection in the Context of Hip-Hop

It has long been hypothesized that a connection exists between the domains of language and music, the idea being that both are cognitively organized and operate in fundamentally similar ways as they each revolve (primarily) around sound and its structure.[47] A common hypothesis in relation to the language–music connection is that the compositions/performances of musicians will reflect the rhythmic and melodic characteristics of their speech prosody (i.e., their intonation). In other words, if a given composer speaks a language/dialect characterized by much melodic and rhythmic variation, their music's melodies and rhythms are expected to exhibit high levels of variation as well. The seminal study in this regard was conducted by Patel et al., who found that British speech and classical music were more rhythmically and melodically diverse than French speech and classical music, showing the patterns of regional variation in the domain of language were reflected in the domain of music.[48] Barring a few exceptions, these findings were replicated in several other linguistic contexts[49] and for vocal rather than instrumental music as well.[50]

Hip-hop and rap were long ignored by researchers interested in the language–music connection. Kautny, however, pondered whether some languages or language varieties might be better suited for certain styles of flow than others due to their rhythmic characteristics,[51] and Thomas suggested that "it could be fruitful to explore the links between [AAE prosodic] features and various styles of music, poetry, and public speaking that African Americans have bestowed upon American culture."[52] Following these suggestions, Gilbers et al. explored whether speech influences rap, specifically in the context of West and East Coast AAE and rap.[53] They found that on average, West Coast AAE speech prosody exhibits more rhythmic and more melodic variation than East Coast AAE speech prosody. A similar pattern was found when comparing West Coast rap flows to East Coast rap flows. Hence, in line with most previous research on the language–music connection, it was concluded that regional variation in the domain of speech is connected to regional variation in music for the AAE/hip-hop context as well.[54]

The Case of 2Pac's Language and Flow

One of hip-hop's most prolific and impactful artists of all time is arguably Tupac "2Pac" Shakur. Despite the fact that he was only twenty-five years old at the time of his tragic murder in 1996, 2Pac managed to leave an indelible mark on the culture, inspiring fans, artists, journalists, and scholars to study his life and his work even to this day. The current section presents such an investigation into 2Pac, one that focuses on the diachronic development of his lyrics, speech accent, and rap flow, combining insights and approaches from several subfields of hip-hop linguistics described earlier in this chapter. It outlines how 2Pac successfully managed to navigate a highly volatile sociopolitical context by actively manipulating his language and music to establish himself as West Coast hip-hop's main advocate in a conflict with his native East Coast hip-hop scene.

2Pac's Role in the East Coast–West Coast Hip-Hop Feud

Born on June 16, 1971 in New York City, 2Pac was a highly successful African-American gangsta rapper, actor, poet and civil rights activist. After moving around the East Coast several times, he moved to California's Bay Area in 1988 at age 17. There, he would establish himself in the West Coast hip-hop scene, releasing his first studio album in 1991 and later moving to Los Angeles to further pursue his career in music and film. Despite his move to California, 2Pac long maintained a good relationship with the East Coast's hip-hop scene, but this relationship turned sour on November 30, 1994, when 2Pac was shot five times in a Manhattan recording studio. He survived the attack, but grew increasingly paranoid that his New York friend and fellow rapper Biggie Smalls and Biggie's Bad Boy Records label mates had set him up. Frustrated and paranoid, 2Pac was stuck in a jail cell soon after the shooting, as he had been sentenced to one-and-a-half to four-and-a-half years in prison in an unrelated case.

In 1995, while 2Pac was still stuck behind bars, an already ongoing conflict between hip-hop's East and West Coast scenes started turning increasingly grim, as Death Row Records – the leading West Coast gangsta rap label at the time – openly antagonized Bad Boy Records, with several violent altercations between the two scenes ensuing. The regional feud escalated even further when Death Row offered to post 2Pac's $1.4 million bail on the condition that he sign with them. 2Pac agreed and immediately went to Los Angeles to work on his next album. There, he immersed himself in Los Angeles's gang-infused hip-hop scene and took charge in the ongoing East Coast–West Coast feud, attacking not just Biggie and Bad Boy Records, but the East Coast scene as a whole on behalf of the West Coast. In the process, 2Pac successfully convinced the West Coast scene to accept him as one of their own, and ironically enough, this turned 2Pac into the West Coast's de facto leader in the war against his home region.

2Pac's involvement in Los Angeles gang politics eventually caught up with him on September 7, 1996, when he was gunned down in a drive-by shooting in Las Vegas. Six days later, 2Pac succumbed to his injuries and passed away at the age of 25. His death was soon followed by the equally tragic murder of his friend-turned-adversary Biggie on March 9, 1997, an event that would finally set in motion the end of the violent bicoastal conflict.

To understand the social and sociolinguistic context 2Pac had to maneuver during the East Coast–West Coast feud, two key concepts of hip-hop culture – regional identity and authenticity – need to be discussed as well as the role that language and music play in regard to these. To members of the hip-hop community, where they are from determines a crucial part of their identity, and this regional identity is often actively expressed to "represent." One of the best ways of representing is through the use of a regional accent and lexicon, and by referencing local customs and places in one's speech.[55] Rappers, in addition to their speech accent, have another way of expressing their regional affiliation: regionally distinct rap flows.[56] Moreover, due to the importance hip-hop assigns to authenticity, pretending to be something you are not can lead to a loss of reputation.[57] As such, representing for a different region than you are originally from – for instance by using a regional accent or flow not native to you – would be a significant challenge for anyone engaged with hip-hop culture.

The observations just discussed raise the following questions: what happened to 2Pac's lyrical content, AAE speech accent and music after he became West Coast hip-hop's leader? Were his lyrics, speech and music affected by his role in the bicoastal conflict, and, if so, were these changes the result of subconscious cognitive processes or of 2Pac's conscious linguistic and musical choices? And how did 2Pac avoid being seen as inauthentic while trying to reposition himself in hip-hop's highly territorial politics?

2Pac's lyrics

Qualitative discourse analysis of 2Pac's lyrical content reveals the effects of 2Pac's involvement in the East Coast–West Coast feud. Being based in California his whole career, he always represented for the West Coast in his lyrics, including during the pre–Death Row era. For instance, 2Pac would proudly announce his connection to Oakland on songs like "Representin' 93" and "Nothing but love."[58] However, he would also represent for his New York roots: before adopting his moniker 2Pac, he went by the name of MC New York, and on songs like "Old school," he specifically praised the New York hip-hop that shaped him.[59]

A drastic change in 2Pac's lyrical content can be noted after he signed with Death Row, however. In this period, 2Pac doubled down on his allegiance to the West Coast: his lyrics not only became more pro–West Coast, with songs like "California love" and "To live & die in L.A." being filled with positive references to Californian places and West Coast hip-hop culture, they became overtly anti–East Coast as well.[60] Some slights directed at the East Coast were relatively subtle, for instance when 2Pac mocks

New York hip-hop fashion trends and refers to the Westside as the "real side" on "Heartz of men."[61] Other slights are much more extreme, most notably on the diss song "Hit 'em up," when 2Pac disrespects and threatens the entire New York scene: "This is how we do it on our side / Any of you niggas from New York that want to bring it: bring it / [...] We gon' kill all you motherfuckers."[62] Commenting on his lyrics, 2Pac said the following in a 1996 interview with Vibe Magazine:

This is not a new allegiance to the West Coast. I been on the West Coast all this time. [...] It's just that by me keeping it real, I always said where I came from. I always gave New York they props. On *Me against the world*, I took a whole song to give it up [for New York]. So now on the next album, when I want to give it up for my home – where I'm at – everybody got a problem?[63]

These remarks reveal that 2Pac was aware of his bicoastal identity and how he navigated it lyrically. As such, a clear change of direction in this regard could be considered part of a conscious effort to adjust his image in the context of hip-hop's regional politics.

2Pac's Speech Accent and Rap Flow

Considering that changes to 2Pac's regional identity and regional affiliations were reflected in his lyrics, the question remains whether this effect could also be observed in his speech accent and rap flow, two other domains used to "represent" for your region. In other words, did 2Pac's AAE accent and flow sound more West Coast–like in his Death Row era than in his pre–Death Row era?[64]

Regarding 2Pac's speech accent, it turns out that such an effect is indeed visible. A diachronic phonetic analysis of 2Pac's speech in interviews between 1988 and 1996 revealed that 2Pac's vowels gradually became longer (and hence more West Coast–like) over time in his pre–Death Row era, an observation in line with standard patterns of second dialect acquisition through immersion. While signed to Death Row, however, his rate of assimilation to West Coast AAE norms increased substantially: from an average yearly increase of 2.31 percent in the pre–Death Row period to an 18.86 percent increase while he was at Death Row. Analyzing 2Pac's prosody (in terms of rhythmic and melodic variation) as it developed over time reveals that his intonation became more West Coast–like as well – specifically in terms of rhythmic variability – especially after signing to Death Row.

Regarding flow, a diachronic analysis of melodic and rhythmic variation in 2Pac's rapping across the span of his career also revealed his style of rapping became more West Coast–like as time progressed, especially when comparing music from 2Pac's Death Row era to his earlier work. Not only did his rapping become significantly more melodic, the rhythmic patterns in his rapping also became more variable. The latter is illustrated by the average rhythmic heat maps presented in Figure 4.1.

They show how 2Pac, on average, did not gravitate to particular notes as much in his Death Row period compared to the period before (i.e., fewer dark-colored sixty-fourth notes for the Death Row era; see Figure 4.1b), similar to how West Coast rappers typically do not gravitate to particular sixty-fourth notes as much as East Coast rappers do (Figure 4.1a). In other words, 2Pac's timing in his rapping became more variable, similar to the typical timing of his West Coast peers.

Connecting the diachronic data on 2Pac's speech and flow shows that 2Pac's acquisition of a second *musical* regiolect followed a pattern similar to his acquisition of a second *linguistic* regiolect. This connects the study's findings to the literature on the language-music connection in a hip-hop context. Moreover, the increased assimilation rates in his Death Row period suggest that 2Pac purposely manipulated his accent and flow to sound more West Coast–like, especially since there were regular instances of 2Pac 'overshooting' West Coast targets (i.e., his speech and rapping were even more extreme than the speech and rapping of his West Coast peers). This observation, as well as 2Pac's own claims that he typically took a method-acting approach to his acting and songwriting – "I just threw myself around that L.A. crowd, learned the language, learned the culture"[65] – further strengthens the idea that 2Pac intentionally used his speech and his rapping to establish his West Coast identity.

Conclusion

This chapter has attempted to highlight (far from comprehensively) a variety of linguistic approaches to the study of hip-hop music and culture, focusing specifically on sociolinguistic work revolving around AAE and HHNL, discourse analysis of rap lyrics, and musicological work on flow that makes use of linguistic theories, insights, and methodologies. The chapter's discussion of the development of 2Pac's lyrics, speech, and music over time showcases each of the aforementioned approaches in one way or another, demonstrating that these different linguistic

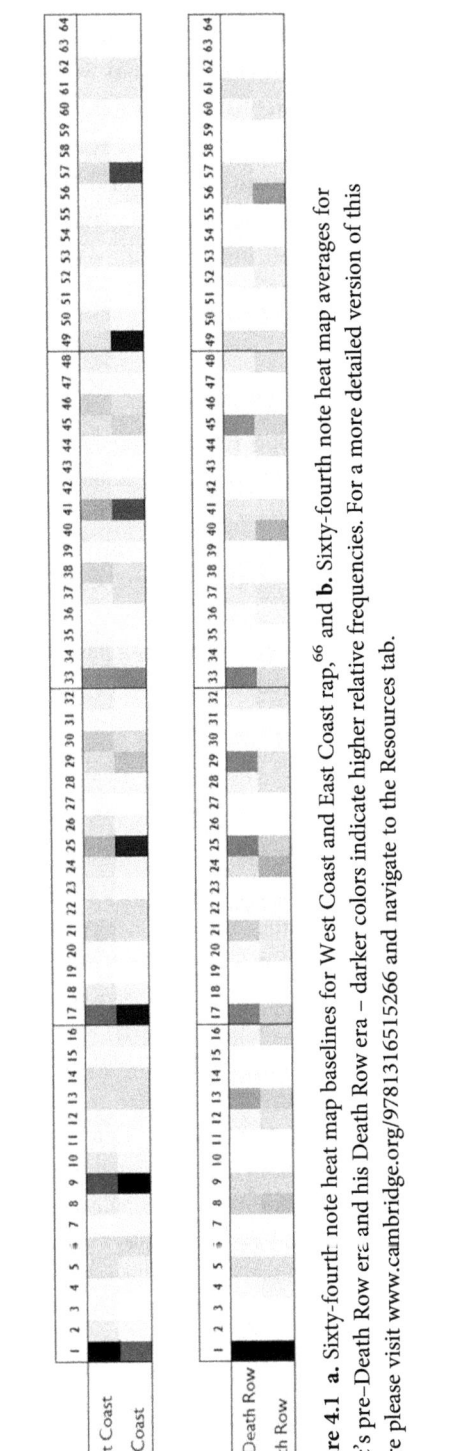

Figure 4.1 a. Sixty-fourth note heat map baselines for West Coast and East Coast rap,[66] and **b.** Sixty-fourth note heat map averages for 2Pac's pre–Death Row era and his Death Row era – darker colors indicate higher relative frequencies. For a more detailed version of this figure please visit www.cambridge.org/9781316515266 and navigate to the Resources tab.

perspectives do not just have to be used in isolation, but that they can inform and strengthen each other as well. To conclude, hip-hop linguistics, ever since it was established as a field by the likes of Marcyliena Morgan and H. Samy Alim, has made many a valuable contribution to hip-hop scholarship in a broader sense, and given the recent surge in hip-hop linguistics research and linguistics-influenced hip-hop scholarship, it is likely that it will continue to do so in the future.

Notes

1. Big L (2000). *Ebonics (Criminal Slang)*. CD. Universal Music Distribution, Rawkus Records, & Flamboyant Entertainment.
2. 50 Cent (2003). *Like My Style*. CD. Interscope Records, Shady Records, Aftermath Entertainment, & G-Unit Records.
3. Eminem (2000). *The Way I Am*. CD. Aftermath Entertainment & Interscope Records.
4. While I – a white man researching Black culture, music, and language – never use the n-word in my own speech or writing, I have opted not to censor the n-word in quotes in order to stay true to the words of the artists cited.
5. Lil Wayne & D-Smith (2008). *Shoot Me Down*. CD. Cash Money Records & Universal Motown.
6. Bad Meets Evil (2011). *Fast Lane*. CD. Shady Records & Interscope Records.
7. 60 Minutes (2010). "Rhymetime with Eminem." YouTube. Retrieved from www.youtube.com/watch?v=_kQBVneC30o [Date accessed: May 1, 2024].
8. Morgan, M. "'Nuthin' but a G Thang': Grammar and Language Ideology in Hip Hop Identity" in S. L. Lanehart, ed., *Sociocultural and Historical Contexts of African American English* (Amsterdam: John Benjamins, 2001), pp. 187–209.
9. Ibid., p. 188.
10. Gilbers, S. (2021a). "African-American English Regiolects and Hip-Hop: Comparing East Coast and West Coast Vowel Duration" in S. Gilbers, Ambitionz az a ridah: 2Pac's Changing Accent and Flow in Light of Regional Variation in African-American English Speech and Hip-Hop Music. Groningen: Groningen Dissertations in Linguistics, pp. 41–50; Morgan (2001).
11. Gilbers, S., Hoeksema, N., de Bot, K., & Lowie, W. "Regional Variation in West and East Coast African-American English Prosody and Rap Flows," *Language and Speech*, 63/4 (2020): 713–745.
12. Blake, R. & Shousterman, C. "Diachrony and AAE: St. Louis, Hip-Hop, and Sound Change outside of the Mainstream," *Journal of English Linguistics*, 38/3 (2010): 230–247.
13. Ibid., p. 230.

14. Alim, H. S. "Hip Hop Nation Language" in E. Finegan & J. Rickford, eds., *Language in the USA: Themes for the Twenty-First Century* (New York: Cambridge University Press, 2004), pp. 387–409; Alim, H. S. "Hip Hop Nation Language: Localization and Globalization." In J. Bloomquist, L. J. Green, & S. Lanehart, eds., *The Oxford Handbook of African American Language* (Oxford: Oxford University Press, 2015), pp. 850–862.
15. Alim (2015), p. 850.
16. Ibid.
17. Ibid., p. 851.
18. Cutler, C. *White Hip Hoppers, Language and Identity in Post-Modern America* (New York: Routledge, 2014).
19. Alim, H. S., Ibrahim, A. & Pennycook, A., eds. *Global Linguistic Flows: Hip Hop Cultures, Youth Identities, and the Politics of Language* (New York: Routledge, 2009).
20. Terkourafi, M. *The Languages of Global Hip Hop* (London: Continuum, 2010).
21. Ross, A. S. & Rivers, D. J., eds. *The Sociolinguistics of Hip-Hop as Critical Conscience: Dissatisfaction and Dissent* (Houndmills, UK: Palgrave Macmillan, 2018).
22. Alim (2015), p. 858.
23. Alim, H. S. "Straight outta Compton, Straight aus München: Global Linguistic Flows, Identities, and the Politics of Language in a Global Nation" in H. S. Alim, A. Ibrahim, & A. Pennycook, eds., *Global Linguistic Flows: Hip Hop Cultures, Youth Identities, and the Politics of Language* (New York: Routledge, 2009), pp. 1–24.
24. Hemphill, T. (2019). "Rap Almanac." Tahir Hemphill Studio. Retrieved from https://tahirhemphill.com/portfolio/work5/ [Date accessed: May 1, 2024].
25. Setaro, S. (2013). "Rap Stats: Breaking Down the Words in Rap Lyrics over Time." *Genius*. https://genius.com/Sameoldshawn-rap-stats-breaking-down-the-words-in-rap-lyrics-over-time-annotated [Date accessed: May 1, 2024].
26. Daniels, M. (2019). "The Largest Vocabulary in Hip Hop." *The Pudding*. Retrieved from https://pudding.cool/projects/vocabulary/index.html [Date accessed: May 1, 2024].
27. Reuneker, A., Waszink, V., & van der Wouden, T. (2017). Sanskriet op de beat: De grootste woordenschat in nederhop. Neerlandistiek. Retrieved from https://neerlandistiek.nl/2017/04/sanskriet-op-de-beat/ [Date accessed: May 1, 2024].
28. Gilbers, S. (2018a). "How the Financial Crisis Changed Hip-Hop" in A. S. Ross & D. J. Rivers, eds., *The Sociolinguistics of Hip-Hop as Critical Conscience: Dissatisfaction and Dissent*. Houndmills, UK: Palgrave Macmillan, pp. 163–189.
29. Ibid.
30. Kreyer, R. "'Now Niggas Talk a Lotta Bad Boy Shit': The Register Hip-Hop from a Corpus-Linguistic Perspective" in C. Schubert & C. Sanchez-Stockhammer eds., *Variational Text Linguistics* (Berlin: De Gruyter Mouton, 2016), pp.

87–110; Werner, V. (2019). *Assessing Hip-Hop Discourse: Linguistic Realness and Styling. Text & Talk*, 39/5: 671–698.

31. E.g., Oddekalv, K. A. (2022). "What Makes the Shit Dope?" Doctoral dissertation. Oslo: University of Oslo; Ohriner, M. (2016). "Metric Ambiguity and Flow in Rap Music: A Corpus-Assisted Study of Outkast's 'Mainstream'" (1996). *Empirical Musicology Review* 11/2: 153–179; Ohriner, M. (2019a). "Analysing the Pitch Content of the Rapping Voice," *Journal of New Music Research*, 48/5: 413–433; Ohriner, M. (2019b). "Flow: The rhythmic voice in rap music" (New York: Oxford University Press).
32. E.g., Adams, K. (2015). "The Musical Analysis of Hip-Hop" in J. A. Williams (Ed.), *The Cambridge Companion to Hip-Hop*. Cambridge: Cambridge University Press, pp. 118–134; Connor, M. E. (2018). *The Musical Artistry of Rap*. Jefferson: McFarland; Krims, A. *Rap Music and the Poetics of Identity*. (Cambridge: Cambridge University Press, 2000).
33. Gilbers et al. (2020) p. 715.
34. E.g., Connor (2018); Edwards, P. (2013). *How to Rap 2: Advanced Flow and Delivery Techniques* (Chicago: Chicago Review Press); Komaniecki, R. (2017). "Analyzing Collaborative Flow in Rap Music," *Music Theory Online*, 23/4: 1–19; Krims (2000); Ohriner (2016); Ohriner (2019b).
35. Ohriner (2016).
36. Ohriner (2019b), p. xxiii.
37. Gilbers et al. (2020).
38. Ibid.
39. E.g., Adams (2015).
40. Setaro, S., Kross, J., & Griffin, W. M., Jr. (2014). "Episode 65: Rakim." The Cipher Show. Podcast retrieved from http://thecipershow.com/episode/65/ [Date accessed: May 1, 2024].
41. Edwards (2013).
42. Ohriner (2019a).
43. Gilbers et al. (2020).
44. Ibid.
45. Ohriner (2019a).
46. Ibid.
47. Patel, A. D., Iversen, J. R., & Rosenberg, J. C. "Comparing the Rhythm and Melody of Speech and Music: The Case of British English and French." *Journal of the Acoustical Society of America*, 119/5 (2006): 3034–3047.
48. Patel et al. (2006).
49. See Hansen, N. C., Sadakata, M., & Pearce, M. "Non-linear Changes in the Rhythm of European Art Music: Quantitative Support for Historical Musicology." *Music Perception*, 33 (2016): 414–431.
50. E.g., Lee, C., Brown, L., & Müllensiefen, D. *The Musical Impact of Multicultural London English (MLE) Speech Rhythm. Music Perception*, 34 (2017): 452–481.

51. Kautny, O. "Lyrics and Flow in Rap Music" in J. A. Williams, ed., *The Cambridge Companion to Hip-Hop* (Cambridge: Cambridge University Press, 2015), pp. 101–117.
52. Thomas, E. R. "Prosodic Features of African American English" in J. Bloomquist, L. J. Green, & S. L. Lanehart eds., *The Oxford Handbook of African American Language* (Oxford: Oxford University Press, 2015), pp. 420–438.
53. Gilbers et al. (2020).
54. Ibid.
55. Forman, M. *The 'hood Comes First: Race, Space, and Place in Rap and Hip Hop.* (Middletown: Wesleyan University Press, 2002); Hess, M. "Introduction: 'It's Only Right to Represent Where I'm From': Local and Regional Hip Hop Scenes in the United States" in M. Hess, ed., *Hip Hop in America: A Regional Guide* (Santa Barbara: Greenwood Publishing Group, 2009), pp. vii–xxix; Morgan (2001).
56. E.g., Edwards (2013).
57. Hess (2009); Morgan (2001).
58. 2Pac (1993). *Representin' 93*. CD. Jive Records & Interscope Records; 2Pac (1993). *Nothing but Love*. CD. Interscope Records.
59. 2Pac (1995). *Old School*. CD. Interscope Records, Atlantic, & Out Da Gutta Records.
60. 2Pac, Dr. Dre & Roger Troutman (1995). *California Love*. CD. Death Row Records & Interscope Records; Makaveli (1996). *To Live & Die in L.A*. CD. Death Row Records & Interscope Records.
61. 2Pac (1996). *Heartz of Men*. CD. Death Row Records & Interscope Records.
62. 2Pac & The Outlawz (1996). *Hit 'em Up*. CD. Death Row Records & Interscope Records.
63. Vibe Magazine (2013). "Tupac Shakur – The Lost Interview, Pt. 1." YouTube. Retrieved from www.youtube.com/watch?v=P19nehRgbys [Date accessed: May 1, 2024].
64. For details on the studies reported in this section, see Gilbers, S. (2018b). "The Linguistic and Lyrical Development of 2Pac in Relation to Regional Hip-Hop Identity and Conflict" in A. S. Ross & D. J. Rivers, eds., The Sociolinguistics of Hip-Hop as Critical Conscience: Dissatisfaction and Dissent. Houndmills: Palgrave Macmillan, pp. 13–36; Gilbers, S. (2021b). "How 2Pac's Prosody and Rap Flows Changed: A Case Study on Linguistic and Musical Second Dialect Acquisition" in S. Gilbers, *Ambitionz az a ridah: 2Pac's Changing Accent and Flow in Light of Regional Variation in African-American English Speech and Hip-Hop Music*. Groningen: Groningen Dissertations in Linguistics, pp. 125–173.
65. Spady, J. G., Alim, H. S., & Lee, C. G. *Street Conscious Rap* (Philadelphia: Black History Museum Pub, 1999), p. 563.
66. Reprinted from Gilbers et al. (2020), p. 738.

5 | Pioneers, Postmodernisms and Aesthetic Experience

A Brief History of Aesthetic Approaches to Rap Music

MAX RYYNÄNEN AND PETTERI ENROTH

Introduction

Today, cultural studies largely dominates academic discussions of rap music and hip-hop culture. In this chapter, however, we show that it was aesthetics that provided rap and hip-hop with their first arena of theoretical reception, from 1984 to the 2000s. The time for bringing this up is long overdue, as the current situation is odd: when we read the history sections of rap research articles or meet scholars from cultural studies who are into rap, it is often the case that they, to our shock, do not even know these pioneering texts. We have even heard claims that hip-hop studies started at the turn of the millennium! Such claims seem all the more backward to us since we both, like so many others, entered the realm of aesthetics through Richard Shusterman's ground-breaking work on rap in the 1990s and early 2000s; this is how one most likely got to know about aesthetics in those days. Aestheticians held rap lectures[1] and took part in public rap discussions. For example, Shusterman applied his theories to scene discussions early on by writing pieces in the early 90s for *The Journal of Rap Music and Hip Hop Culture*, edited by ex-Panther George Ware, and featuring, for example, columns by Chuck D of Public Enemy.

What the present situation says about the power relations between cultural studies and the much smaller field of philosophical aesthetics is an intriguing issue in itself: scholars in cultural studies talk about marginal culture and power structures but keep working against smaller, less-central scholarly disciplines. However, we would like to think this is not because of the size of cultural studies' collective academic ego, but rather a more or less accidental miscommunication – one we wish to correct – or something that is just typical of power relations: New Yorkers do not know the cultural scene in Philadelphia, but vice versa they do.

In what follows, we present a brief survey of the relationship of aesthetics and rap, with some notes towards the larger culture of hip-hop. We use 'aesthetics' in a somewhat applied form, meaning both contributions from academics who explicitly and mainly work in the domain of philosophical aesthetics and texts that we see as focusing decisively more on aesthetic matters than, say, those of representation, identity and other topics characteristic of cultural studies: as James Edward Ford III has noted, there is a hegemonic tendency to disregard the aesthetic elements in some classical contributions to hip-hop studies,[2] so the choice of what suits the scope of our text is actually not hard to make.

In addition to showing that aesthetics, which often has a rather conservative academic brand,[3] was a surprisingly radical field regarding rap scholarship, we also call for fellow academics interested in rap and hip-hop to go back to these texts and revive a discussion of the music and culture informed by philosophical aesthetics. In the conclusions, we make short initial remarks as to possible starting points for that.

A Historical Overview of the Aesthetics of Rap

Some very brief notes on the history of rap music and its main practices are called for. First of all, many people like to mark the birth of rap music as August 1973; that is, Kool Herc's sister's birthday block party on 1520 Sedgwick Avenue in the Bronx, New York. For the purposes of this chapter, we do not see a need to rethink this conception, but it is good to note that toasting and talking on music had a history before the mentioned date, even in diasporic music cultures that had roots in Africa. Forerunners in what was to become rap's first local scene, such as James Brown, Pigmeat Markham, Amiri Baraka, Gil-Scott Heron, U-Roy and Isaac Hayes, were already quite at it before Grandmaster Flash, Sha-Rock and others formed the music's basic codes, like the later manner of focusing on breakbeats and talking/rapping. From another perspective, some sound art pieces, like William S. Burroughs's reel-to-reel tape experiments in the 1950s, could be seen as anticipating the vigorous manipulation of material sound recordings by hip-hop DJs. However, the differences might be more interesting than similarities here; for instance, in Burroughs's practice, as opposed to the DJs', there is no element of an artistic, controlled craft, but a Dada-esque focus on automatism.

There is no space to really elaborate on the following thought here, but if one focuses on rap as the specific vocal element of music, it is interesting to note how many rap-like practices can be detected globally. In addition to the well-documented West African roots of rapping, for instance, Sanskrit recitals of religious texts emphasise rhythm and form a rappish beat. In Europe, Karelian oral poetry, for example (before modernisation), used to be rhythmically spoken and used for battling.[4] It is, in fact, worth asking whether contemporary rap as a major commercial enterprise, dominated by a strong Anglo-American culture, overshadows the cultural diversity of all the rap-like practices that have detectable aesthetic and practical connections, but nonetheless, the whole question would not arise if rap had not become the contemporary cultural popular music practice it is. Still, rap, framed as a globally considered cultural phenomenon, could actually help us to see some cultural similarities.

Whereas 'rap', thought of in this broad sense, was the dominant cultural practice in the aforementioned Sanskrit and Finnish examples, as a modern phenomenon with its current specific name and an inherent connection to turntables, African-American (and other) hits, and the cultural context of the Bronx, it grew up as an underdog. This applies both to its position, first, in terms of the field of (popular) culture and later, as the music itself grew bigger, in academic reception, as rap music was the number-one shooting target of many intellectuals.[5]

However, positive attempts to approach it soon became commonplace as well: rap was for many not just a new style of music but was seen by some as a new art form, half-independently, as it were, from prevailing forms and conceptions of 'music', or as a holistic aesthetic concept. The oldest text in this vein of aesthetically sensitive philosophical tackling we have found is Esa Sironen's 'Hip-hop don't stop' from 1984. In a manner reminiscent of Walter Benjamin's analyses of modernity and everyday urban culture, as well as Herbert Marcuse's treatment of the hippie movement,[6] Sironen saw rap music as a new way of coping with aesthetic reality, organically producing an aesthetic alternative to mass culture by appropriating it. Rap music displaced and twisted elements of earlier music, mostly funk and soul, to its own ends to create something entirely new. As an aesthetic construct, Sironen saw it as a reaction to fast-paced, technologically driven urbanisation in a situation where life between economical suppression, ethnic oppression and urban fragmentation had to find support from new cultural formations. Sironen also accentuated, in a post-humanist fashion, the way birds have changed their singing in heavy urban conditions: Naming the great tit, whose singing had become shorter and faster in cities, he asked if rappers and hip-hoppers had somehow found a way to artistically appropriate urban pace and noise in a similar way.[7]

The same year, David Toop's outlawish *The Rap Attack* (1984) brought in a scene-driven history of rap where the African roots of the art were deeply acknowledged. Toop traced the history of rap back to the *galalas* (Nigeria) and *griots* (West Africa), and their cultural echoes in the United States, including verbal games like *the dozens* in the Southern States; their even more rhyme-driven versions in Harlem, New York; and the *signifying songs* of New Orleans.[8] Toop's object of research, then, was the cultural chain that eventually laid eggs on the record player of 'professor' Grandmaster Flash in the Bronx, and the chain of musical and aesthetic inspirations and impacts that followed after that.[9] In other words, although not an aesthetician in an academic sense, Toop gave rap first and foremost an aesthetic history. The way he directed a programmatic gaze at the West African way of understanding 'art' only and inherently as part of life – instead of a special, cut-off area of expertise – is just one example of the instances of philosophical aesthetics in the book.

In the 1990s, the 'new art form' and 'new cultural form' discourse grew into a mainstream matter in aesthetics by Richard Shusterman's initiation. He was the first aesthetician – in the academic sense – to approach rap music with systematic seriousness. Shusterman's starting point for this was to revive, for the first time, John Dewey's experience-centred aesthetics as articulated in *Art as Experience* (1934). For Dewey, one of the founding pragmatist philosophers,[10] 'art' was by definition a matter of a certain kind of engaged and imaginative aesthetic experience instead of specific forms, contents or institutional workings. In Shusterman's application of this pragmatist stance, listening and dancing to rap neatly fit the idea of such 'engaged' aesthetic experience, as opposed to a (Kantian) contemplative or disinterested experience. He explored the essential aesthetic features of rap music, like sampling, the use of breakbeats, scratching and punch phrasing. More broadly, with the help of his rap analyses, he highlighted the way the popular arts were naturally and readily included in philosophical aesthetics when this type of experience-based thinking prevailed. This was far from evident at the time Shusterman was writing his seminal works, although there was a rising dissatisfaction among aestheticians with the way the popular arts were treated, and the whole highbrow/lowbrow dichotomy.

Shusterman's *Pragmatist Aesthetics: Living Beauty, Rethinking Art* (1992) included two chapters on rap music that had appeared earlier in journals, in slightly different forms. 'The Fine Art of Rap' (orig. 1991)[11] was a detailed art philosophical exposition into the practices of rap. 'Form and Funk: The Aesthetic Challenge of Popular Art' (orig. 1991)[12] was a more general overview of the bad treatment that popular culture had typically received from traditional aesthetics, but it also delved into the problematics of rap. The importance of Dewey for Shusterman's project should be further highlighted: in the aforementioned *Art as Experience*, Dewey had mentioned, for example, working songs as important for old-time workers to keep the rhythm of the work, and he accentuated the artistic potentials of jazz as an everyday art in a way that was radical, considering the white academic context in which he worked. Indeed, one reason for reviving Dewey's holistic concept of experience was for Shusterman to question the whole idea of (highbrow) 'art'. This did not mean the simple dismissal of the latter, but more like a relativisation: Shusterman aimed to show connections between rap music and the type of arts that were legitimately called art with a capital A, and more specifically, as connected to the fresh tenet of the time, postmodernism. While traditional art debates that debased popular culture were often quite abstract, focusing on obscure concepts like 'real satisfaction',[13] the postmodernists had explained in quite an amount of detail what the new thing in art was about, naming, for example, intertextuality and collage. However, they never really included African American or global cultures into what they wanted to discuss as postmodernist culture.[14] On the other hand, African American intellectuals themselves did use the term, in *The Journal of Rap Music and Hip Hop Culture* and elsewhere, so Shusterman merely took it over and showed concretely how rap was intertextual and how it collaged popular music.[15]

He elaborated on the topic in his 'L'esthétique postmoderne du rap' (1992), discussing rap music from the point of view of Oswald de Andrade. De Andrade's famous idea of cultural cannibalism, a Brazilian avant-garde concept and practice he presented in 1928,[16] was based on the idea that Brazilians, who were under constant colonial pressure, should welcome European/Western culture in the same way as the Tupi tribe was said to have done when they ate a missionary in the 1500s. This 1920s manifesto-esque way of thinking about culture saw the invasion as unavoidable, and the idea was that by eating all the culture that came, there was a way of handling it, perhaps appropriating it, but most importantly staying true to some local traits of culture, too. A DJ in rap, Shusterman thought, did the same: they took up the more commercial music that surrounded them and kind of ate it, took control of it, and gave it a new edge.[17] What was once, for instance, mainstream disco or Aerosmith's 'Walk This Way' (Run DMC's members did not even know what they were sampling when they made their version of it) hence became hip-hop and rap music.[18] So, de Andrade's originally quite bourgeois idea gained a more street-wise application in hip-hop culture. Again, Shusterman can be criticised here for applying a straightforwardly dualist mainstream/underdog framework to rap and consequently downplaying the role of earlier African American music, specifically funk and soul, for its practices and aesthetics. Most of the popular early samples were not taken from disco, rock, or other mainly white mainstream genres, but rather from funk and soul tracks. These might have been hits in Black America, but they were definitely not mainstream hits, and sometimes these sampled tracks were even obscure within the African American mainstream, as is the case with the now iconic Amen Break, sampled from a little-noticed B-side track 'Amen Brother!' to the soul band The Winstons' 1969 single 'Color Him Father'. Still, Shusterman's idea of hip-hop as cultural cannibalism is not at all irrelevant.

So, Shusterman wanted to show that everything that people talked about as postmodernism in the arts was a reality in rap music too, from lyrical appropriation and the playful cut-and-paste of both old texts and music to irony. Tim Brennan criticised the enterprise and saw Shusterman as appropriating rap music, taking it from the ghetto to the white intellectual sphere.[19] Shusterman answered, first, that the original ghetto music was in fact Klezmer in 1500s Venice, as the Jewish population was closed into their own quarters by a Venetian administrative decision in 1516.[20] Moreover, and perhaps more acutely, he pointed out that African American intellectuals themselves used the word postmodernism and bought the general idea of rap and hip-hop culture as a postmodernist practice.[21] Further, it would be quite a stretch to say that, for instance, R. A. Potter's claim that the ethos of African-American jazz can be understood as an instance of artistic modernism, which was then followed by hip-hop's postmodernism,[22] is an appropriation rather than a reflection on some matters that were actually already there, in the culture itself. Jazz's modernist twang is exemplified, for example, by its inner hierarchies, where experimental free jazz is commonly seen as the most progressive and therefore valuable, and clubbed-up acid jazz as the artistically poorest strain.

Shusterman has also been criticised for the whole idea that not only could aesthetic theory be applied to rap and hip-hop culture, but that it was in fact beneficial and wanted for the music and the culture. Against him, Herbert Grabes claimed that rap music seemed to thrive pretty well even without artistic support.[23] This is, of course, true, but Grabes's claim is rather confused about the potential benefits and impacts of theoretical attention. It is not the same as academic-institutional taming. For example, painting could well thrive without theory, too: marketplaces are full of paintings, not to even delve into present-day Instagram accounts where self-taught artists pose according to cultural clichés about what 'artists' are like. The point is that the way some painters have had a safe space and other grains of freedom gained from having an art scene and institution supporting them, in which theories and philosophies of art have had a major role, provides different and surprising artistic opportunities, directions and considerations.

Missed Encounters

Later, the aforementioned possibilities for applying an aesthetic perspective on rap went shockingly under the radar – even for those who wished for such things. Attempts have not been completely absent, but because of some strange scholarly miscommunication that is probably too difficult to trace and pinpoint now, they have remained clustered. As early as in 1995, Mtume ya Salaam wrote in his 'The Aesthetics of Rap' that there was not really any discussion about the aesthetic features of rap music, for example, flow.[24] He was obviously unaware of the pragmatist debate on rap music, and focused on discussing again, as if starting from scratch, its special aesthetic features. Marvin Gladney, also in 1995, wrote that rap music was like its own artistic voyage, with more of a bearing on the Harlem Renaissance, a black art movement in the 1920s, than anything else; that is, he referred to it art-philosophically, as an kind of avant-garde movement, and not a new style of music.[25] Much more recently, in 2015, Emery Petchauer noted that in the context of hip-hop education, both theory and praxis have shifted 'from understanding hip-hop solely as content to understanding hip-hop also as aesthetic form'.[26] He situates and analyses 'ruptures, layers, samples' and 'percussive disruption' as the central aesthetic forms of hip-hop through which its educational value in urban contexts can be understood and applied.

One cannot help but think that Petchauer's and others' work would have been easier and more rewarding had someone presented to them both the '90s aesthetics discussion and ways of approaching scholarly works that are not specifically academic aesthetics but focus on aesthetic matters. Such calls are indeed still being made, since the aesthetic turn in hip-hop education described by Petchauer has not apparently reached the wider pool of hip-hop scholars. James Edward Ford III, in 2019, expressed his desire to break out of the 'limited purview of Hip-Hop Studies' because the 'most pioneering dimension' of classics in the field 'has faded from view – their sensitivity to the aesthetic, historical, and political "noise" overwhelming Western standards of creating, feeling, and knowing'.[27] As for the classics, Ford names 'Tricia Rose's *Black Noise*, Imani Perry's *Prophets of the Hood*, Murray Forman's *The Hood Comes First*, and Ronald Judy's "On the Question of Nigga Authenticity"'.[28] Thinking about early rap theory, Ford's comment shows stingingly how far academic rap and hip-hop discussion has come from its beginnings in aesthetics, and how later waves of cultural studies theorising almost completely overshadowed them. This scholarly rupture is a shame, since keeping aesthetics in sight could have been helpful for all parties of an intellectually minded audience of hip-hop.[29]

A few more clustered contributions in the vein of rap aesthetics are worthy of mention. In 2005, Shusterman returned to the topic by discussing 'violence' as an aesthetic method in rap music; that is, cutting and 'bruising' music for one's own artistic interest.[30] During the same decade, Wojciech Małecki and Stefán Snævarr discussed (and/or criticised) Shusterman for being too romantic about popular culture in general, and claimed that the aesthetic and cultural effects of popular culture and visual culture are often negative. There were also some smaller notes, like those of Martti Honkanen, who noted rap's connection to the rhythm of driving (a lot of rap music is made to be listened to in cars),[31] and Ossi Naukkarinen (1999), who plumped upon hip-hop as a side matter in his discourse on what he calls 'popular culture environments' (where rap music often dominates, from skateboard practice to fashion shops).[32]

Other than these contributions, rap music disappeared for a long time from aesthetics, just as aesthetics disappeared from the scene of rap scholarship. Today, the scholarship is much more about identities, religion, and feminist analysis – for the good, of course, too – but we feel 'rap as art' is a perspective that is worthy of a comeback.[33] As shown, we have not been alone, but most importantly, rap and hip-hop culture simply deserve and call for more sustained and systematic aesthetic attention – and knowledge about it would help many contemporary scholars.

Going Forward: Two Angles

As space is limited, we will refer to two possible, somewhat opposing, directions for re-applying aesthetics to rap and hip-hop culture.

Ossi Naukkarinen noted that popular music and popular culture are often more about environments and settings than objects, so they could be approached through environmental aesthetics, a branch of aesthetics established in the 2000s.[34] He refers to four tenets of environmental aesthetics: (1) *The lack of a clearly delimited object* in favour of 'symbiotic compounds'; (2) *The changing nature of the object of study*; (3) *The multi-sensory character of experience*; and (4) *Engagement with the environment*.[35] It should be pretty clear how rap could be perhaps even the most appropriate instance of popular culture for such analysis. Further, Naukkarinen's suggestion can be expanded: rap and hip-hop culture could be taken to the sphere of everyday aesthetics, an even more recent vein of research.[36] How is hip-hop incorporated into the everyday life of different social strata? When does it stand out, and when does it become simply an enabling background, or a 'tool for living', as Arto Haapala put it?[37] An example of the everyday ubiquity of rap music is presented by a common trope of internet memes, where white, middle-class people make fun of themselves for listening to gangsta rap while driving to their nine-to-five desk jobs.

On the other hand, as Naukkarinen also acknowledges, rap is often *primarily* auditory. This is as evident in a vinyl-lover's ecstatic immersion into the dark and distorted pulse of an RZA-produced beat, a teenager as fascinated by the ice-cold testimony of Missy Elliott in their headphones as in the hypnotic booming of an underground club setting. Hence, a phenomenological, object-centred approach is very much relevant for rap. Here, it is good to note Shusterman's words about the sonically holistic quality of hip-hop: 'No notational score could transmit [rap's] crazy collage of music, and even the lyrics cannot be adequately conveyed in mere written form, divorced from their expressive rhythm, intonation, and surging stress and flow.'[38] Also, as touched upon earlier, books like Tricia Rose's classic *Black Noise* are rife with points of departure for a phenomenological aesthetics of rap. However, to our knowledge the only systematic attempt along these lines has been David A. M. Goldberg's study, where he proposes 'a prototype analytic framework for rap that (1) foregrounds the phenomenological and aesthetic encounter with the sonic energy that remains the core experience of rap music; and (2) considers that encounter without segregating vocals, lyrics, and music'.[39]

We took up Naukkarinen and Goldberg's quite recent suggestions as they represent two different poles of aesthetic analysis: an environmental, (everyday) life-oriented one, and an object-oriented one. Further elaboration must be done somewhere else than in this chapter, but we think it is clear that, taken together with the early tradition of aesthetics of rap, these two perspectives could form into something powerfully new in the sphere of rap and hip-hop studies.

Notes

1. See Jos de Mul's rap lecture at Amsterdam Paradiso in 2005: https://vimeo.com/31428499.
2. James Edward Ford III, '"The Unclean Break": Re-Imagining the Sound of Hip-Hop', *College Literature* 46/1 (2019): 269–274.
3. See e.g. Rita Felski, 'The Role of Aesthetics in Cultural Studies', in *The Aesthetics of Cultural Studies*, edited by Michael Bérubé (Malden: Blackwell, 2005), pp. 28–43.
4. For more on this, see Max Ryynänen, 'Can the (Non-)Subaltern (Understand) Rap? Rap as Vernacular Critical Theory', *Journal of Asia-Pacific Pop Culture* 6 (2021): 213–229.
5. Richard Shusterman, *Pragmatist Aesthetics: Living Beauty, Rethinking Art* (London: Blackwell, 1992), p. 201.
6. Hebert Marcuse, *An Essay on Liberation* (Boston: Beacon Press, 1969).
7. Esa Sironen, '"Hip-hop don't stop": Katujen uutta kulttuuria', *Keskisuomalainen* (Nuorisoliite), 31 August 1984. Republished in Lauri Mehtonen and Esa Sironen, *Aistimellisuus, sivistys ja massakulttuuri: Fragmentteja eräästä projektista 1977–1987* (Jyväskylä: Jyväskylä University, Department of Philosophy, Vol. 34, 1987), pp. 127–132.
8. David Toop, *The Rap Attack: African Jive to New York Hip Hop* (London: The Works, 1995); see also Claudia Mitchell-Kernan, 'Signifying, Loud-Talking and Marking', in *Rappin' and Stylin' Out: Communication in Urban America*, edited by T. Kochman (Urbana: University of Illinois Press, 1972), pp. 315–355.
9. See also G. S. Holt, '"Inversion" in Black Communications', in *Rappin' and Stylin' Out: Communication in Urban Black America*, edited by T. Kochman (Urbana: University of Illinois Press, 1972), pp. 152–159, and in the same book, William Labov, 'Rules for Ritual Insults', pp. 265–314.
10. Pragmatism is a non-foundationalist, experience-driven and impact-oriented school of philosophical thinking. See e.g. Richard Shusterman, *Pragmatist Aesthetics*.
11. Richard Shusterman, 'The Fine Art of Rap', *New Literary History* 22/3 (1991): 613–632.
12. Richard Shusterman, 'Form and Funk: The Aesthetic Challenge of Popular Art', *The British Journal of Aesthetics* 31/3 (1991), p. 213, DOI: https://doi.org/10.1093/bjaesthetics/31.3.213.
13. See Shusterman, 'Form and Funk'.
14. See e.g. bell hooks, 'Postmodern Blackness', in *Yearning: Race, Gender and Cultural Politics* (Boston, MA: South End Press, 1990), pp. 23–31.
15. Shusterman, *Pragmatist Aesthetics*, chapters 7 and 8.
16. Oswald de Andrade, 'Cannibalist Manifesto', translated by Leslie Bary. *Latin American Literary Review* 19/38 (1991): 38–47.

17. Richard Shusterman, 'L'esthétique postmoderne du rap', *Rue Descartes* 5/6 (1992): 209–228.
18. Loudwire, dir. Graham Hartmann. 2016. DMC: The Real Story of Aerosmith + Run-D.M.C.'s 'Walk This Way'. www.youtube.com/watch?v=5ikJrtxRovI. Accessed 30 August 2023.
19. Tim Brennan, 'Off the Gangsta Tip: A Rap Appreciation, or Forgetting about Los Angeles', *Critical Inquiry* 20 (1994): 663–693.
20. Richard Shusterman, 'Ghetto Music', *JOR Quarterly: The Journal of Rap Expression and Hip Hop Culture* 2/1 (1992): 11–18.
21. *JOR* and Shusterman were from Philadelphia, and this connection, together with the strong presence of pragmatism in Temple University (which was as close to the large and devastated ghetto of North Philadelphia as one could academically get) probably made this exchange possible. If rap originated in New York, its aesthetics, theoretically speaking, and hence its sustained and systematic academic reception in general, gained its first big spark and kickoff in the North Side of Philadelphia.
22. Russell A. Potter, *Spectacular Vernaculars: Hip-Hop and the Politics of Postmodernism* (Albany: State University of New York Press, 1995).
23. Herbert Grabes, 'The Revival of Pragmatist Aesthetics', in *Pragmatism and Literary Studies: Yearbook of Research in English and American Literature*, edited by Winfried Fluck (Narr Verlag: Tübingen, 2002), pp. 137–149.
24. Mtume ya Salaam, 'The Aesthetics of Rap', *African American Review* 29/2 (1995): 303–315.
25. Marvin Gladney, 'The Black Arts Movement and Hip-Hop', *African American Review*, 29 (1995): 291–301, p. 293.
26. Emery Petchauer, 'Starting with Style: Toward a Second Wave of Hip-Hop Education Research and Practice', *Urban Education* 50/1 (2015): 78–105, p. 78.
27. Ford, 'The Unclean Break'.
28. Ibid., p. 270.
29. Neither does Julius Bailey's *Philosophy and Hip-Hop: Ruminations on Postmodern Cultural Form* (New York: Palgrave MacMillan, 2014), even though its name mentions 'postmodern [...] form', taking advantage of the work already done in aesthetics. The book has, though, other nice takes on rap, like the reading of it as an African-American extension of Jürgen Habermas's 'public sphere' (see p. 11).
30. Richard Shusterman, 'Rap Aesthetics: Violence and Keeping It Real', in *Hip Hop and Philosophy*, edited by D. Darby and T. Shelby (Chicago: Open Court, 2008), pp. 53–64.
31. Martti Honkanen, 'Tien estetiikka ja tietaide', in *Ympäristö, arkkitehtuuri, estetiikka*, edited by Arto Haapala, Martti Honkanen and Veijo Rantala (Helsinki: Gaudeamus, 1995), pp. 51–57.
32. Ossi Naukkarinen, 'Aesthetics of Popular Culture as Environmental Aesthetics', *Popular Inquiry* 1 (2017): 3–15.

33. B. L. Love, *Hip Hop's Li'l Sistas Speak: Negotiating Hip Hop Identities and Politics in the New South* (New York: Peter Lang, 2012).
34. See e.g. Allen Carlson, 'Environmental Aesthetics', in *Stanford Encyclopedia of Philosophy*: https://plato.stanford.edu/entries/environmental-aesthetics.
35. Naukkarinen, 'Aesthetics of Popular Culture as Environmental Aesthetics', pp. 11–12.
36. See e.g. Andrew Light and Jonathan Smith, eds., *The Aesthetics of Everyday Life* (New York: Columbia University Press, 2005).
37. Arto Haapala, 'The Everyday, Building, and Architecture: Reflections on the Ethos and Beauty of our Built Surroundings', *Cloud-Cuckoo-Land* 22/36 (2017): 171–182, pp. 180–181.
38. Shusterman, *Pragmatist Aesthetics*, p. 209.
39. D. A. M. Goldberg, 'Beats, Rhymes, and Life in the Ocean of Sound: An Object-Oriented Methodology for Encountering Rap Music', *Biography* 41 (2018): 587–606.

6 | The Literary Singularity of Roots Manuva's *Awfully Deep*

RICHARD BRAMWELL

Hip-hop has received considerable critical attention over the last forty years and is often celebrated for its political and cultural significance within youth subcultures. Although scholars frequently emphasise rap's relation to the lives of socially and economically marginalised young people, they often neglect to give sufficient attention to the aesthetic value of rap lyrics. This is, in part, due to the success of cultural studies and its influence on academic discourse and mainstream debates on contemporary art. However, I suggest that alongside considerations of the social, cultural and political significance of rap artists' work, global rap studies needs to address rap's formal qualities. This will aid our understanding of the pleasure that is found within this oral-poetic form and how rap artists produce their effects. Rap is the most popular poetic form in the world, and it may very well be that it is in the aesthetic qualities of this cultural form that scholars will find much of lasting value.

In the English education system, school inspectors have observed that in spite of a relative weakness in poetry teaching (in comparison with other areas of literacy teaching), pupils are clear about what they liked about poetry, and suggest that 'positive attitudes towards poetry may well reflect its place in contemporary culture, including rap'.[1] This oral-poetic form has had a significant impact on contemporary English literary culture. In one example, Kate Tempest first performed at open mic events at Deal Real Records, an important hub within the UK hip-hop scene,[2] before going on to receive the Ted Hughes Award for New Work in Poetry in 2012. In the context of the United States, Brent Wood has suggested that the reasons for the lack of scholarly attention to rap 'include cultural differences between Euro-American and African-American sensibilities, the reluctance of academic poets and critics to embrace popular culture, and the inability of print-based analysis to deal adequately with oral artistry'.[3] However, Bradley's critique of the trend amongst 'modern literary poets' in moving away from the fulfilment of popular expectations regarding rhyme and meter in poetry towards 'experimentation with a broader range of formal possibilities',[4] suggests that the divergence between the formal experimentation in contemporary poetry and the formal qualities responsible for rap's popularity may be one reason for the lack of attention given to rap by literary critics. I have written elsewhere on the role that rap can play in the production of collective identifications and autonomous spaces. I want to argue, here, that literary studies needs to attend to the formal qualities of rap artists' creative work. Furthermore, through engagement with the particular qualities of rap songs, studies of global rap will develop a stronger understanding of how pleasure, identification, and meaning are produced through rap.

In this chapter I examine the work of Rodney Smith in a manner that is open to the literary value of his lyrics. I draw upon Timothy Clark's notion of literary singularity in order to highlight the need for a close analysis of Smith's work. In *The Poetics of Singularity*, Clark criticises the culturalist turn in literary studies, which he claims reduces 'all intellectual positions to stances within a certain model of cultural politics'.[5] He goes on to argue that within this paradigm:

To understand a text is taken to mean placing it within the various competing discourses of its time and (or) our own time, discourses being understood instrumentally as competing ways of representing or constructing reality, each reflecting or producing various kinds of identity, often defined in terms of ethnicity, nationality, religious affiliation, class or gender. The assumption is that once one has cashed in a text in terms of its cultural politics (so understood) nothing worthwhile is left to say about it.[6]

The Poetics of Singularity schematises a school of singularity which has been attentive to literary texts' resistance to being described in general categories. Clark places this school in opposition to the dominant paradigm and claims that this alternative thinking can, through 'the notion of discontinuity inherent in singularity' enable a jump out of the 'use of cultural identity as a principle of explanation'.[7] While I do not entirely accept Clark's criticism of the reductive impact of cultural theory on literary studies, and suggest that a sound understanding of social, cultural, and historical context can enhance the reading of literary texts, in this article I want to draw on Clark's notion of singularity in order to bring to the foreground the literary value of Smith's work.

Clark identifies Jacques Derrida as the presiding figure in arguments that 'literature should finally be valued ... because it is inassimilable to fixed stances or cultural programmes'.[8] In 'This Strange Institution Called Literature', Derrida states:

The space of literature is not only that of an instituted *fiction* but also a *fictive institution* which in principle allows one to say everything. To say everything is no doubt to gather, by translating, all figures into one another, to totalize by formalizing, but to say everything is also to break out of prohibitions.[9]

Derrida refers to a space which precedes the general categories that critics (such as Clark describes) might seek to impose upon literary texts, or translate them into. In his reading of 'Fable' by Francis Pong, Derrida identifies an 'instability [that] constitutes that very event – let us say, the work – whose invention disturbs normally, as it were, the norms, the statutes, and the rules'.[10] Clark argues that rather than being reducible to a set of discourses, for example those of race, gender or class, the literary work may be understood as a space which 'cannot be fully understood theoretically but must be engaged in its specific performance'.[11] I also wish to draw on the work of Giorgio Agamben who, in contrast to Derrida, locates literature's singularity in 'the tension and difference between sound and sense'.[12] In his discussion of 'the end of the poem' Agamben highlights enjambment as the 'opposition of a metrical limit to a syntactical limit' and a defining feature of poetry.[13] In the poetic disruption of the coincidence of the semiotic and semantic spheres is a space which allows new possibilities and the end of the poem is identified as the 'source or condition of possibility'.[14] Through a close analysis of Rodney Smith's work I aim to direct critical attention to rap's literary value and highlight some of the qualities that make this oral-poetic form significant to contemporary British culture. In this gesture of openness to rap's literary qualities, it is important to retain the significance of its performed, oral character. Bradley (2009) argues that rap's 'dual rhythmic relationship' with the beat is a fundamental characteristic of this oral-poetic form.[15] I want to expand on Agamben's distinction between sound (the semiotic) and sense (the semantic) in poetry, in order to highlight the distinction between the musical (semiotic-performative) and oral (semiotic-poetic) qualities that produce rap's literary value. I begin my analysis with 'A Haunting', the sixth track on Roots Manuva's third album, *Awfully Deep*.[16]

'A Haunting' opens with a Tam-Tam, or gong. There is a rolled attack which is left to decay for fifteen seconds, to near complete silence. The song begins, then, with an ending. As a result of the attack (the beginning of a note) being rolled, the beginning of the track is difficult to pinpoint and is almost immediately overlapped by its after effect, the long decay. An attempt to identify the beginning would involve making a judgement as to whether it is the initial contact with the Tam-Tam by the object used to strike it, the final contact between the two objects, or the entire rolled attack along with the prolonged decay. Indeed, the song could be considered to begin after this, but that raises the question of the Tam-Tam's purposiveness in relation to the rest of the track. This single, but complex sound has no semantic element and is a purely semiotic event. However, it contributes to an aesthetic of haunting, with the prolonged reverberation foregrounding the after-effect of an initial event which itself is difficult to distinguish from its effect. Once the sound has almost completely decayed it is followed by a regular bass-line accompanied by a horn for eight bars, the last two bars of which are punctuated by Roots Manuva's voice. The words spoken are identifiable as words, though which words they specifically are is difficult to identify. These eight bars last another fifteen seconds, the regular beat contrasting with the gradual decay of the Tam-Tam. The ninth bar, which now introduces drums to the track, opens with Roots Manuva singing a purely semiotic 'oo-oh' sound. There are a series of juxtapositions in the prolonged opening of 'A Haunting' which include the slow decay of the Tam-Tam, the regular bass-line, the obscured spoken words, and the sung words which rise and fall in pitch.

Though at this stage the song has not articulated any clear meaning, I wish to venture the tentative suggestion that the regular rhythm in the eight bars contrasts a form of temporalisation with the prolonged decay that preceded it. Furthermore, the purely semiotic sung sound contrasts the oral foregrounding of the semiotic with the closer relation between the semiotic and semantic in the words which precede it. It is significant that the *meaning* of those words cannot be identified but that they *are* words can. There is a closer relation between the semiotic and semantic but not a coincidence. The first forty-five seconds of the track contrasts forms of temporality, the tension and difference between the semantic and semiotic, as well as the relation between the semiotic-performative of its musical performance and the semiotic-poetic of its oral performance. However, the sound produced by the Tam-Tam and the eight bars of bass coupled with a horn, which both last fifteen seconds, cannot be said to have a definite meaning any more than can the obscured words. In attempting to engage with 'A Haunting' in its singularity it might be useful to recall that, just as the Tam-Tam resists being assigned a specific meaning, the track's play with the relation between the semantic and semiotic in its series of juxtapositions in the opening does not set up rigid oppositions but allows the exploration of difference and various forms of, and potential for, meaning.

The opening lines of the rap clearly contrast with the obscured words that preceded them. However, if we are to seriously consider Clark's call for a 'minute discipline of following [the literary work's] terms',[17] we should note that this very discontinuity may be significant. There has been a shift from the play of the semiotic, and the impossibility of meaning signalled by the rolled attack of the Tam-Tam, to a coincidence between the semiotic and semantic in the rapper's spoken words. Indeed, these opening lines are accompanied by another attack of the Tam-Tam, but this time the attack is not rolled. This point could be considered a new beginning, and this position would allow us to feel more secure in the suggestion that the purpose of the rolled attack allows us to engage with notions of temporalisation and beginning. It would be important, at the same time, to also bear in mind that this may involve a change in position (even if that change is only to be more secure within our current position). The Tam-Tam and obscured words' resistance to being specifically defined in this way could equally be understood to enable us to engage with the very act of attempting to join the semantic and semiotic. The first verse is given below; I have placed the line endings to coincide with the end of each two-bar phrase:

Rebel I with fortitude come see the dude exude – the rudiment cement baptism. No arguments, cause I know the blokes who terminate. They do it for the joy and they don't need no pape's. While I count the shillings, best know there's many willing, to drill out the laws 'til the nonsense pauses. Down for the essence the Rebel I causes. With synchronicity goat skin paraphrase, mystic maze of sonic mathematics the acrobatics on the tight rope that near broke the spine time for time, line for line, random as the wind chime, deep sublime risen above, written in dub, the dub wise, pommes frites or French fries. International passion of whom new life in the womb.

The verse begins with the foregrounding of the 'subject or object of self consciousness' (OED). The construction of the self as disobedient to higher authority can be associated with the impossibility of fixing any specific meaning to the Tam-Tam or the series of juxtapositions which took place. The 'Rebel I' is further characterised as possessing moral courage. At this point the rap appears to privilege the semantic over the semiotic in its construction of the 'Rebel I'. The description of the 'Rebel I' is followed by a caesura which separates it from 'the rudiment/cement baptism'. This phrase is also internally divided as a result of running over the end of the second bar; there is a disruption at the semantic level by the semiotic-performative. However, there is also a tension between this disjuncture and the use of rhyme to join the last word of one line, 'rudiment', with the first word of the following line, 'cement'. At this point we can see the way in which the work semiotically performs the semantic, cementing the lines through the use of 'cement'. In contrast to Agamben's statement 'that poetry lives *only* in the tension and difference between sound and sense',[18] Roots

Manuva's poetics involve a play with the tension and difference as well as coincidence between the semiotic-performative, semiotic-poetic and semantic. We can contrast this cohesion through rhyme of what had been disrupted at the semiotic-performative level, to the resistance to semantic coherence of the opening of the track. Furthermore, the foregrounding of the semiotic coincidence with the semantic to produce both cohesion and coherence contrasts with the privileging of the semantic over the semiotic during the first line. If earlier we experienced a lingering poetic tension between sound and sense, here we find an inventive performance of its coincidence.

As we can see from the way in which I have transcribed 'A Haunting', the ending of the first line, 'rudiment', emphasises rough beginnings or first principles. However, when the rap is heard rather than read, this emphasis seems to be produced by the caesura. Although Agamben privileges enjambment as the device which distinguishes poetry from prose, there is a complement between the caesura which precedes the words and the use of enjambment, produced by the running over the temporal (or semiotic-performative) limit of the bar. Agamben identifies the space of poetry as the 'condition of depriving it of the possibility of a lasting accord between sound and sense'.[19] Ending the bar with 'rudiment' can be seen as an exploration of the impossibility of beginning in the space produced by the discord between sound and sense. One way of viewing the beginning of the next line is that there is a return to the privileging of the semantic over the semiotic. However, there is a new possibility in this word, to the extent that it appears to be valued more for its form than any meaning it may have outside the rap. Just as the unintelligible words prior to the rap appear to be present merely as words, 'cement' seems to have been invented, within the rap, for the primary function of cohering these lines. Following that, it is then employed to strengthen the 'fortitude' of the 'Rebel I'. The use of enjambment to create new meaning contrasts with the coincidence of the semiotic-performative limit of the bar in the second line and the word 'terminate', which is unrhymed, along with the syntactical limit of the end of the sentence. This coincidence of limits produces a semiotic performance of the termination. In addition to performing the cementing and termination of lines, this verse, while referring to 'sonic mathematics' in one of its longest lines, pushes the number of syllables that can fit into the bar to the limit, threatening to break the semiotic-performative 'spine'. Roots Manuva's exploration of coming to meaning involves a self-conscious use of the limits of, and interplay between, the semantic, semiotic-performative, and semiotic-poetic.

If this rap is brought together through a complex interplay of the semantic, semiotic-performative, and semiotic-poetic (in contrast to

Agamben's assertion that poetry lives in the tension between the poetic and semantic), then what is the significance of this to the theme being developed in the first line? In addition to the use of homophony, linking rudiment and cement, there is a semantic connection between cement and fortitude, in the latter word's sense of physical and structural strength. There is also a connection between fortitude and a sense of morality that is carried by 'baptism'. Not only does 'cement' function to cohere the two lines, it also strengthens the characterisation of the subject of the first line. If this is the case 'baptism' possibly introduces a tension between its link with ritual and the construction of a subject that rejects higher authority. 'Rudiment' may be associated with the notion of first principles and either rough or important beginnings. This again provides a semantic connection with baptism and initiation. The second line ends 'No arguments, cause I know the blokes who terminate', again producing a coincidence between the semantic and performative. The vernacular 'blokes' and 'dude' earlier appears to strengthen the connection between 'Rudiment' and 'Rudie'. However, 'baptism' seems to have its significance constrained to initiation. That constraint is reinforced by the semiotic and semantic termination at the end of the bar and the desire expressed later to 'drill out the laws'. The phrase also recalls the sound of the Tam-Tam, the rolled attack along with the prolonged decay. The track attempts to produce a space outside external laws and is resistant to higher authority, privileging what it presents as 'the essence the Rebel I causes'. While I do not have the space here for an exhaustive reading of 'A Haunting' it is possible to identify ways in which it resists being categorised in general terms. The track engages with the process of coming to meaning, poetic invention, and the tension between the semantic, semiotic-performative, and semiotic-poetic. There is also a play with forms of temporalisation and the use of words purely for their sound as well as to invent new meaning within the space the track creates. Significantly there is also an emphasis on beginning, self-consciousness and resistance to authority. There is a resistance to being explained in predetermined categories and 'to break out of prohibitions'.[20] I shall now turn my analysis to the other tracks on the album in order to explore the wider themes of *Awfully Deep*.

The title track of the album, 'Awfully Deep', opens with a slow drum beat and a high-pitched drilling sound. This is followed by a whirring or pulsating noise, then the chorus. The refrain 'Things are getting awfully deep/ Awfully deep, I can't get no sleep' is accompanied by a synthesised pulsating along with the same beat and drilling that the track begins with. The layering of these synthesised sounds on top of one another significantly differs from the use of acoustic instruments in 'A Haunting'. There is an ominous sense of disorientation produced by this layering, which can be linked to the prolonged periods of involuntary consciousness referred to in the chorus. The opening line of the first verse, 'I don't do mind games, I'm frame by frame' builds upon this disorientation by associating the mind with technology. The rapper goes on to describe himself in technological terms, perhaps not referring to his persona, Roots Manuva, but to the digital media upon which his voice is recorded: 'I'm eighteen bits, I'm forty-eight hertz.' The disorientation, which is associated with technology here, later becomes associated with morality:

A terrible phase is spendin' money wi' whores.
A pastor say we shouldn't do that shit
so we sit down, reflect on all the sins we commit.
How many Hail Marys? Cut down on the dairy?
Away with the fairies, how much do my fare be?
Two travel-cards, my life's so hard
I don't know my inch, from my foot to my yard.
Botch my body card, make you part of me, pa.

The manner in which the pastor's reprimand is represented, 'we shouldn't do that shit', suggests an ironic disposition towards religious authority. Following earlier references to things which belong to the rapper and the repeated use of 'my', the reference to '*a* pastor' (my emphasis) indicates a more distant association with this figure of religious authority. Furthermore, there is a sense that one can gain additional pleasure by reflecting upon past sins. Penance is associated, through rhyme, with superstition, financial exchange, and dieting. The successive rhyming gives the impression that all these elements are interchangeable. The penultimate line builds upon the theme of disorientation by conveying the rapper's inability to choose a scale to apply to his life.

The second and third verses continue the theme of disorientation, though now focusing more directly on the theme of mental health. While the lyrics are repeated in differing tones by voices in the background throughout the track at various points, in the second and third verses this becomes more apparent, adding to the aesthetic of disorientation. Along with the continuation of this theme, the second verse develops the themes of measurement and resistance to authority.

My sanity's back on the line again
Last year, I said I wouldn't rhyme again
But I'm, back for punishment, time again

> If I should lose my good mind again
> Tell my management not to waste good money
> Sendin' me away to the farms of the funny.
> Them places only make me worse,
> They full'a, crooked doctors and kinky nurses
> That poke you in the arse, and measure your schlong
> Put that tape measure down, that practice is wrong.
> They thought I didn't know what was goin' on
> But I, knew the coup though the drugs was strong
> Chloro- Polma- Oxidisa- what?
> Tell me doctor, why I got purple snot?
> I'm feelin' happy when I know I'm sad
> And now they wanna certify me mad.

The first four lines of the verse relate the rapper's mental state, or 'sanity', with rap. His 'mind' is connected semantically and semiotically to 'rhyme', 'time', and the poetic 'line'. The possibility of losing this connection with music is accompanied by the threat of being sent to 'the farms of the funny', followed by a challenge to the mental health profession: in contrast to the rapper, who is 'on the line', the doctors and nurses are described as 'crooked' or 'kinky' indicating some form of deviance. This implication is reinforced by the instruction to 'put that tape measure down, that practice is wrong'. At the same time that he most directly confronts authority in this track the rapper also criticises attempts to measure or categorise human beings. Furthermore, the knowledge of the doctors and nurses is challenged by the rapper's insight into his own condition and awareness of their activity. The penultimate line contrasts emotion and reason as forms of knowledge. In the opening of the final verse there is a quoted reference to the artist, Rodney Smith, as an historical figure: 'They said, "Mr Smith, please calm down."' This contrasts with the reference, in the first verse, to the disembodied digitised voice of the rapper's persona. Along with the association of Roots Manuva's mind with rap music, in the second verse, these references complicate the distinction between artist and persona. I have used the term rapper to incorporate both the artist and the persona that the artist uses in his work. In 'Awfully Deep' we can see a play with the relation between the rapper and his work in which the distinction between artist, persona, and work is problematised alongside a resistance to the attempts of figures of authority to categorise or measure human beings.

In addition to problematising the nature of Rodney Smith's relation to 'Awfully Deep', the tensions produced by competing forms of knowledge also contribute to the track's theme of disorientation. Though the final verse begins by quoting the rapper's doctors, their scientific rationality is challenged by other ways of 'seeing things'. Both Christianity and Voodoo are referred to as the rapper faces his own 'painful truth'. The rap ends with a reiteration of the significance of Voodoo as an explanation for the pain suffered by the rapper and his attempt to escape: 'voodoo in the hills and I'm running from ghosties'. Along with dieting, religious penance and superstition, as interchangeable methods for correcting the rapper's lifestyle, the opposition of explanatory frameworks for understanding Roots Manuva's mental state can be seen as a resistance to dominant discourses and a privileging of subaltern forms of knowledge.

Like 'Awfully Deep', 'Colossal Insight' moves from focusing on a meditation upon the self in the first verse, towards the theme of the relations between the self and others in the later verses. The rap opens with an unorthodox address to God and proceeds to consider the rapper's lifestyle:

Gracious Lord, my mega-almighty
I know I been slightly, out your path.
Feelin' the cold draft, of the bleak winter
Splinters in my soul, I'm out of control and I know
that I should cut down this drinkin'
Too many late nights and, wayward thinkin'
Compellin' a man to plan two shennanigans
They boy me out, I got to be the man again
'cause I didn't rhyme to get me rich
but I'm a scally, two twos you'll find I switch
Hurt and pain made me, nothin' came to save me
I walk with disaster, prefer to be plastered.
Time's my master don't ask me for jack turd
all I owns is my balls and my word.
No-body heard'a me, 'cause I'm a new man.
I got this new plan, to get these new grands.

The peculiar language used in this address suggests a lack of deference to higher authority, represented by the 'mega-almighty'. There is an irony in the rapper's confession that he is 'out of control' as the claim contributes, with 'soul', to an internal rhyme, demonstrating the level of skill and control the artist has accomplished. However, the mournful 'o' sound of 'know', 'soul', and 'control' suggest a yearning, possibly for a path to be guided by. This irony, along with the unconventional address to 'Gracious Lord,' can be linked to his admission 'I'm a scally, two twos you'll find I switch', drawing attention to the rapper's ambivalence. This is followed by a rejection of religion. Rather than declaring allegiance to the 'mega-almighty' the rapper asserts that pain and disaster are the forces that form him and claims 'Time' as his 'master'. Roots Manuva's construction of Time, which is associated with music, rapping, and the mind in both 'A Haunting' and 'Awfully Deep', is identified here as the rapper's 'master'. However, the nature of this relationship appears not to be a simple opposition of a dominant Time with subordinate rapper. He asserts his ability to use time as a guide, through the assertion that 'all I owns is my balls and my word', and in the interplay between his control of language through rapping and use of temporalisation against the syncopations of the musical beat. This verse is followed by a criticism of fame and responses to the rapper's success. The repeated use of 'like', in the opening lines of the second verse, conveys a sense of inarticulacy and repetitiveness in those who are enamoured by celebrity. Though he states that he is 'just the same type' there appears to be an irony in this statement. The 'scally' rapper adopts a critical distance 'observin' this world' and caricatures this 'type' of person. Roots Manuva questions this 'game', then criticises the media in a world of changing perceptions. This is followed by Roots Manuva's disengagement from that world, his rejection of attempts to be categorised and an expression of 'love for every one of them scenes' that nevertheless are not considered restrictions for the rapper.

Paul Gilroy discusses, in *The Black Atlantic*, the way in which black cultural forms produce a sense of 'sameness by introducing a syncopated temporality – a different rhythm of life and being'.[21] Roots Manuva's repeated invocation of time conveys the sense of a critical perspective gained through linguistic and musical innovation. We can see in *Awfully Deep* the themes of resistance to categorisation and the association of time and music with the rapper's mental state. Building upon the theme of coming to meaning in 'A Haunting', both 'Awfully Deep' and 'Colossal Insight' engage in a rebellion against and deconstruction of authority and categorisation, which is followed by a disengagement from and critical orientation towards dominant discourses. The themes of these rap songs are reinforced by their inventive performance (such as 'cement' in relation to cohesion and moral strength), which allows the possibility of producing new meanings that cannot be described within pre-existing categories.

Through a close analysis of these texts I have attempted to draw attention to the literary singularity of Roots Manuva's work. It is clear from children's responses to rap in schools, the contribution that emcee culture has made to contemporary genres such as grime, and from the mainstreaming of rap in popular music culture, that a great deal of pleasure is found within English rap. The popularity of this oral-poetic form raises an important challenge to English studies, which has not developed the analytical tools necessary to address rap on its own terms. To address this challenge, I suggest that literary critics need to attend to the singularity of rappers' works *and* to engage with the various contexts within which those oral-poetic works are produced and performed. Alongside an appreciation of the singularity of rappers' songs, scholars need to develop an interdisciplinary approach to rap in performance. The relation between the lyrical, musical and the social needs further consideration in accounts of rap culture. Global rap studies will develop the methods necessary to engage with rap, on its own terms, through a stronger engagement with performance studies, literary studies, linguistics, musicology, aesthetics and cultural studies.

Notes

1. OFSTED *Poetry in Schools: A Survey of Practice* (London: HMI, 2007).
2. Bramwell, R. 'Council estate of mind: the British rap tradition and London's hip-hop scene' in Justin Williams, ed., *The Cambridge Companion to Hip-Hop* (Cambridge University Press, 2015).
3. Wood, B. 'Understanding rap as rhetorical folk-poetry', *Mosaic* 2/4 (1999): 129–146, p. 129.
4. Bradley, A. *Book of Rhymes: The Poetics of Hip-Hop* (New York: Basic Civitas, 2009), p. 10.
5. Clark, T. *The Poetics of Singularity* (Edinburgh: Edinburgh University Press, 2005), p. 1.
6. Ibid.
7. Ibid.
8. Ibid.
9. Derrida, J. '"This Strange Institution Called Literature": An Interview with Jacques Derrida' in *Acts of Literature* (New York: Routledge, 1992a): 33–75, p. 36.
10. Derrida, J. 'From Psyche' in *Acts of Literature* (New York: Routledge, 1992b): 310–343, p. 326.
11. Clark (2005), p. 3.
12. Agamben, G. *The End of the Poem* (Stanford: Stanford University Press, 1999), p. 112.
13. Ibid., p. 109.

14. Ibid., p. 111.
15. Bradley (2009), p. 14.
16. Roots Manuva (2005) *Awfully Deep* Big Dada, Banana Clan: BDCD072X.
17. Clark (2005), p. 4.
18. Agamben (1999), p. 109 (emphasis added).
19. Ibid., p. 114.
20. Derrida (1992a), p. 36.
21. Paul Gilroy *The Black Atlantic* (London: Verso, 1993), p. 202.

7 | The French (Hip-Hop) Revolution Is Yet to Come

A Sociology of Rap Music in France

KARIM HAMMOU AND MARIE SONNETTE-MANOUGUIAN

The sociology of culture offers a variety of methodological and theoretical resources to understand hip-hop. Over and above the content of its musical output, this discipline allows us to take seriously the relationships and social contexts which give full meaning to the practices related to rap. The production perspectives in sociology remind us that rap is not just a form of expression for social groups, but the product of complex cultural industries, where both alliances and conflicts are played out, sometimes in unexpected ways. The sociology of taste and cultural practices helps us to appreciate the diversity of audiences and their relationship to this music, but also the points of convergence in the forms of subjectivation fuelled by it. Finally, the sociology of artistic worlds reveals how musical worlds are inseparable from other media, and from political or legal arenas. Over and above these insights into artistic phenomena, sociology encourages us to devote sustained empirical attention to power struggles, and in particular to the hierarchies of age, class, gender, and race which play a role in our everyday lives.

As a genre derived from the tradition of African-American music, French rap has inherited a part of its organisational structure from the American music industry, characterised by the contrast between 'Black' music and 'White' music. France's own history of musical racialisation has also had an impact: from the interwar period onwards, the French music industry exploited the exoticism associated with both African-American music and the French colonial imaginary.[1]

During the early 1990s these processes of racialisation became increasingly complex. The practice of French rap began to receive significant media coverage from the autumn of 1990.[2] This mediatic zeal was spurred both by the commercial success of the compilation *Rapattitude* as well as by social events, sources of stigma with which rappers were being associated. These heterogeneous events – inner-city riots, the proliferation of graffiti on the Paris metro network, high-school demonstrations against violence, and gang warfare in the Île-de-France – brought the 'question of the *banlieue*'[3] back into the public eye, a subject on which rappers often expressed their opinions. These events also exacerbated an issue which had become a recurrent theme in the works of certain hip-hop artists since the 1980s: the critique of persistent racist inequalities, despite the universalist rhetoric of equality for all citizens upheld by the French Republic.[4]

During its first few decades in France, rap was construed as an 'othered' form of music, symptomatic of social problems. This otherness was therefore conceived as representative of rappers as 'young people from the *banlieue*'. This characterisation was portrayed in relation to hierarchies of age and class but was primarily linked to the geographic imaginary of the *banlieue* as a symbolic locale of unrest. This 'othering' was also racialised: the focus in media reports and debates on the question of immigration and racism suggested that the concept of 'young people from the *banlieue*' was used as a euphemism to designate a non-White working-class youth, typically represented by a caricature of 'North African youth'.[5] This new racialisation of rap mobilised the stereotype of the Arab man,[6] a stereotype constructed over the course of French colonisation, and particularly during the Algerian war of independence. French rap was therefore no longer associated solely with the racialisation taking place in the United States and the fear of it being imported:[7] it was also defined by reference to the internal boundaries in France contrasting racialised people with the majority group.

In this article, we offer an overview of the various spaces which have led to the racialisation of rap music in France using tools available to cultural sociology. By seizing on opportunities to exploit a commercial niche, the music industry helped in the building of a racialised professional segment, one which would later become a central pillar of its business. In the first section, we will explore this process using the 'production of culture perspective' in cultural sociology.[8] Rap audiences have long been the object of social representations which present them as exclusively popular; in the second section, we will, however, demonstrate how they have in fact been diversified from the outset. Indeed, their massification over the last twenty years is not contradictory to the capacity of rap to serve as a formative medium[9] for contemporary self-understanding in France. Finally, in the third section, we will examine the political, legal, and mediatic racialisation processes which have incited moral panic[10] relating to rap and rappers, such as lawsuits or attempts to censor their work.

The New Golden Age of a Racialised Professional Segment

In 2017, hip-hop music in the broad sense (including rap, contemporary RnB, ragga, reggaeton, etc.), both in French and otherwise, represented a turnover of at least 250 million euros in France. Ticket sales for concerts totalled 74 million euros (8 per cent of all box office receipts); physical music sales had revenues of 60 million euros (15 per cent of the total); and digital music sales reached 100 million euros (33 per cent of total turnover).[11] French-language rappers generated most of this economic activity (as they have done since the 1990s) in a French recorded music market which remains one of the most protectionist in Europe.[12]

During the first golden age of French rap, at the end of the 1990s, estimates suggest rap's market share of the recording industry turnover stood between 7 and 8 per cent. While the scale of the hip-hop music market in France is still modest when compared to the United States,[13] the share of hip-hop revenue within the whole French recorded music industry now exceeds 20 per cent, a share which for the first time is comparable to that seen in the United States.[14] However, French rap has not been integrated into French popular music or song writing: it, instead, continues to be closely related to postcolonial minorities. How can we explain this tour de force which has transported a musical genre associated with minority groups to the very heart of the French music industry and the source of its greatest contemporary hits?

This process is firstly explained by the ability of hip-hop artists and entrepreneurs to create and maintain their 'own proper places',[15] by which we mean structures offering hip-hop artists and activists a sense of relative autonomy.[16] This structuring of a network of actors helps counterbalance the weak position rap artists hold within the recording industry. Consequently, rappers have successively overcome a series of obstacles that impeded the commercial success of rap in France: its rejection by the major radio networks targeting young listeners who, in the mid 1990s, associated rap with a divisive form of music; the wave of contract cancellations among hip-hop artists in major record companies during the crisis spurred by the digitisation of music; increasing competition from related musical genres (US rap, contemporary RnB) in the 2000s; and the recurring suspicions of piracy or fraud which have undermined the credibility of hip-hop artists and entrepreneurs in the eyes of their economic partners.

But the resilience of hip-hop within the French music industry can also be explained by the invention of a unique method of commercial operation during the second half of the 1990s. French rap, in particular, was defined as a cultural good that was no longer seen as just a passing fad or a symptom of social problems, but as an 'oppositional avant-garde', combining a dissenting stance with innovative ambition on the aesthetic level.[17] Within such a framework, music industry players set up a system of catalogues (the Hostile label owned by Virgin Music/EMI is a pertinent example), placing their bets on artistic avant-gardes likely to be commercially successful in the medium term. Both hip-hop's key figures and the major record companies accordingly developed a strategy of 'marketing the margins',[18] often using specialised labels, organising the commercial management of the minority traits given to rap – especially its association with non-White minorities. The imaginary of the 'street', a characteristic of this strategy, became a central pillar of promotional material, as well as the professional[19] and aesthetic[20] discourses which accompany rap in France. From the second half of the 1990s till present, rap has and continues to act as an 'othered cultural good',[21] whose commercial success is directly linked to the exotic attraction or rejection of the minority groups to which rap remains emblematically linked.

Beginning in 2013, a new mode of digital distribution has become central to the music economy: listening via *streaming* platforms, generating income primarily through subscriptions, with secondary revenue from advertising. From 2010 to 2015, turnover generated by French rap within the French record industry was multiplied by a factor of 2.5. In 2018, turnover from recorded music linked to *streaming* (301 million euros) almost equalled that of physical sales (313 million)[22] in France. The resurgence of physical sales of French rap music, and more broadly of hip-hop music, coincided with this growth in streaming. The onset of the digital era therefore put an end to the restrictive broadcasting of hip-hop music for which the television and radio media outlets were responsible.

As a consequence of this growing profitability, the major companies are adopting the same tactics as they did at the end of the 1990s: they are forming partnerships with a number of independent hip-hop producers, and harnessing expertise through the recruitment of professionals in this sector. The music industry is still characterised by the logic of an oligopoly with a competitive fringe: the centre of the oligopoly, dominated by the major record companies, is still able to absorb smaller companies which develop on its periphery (or 'fringe') when they prove to be lucrative.[23]

Born on the fringe of the oligopoly, the social world of French rap works as a professional segment,[24] which is becoming an integral player within the musical industry. It is characterised both by the specialisation of its artistic and economic initiatives in the hip-hop music sector, a circle of colleagueship visible in the numerous 'featuring' collaborations between artists, and the persistent marketing of the margins as inextricably linked to the racialised imaginary of the *banlieue*. Thus, since the 2000s, the social world of French rap has become the core of a much larger racialised professional segment, incorporating a growing number of musical aesthetics which music industry professionals increasingly describe as 'urban'.[25]

Diverse Audiences United by a Controversial Musical Genre

The popularity of rap can be measured by its economic success, but also by the range and diversity of its audiences. In 2018 almost one in three people in France revealed that they listened to rap.[26] This constituted a six-fold increase over twenty years. There are, of course, significant disparities depending on various social characteristics such as age, class, and gender. The impacts of ethnicity are more complicated to tally because they are not covered by specific questions in the survey carried out by the French Ministry of Culture, which sets the standards for knowledge of cultural practices in France. Nevertheless, the process of racialisation remains a key component in the expression of people's taste and distaste for rap as various qualitative studies have shown.

Listening to rap has been a mainly generational phenomenon since the 1990s. This music has played a unifying role for teenagers since the 2000s,[27] a role which helps explain its ability to constantly renew itself as new audiences begin to discover it. In 2018, the majority of people aged under 35 said they listened to rap music; but the genre is now popular among all age groups: 38 per cent of 35–44-year-olds say they listen to it compared to 16 per cent of 45–54-year-olds and 8 per cent of 55–64-year-olds.[28]

In terms of class, the audience of rap has always been socially diverse. In the 1980s, the growth of rap in France was supported both by fractions of the working classes who were passionate about soul and funk music and by a bourgeois cultural avant-garde.[29] By 1997, listening to rap was found to be just as frequent among the children of executives and higher intellectual professions as among those of working-class parentage.[30] During the 2000s, the social dynamics of listening to rap changed substantially: rap became an increasingly popular choice, in both senses of the word. Rap, as we have already outlined, is increasingly heard by all social groups, but it is also most favoured among the working classes.

Although twice as many men as women listened to rap in the 1990s, this gap has been considerably narrowed over the past twenty years. In 2018, 34 per cent of men and 26 per cent of women claimed to listen to rap. Indeed, listening to rap in general is now less of a gendered phenomenon than the manner of its consumption: male involvement in rap is statistically stronger and more durable over time as 26 per cent of the women who stated they listened to rap aged 12 no longer did so in 2018, compared to just 13 per cent of men. Qualitative research helps us to interpret this phenomenon. On the one hand, the female (and queer) audience for French rap sees their tastes and amateurish skills depreciated by the male and heterosexual audiences that surround them.[31] On the other hand, the stereotype of rap as a fundamentally virile form of music allows one to '[embody] a sexuality above all suspicion – that is, explicitly heterosexual and seen as inevitably dominating'.[32] This issue, which is particularly noteworthy among young men, seems to feed into their statistically stronger preference for rap.

This specifically heterosexual factor in the inclination towards rap in France is based on an equation involving not only issues of gender, but also age, class, and race, all of which are encapsulated in the constructed idea of *racaille* (literally 'scum'). This stereotype is associated with racialised young men from impoverished working-class suburbs. Yet, as an idea, it is both appealing and repulsive well beyond the groups to which this figure is usually tied.[33] Rap is one of the major cultural vectors in the development of this stereotypical figure as well as its dissemination and appropriation by various social groups, promoting complex forms of identification and exoticism. We therefore find that the public are just as ambivalent as the commercial player; the image is sustained in both cases by the paradoxical regime of value[34] accorded to an othered cultural good. Being 'othered' is therefore no longer synonymous with the marginalisation of rap but may, on the contrary, actually contribute to its centrality to the French cultural landscape.

Before examining the way rap music fits into these public media spaces, we need to question the reality of this association between rap and postcolonial minorities. Although it is not possible to directly identify the ethnoracial affiliations of rap fans through the survey of cultural practices carried out by the French Ministry of Culture, several elements suggest solid avenues worth investigating. First, the extent of rap's popularity as a musical genre and its economic success refutes the idea that it is a style of music exclusively appreciated by postcolonial minorities. A proclivity for this music is dominant amongst both the youth of the majority population and that of minority groups. However, by focusing on national origin as an imperfect proxy for racialisation,[35] we can find some notable results.

In the population of mainland France as a whole, those who are French by birth say they listen to rap more often than French residents who are foreigners or who have been naturalised. Rap is not, in this sense, a music related to immigration but rather a music closely linked to the national condition. On the other hand, people whose parents were born French listen to rap less often than those with one parent born abroad. By identifying three modalities we can reach conclusions which were specific just to the rap genre in 2018: people with one foreign-born and one French-born parent are those who most often say they listen to rap (44 per cent) ahead of people with both parents born in France (28 per cent), and also of those with two foreign-born parents (32 per cent).

How should we interpret this result? We can hypothesise that it is less the experience of not being French that encourages people to listen to rap than that of being subject to the suspicion of not being French. It is thus a paradoxical national condition that it is marked by a hindered cultural citizenship,[36] which finds an elective affinity with listening to rap. Likewise, the strong attachment to rap that we can detect amongst people living in mainland France, but who were born in French overseas territories, argues the same point.[37] In other words, the experience of discrimination could be a factor leading to an attachment to rap, a hypothesis that the aesthetic history of this musical genre reinforces.

In fact, the everyday experience of racism and discrimination within working-class neighbourhoods is a recurring theme in rap music, often written using the first person singular or plural.[38] This subjective expression of critical social conscience strives for political autonomy and demands radical civic equality for non-White minorities in France. The aesthetic implementation of this radicalism, combined with the social affiliations of rap artists, has led to particularly repressive political treatment of both rap and rappers.

The Intervention of the Political Class and the Criminalisation of Rap

Fuelled by the othering of actors in hip-hop music and their related productions, there are still numerous controversies that continue to court the rap genre, even at the beginning of the 2020s, despite an economic and cultural context which favours this type of music.[39] These are in line with the forms of political illegitimacy and legal criminalisation which were intensified in the 2000s.[40] Under the impetus of political activists or associations, generally regarded as being on the political right or far right, political actors, and/or members of Parliament or the Government regularly generate controversies related to rap, which sometimes result in trials and financial penalties for rappers.

This extensive history of the political and legal delegitimisation of the rap musical genre began in 1995 when complaints were filed against the group Suprême NTM. NTM was convicted for remarks made about police unions on stage during a concert for SOS Racisme at La Seyne-sur-Mer in 1995. Initially, during the first trial in 1996, they were sentenced to a prison term, which was then suspended on appeal in 1997. These recurrent quarrels between rap artists and the police, both within their music and in court, have been ongoing for the three decades since that time.[41]

Since then, numerous court cases have been filed, affecting both famous and little-known rappers alike. From the 2000s onwards, the target of political denunciation took on a new form: initially instigated by a far-right media campaign, members of the parliamentary and/or governmental right-wing groups seized the opportunity, leading to concert cancellations and sometimes taking rappers to court.[42] In the 2000s and 2010s, members of parliament (most often from the right) increasingly used the opportunity of *Questions au Gouvernement* (Question Time) to accuse rap or rappers of 'threatening the French state and people'[43] and to call for certain works to be banned. It is often the exclusion of the supposed rap audience that is at stake in these attacks: it is not just an attack on the artists, but also on their presumed listeners, associated with the working-class and non-White youth coming from the *banlieue*. The image of the rapper is once again associated with that of '*racaille*' and the political actors involved are often the same ones who have popularised the term as a racialising stigma. Rap audiences were portrayed as being both less capable of intelligent decision-making and incapable of interpreting the symbolic uses of artistic words and gestures. Above all, they were seen as being 'ready to take action', which implied that they were incited to violence after listening to a song.[44]

The history of the political criminalisation of rap corresponds to the 'growing audience for a nationalist moral crusade'.[45] By targeting rap and rappers, political leaders are feeding a moral panic,[46] which is to say, a disproportionate reaction seeking to provoke collective indignation at practices considered threats to the values and interests of society. These controversies are actually in line with the political agenda: political leaders are instrumentalising rappers' outputs to condemn undesirable populations deemed threatening to the French Republic.[47] In this way they justify public policies and legislative debates, as was the case in 2005 in a context dominated by events known as the 'riots in the *banlieue*'. The right-wing member of parliament François Grosdidier, along with 201 colleagues, asked the Ministry of Justice to press charges on seven rap groups on the grounds that 'the message of violence from these rappers propagated to uprooted, decultured youth may incite them to incivility, or worse terrorism'.[48]

Since the 2010s, social networking has facilitated the rapid dissemination of questions raised by activists from political organisations or by 'opinion leaders'.[49] Political declarations spread by hundreds of Twitter accounts have found a media outlet leading to consequential decisions for the artists' careers. In 2018 Marine Le Pen (Front National) and Laurent Wauquiez (LR) used Twitter to demand a ban on concerts by Médine planned at the Bataclan, the concert hall targeted during the terror attacks of 13 November 2015. This ban was upheld by Gérard Collomb, then Minister of the Interior, and accepted by the rapper's team following threats of demonstrations. In a context where there is a trivialisation of the discourse identifying racialised people in France as *'racaille'* or, more recently, 'terrorists' hostile to public society,[50] rap artists, seen as emblematic of this new internal enemy, were a choice target for political figures defending a conservative or reactionary political agenda. In response, these artists have turned their stigmatisation into material for their artistic output, and even to promote their activities. Whether as an attraction based on exoticism, or as a demonised figure of rejection, characterised as emblematic of minority groups, rap in the 2010s was still seen to be an othered cultural good.

Conclusion

The experience of discrimination, national and transnational loyalties, and, more broadly, the relationship to politics, have been recurring themes in French rap music since the early 1990s. The emergence of hip-hop music in French popular culture has therefore helped to identify new modes of enunciation, revealing new shared topics, linked especially by the direct and intimate experience of racism. As such, new ways of living and their narratives have found an unprecedented home at the heart of the musical and media landscape. This transition from the invisible to the visible world is what Rancière refers to as political: bringing 'those who have no part'[51] into the sphere of representation: hip-hop artistic practices contribute to a redefinition of the 'distribution of the sensible'[52] in France. But the resistance to this irruption is far from negligible. The ingress of rap into the core of French cultural life calls into question the paradoxes of republican citizenship: is the current economic and political regime compatible with an objective of equality and common dignity? This question results in mostly ambivalent commercial, sensitive, aesthetic and political responses. In the meantime, although rap in France has not yet had its revolution, it continues to function as a counterculture to civic modernity.[53]

Notes

Traduction depuis le français par Edward Lees. Nous tenons à remercier Paroma Ghose pour sa relecture attentive. ['Translation from French by Edward Lees: We would like to thank Paroma Ghose for her careful proofreading.']

1. O. Roueff, *Jazz, les échelles du plaisir. Intermédiaires et culture lettrée en France au vingtième siècle* (Paris: La Dispute, 2013); E. C. Hill, *Black Soundscapes White stages: The Meaning of Francophone Sound in the Black Atlantic* (Baltimore: The Johns Hopkins University Press, 2013).
2. C. Warne, 'Curiosity, Fear and control: The ambiguous representation of hip-hop on French television', in *Group Identities on French and British Television*, M. Scriven and E. Roberts, eds. (New York: Berghahn Books, 2003), pp. 108–118.
3. Meaning literally 'suburbs', the *banlieue* in France is associated with poor people and projects. See H. Boyer and G. Lochard, *Scènes de télévision en banlieues, 1950-1994* (Paris: INA / L'Harmattan, 1998), p. 91.
4. S. Larcher, *L'autre citoyen. L'idéal républicain et les Antilles après l'esclavage* (Paris: Armand Colin, 2014).
5. G. Derville, 'La stigmatisation des "jeunes de banlieue"'. *Communication et langages* 113 (1997): 104–17; S. Bonnafous, 'Où sont passés les "immigrés"?'. *Cahiers de la Méditerranée*, 54/1 (1997): 97–107.
6. T. Shepard, *Sex, France and Arab Men, 1962-1979* (Chicago: University of Chicago Press, 2017).
7. S. Meghelli, '"Fear of a Black Planet". The Transnational Racial Politics of Hip-Hop in France, 1990-1991', in *Hip Hop Français: An Exploration of Hip Hop Culture in the Francophone World*, A.-P. Durand, ed. (London: Rowman & Littlefield, 2020), pp. 29–45.
8. R. A. Peterson and A. Narasimhan, 'The production of culture perspective'. *Annual Review of Sociology*, 30 (2004): 311-334; D. Hesmondhalgh and A. Saha, 'Race, Ethnicity, and Cultural Production'. *Popular Communication* 11/3 (2013): 179–195.
9. T. DeNora, 'Music into action: performing gender on the Viennese concert stage, 1790–1810'. *Poetics* 30 (2002): 19–33.
10. A. McRobbie and S. L. Thornton, 'Rethinking "moral panic" for multi-mediated social worlds'. *British Journal of Sociology* 6/4 (1995): 559–574.
11. K. Hammou and M. Sonnette, eds., *Quarante ans de musiques hip-hop en France* (Paris: Presses de sciences po, 2022).

12. D. Looseley, 'Cultural policy in the twenty-first century: issues, debates and discourse'. *French Cultural Studies* 10/28 (1999): 5–20; H. Dauncey, 'L'exception culturelle'. In *The End of the French Exception? Decline and Revival of the 'French Model'*, T. Chafer and E. Godin, eds. (London: Palgrave Macmillan, 2010): pp. 72–86.
13. In 2017 the music market was worth close to 6 billion US dollars compared to just under 1 billion in France, according to figures from IFPI.
14. In 2017 R&B/Hip-Hop represented 24.5 per cent of total sales by volume (12.8 per cent of physical sales, 17.5 per cent of digital sales, and 29.1 per cent of streamed music) in the United States. Source: Nielson Music.
15. K. Hammou, *Une histoire du rap en France*. Paris: La Découverte, p. 146.
16. S. Baumann, 'A general theory of artistic legitimation: How art worlds are like social movements'. *Poetics*, 35/1, 2007, pp. 47–65.
17. K. Hammou, 'Mainstreaming French rap music'. *Poetics*, vol. 59, pp. 67–81.
18. G. Huggan, *The Postcolonial Exotic: Marketing the Margins*. London: Routledge, 2001; K. Hammou, *Une histoire du rap en France*, pp. 194–207.
19. K. Hammou, *Une histoire du rap en France*, pp. 223–238. See also K. Negus, *Music genres and corporate cultures*. London: Routledge, 2013.
20. A. Pecqueux, *Voix du rap: Essai de sociologie de l'action musicale*. Paris: L'Harmattan, 2007, p. 188.
21. K. Hammou, 'Mainstreaming French rap music'; A. Saha, *Race and the Cultural Industries*, Cambridge: Polity Press, 2018, p. 113.
22. www.insee.fr/fr/statistiques/4238548?sommaire=4238635#tableau-figure1, accessed on 13 November 2021.
23. P. D. Lopes, 'Innovation and diversity in the popular music industry, 1969 to 1990'. *American Sociological Review*, 57/1, 1992, pp. 56–71.
24. R. Bucher and A. Strauss, 'Professions in process'. *American Journal of Sociology*, 66/4, 1961, pp. 325–334.
25. K. Hammou and M. Sonnette, *Quarante ans de musiques hip-hop en France*.
26. Cultural practices survey carried out by the French Ministry of Culture, Deps-doc.
27. S. Octobre, C. Détrez, P. Mercklé, and N. Berthomier, *L'enfance des loisirs: Trajectoires communes et parcours individuels de la fin de l'enfance à la grande adolescence*. Paris: La Documentation française, 2010.
28. K. Hammou and M. Sonnette, *Quarante ans de musiques hip-hop en France*.
29. See especially the role played by the Parisian cultural and musical world in the 1980s, and particularly the Nova radio station, in the development of rap music: K. Hammou, *Une histoire du rap en France*, pp. 64–69.
30. S. Molinero, *Les publics du rap: Enquête sociologique*, Paris, L'Harmattan, 2009, p. 18.
31. P. Higgins, 'Femmes et Queers: des publics subalternes et cachés du rap français?'. *Volume!* 17/2, 2020, pp. 129–146.
32. I. Clair, '"La racaille", a performed figure in French contemporary youth'. *Ethnography*, 22/3, 2021, p. 20.

33. *Ibid.*
34. Or 'two apparently conflicting regimes of value [which] are mutually entangled'. See G. Huggan, *The Postcolonial Exotic: Marketing the Margins.*
35. C. Beauchemin, C. Hamel, and P. Simon, eds., *Trajectoires et origines: Enquête sur la diversité des populations en France*. Paris: Ined Éditions, 2016.
36. J. Beaman, 'Citizenship as cultural: Towards a theory of cultural citizenship'. *Sociology Compass*, 10/10, 2016, pp. 849–857.
37. 50 per cent of the inhabitants of mainland France, but born in French overseas territories, said they listened to rap music compared with 30 per cent of the population as a whole.
38. See the contribution made by P. Ghose to this book. See also M. Sonnette, 'Des mises en scène du "nous" contre le "eux" dans le rap français'. *Sociologie de l'Art,* 23–24, 2015, pp. 153–177.
39. K. Hammou and M. Sonnette, *Quarante ans de musiques hip-hop en France.*
40. M. Sonnette, *Des manières critiques de faire du rap: Pratiques artistiques, pratiques politiques. Contribution à une sociologie de l'engagement des artistes*, Thèse de sociologie, Paris 3 – Sorbonne Nouvelle, 2013.
41. E. Carinos, '"Fuck le 17!": Rap français et forces de l'ordre', in *Droit(s) et hip-hop*, A. Montas, ed. Paris: Mare et Martin, 2020, pp. 105–122.
42. M. Sonnette, *Des manières critiques de faire du rap*, pp. 510–528.
43. K. Hammou, *Une histoire du rap en France.*
44. M. Sonnette, *Des manières critiques de faire du rap*, pp. 537–544.
45. K. Hammou, *Une histoire du rap en France.*
46. A. McRobbie and S. L. Thornton, 'Rethinking "moral panic" for multi-mediated social worlds'.
47. M. Sonnette, 'How politicians use French rap to stoke division', *The Conversation*, 18 August 2021, https://theconversation.com/how-politicians-use-french-rap-to-stoke-divisions-165567, accessed on 15 April 2022.
48. 'Des parlementaires réclament des poursuites contre des rappeurs': www.lemonde.fr/societe/article/2005/11/24/des-parlementaires-reclament-des-poursuites-contre-des-rappeurs_713789_3224.html, accessed on 10 November 2021.
49. J. Boyadjian, 'Twitter, un nouveau "baromètre de l'opinion publique?"'. *Participations*, 8, 2014, pp. 55–74.
50. P. Durand and S. Sindaco, *Le discours 'néo-réactionnaire'* (Paris: CNRS Éditions, 2015); C. Guibet-Lafaye, 'Radicalisation: de l'adversaire à l'ennemi'. *Regards Sociologiques*, 68/53–54, 2019, pp. 169–192.
51. J. Rancière, *Disagreement: Politics and Philosophy* (Minneapolis: University of Minnesota Press, 1998) p. 9.
52. J. Rancière, *The Politics of Aesthetics: The Distribution of the Sensible* (London: Bloomsbury, 2004).
53. P. Gilroy, *The Black Atlantic: Modernity and Double Consciousness* (London: Verso, 1993).

PART III

Applications of Rap

8 | Lords of the Mic

Live Collective Performance in Grime Music

ALEX DE LACEY

Introduction

Grime music emerged at the turn of the millennium. Performed by MCs and DJs, it is a vital and vibrant form with unrelenting energy. MCs spit lyrics (bars) over a constantly shifting canvas of instrumental tracks. These are chosen ad hoc by the DJ, who – if they are any good – tries to match the beat with the intent and direction of their sparring partners on the microphone. These relationships are often harnessed in a group setting, around 'crews'. Sociologist Joy White sees crews as central to grime, acting as a 'space that provides an opportunity to learn your craft and develop tacit knowledge about the scene and how it operates'.[1]

Over the past twenty years, grime has become one of the most prominent genres within the United Kingdom. South London MC Stormzy is an international star. He headlined Glastonbury, the UK's largest music festival, in 2019 and set up a scholarship for Black students at the University of Cambridge. North London's Skepta has three Top 5 albums, and in 2017 he collaborated with Canadian rapper Drake on *More Life*, an album that broke Spotify streaming records. There are now grime scenes in Brazil, Australia and Japan. But despite grime's success, the genre's core principles remain unchanged.

This chapter focuses on live collective performance in grime music. In particular, it explores the spaces where grime is performed, paying attention to the specificity of these contexts, and their impact on group practice.

The idiosyncrasies of global rap forms are often contingent on, or at least informed by, the spaces and the political climate in which they are created. Hip-hop in Tanzania, for example, has historically been produced in spaces of alterity, with local radio its key site for dissemination. This is owing to long-standing alignment between owners of large-scale national radio stations and the governing Chama Cha Mapinduzi party.[2] In post-socialist Albania, hip-hop took hold through a bustling import market of 'inexpensive cassettes [from] American artists', with state broadcasters (again) taking time to adapt, 'tend[ing] to favour rock and pop styles'.[3]

For grime music, its grounded ecosystem of youth clubs, pirate radio stations and raves – functioning outside the punitive gaze of New Labour Britain – is critical for understanding the form's performance practice, artist etiquette and improvisational schema.

This chapter is split into three sections. Firstly, it positions grime as genre, demonstrating how antecedent forms – principally hip-hop and Jamaican dancehall – inform its collaborative, yet vehemently competitive nature. Secondly, it will offer an overview of its key arenas (radio, raves, record shops), unpacking how grime thrived within a 'Black Public sphere' outside of heavy censorship and racialised policing of mainstream public fora. Finally, it will focus on a particular performance that characterises grime's improvisatory framework. Taken from 2007, this acclaimed 'Birthday Set' for East London MC Ghetts possesses all the hallmarks of grime performance. In doing so, this chapter will demonstrate dense interconnectivity between grime's contexts for performance, offering insight into the ways in which the crew acts as the central fulcrum for new creative work.

Origins

Grime music is a Black British musical form. This status is of course partly attributed to grime's predominantly Black (often male) practitioner base, but it is grime's performance style, and its indebtedness to other genres of Black music that cements this position. While there is a particularity to grime that sees it markedly differ from its predecessors – in tempo, interpersonal relations and improvisatory gait – there are commonalities that help frame grime within wider Afrodiasporic musical practice. Like many genres, it is influenced by locally immediate forms, but also other musics from what Paul Gilroy heuristically calls the 'Black Atlantic'. Jamaican sound system culture and hip-hop loom large, with both genres' competitive spirit seeping into the mentality of grime MCs and DJs.

(i) Dancehall and Hip-Hop

The traditions of 'clashing' and 'battle rapping' respectively are core to grime's character. Battle rap's origins are generally located in the 'dozens', a homosocial game of name calling and provocation that has ancestral ties to Black Atlantic proverbial exchange.[4] For East London grime MC Scissor[5]: 'all the best rappers are those that battle. Busta Rhymes, Eminem. They were all battling before. On the street and in the clash.'

But while battle rap has an influence on grime – notwithstanding commonalities with hip-hop production most clearly evidenced in the so-called 'double time' work of Timbaland and New Orleans bounce – Jamaica stands tall.

Many grime artists reference Sting, a prestigious dancehall event held annually at Portmore, as formative for both performance, and their approach to clashing. West London MC Swarvo sees popular grime rave Eskimo Dance as indebted to the 'Jamaican Yardie stage show'.[6] Furthermore, dancehall MCs such as Vybz Kartel, Beenie Man and Elephant Man are mentioned regularly in grime lyrics: Scare Dem Crew were named after Elephant Man's own roster; while Skepta professed on 2007 track 'I Spy' to 'run tings like Ninjaman and Kartel in Jamaica'.

Perhaps the most explicit reference to dancehall's ever-presence in grime is Skepta's 'Stageshow Riddim'. Released in 2007, the track sonically hearkens back to legendary sound clashes, with snippets of live shows interspersed with a breakneck instrumental. In keeping with tradition, it was also vocaled by a significant number of MCs including Southeast London's Merky Ace, North London's YGG, and Skepta himself. 'Re-licks', as they're known in dancehall, are a staple in grime, with tracks such as D Dark's 'Lake Days' and Jammz and Jack Dat's 'French Montana Riddim' getting the version excursion treatment.[7]

Clashing itself is also crucial for grime (see Chapter Two). While entire collectives can sometimes compete, in grime considered emphasis is placed on the MC's one-to-one clashing capabilities. Producer and MC Jammer set up Lord of the Mics with filmmaker Ratty in 2004, pitting MCs against each other in lyrical battles. The franchise released seven series, with luminaries such as P Money, Kano and Tinchy Stryder all participating. In addition to formalised clashes, impromptu wars of words also occur, with battles taking shape either in situ at radio stations, or bubbling up over time with 'sends' posted to YouTube that seek to critique their opponent's character.[8]

These 'ritualised verbal form[s] of combat' are central to the form. Crucially, though, these are balanced against the need to fashion a successful and enlivening performance. Thus, a potent combination of competition and camaraderie, handed down to grime from hip-hop and dancehall, undergirds the performance space.[9]

(ii) Club Culture

In addition to these longstanding influences, grime was more immediately impacted by a thriving Black electronic dance music circuit that dominated British clubs throughout the 1990s. Hardcore, Jungle, and latterly UK garage all have a part to play in making sense of grime artists' approaches to their craft. Prior to the genre's codification, many of its key players were seasoned across multiple styles, with DJ Slimzee, a co-founder of East London radio station Rinse acknowledging a natural progression: 'I've been DJing since 1992. So I was playing hardcore them times then. Then jungle. Into garage. Then grime'.[10]

In terms of musical influence more specifically, grime is indebted to jungle for the character of its MCing. Jungle's heightened pace, oscillating between 165bpm and 180bpm, was well suited to the fast-chat style initially pioneered by UK dancehall artists Smiley Culture, Tippa Irie and Peter Kind in the 1980s. Jungle MCs had strong partnerships with their DJ, and engaged in antiphonal dialogue with audience members, be it at the rave or over the airwaves. Figures such as Stevie Hyper D, Shabba D, Skibadee and MC DET are considered foundational for grime.

The urgency and space afforded by jungle tracks offered MCs room to really expand their lexicon, working complex multisyllabic rhyme patterns into their routines. This approach was largely abandoned in the early days of UK garage, which often favoured 'gospelly piano riffs' and 'soulful lead vocals' of its US counterpart. However, this commitment to MCing practice as documentation, dancehall co-ordination and fiery provocation reared its head once again as garage took a turn towards what would be known as grime in the very early 2000s.[11]

The rise of garage crews, most notably South London collective So Solid Crew, who received a UK Number One with '21 Seconds' in 2001, acted as a catalyst for this new direction. Other notable groups include North London's Heartless Crew, and East London's Pay As U Go collective, whose track 'Know We' – officially released in 2001 – perhaps best captures grime's sonic character: its hook, laden in patois, is grounded in battle rap provocation; MCs Major Ace and Wiley demonstrate double-time fast chat flows; while Maxwell D offers intertextual reference to English reggae singer Sweetie Irie.

Spaces, Sites, and Rites

Grime, then, is a form founded upon the Jamaican stageshow, re-rendered for the fast pace of the United Kingdom's inner cities. As such, it is a potent live performance form, with multiple arenas for its dissemination.

Dominant perspectives on performance practice have historically located creative practice within the confines of a concert hall or theatre. Skilled performers recreate works by composers whose autonomy is often unquestioned, sometimes at the expense of creativity.[12] This reading is insufficient for grime, a form that is built collaboratively. Christopher Small's *Musicking* famously dismantled the autonomy of the concert hall, signalling a move towards the everyday nature of interaction, and the many actors that excite the performance environment. This collaborative approach resonates with sound system culture. Jones and Pinnock's ethnography of Birmingham-based sound system Scientist notes a three-way relationship between the studio where tracks are cut, the sound system itself – with its crew of engineers, the selector and the MC – and the audience.[13] Julian Henriques goes further, highlighting actors whose involvement transcends the immediacy of the performance itself, such as the maintenance crew, or 'boxmen'. For Henriques, this reaffirms a need for 'the widest possible definition of what constitutes performance' and an appreciation of 'every necessity required for the performance to take place rather than only those on stage in front of the audience'.[14] This acknowledgement of the wider performance ecology speaks to grime's interconnected community of pirate radio engineers, DJs, MCs, rave promoters, and videographers.

Simon Reynolds' writing on the 'hardcore continuum' pays close attention to the interconnected elements that constitute these genres' performance network(s). Reynolds' work on UK garage evokes the synergetic relationship between club, pirate radio and the record shop. New tracks would be tested over the airwaves, before being debuted in the clubs. Records for were found through 'hang[ing] out at a garage shop like Rhythm Division'. For Reynolds, this music was about 'vibe' and this vibe was built through engagement in this 'subcultural engine, an urban folkway with its own privileged sites and rites'.[15]

Grime music's basis within these forms means that its performance environment is similarly bound to a multifaceted network of 'sites'. Richard Bramwell has written on how these spaces can be situated within a Black Public Sphere.[16] For Bramwell, this liminality is reflective of the socioeconomic pressures faced by the predominantly working-class Black youth who engaged in grime practice at its outset. Similarly to other Black musical forms, such as Dancehall which faced difficulties following the 1997 Noise Abatement act, grime has faced censorship that delimited the spaces in which it could be performed.[17]

Form 696 has become synonymous with grime event closures. In 2019, a large-scale study by Mykaell Riley deemed the document, issued by the Metropolitan Police to assess the safety of events, to have been used punitively against grime events, resulting in cancellation.[18] Beyond the rave, pirate radio stations were often raided by the police. Skepta's track 'DTI' is named after the Department of Trade and Industry, whose firm hand ensured the impermanence and enforced closure of many radio stations.

However, these restrictions contributed to positive outbursts of creativity. Bramwell draws on Michael Dawson's writing on Black counterpublics, presenting an innovative, interconnected space in which budding practitioners would exchange ideas over Bluetooth between mobile phones, create beats on 'cracked' copies of digital audio workstations such as Fruity Loops, and sharing the results at local youth centres, radio (when it was running), and raves.[19]

This resilience resulted in a circuit that functioned outside of the mainstream (aside from municipal backing available through Youth Centre provisions). The means by which artists worked within this network, and ascended through the ranks, are captured well in an interview between N.A.S.T.Y Crew member Sharky Major and DJ Logan Sama: 'We used to go around peoples' yards and record a bedroom tape . . . I had my regular dons and I started linking [East London MC] D Double E and I was going to a few older guys' yards [to record tapes] . . . we used to do sets in a church club. Those were the days for us, what moulded it. Me and Double would go around to bare different houses and link [East London MC] Kano on that circuit . . . [then] more people started doing radio sets'.[20]

This quote emphasises the trophic separation between avenues of expression, with artists working their way up from the bedroom set to the community centre, and then onto radio. Once there, artists could promote new singles, dubplates and upcoming raves. Resilience and resolve were required to get to this point. 'It was any way', recalled Logan Sama. 'Any which way in which you could string up a pair of decks and some speakers'.[21]

Case Study – F**k Radio

Grime's entrepreneurial ingenuity, creative resolve in the face of censorship, and improvisational performance structure were realised on a day-to-day basis throughout the 2000s. Sama's allusion to getting things off the ground by any means necessary was profoundly apparent across London's dense network of pirate radio stations. With a particular concentration in East London, stations such as Rinse FM and Deja Vu FM hosted a plethora of prominent crews. During this early period, much of grime's performance schema was refined and developed.

Radio's role as a site for creative experimentation is unique, owing to its 'tripartite system of improvising practitioners, active listenership, and interconnected performance network'.[22] Mutual excitation from the wider network combines with the freneticism of the live arena and dynamic of the MCs and DJs in attendance. This environment is insatiably generative. Artists listen and create together in situ. To capture this interplay, this section focuses on a heralded radio 'set' from October 2007. Held in honour of Ghetts' twenty-third birthday, the performance features several MCs working under the stewardship of DJ Unique. Multiple crew affiliations are on show, with tension and tenacity in equal measure.

Hosted at AIM Studio in Southeast London, Ghetto's Birthday set was one of a series of performances recorded for 'F**k Radio'. This space was set up by artists themselves – with the permission of studio owner Danny C – in response to 'too many MCs drawing too much attention and causing trouble [leading stations to] begin limiting sets'.[23] The set is relatively rare for the period, since it was filmed in its entirety by grime documentarian Risky Roadz. This means that both visual and musical cues can be observed.

The performance suitably opens with Ghetto on the microphone, shouting out everyone who made it possible: 'Big up my mum, it's my birthday I made it to 23, what's good? DJ Unique on the deck right now, F**k Radio resident'. It then opens out into an hour-long performance with no interruption, aside from well-placed reloads[24] by DJ Unique that acknowledge the contribution of the MCs. There are three key aspects of grime performance that are captured across the sixty minutes, and these will be focused on in turn. Firstly, how competitiveness dovetails with camaraderie. Secondly, the intergeneric allusions that characterise and stimulate grime performance. Finally, the DJ's technical cachet. Unique is the ultimate arbiter, choosing what tune to play next, and how to fashion excitement through DJ tactics. His selection, use of chopping and cutting will be explored.

(i) Competitiveness and Camaraderie

Grime is often at its best when it is on the verge of collapse. Business theorist Bernhard Burnes researched how the best run companies 'operate at the edge of chaos by relentlessly pushing a path of continuous innovation'. This push, however, is dangerous: an 'inject[ion] of so much novelty and change into their normal operations [causes them to] constantly risk falling over the edge'.[25] Striking a balance between stability and innovation is key. This is complicated by daring interchange and disputes that arise between collaborators (friendly or otherwise). On this occasion, artists were present from East London's Nasty Crew (specifically its younger faction), South London's OGz, and the Movement, a wider amalgamation of MCs from across North and East London.

After the excitable intro from Ghetts, there's an immediate display of affinity between the East London MC and Dagenham's Devlin. Both MCs are part of the Movement, and they collaborated for the Movement album *Tempo Specialists* (2006) and solo records such as *Ghetto Gospel* (2007). According to archivist Jesse Bernard, 'the Movement was a point in time where a group of talented individuals embraced collectivism ahead of personal gain'. This display at F**k Radio was evidence of their shared vision.[26]

At choice moments they encourage each other to contribute and back up their lyrics. Three minutes in Ghetts remarks: 'Ay Devs, they didn't know Ghetts, spitting ... since house and garage I've been down with bars'. Devlin immediately backs up these lyrical assertions. This favour is returned shortly afterwards with Ghetts accentuating the end of each of Devlin's rhymes.

Twenty minutes into the performance, Devlin takes over from Ghetts. There's a brief pause. Devlin checks the microphone is working, and Ghetts interjects: 'you know what we guna do, you know what we guna do, we're guna do that thing. Watch'. Devlin then launches into a dense passage that invokes his fellow performer: '*Test the team, it's Devs and G, running up on sets to squeeze, rest in peace, the best achieved, test in me, can't stop what I am destined to be, I will decimate teams, I am a threat to the scene . . .*'

After this dense multisyllabic passage, Ghetts comes through with his own contribution. Straight after, Devlin flips the rhyme scheme: '*It's Ghetts and Devs, you wanna put the metal to your head, pull the trigger now you're dead*'.

This passage demonstrates a deep, attenuated connection between the two MCs. It's crucial to acknowledge that while aspects of grime performance are pre-planned – most lyrics are written, and DJs might have an idea of what they're going to play – the way they are chosen and employed is completely improvised. Ghetts saw an opportune moment where both Devlin and himself were at the microphone. Using a short sentence that doesn't even indicate what *that thing* is, both performers enter into a frenetic back-and-forth routine only achievable through regular practice hours at radio.

In addition to the articulation of close ties, latent feuds also come to a head at radio, often in ways that are musically productive. On occasion, disagreements can boil over, as documented by Troy 'A Plus' Miller on his *Conflict DVD* (also see Chapter 16) where grime pioneer Dizzee Rascal and his opposite number Crazy Titch took to the roof of Deja Vu FM to settle their dispute.[27] While some of the disagreements on show at F**k Radio were similarly overt – with exchanges and glances between the South London contingent and the East London MCs – there was an intricate battle at play between North London MC Chipmunk and members of Nasty crew.

Chip was still in school at the time, but by this point he had already become one of the most well-known MCs on the circuit. He takes the microphone early on and enters with a characteristic line: 'I be going on sho'. Immediately after Chip enters, a proto-clash emerges. Lil Nasty takes Chip's lyric and repurposes it with a provocation. The rhythmic commonalities between the two passages are striking (see Figures 8.1 and 8.2), with difference only apparent through a disrupted second bar from Nasty which directly refutes Chip's assertion. The pointed 'Nah', in response to the question of 'are we going on sho?', is the most direct indication of the disagreement. The encounter is made further apparent by this rhythmic similarity. Not only is Lil Nasty 'indirecting' Chipmunk, but he is also using Chip's own flow to do so. This level of dense intertextual referencing is common in grime, and suitably elicits a response.

Chip then goes on the offensive with a much more pugnacious lyric, asserting that: 'man will get had up, I'm on a music ting not road but if man

Figure 8.1 Chipmunk on F**k Radio

Figure 8.2 Lil Nasty on F**k Radio

hype you will get bad up'. Whoops are heard in the background. One MC calls to 'allow it' and settle down, but Chip continues regardless. At this juncture, it feels like it's about to boil over. But then Lil Nasty enters with a verbal acknowledgement that it's strictly lyrics: 'selecta, let's do this. Hold tight Chipmunk, we does this'. This comment doesn't stop the battle from re-emerging later on in the performance. Twenty-five minutes afterwards, Chip takes Griminal's flow (Lil Nasty's brother), to assert 'you know what I'm on, said you wanna clash, it's already long'. But the disagreement remains lyrical.

A long-standing tradition of artists lyrically 'killing' opposing performers stretches back to Jamaican dancehall, and is referenced on record by Barrington Levy, with 1984's 'Murderer'. This is a battle for lyrical supremacy. Whether grime artists are close friends or arch-rivals, competition is ever-present. This stimulant of creative practice maps out an enduring tension between divergent individuality and collective fervour. Similarly to the hip-hop cipher, which H. Samy Alim writes of as a 'communal and competitive' space, a balance must be struck.[28] Unlike many ciphers, though, where artists take turns to spray their best 32-bar, individuals are afforded opportunity to converge and combine, either with a fellow MC or the DJ, often resulting in moments of climactic energy.

(ii) Intertextual Reference as Generative

The preceding interaction between Chipmunk and Lil Nasty was catalysed by clever provocation, using their rival's own lyrical patterns against them. Signifying, and riffing off ideas of others, is a recognisable characteristic within many Afrodiasporic forms. Intertextuality in hip-hop is familiar territory, with Justin Williams writing that (one of) its defining characteristics is the 'overt use of pre-existing material to new ends'.[29] Rappers may offer a lyrical adage to a bonafide great – like Biggie Smalls – and this can strengthen or articulate a bond to hip-hop's wider community. Particularly in global manifestations of rap, such as in Australia, this signifies a link to a 'transnational hip-hop nation'.[30]

In grime performance exchanges are much more local, and function as generative intra-ensemble tactics. Similarly to Ingrid Monson's mapping of the 'intermusical', crews work within an open sphere of 'musical allusions' that are 'interactionally produced'. These allusions span the full spectrum of interaction and communication.[31] They can be elementary, such as

Figure 8.3 Griminal on F**k Radio

Figure 8.4 Ghetts on F**k Radio

mentions of each other, or they can be intricate homages that elicit musical responses and embolden the communal bind.

This was made abundantly clear in an exchange between Ghetts and Griminal midway through the performance on F**k Radio. Less than a minute after a fiery contribution from Griminal, Ghetts takes over on the microphone and acknowledges his sparring partner (see Figures 8.3 and 8.4). Like the exchange between Chipmunk and Lil Nasty, the similarities are immediately apparent, both rhythmically and in terms of cadential falls. Ghetts' slight alteration to say he's 'like Grim', coupled with an equally potent simile about being hard as a brick, take the spirit and intent of Griminal's passage and repurpose it for his own tongue.

Importantly, here, there is an indication of shared geography. Both artists assert that you can find them in Greengate, a neighbourhood in Plaistow, East London. This speaks both to conviviality but also locational claustrophobia, or 'neighbourhood nationalism' that dogged grime in its early years.[32] Joy White's study of grime in Newham – the wider borough where Greengate is located – documented 'postcodes and poverty corralling young black lives into ever smaller spaces'.[33] While this isn't the only marker of alignment, Ghetts' decision to spit this lyric straight after Griminal fashions an inextricable tie, both musically and geographically. The warmth with which Griminal received Ghetts' response demonstrates how this intermusical referencing can actively reinforce relationships and elicit change in the unfolding performance.

(iii) DJ Unique on the 1s and 2s

This chapter has so far focused on the intricacies of MC interplay. However, these interactions are continually bolstered by the DJ. In many ways, the DJ is the core figure since they have control over track selection, who is allowed to attend their set and whether to reload a tune. Macro-decisions and indications of a performance's wider trajectory are primarily proposed by the DJ, since the DJ (for the most part) is fixed while MCs move in and out of the foreground as the microphone is passed around to whoever is in attendance.

Because of this, MCs' and DJs' responsibilities in grime can be broadly mapped onto soloists and rhythm section members in jazz.[34] MCs act as 'temporary leaders' relying on the DJ 'to provide signposts for the performance direction'. Because of this, MCs pay close attention to each other and the DJ, listening out for aural cues or physical indications, making musical decisions based on the state of play.

Mediating between being supportive and combative is a fine art, and there are three broad ways in which grime DJs can shift between approaches while working with MCs: firstly, selection and speed of selection; secondly, responsiveness to MC's expectations; thirdly, through techniques and punctuation, such as chopping and cutting. For the entire hour DJ Unique presided over proceedings, all these factors were at play. I want to focus on Unique's technical cachet, and how he enlivened the situation through dynamic – sometimes combative – DJing practice.

A DJ's speed of transition can have a significant impact on the feel of a set. A great deal of grime tunes are built around 'eight-bar switch ups' – one of its early names was eight-bar[35] – but the speed with which tracks are moved through can help further momentum. DJ Unique opens the set with a track from JME, but shifts to a production from Rapid as soon as Devlin takes over the microphone from Ghetts. The combined novelty of Devlin and the instrumental adds exponentially to the trajectory. Within 24 bars, Unique has another acetate cued up and this is abruptly cut in, allowing for an 8-bar transition before Ghetts re-arrives. This exchange happens in the space of less than 45 seconds, with Unique closely listening to the MC's contributions. In grime, lyrics are often assembled in 16s and 32s. Thus, Unique pre-planned for the new track to combine with Ghetts' entry.

Further to this are the more percussive aspects of DJ craft. Chopping is vital. This technique involves swiftly cutting between two channels on the mixer, each playing an instrumental, so that the tracks instantaneously fade in and out of prominence through the speakers. This can be done either with the crossfader or the channel faders (the latter more common in grime). Oftentimes, MCs will sit back while a DJ is chopping, but Unique creates extra percussive layers with a particular brand of chopping, known as 'punching', where you bring one track in and out of focus, often on the first and third beat. These acts typically culminate with a full release of the track that had previously only been exposed in snippets.

Chopping is highly stimulating and arduous in equal measure, often relying on a close working relationship between the artists present. In conversation with North-West London DJ Eastwood, he spoke to both an artist's *level* and *familiarity* as fundamental for pulling off these interventions:

> There's been times where you do that [chop in a track] and the MC gets confused and loses his rhythm. He starts stuttering, forgets his lyrics, then blames it on the DJ. When you're around good good MCs . . . they're so on point they can catch any beat.[36]

Eastwood brings to light this balance, between being combative to garner a reaction, while also complementing the MCs and their capacity to rise to the occasion.

All these factors in combination are captured in a highly memorable moment from the performance, which took place 20 minutes in. Entering over an upbeat two-step instrumental from Chunky Bizzle, Griminal picks up the baton and keeps running. Almost instantaneously, Unique starts to chop in a half-time feel instrumental from Maniac entitled 'Shangandy'. Over eight bars the tracks intersect and battle for sonic dominance, with Unique cleverly setting up a transition.

As soon as 'Shangandy' is left to breathe, space opens up for Griminal to really soar. Instead of battling against a densely percussive texture, he is faced with a dark, brooding instrumental that affords him room to roam. This is bolstered by cutthroat punching from Unique that sees the instrumental cut in and out every two beats, with Griminal resolutely in the foreground. At the fourth time of asking, the energy reaches a point where the room is in the throes of a welter, and Unique reloads the track, pulling back the instrumental to start it from the top. A cry of 'run that again!' from Ghetts is met with cheers and claps, as the performance begins anew.

This creative climax could only have been achieved through close-knit group interaction. Both artists showed improvisational flair to react to each other's performance directions, resulting in a moment where the track simply had to be brought back. This intersection of divergent individuality from Griminal and lightning-fast reactions from Unique – achieved through quick selection of an appropriate follow-up track, ferocious chopping and punching – combined to fashion a moment that exceeded the sum of its parts. These moments characterise grime, and its resolutely group-based improvisatory gait. They can be reached in a number of ways, either built towards iteratively as part of an interrelated improvisatory process, or emerging suddenly through remarkable points of convergence.

Conclusion

Grime music is a group-based form, developed within high-pressure settings such as youth clubs and pirate radio stations. Both the crew formulation, and these settings, provide communal ground to interact and create anew. Specifically, crews and their wider connections (such as the artists who convened for Ghetts' birthday) function as communities to fashion passages of play, try out new lyrics, and inculcate energy through deft interplay that is augmented through intertextual referencing and creative techniques.

The radio setting brings chaos and coherence in equal measure, while enduring tensions between individuals and the wider collective necessitates what P Lakes[37] called 'sharpening steel against steel'. This intensity fosters a clamour for new ideas, and these are often developed in situ and premiered over the airwaves to a clued-on listenership who feedback into the ongoing process.

For DJs and MCs, prescience is paramount. Prediction of a fellow performer's next move is required to arrive at a point of communion. This was evidenced time and again by DJ Unique who lined up instrumentals so they would arrive with a new artist's entry, selecting tracks that would fit the flow and approach of the MC next in line.

What makes grime distinct from its forebears is the sheer number of permutations and figures engaged in these interactions. Twelve artists were present at F**k Radio, with varying affiliations. Each arriving with their lyrics – Unique with a bag of vinyl records – the hour ahead of them was not predetermined. Nonetheless, the ensemble (with all its internal disagreements and disputes) was able to improvise collectively for over an hour, fashioning moments of interplay that were scintillating, but never to be repeated. Griminal's interaction with Unique was stand-out, but it was not pre-planned. And yet, its enactment is remembered to this day, canonised through radio rips posted online, and *X* (formerly Twitter) threads.

Anchored in Jamaican dancehall and US rap, grime music is a form that thrives in a collective setting. Its rotating roster of collaborators, vehement multi-directionality, and vital, thriving network of radio, record shops and raves has galvanised the form across two decades. In 2021, Ghetts reached Number 2 in the UK Charts with an expansive album for Warner Records, entitled *Conflict of Interest*. This may be seen as his crowning glory. But the skills, attitude and approach that enabled him such flexibility as an artist, was fostered back at F**k Radio in 2007, in a makeshift studio in Southeast London.

Notes

1. White, Joy. *Urban Music and Entrepreneurship: Beats, Rhymes and Young People's Enterprise* (London: Routledge, 2017) p. 4.
2. Perullo, Alex. 'Hooligans and heroes: Youth identity and hip-hop in Dar es Salaam, Tanzania', *Africa Today*, 51/4 (2005): 85.
3. Tochka, Nicholas. 'Cosmopolitan Inscriptions? Mimicry, Rap and Rurbanity in Post-Socialist Albania'. In Miszczyński, Miłosz, and Adriana Helbig, eds., *Hip Hop at Europe's Edge: Music, Agency, and Social Change* (Bloomington, IN: Indiana University Press, 2017) p. 167.
4. Abrahams, Roger. 'Playing the Dozens', in Alan Dundes, ed., *Mother Wit from the Laughing Barrel: Readings in the Interpretation of Afro-American Folklore* (Oxford, MS: University Press of Mississippi, 1993) p. 295.
5. Name anonymised.
6. Personal Interview, July 2017.
7. Sparks, Marvin. *Run the Riddim: The Untold Story of 90s Dancehall to the World* (London: No Long Stories, 2021) p. 72.
8. Pre-YouTube sends would often debut on pirate radio.
9. Alim, H. Samy. *Roc the Mic Right: The Language of Hip Hop Culture* (London: Routledge, 2006) p. 101.
10. Pritchard, Will. 2019. 'White Label Goods: How Vinyl Culture Shaped Grime', 2 April 2019 [Date accessed: 1 May 2024].
11. Boakye, Jeffrey. *Hold Tight: Black Masculinity, Millenials and the Meaning of Grime* (London: Influx Press, 2017) p. 50.

12. Vervliet, Stijn, and Bart Van Looy. 'Bach's Chorus Revisited: Historically Informed Performance Practice as "Bounded Creativity"', *Early Music* 38/2 (2010): 206.
13. Jones, Simon, and Paul Pinnock. *Scientists of Sound: Portraits of a UK Reggae Sound System* (Poland: Bassline Books, 2018) p. 4.
14. Henriques, Julian. *Sonic Bodies: Reggae Sound Systems, Performance Techniques and Ways of Knowing* (London: Continuum Press, 2011) p. 45.
15. Reynolds, Simon. 'The Wire 300: Simon Reynolds on the Hardcore Continuum Series #6: Two-Step Garage (1999) – The Wire'. The Wire Magazine – Adventures in Modern Music. www.thewire.co.uk/in-writing/essays/the-wire-300_simon-reynolds-on-the-hardcorecontinuum-series_6_two-step-garage_1999_ [Date accessed: 6 December 2019].
16. Bramwell, Richard. *UK Hip-Hop, Grime and The City: The Aesthetics and Ethics of London's Rap Scenes* (London: Routledge, 2015) p. 18.
17. Niaah, Sonjah Stanley. *DanceHall: From Slave Ship to Ghetto*. Illustrated edition (Ottawa: University of Ottawa Press, 2010) p. 10.
18. Riley, Mykaell. 'State of Play: Grime', Ticketmaster, October 2017. http://blog.ticketmaster.co.uk/stateofplay/grime.pdf, p. 59 [Date accessed 15 February 2019].
19. Bramwell (2015), p. 18.
20. Sama, Logan. 2019. '009 – Sharky Major', Keepin It Grimy Podcast, 20 May 2019, https://open.spotify.com/episode/7xPSj8MnIlZm0zER8r0vgK?si=xsItH9ARRCeCkZB8gZm9Tg, 22:00 [Date accessed: 2 February 2022].
21. Ibid., 22:30.
22. de Lacey, Alex. 'Pirate Mentality: How London Radio Has Shaped Creative Practice in Grime Music', *Radio Journal International Studies in Broadcast & Audio Media*, 19/1 (2021): 197–215, https://doi.org/10.1386/rjao_00041_1, p. 203.
23. RSKY. 2008. *F**K Radio*. J Clarke Enterprise. DVD.
24. The reload involves restarting the track from the beginning after a significant reaction (typically from the audience).
25. Burnes, Bernhard. 'Complexity Theories and Organizational Change', *International Journal of Management Reviews*, 7/2 (2005): 80–81.
26. Bernard, Jesse. 'The Lasting Impact of The Movement', 30 July 2019. https://trenchtrenchtrench.com/features/the-lasting-impact-of-grime-outfit-the-movement [Date accessed: 16 February 2020].
27. See Hancox, Dan, 'Pirates and Olympians: DejaVu FM and the Copper Box Arena', in Alberto Duman, Dan Hancox, Malcolm James and Anna Minton, eds., *Regeneration Songs: Sounds of Investment and Loss from East London* (London: Repeater Books, 2018): 191–202.
28. Alim (2006), 101.
29. Williams, Justin. *Rhymin' and Stealin': Musical Borrowing in Hip-Hop* (Ann Arbor, MI: University of Michigan Press, 2013) p. 1.

30. Maxwell, Ian. *Phat Beats, Dope Rhymes: Hip Hop Down Under Comin' Upper* (Middletown, CT: Wesleyan University Press, 2003) p. 50.
31. Monson, Ingrid. *Saying Something: Jazz Improvisation and Interaction* (London: University of Chicago Press, 1996) p. 188.
32. Back, Les. '"Neighbourhood Nationalism": Youth, Race, Nation and Identity', in *New Ethnicities and Urban Culture* (London: Routledge, 1996) p. 49.
33. White (2017), p. 259.
34. See Berliner, Paul F., *Thinking in Jazz: The Infinite Art of Improvisation* (London: University of Chicago Press, 1991) p. 358.
35. Mason, Matt, 'Interview with DJ Slimzee', *RWD Mag*, Issue 13 (September 2002): p. 28.
36. Personal interview, May 2017.
37. Name anonymised.

9 | Hip-Hop and Mental Health

Perspectives from Psychiatry, Psychology, Public Health, and Neuroscience

AKEEM SULE AND BECKY INKSTER

The Origins of Hip-Hop Music and Culture

Hip-hop's connection with mental health extends far back in history to African culture and the subsequent trauma from transatlantic slavery, from which many narratives around vulnerability and resilience arose.[1] In West Africa, the Yoruba tribe of modern Nigeria had oral traditions of 'Oriki', much like the Griots, expressing heritage through poetry and songs often as riddles, proverbs, and folk tales, which is not dissimilar from modern MCs who rap today. Such traditions were brought into reggae and calypso in the West Indies, all of which contributed to the emergence of hip-hop in the 1970s from the neglected South Bronx, New York City, USA. This period was extremely turbulent for many African American and Latino families who were frequently exposed to poor housing, poverty, illicit substances, over-policing, and increased incarceration – particularly of African American and Latino males – that further fractured family cohesion. Such factors also increased the risk of developing mental health issues and psychiatric illnesses.[2] How hip-hop culture emerged from this situation is remarkable. Like the griots before them, hip-hop artists became 'street epidemiologists' providing social commentaries on their harsh environments, yet also expressing messages of hope, resilience and healing.[3]

Mental Health Definitions and Care Delivery

An informed discussion needs to be had on how hip-hop music and culture can contribute to a better understanding of mental health, psychiatry, psychology, public health, and neuroscience.[4] In doing so, it is important to understand definitions related to mental health and the potential models that underpin such concepts. With this understanding we can explain the role of hip-hop as a vehicle for supporting mental health, promoting resilience, and improving mental healthcare delivery. The World Health Organisation (WHO) Constitution defines 'Mental Health' as 'a state of well-being in which an individual realizes his or her own abilities, can cope with the normal stressors of life, can work productively and is able to make a contribution to his or her community'.[5] The WHO Constitution emphasises social and psychological factors in causing poor mental health, such as violence and persistent socio-economic pressures. The WHO Advisory Group for the International Statistical Classification of Diseases and Related Health Problems 10th Revision defines a 'Mental Disorder' as 'a clinically recognizable set of symptoms or behaviours associated in most cases with distress and interference with personal function'.[6] These definitions indicate that multiple professionals with different training play important roles in helping people with poor mental health. While psychiatrists have medical degrees and prescribe medicines, other roles include psychiatric pharmacists, psychiatric nurses, clinical psychologists, social workers, therapists, counsellors, coaches, and so on. In the UK, mental healthcare is provided at the primary level (i.e., acting mainly as preventative), secondary level (i.e., for early detection and treatment), or tertiary level (i.e., involving specialist treatment). Hip-hop is already being integrated across all levels as we discuss next.

The Origins of Hip-Hop Therapy

Hip-hop therapy was the name given by Dr Edgar Tyson, who is known as the pioneer responsible for creating its foundational model in 1996.[7] In this model, hip-hop culture is used by mental health professionals to foster therapeutic relationships to promote recovery and well-being. Hip-hop therapy uses a heterogenous approach of different models, such as cognitive behavioural therapy, music therapy, and narrative therapy, all combined in culturally relevant ways to provide an ethos for working with often overlooked and disadvantaged communities (e.g., homeless youth, and youth involved with the criminal justice system). Given that hip-hop culture is the dominant form of pop culture at present, it can impact a much broader population of people with mental health problems. Hip-hop therapy must be understood within a broader context of hip-hop culture, which incorporates five elements of hip-hop including 'knowledge', which is championed by artist, KRS-ONE, who focuses on 'hip-hop as a consciousness' rather than focusing on the material aesthetics. When the emphasis is specifically on rap music as a therapeutic tool, the term 'rap therapy' is more appropriate,[8] which is a term given by psychologists and counsellors using rap music to explore issues around problematic behaviours and promoting mental well-being by discussing song lyrics, writing songs, and so on. The importance of having a deeper contextualised appreciation for songwriters' lived experience is well-documented. For example, one study observed that 'although the lyrics presented violent and misogynistic imagery, the music revealed a dystopian soundscape with bottomless bass tones, sirens, and other warlike sound effects. The combined image revealed a songwriter trying to survive in their neighbourhood by any means necessary, and where vulnerability had to be hidden as an instinctual tactic for survival.'[9]

Our Hip-Hop Psych Initiative

Hip-hop therapy is generally delivered in secondary and tertiary settings because people are already mentally unwell; however, there is scope to intervene at the primary level. Our initiative, Hip-Hop Psych, has focused on primary care by engaging with both health professionals and the public. We dissect hip-hop lyrics for mental health themes and translate credible medical information in accessible, culturally relevant ways. We deliver interactive presentations incorporating medical and neuroscientific research in a variety of settings, such as prisons, lecture halls, festivals, nightclubs, and academic conferences. This creates new spaces for discussion and debate about mental health from different viewpoints, especially from hard-to-reach audiences. We also discuss race and gender issues around provider care and broader social injustices (e.g., reproductive justice). Furthermore, Hip-Hop Psych helps the medical community understand how mental health is portrayed in hip-hop, which offers different perspectives for health professionals, helping them to build empathy with those whose experiences differ from their own. Such knowledge might help health professionals be more aware and prepared for discussions with patients about potential trends related to hip-hop icons, such as contagion effects of suicide, self-harm, and self-medication.[10]

At the core of our initiative, we apply what is known to the medical community as 'the biopsychosocial model'. This model underscores the importance of thinking about how multiple factors integrate (i.e., biology, psychology, and socio-environmental).[11] To illustrate our approach, in Kendrick Lamar's song 'Swimming Pools' the character describes and relates to the biopsychosocial model of alcohol misuse, stating why people drink alcohol: 'they like "the way it feels" (biological), to "kill their sorrows" (psychological), or to "fit in with the popular" (social)'.[12] Another example of our approach is outlined in our paper, entitled 'Eminem's Character, Stan: A Bio-Psycho-Social Autopsy'.[13]

Lyrics Analysis

We briefly demonstrate how we dissect lyrics across a range of mental health topics. For example, our paper 'Social Adversity Portrayed by Tupac and Eminem' examines lyrics from the song 'Death Around the Corner' by Tupac Shakur in relation to themes around paranoia, psychosis, drug use, urbanicity, social defeat, and Post-Traumatic Stress Disorder (PTSD).[14] In this song, it appears Tupac's character is preoccupied with paranoia about a perceived threat to him and his family. The character describes his harsh urban environment as being where the 'skinny' (i.e., weak/subordinate) people 'die' (i.e., are killed, exploited, or become irrelevant). The environment appears to be a place where vulnerable individuals develop social defeat, which is a risk factor for psychosis. Selten and Cantor-Graae defined social defeat as being an experience of 'subordinate/outsider status', and could precipitate psychosis in the long term, especially in urban areas where there is greater social competition.[15] Preclinical studies have investigated the social defeat model, whereby a male rodent is presented with an intruder rodent, and the latter demonstrates submissiveness. This behaviour has been associated with hyperactivity of the dopaminergic system in the mesocorticolimbic pathway in the intruder rodent's brain. Furthermore, Tupac mentions his character's use of 'endo' (i.e., cannabis) and how it relieves his stress and paranoia; however, he then says, 'too much weed (i.e. cannabis) got me paranoid, stressed'. While these lyrics appear contradictory, Di Forti and colleagues found an increased risk of developing first episode psychosis following use of 'skunk', which has a high percentage of delta-9-tetrahydrocannabinol (i.e., THC) and a low percentage of cannabidiol.[16] Whilst THC is psychotic-inducing, cannabidiol is anxiolytic (i.e., a medication or other intervention that reduces anxiety)[17] and has anti-psychotic properties. We therefore speculate that it depends on the type of cannabis that Tupac's character has smoked, which could explain both increases in paranoia and relief from it. There are additional childhood factors placing the character at risk, such as references to his mother's alcohol misuse while breast feeding, which could have had a long-lasting negative impact on his developing brain. Evidence has shown that childhood adversity can alter brain structure and function through underlying biological mechanisms. For example, a molecule called brain-derived neurotrophic factor protein (BDNF) plays a key role in brain development, particularly in a brain region called the hippocampus, which plays a key role in learning and memory. Evidence has shown that childhood adversity is associated with compromised BDNF signalling and a smaller hippocampus volume.[18] BDNF is also critically involved in the regulation of the hypothalamic–pituitary–adrenal (HPA) axis. When the HPA axis is hyperactive this increases the production of a stress hormone called cortisol and can also lead to compromised dopamine levels (a hormone associated with goal-oriented activity and pleasure). These changes could consequently lead to the development of psychosis in later life, possibly via epigenetic mechanisms (e.g., DNA methylation).[19] An alternative view of Tupac's character's presentation is that he is experiencing PTSD symptoms after witnessing life-threatening situations while living in a violent environment: 'I seen too many murders.' Therefore, as the character frequently looks out the window, his paranoia is instead viewed as hypervigilance and hyperarousal, which are prominent symptoms of PTSD. Mentioning that death is around the corner could be referencing flashbacks (i.e., reliving violence) and his use of cannabis could be for self-medication. This song also raises issues around moral injury and transgression as the character lives in a harsh environment that challenges his ethical principles where he must protect himself and his family from violence by using violence against others within his community.

In contrast to risk factors, other hip-hop narratives contain messages of overcoming adversity as described in our paper: 'Hip-hop's Survival Anthems: Incarceration Narratives and Identifying Resilience Factors in Maino's Lyrics'.[20] We illustrate how Maino's lyrics exemplify protective factors, such as positive visual imagery, stress inoculation, cognitive reframing, and locus of control. In brief, Maino served a ten-year prison sentence from age sixteen where he experienced periods of 'isolation' in a 'special housing unit' inside a non-rehabilitative setting. After prison, Maino became a successful rapper, entrepreneur, and actor. A leading definition of resilience proposed by Rutter in 2006 states that resilience is 'an interactive concept that is concerned with the combination of serious risk experiences and a relatively positive psychological outcome despite those experiences' and Rutter later defined the term 'turning point' as occurring when 'a discontinuity with the past removes disadvantageous past options and provides new options for constructive change'.[21] Incarceration arguably removed Maino from crime, enabling him to alter his trajectory; however, incarceration can have deleterious effects on mental health. Using his song lyrics as indicators, we feel that Maino survived – not thrived from – these experiences. Maino's character exhibits an internal 'locus of control' in the lyrics 'you take all this from me and I'm still gon survive', hence believing that his abilities to endure and thrive are in his control and not due to other people or circumstances.[22] 'Stress inoculation' is a gradual, increased exposure to stress that enables a person to manage situations better by gradually adapting and overcoming problems (defined by Lyons, Parker, Katz and Schatzberg in 2009), which is also evidenced in his lyrics 'picture you wasting your life, picture you facing a charge, picture you beating the odds'.[23] There is also evidence of positive visual imagery, defined by Holmes and colleagues in 2009, which protects against depression by supporting a person to cultivate positive images of what their future might hold if it went well, as shown in Maino's lyrics 'when I think that I can't I envision Obama I envision them diamonds I envision Ferraris'.[24] It is important to note, however, that systemic issues and environmental factors are often beyond the control of individuals, such as discrimination and poverty, and therefore resilience should not be solely placed on an individual to take responsibility.

Hip-hop artists' lyrics also show alignment with neuroscientific findings. For example, Kid Cudi's lyrics 'People say that bad memories cause the most pain, but it's actually the good ones that drive you insane' mirror findings from a study showing that those who experienced prolonged and complicated grief (exceeding 12 months) had increased brain activation in both the 'pain pathway' and 'reward pathway' when exposed to grief-related words compared to participants who had non-complicated grief (a much shorter period of grief) who only showed activation in the 'pain pathway' – not in the 'reward pathway'.[25] A key brain region activated in the complicated grief group was the nucleus accumbens, which is associated with reward anticipation. Kid Cudi's character could be having a hard time letting go of a lost loved one, partly by holding on to positive memories in an unhealthy way that kept his brain in 'anticipation mode' of hoping to see his lost loved one, yet still knowing it's not possible, which could exacerbate and prolong this painful experience, thereby putting the character at increased risk of developing psychiatric co-morbidities, such as depression.

Hip-Hop and Public Mental Health

In recent years, hip-hop has played an important role in promoting public health, such as by mobilising resources for vulnerable populations during the Covid-19 pandemic.[26] Artists are now addressing stigma in more candid ways by encouraging people to seek resources and consider treatment.[27] The rapper Logic partnered with the National Suicide Prevention Lifeline on a song entitled '1-800-273-8255' about a suicidal hotline caller receiving support. After several live performances of this song, a scientific study found that Lifeline received an excess of 9,915 calls (i.e., an increase of 6.9 per cent over the expected number of calls) and reported a reduction of 245 suicides over the same period (i.e., 5.5 per cent below the expected number of suicides).[28] In contrast to a public health term known as the 'Werther effect', which is the emulation of suicide after a widely publicized suicide (which is most noted in the adolescent population and predominantly linked to celebrities), the authors observed what is known as the 'Papageno effect' after Logic's performances, which triggered a positive contagion from the messages of survival and hope.[29]

In contrast, certain lyrics by some hip-hop artists have arguably contributed to negative public health messaging by normalising poor self-care, ignoring destructive mental health symptoms, promoting self-medication, and suicidal ideation.[30] For example, within the subgenre known as 'Emo-Rap' rappers like Lil Peep, Lil Uzi Vert, and Juice WRLD have openly articulated their mental health struggles and attempts to cope and manage their symptoms; however, this also raises concerns that it could increase the risk of negative contagion (i.e., the Werther effect) to the broader public. Self-medication is a serious risk in hip-hop culture, as was exemplified by the tragic death of rapper Mac Miller from an apparent accidental drug overdose who had released a song two months prior to his death called 'Self-Care' with lyrics such as 'Self-care, I'm treatin' me right ... we gonna be alright'.

How to delineate positive versus negative contagion in hip-hop lyrics raises issues around censorship versus self-expression. This is further complicated given that what might be perceived as a positive message for one person's recovery could have neutral or harmful consequences for others. This debate is exemplified in the song 'Cleaning Out My Closet' by Angel Haze as she speaks very candidly about her experiences of childhood sexual abuse.[31] The first several minutes of the song describe this encounter of abuse with vivid negative visual imagery, intense affective prosody, and explicit language, which could be extremely triggering for some individuals; however, it could also be seen as healing for others as they relate to someone who has experienced something painfully similar. The song ends with messages about survival and resilience: ' ... I'm just standing living breathing proof look at me now I made it through everything ... there's a way from the ground, the makings of a legend are often hidden in trials so just be strong ... '. Therefore, prioritising health communication research is urgently needed to help artists achieve safe portrayals of mental health in their lyrics, but in ways that uphold artistic expression. As one way forward, Hip-Hop Psych is working directly with hip-hop artists, in part through a collaboration with a music-led mindfulness app called Spoke,[32] to provide knowledge to artists about mental health, the biopsychosocial model, and neuroscience research. This 'upskilling' and 'task-sharing' approach can help to inspire the development of lyrical content in safe, evidence-based ways while still respecting the culture and the artists' ability to authentically connect and communicate with their listeners.

We argue that hip-hop lyrics could be used as a primary source of data to help identify public health trends reflecting societal change. Throughout the genre's history, hip-hop lyrics have made regular references to factors that impact mental health, such as drugs[33] and financial hardship. For example, when the American economy entered a recession in 1990, the poverty rate climbed and peaked at 27 per cent in 1993 in New York City.[34] Within this socioeconomic context, Hip-Hop Psych examined the frequency of the use of the words 'broke' and 'suicide' in lyrics across artists across time. We observed curves that climbed and peaked for these words that were similar to what was observed when poverty rates had peaked in New York City around 1993.[35] Hip-hop artists were reflecting the consequences of their changing environments and the impact it has on their state of mind.

Neuroscience and Evidence-Based Research

Numerous studies across a range of contexts and health conditions have shown that music interventions can improve psychological and physiological stress-related outcomes.[36] However, little research has been done within the cultural context of hip-hop. Notwithstanding the stigma that surrounds this genre, this is surprising given hip-hop's connection with authentic storytelling about experiencing adversity and overcoming hardships – all of which can shape the brain's synaptic structure and function. One functional magnetic resonance imaging (fMRI) study found that engaging in hip-hop freestyle rapping was associated with changes in brain activity in healthy participants.[37] By comparing a group who engaged in spontaneous freestyle rap with a group who engaged in a conventional rehearsed performance,[38] the authors found that brain activation in the freestyle rapping condition was associated with increased activation in the medial prefrontal cortex (MPFC), which is a region associated with motivations, intentions, goal setting, and drive. Simultaneously, the authors observed a decrease in activation in the dorsolateral prefrontal cortex (DLPFC), an area that manages higher-level executive functions and consciously monitors and adjusts behaviours to ensure that goals align with actions. Typically, the MPFC sends brain activity signals to the DLPFC, which in turn sends signals to the motor control brain regions to implement actions. However, during spontaneous freestyle rapping the MPFC bypasses the executive control of the DLPFC and sends brain signals directly to a premotor region that combines cognitive and affective information to carry out behaviour. In summary, freestyle rapping is an internally motivated behaviour that is driven by MPFC activation, and this is atypical as it occurs in the absence of conscious volitional control via DLPFC inhibition. The study reported several additional brain regions that were associated with freestyling,[39] and several of these brain regions have been previously implicated in mental health conditions. Therefore, understanding the neural mechanisms underlying freestyle rapping and cognitive flexibility in mental health intervention contexts should be investigated in future studies.

Furthermore, evidence to support the clinical effectiveness of hip-hop music interventions was shown in a feasibility study led by Hip-Hop Psych in collaboration with Key Changes and academics. This study involved eight mental health service users with moderate-to-severe mental illness, and it evaluated the psychological and physiological impact of socially prescribed hip-hop lyric writing and studio recording sessions. This study observed a significant reduction in self-reported rating of negative emotional affect after completing the music intervention. This study further demonstrated the feasibility of safely using technology to collect real-time physiological data in a trusted setting, which is important from an ethical perspective given the potential issues around surveillance and monitoring (e.g., paranoia, psychosis, history living in prison, etc.). Randomised control trials will be an important next step in validating these preliminary findings.

Language disturbances have been consistently associated with mental health conditions, such as depression and schizophrenia spectrum disorders. For example, a common symptom of psychosis is disorganized thinking, and incoherent or illogical speech. Rapping and rhyming contain important features that could help identify language disturbances. Rapping and freestyling often involve describing emotionally important experiences and cognitive beliefs, and therefore contain linguistic and extra-linguistic information that can be analysed using automated natural language processing methods to characterize disturbances, for example, in semantic coherence (e.g., derailment and tangentiality) and syntactic complexity (e.g., concreteness) to predict, for example, subsequent psychosis onset. Neural systems related to emotions and language perception overlap with brain regions that have been associated with poor mental health.[40] Furthermore, even listening to songs and comprehending complex wording and messages can be cognitively demanding (e.g., figurative meaning of proverbs and metaphors). Disturbances in figurative meaning have been reported in patients with schizophrenia spectrum disorders along with their underlying neural correlates.[41] In addition to language, other forms of information could be important in hip-hop therapeutic contexts, such as speech prosody as an indicator of vocal psychopathology (i.e., 'It's not what you say, it's how you say it'). Hip-hop music often involves strong speech prosody (e.g., Tupac Shakur often portrayed anguished suffering in his tone, and Kanye West expressed a yearning tone in his song 'Donda', which makes reference to his late mother). In the scientific literature, there is general agreement that emotional prosody – across heterogeneous tasks – is impaired in patients with schizophrenia spectrum disorders and that other non-emotional prosody difficulties with communicative situations exist as well.[42]

While data science and technology offer vast opportunities to collect person-centred, culturally sensitive data that could be relevant within clinical settings and beyond, collecting personal data must be done respectfully, inclusively, ethically, and only once trust has been established and maintained. These various forms of data could help improve the detection of mental health problems and offer more customised support interventions for high-risk groups. For example, changes in language patterns could be used to better predict first episode psychosis. Data sources could also be used to inform and support recovery and rehabilitation. For example, voice modulation rapping interventions could help patients with schizophrenia spectrum disorders who experience severe difficulties in interpersonal communication to develop their social cognition skills. Additional data sources related to other elements of hip-hop culture should be scientifically examined, such as body motion detection measurements while breakdancing or body popping to examine associations with shifts in mental states and the impact of hip-hop beat making and sound-based treatments, especially given hip-hop's numerous sub-genres. In conclusion, we believe that hip-hop will help expand and evolve an existing literature that seeks to develop effective tailored treatments across a range of mental health conditions for improving emotional dysfunction and reframing cognitive distortions.[43]

Conclusion

We argue that hip-hop is playing a hugely influential role in mental health. It can help people translate their experiences and inner thinking, and it can also help shape perceptions, challenge opinions, bridge communication, and help to understand other people's viewpoints. Hip-hop music and culture have, however, also contributed negatively to individuals and society, which needs careful consideration.

Given that 75 per cent of mental health problems are established by age 24,[44] and that hip-hop is especially embraced by young people, this culture opens a vital window to intervene and provide support. Hip-hop is an important vehicle for engaging with hard-to-reach groups, for example from ethnic minority communities, who face many barriers in accessing mental health services. Furthermore, using hip-hop in therapeutic settings could play a critical role in supporting individual autonomy by enabling more evenly balanced conversations with health professionals. Early evidence is laying the groundwork to understand the therapeutic role that hip-hop can play in mental health interventions; it could help further our understanding of the neural underpinnings of mental illnesses and recovery, and it has been a major driving force for positive public mental health. So long as the conversation is out there and moving forward in a safe, effective, and inclusive way, then hip-hop in mental health holds a lot of promise for the future.

Notes

1. 'Hip Hop Psych presentation at the Arts and Mental Health symposium, The Dust of Everyday Life, Glasgow, 20 April 2017'. https://soundcloud.com/mentalhealtharts/dust-2017-hip-hop-psych [Date accessed: 11 April 2023].
2. Sule, A., and Inkster, B. 'A Hip-Hop State of Mind', *Lancet Psychiatry*, 1/7 (2014) pp. 494–495.

3. Inkster, B., and Sule, A. (2015) 'Drug Term Trends in American Hip-Hop Lyrics', *Journal of Public Mental Health*, 14(3): 169–173. DOI: https://doi.org/10.1108/JPMH-05-2015-0019.
4. Sule and Inkster (2014).
5. 'World Health Organisation Mental Health Key Facts'. www.who.int/en/news-room/fact-sheets/detail/mental-health-strengthening-our-response [Date accessed: 11 April 2023].
6. 'A Conceptual Framework for the Revision of the ICD-10 Classification of Mental and Behavioural Disorders'. International Advisory Group for the Revision of ICD-10 Mental and Behavioural Disorders. www.ncbi.nlm.nih.gov/pmc/articles/PMC3104876/ [Date accessed: 11 April 2023].
7. Viega, M. 'Exploring the Discourse in Hip Hop and Implications for Music Therapy Practice', *Music Therapy Perspectives* 34/2 (2015).
8. Alvarez, T. 'Beats, Rhymes, and Life: Rap Therapy in an Urban Setting' in Hadley, S., Yancy, G., eds., *Therapeutic Uses of Rap and Hip Hop* (New York: Routledge, 2011).
9. Viega (2015).
10. 'How Hip-Hop's Progressive Narratives Are Helping to Tackle Mental Health Stigma'. Akeem Sule and Becky Inkster. https://blogs.bmj.com/bmj/2020/12/09/raps-battle-with-mental-health-how-hip-hops-progressive-narratives-are-helping-to-tackle-stigma/ [Date accessed: 11 April 2023].
11. 'Biopsychosocial Model'. https://en.m.wikipedia.org/wiki/Biopsychosocial_model [Date accessed: 11 April 2023].
12. Sule, A., and Inkster, B. 'Kendrick Lamar, Street Poet of Mental Health', *Lancet Psychiatry*, 2/6 (2015) pp. 496–497.
13. Sule, A., and Inkster, B. 'Eminem's Character, Stan: A Bio-Psycho-Social Autopsy', *Journal of Hip Hop Studies*, 4/1 (2017) pp. 43–49; Akeem Sule and Becky Inkster. www.hiphoppsych.co.uk/pdf/eminem_stan.pdf [Date accessed: 11 April 2023].
14. Sule, A., and Inkster, B. 'Social Adversity Portrayed by Tupac and Eminem' www.hiphoppsych.co.uk/pdf/hhp_tupac_eminem_freestyle_mixtape_essay.pdf (2015) [Date accessed: 11 April 2023].
15. Ibid.
16. Ibid.
17. 'Anxiolytic'. https://en.wikipedia.org/wiki/Anxiolytic [Date accessed: 11 April 2023].
18. Frodl, Thomas et al. 'BDNF Val66Met Genotype Interacts with Childhood Adversity and Influences the Formation of Hippocampal Subfields', *Human Brain Mapping*, 35/12 (2014): 5776–5783. DOI: https://doi.org/10.1002/hbm.22584.
19. Ibid.

20. Sule, A., and Inkster, B. 'Hip-Hop's Survival Anthems: Incarceration Narratives and Identifying Resilience factors in Maino's lyrics', *Forensic Science International Mind and Law* 1 (2020).
21. Rutter, M. 'Implications of Resilience Concepts for Scientific Understanding', *Annals of the New York Academy of Sciences* (2006) p. 1094.
22. Sule and Inkster (2020).
23. Ibid.
24. Ibid.
25. Ibid.
26. Sule, A., and Inkster, B. 'A Public Health Perspective on Hip-Hop's Response to the COVID-19 Pandemic: Experiences of Illness, Spread of Misinformation, and Mobilization of Resources', *Public Health in Practice* 2 (2021). DOI: https://doi.org/10.1016/j.puhip.2021.100078.
27. Sule, A., and Inkster, B. 'How Hip-Hop's Progressive Narratives Are Helping to Tackle Mental Health Stigma', *BMJ*. https://blogs.bmj.com/bmj/2020/12/09/raps-battle-with-mental-health-how-hip-hops-progressive-narratives-are-helping-to-tackle-stigma [Date accessed: 11 April 2023].
28. Niederkrotenthaler, T., Tran, U., Gould, M., Sinyor, M., Sumner, A., Strauss, M., Voracek, M., Till, B., Murphy, S., Gonzalez, F., Spittal, M., and Draper, J. 'Association of Logic's Hip Hop Song "1-800-273-8255" with Lifeline Calls and Suicides in the United States: Interrupted Time Series Analysis', *British Medical Journal*, 375 (2021) p. 8319.
29. Ibid.
30. Sule and Inkster (2020).
31. Sule and Inkster (2020).
32. 'Spoke'. www.spoke.world [Date accessed: 11 April 2023].
33. Inkster, B., and Sule, A., *Drug Term Trends in American Hip-Hop*. https://www.emerald.com/insight/search?q=Drug+Term+Trends+in+American+Hip-Hop+&showAll=true [Date accessed: 11 April 2023].
34. Levitan, M., and Wieler, S. 'Poverty in New York City, 1969–99: The Influence of Demographic Change, Income Growth, and Income Inequality'. www.newyorkfed.org/medialibrary/media/research/epr/08v14n1/0807levi.pdf [Date accessed: 11 April 2023].
35. Inkster, B., and Sule, A. *Money, Mental Health & Hip-Hop*. Kindle Direct Publishing (2023).
36. Martina de Witte, Anouk Spruit, Susan van Hooren, Xavier Moonen, and Geert-Jan Stams, 'Effects of Music Interventions on Stress-Related Outcomes: A Systematic Review and Two Meta-analyses', *Health Psychology Review*, 14/2, (2020): 294–324.
37. Liu, S., Chow, H., Xu, Y. et al. 'Neural Correlates of Lyrical Improvisation: An fMRI Study of Freestyle Rap', *Scientific Reports* 2 (2012).
38. Ibid.
39. Ibid.

40. Liebenthal, E., Silbersweig, D., and Stern, E. 'The Language, Tone and Prosody of Emotions: Neural Substrates and Dynamics of Spoken-Word Emotion Perception', *Frontiers in Neuroscience*, 10 (2016).
41. Kircher, T., Leube, D., Erb, M., Grodd, W., and Rapp, A. 'Neural Correlates of Metaphor Processing in Schizophrenia', *NeuroImage*, 34 (2007) pp. 281–289.
42. Lucarini, V., Grice, M., Cangemi, F., Zimmermann, J. T., Marchesi, C., Vogeley, K., and Tonna, M. 'Speech Prosody as a Bridge Between Psychopathology and Linguistics: The Case of the Schizophrenia Spectrum', *Frontiers in Psychiatry*, 11 (2020).
43. Bąk, H. *Emotional Prosody Processing for Non-Native English Speakers: Towards an Integrative Emotion Paradigm*. Springer International Publishing (2016).
44. 'RCPCH State of Child Health: Prevalence of Mental Health Conditions'. https://stateofchildhealth.rcpch.ac.uk/evidence/mental-health/prevalence/ [Date accessed: 11 April 2023].

10 | The Beat of the Gavel

Rap, 'Race', and Criminal Injustice

LAMBROS FATSIS

Rap music is routinely policed as a symbol of trouble and a source of danger, through legal penal[1] tactics that accuse rappers of glamourising, glorifying, inciting and even causing violent crime.[2] Stripping it of its artistic nature and ignoring its performative genre norms, police, prosecutors and judges target rap as literal, autobiographical testimony – to adduce lyrics, videos and still images as 'evidence' of criminal wrongdoing; thereby putting an entire music genre 'on trial'.[3] So popular has this criminalising trend become, that a New York Senate State Bill was (nick)named: the 'Rap on Trial' Bill[4] – speaking volumes for how institutionalised the war against rap has become. Despite such fair-minded legislation, which emerged as an antidote to the unjust penalisation of rap, the crusading zeal with which rap music continues to be apprehended as a 'crime', shows no signs of abating.

Written against the backdrop of such punitive fervour, this chapter offers a flickering snapshot of how rap music is summoned to the defendant's seat – by unearthing the legalistic arsenal that criminalises rap(pers), while also exposing the discriminatory logic that makes the racialised, state-sanctioned criminalisation of Black[5] music genres possible in the first place. Nowhere is such 'condemnation of Blackness'[6] more audible than in the discriminatory suppression of UK drill music – by anti-Black policies and politics of law and order that police human difference ('race') through the political category of 'crime'.[7] Following a broad-brush description of UK drill music, the remainder of this chapter will focus on legal penal processes through which this latest rap subgenre is cast (out) as criminogenic.[8] Arguing that the selective, racialised criminalisation of UK drill music offers a unique register through which to understand the racialisation of 'crime' and the criminalisation of 'race',[9] this chapter ends with a concluding bar that ... spits truth to power[10] – as an oppositional coda that denounces racist legal penal processes that police the beats and make crimes out of rhymes rather than protect 'the public' against danger.[11]

What's That Sound? Introducing UK Drill Music

UK drill music, a British offshoot of Chicago drill, broke into the mainstream in 2018 – through lurid headlines that described it as the 'demonic'[12] and 'nihilistic'[13] 'knife crime rap'[14] that ostensibly provided 'the soundtrack to London's murders',[15] while also 'spreading a message of hatred and violent revenge'.[16] (Mis)interpreting this new rap subgenre's dark, gritty, deep-bass, punchy 808-generated beats[17] as menacing – and mistaking its provocative bars (lyrics) for real threats of violence – UK drill continues to haunt the penal imagination as a criminal enterprise (which it is *not*), rather than an art form (which it actually *is*). Lacking appropriate knowledge of or literacy in rap *lore*, cops, prosecutors and judges have therefore reduced drill to little more than the object and subject of criminal *law*.[18] As such, drill was indelibly linked to and marked by associations with violence at the outset – although that very same genre is also celebrated as a commercially successful asset to the popular music industry; through chart-topping hits, sold-out gigs, headlining festival line-ups and endless playlists on YouTube and Spotify. This is not to deny, justify, downplay or condone any of the violence (or misogyny) in some but by no means all drill music. Rather, it is to stress that drill is *selectively* singled out for lyrical content that is otherwise overlooked, tolerated or excused in other music genres[19] and different art forms too.[20] First-person narratives that may be partly or purely performative, fictional, hyperbolic or fabricated even – as is the case with many other music lyrics or literary works – make drill vulnerable to accusations of violence, 'gangsterism' and 'criminality', even though rappers consciously exploit such 'outlaw narratives'[21] as a sought-after commodity to be consumed online by followers whose clicks, views, likes and shares can and *do* bring fame and material rewards too.[22] In short, this is a story of a new rap subgenre emerging – only to find itself mired in and threatened by old stereotypes that refuse to see, let alone listen to, Black music outside a legal penal context.

Sounds Bad: Prosecuting Rap Music Beat by Beat

Having introduced and situated the emergence of UK drill in the legal penal context that made a public enemy out of it, this section offers an overview of the various ways rap enters the courtroom as a source of criminal evidence. To do so, the main legal arguments that are made to prosecute UK drill are outlined to reveal the normalised, legalised and institutionalised racist ideology that undergirds, justifies and (re)produces such legalistic sophistry and criminal injustice. While the preceding parts of this chapter have already sketched the broad contours of the legal(ised) criminalisation of rap subgenres like drill, what follows is a head-on confrontation with the specific tools and tactics that legal penal functionaries marshal to charge rappers with the offence of making music they (pre)judge as distasteful and harmful.

'Criminally-Minded'

The repudiation of UK drill as an inherently and quintessentially violent music genre that encourages, celebrates and even enables acts of serious (youth) violence is vividly illustrated by the use of lyrics, music videos and still images obtained from music videos: as direct evidence of wrongdoing, as confessions to an offence, or as expressions of intent to commit an offence. The use of such material, however, is also used indirectly. A case in point is the imposition of Criminal Behaviour Orders (CBOs). Such 'ancillary orders'[23] require drill artists to inform the police twenty-four hours in advance of their intention to publish any videos online while also demanding that they give a forty-eight-hour warning of the date and locations of any planned live performance. But they can also prevent suspects from associating with certain people, entering designated areas, wearing hoods, or using social media and unregistered mobile phones. The police also request the removal of drill music videos from YouTube[24] and monitor the playing of UK drill music on air by requesting radio stations to pluck drill tracks out of their playlists – as the Met Deputy Commissioner, Sir Stephen House disclosed at a Police and Crime Committee meeting of the London Assembly.[25] The Metropolitan Police has even formed a Drill Music Translation Cadre, consisting of police officers who act as rap expert witnesses, decoding lyrics and translating them into evidence for the prosecution.[26] Such heavy-handed measures could be justified, if substantive, reliable, tangible and concrete evidence existed to support them.[27] In the absence of such evidence, however, the dictates of the legal penal system stand in for evidential facts – in ways that have alarmed law reform and human rights organisations,[28] leading legal professionals,[29] defence counsels, the expert witnesses they instruct, as well as social scientists, rap experts and legal scholars.[30]

'Gang-Affiliated'

UK drill is also blamed for and targeted as little more than a front for gang membership and collective offending despite a thin evidence base and a number of troubling implications. Such a prosecutorial strategy is enabled by so-called gang injunctions which, under Section 34(5) of the Policing and Crime Act 2009, allow legal penal agencies to define acts as gang-related – provided that the targeted group (a) 'consists of at least 3 people', (b) 'uses a name, emblem or colour or has any other characteristic that enables its members to be identified by others as a group', and (c) 'is associated with a particular area'. In the context of drill music, this means that anyone who raps on camera with at least two other people, wearing T-shirts with the drill collective's name or logo in their neighbourhood, can be identified as a gang member and prosecuted as such. Inferring gang association through appearances in drill videos that circulate on social media is hardly evidence and complicated further by the fact that the pose, imagery and performance of 'gang lifestyles' have been a staple in various rap subgenres (drill included) since the emergence of gangsta rap in the 1990s. Worse still, gang association *cannot* be inferred through appearances in videos with known gang members, when there can be many innocent reasons for associating with gang members, including musical collaborations, or kinship and friendship ties.[31]

'Bad Characters'

When all else fails, drill music material is relied on as evidence of the defendants' 'bad character', or to denote involvement in 'joint enterprise'.[32] Section 98 of the Criminal Justice Act, 2003 defines bad character evidence as 'evidence of, or of a *disposition towards*, misconduct' rather than evidence which 'has to do with the alleged *facts* of the offence with which the defendant is charged' (emphasis added). As for joint enterprise, it is a legal doctrine that allows the court to show a link or association between defendants. Given the broad scope of such legislation, it is possible to convict individuals of crimes *without* committing the criminal act they are charged with, or even being at the scene of the crime. To introduce such 'evidence' in court, prosecutors present such material in conjunction with witness statements that are produced by relevant 'experts' (usually police officers, 'gangs experts' and forensic linguists), who may also be instructed to give evidence in court. The arguments that such cases are usually based on, involve a matter-of-fact presentation of drill-related material – without adequately interrogating the artistic, literary or fictional nature of the 'evidence' that is brought before judges and jurors.[33]

Spitting Truth to Power

Reflecting on the regular use of such prosecutorial strategies against rap(pers), the racist ideology that informs and sanctions such practices remains invisible, without subjecting such legalistic trickery to the critique it deserves. This involves (a) challenging the evidential weight of such 'evidence', (b) questioning the expertise of those who are instructed as such by the prosecution, and (c) highlighting the problems with interpreting drill lyrics and videos in a courtroom setting and in a strictly law enforcement context. What is presented as evidence-led attempts to prosecute those who are suspected of wrongdoing based on the music they produce, therefore, sounds a warning against the dangers of drawing on drill-related material – without scrutinising the admissibility and relevance of such material, which reproduce racist stereotypes about Black music genres and 'criminality' instead of upholding high standards of evidence. Even the relevant Criminal Procedure Rules, Criminal Practice Directions and Crown Prosecution Service guidelines could, in theory, challenge such racialised criminalising practices, were they used to do that. Without challenging criminal injustice on those grounds, however, drillers remain vulnerable to processes of gathering and presenting 'evidence' that has insufficient weight to withstand scrutiny, given that it is richer in prejudicial impact than evidential/probative value.[34] This is made worse by the fact that the success and impact of such evidence depend on making an emotive case to the jury by portraying defendants in a negative light or whether the drill-related material used is even connected to the charges brought against the defendant.[35]

None of this would be possible were it not for anti-Black policies and politics of law and order that perceive and pursue Black Britons as 'permanent suspects',[36] whose forms of creative expression are perceived and policed as 'aesthetically "out of tune", culturally "out of place" and politically "out of order"'.[37] Drill music is just the latest example in a long history of criminalising Black music(s) from the era of colonial slavery to the present day.[38] Just as earlier Black music genres were policed as audible signs of rebellion, insurrection and disorder, it would not be an exaggeration to suggest – as Murray Lee does[39] – that drill is prosecuted in the way that it is, precisely because it 'challenges, transgresses, confronts, goads, and subverts mainstream society and culture, police and agents of social control, and even the aesthetic sensibilities of mainstream music and the music industry'.[40] Calling, as Lee commendably does, for a 'musicriminology' that is attuned to questions of culture and power, rap scholars should draw on the music to spit truths to power against rap-illiterate colleagues and legal penal practitioners – who only see danger in rappers' rhymes. Rather than 'hear the singer, they analyse the lyrics; rather than hear the drum, they study the song title'[41] – ignoring rap as a cultural practice that speaks of, as well as to rappers' inventiveness, creativity, and artistic imagination; just as it opposes the dominant socio-cultural and political order that polices it as 'noise to be eliminated rather than as music to be appreciated'.[42]

Notes

1. The neologism 'legal penal system' – not unlike the abolitionist catchphrase 'criminal legal system' – is coined here to problematise, refute and refuse the term 'criminal justice system', insisting that the latter is a system of laws that (literally) *creates* 'crime' – both as a concept and a reality – through turning certain activities into punishable offences. This is not to deny that violence and harm exist, or that there are people who commit violent acts that cause harm. Rather, it is to stress that 'crime' is a political category that condemns, stigmatises, marginalises and racialises violence as the inherent trait, individual anomaly, cultural pathology and personal responsibility of 'deviant' individuals and groups. Notions like 'law' and 'justice', therefore, are not understood here as interchangeable or synonymous. As Ben Quigley (2007: 15) argues, '[w]e must never confuse law and justice. What is legal is often not just. And what is just is often not at all legal'. Legal practitioners, therefore, do not (necessarily) observe principles and ideas of 'justice', but enforce 'the law'; the technical and legal(istic) restrictions on the behaviour, actions and activities of 'the public'. While 'justice' denotes and embodies notions and ethical standards of fairness, 'the law' is 'the technical embodiment of attempts to order society' (Williams, 1993: 139). What we refer to or think of as 'the law', therefore, simply refers to 'written law, codes, [and] systems of obedience' (Williams, 1993: 138), *not* that higher, 'just' ethical plane that we think that the law signifies or stands for. For that reason, the term 'legal penal system' is used throughout this chapter to stress that the state's juridical infrastructure delivers punishments, not justice – using 'the law' as an instrument of political (mis)rule. See Quigley, B. (2007) 'Letter to a Law Student Interested in Social Justice'. *DePaul Journal for Social Sciences* (1)1: 7–28 and Williams, P. J. (1993) *The Alchemy of Race and Rights*. London: Virago.

2. For an overview of such accusations, see Fatsis, Lambros 'Decriminalising Rap Beat by Beat: Two Questions in Search of Answers', in Peters, Eleanor (ed.) *Music in Crime, Resistance, and Identity* (London: Routledge, 2023a) pp. 63–77.
3. Kubrin, Charis and Nielson, Erik 'Rap on Trial', *Race and Justice* 4/3 (2014): 185–211; Erik Nielson and Andrea Dennis *Rap on Trial: Race, Lyrics, and Guilt in America* (New York: New Press, 2019); J. I. Lerner and Charis Kubrin 'Rap on Trial: A Legal Guide for Attorneys', *UC Irvine School of Law Research Paper* 35 (2021). For a digital compendium to scholarly research related to 'rap on trial', see Charis Kubrin's valuable website: https://endrapontrial.org/research/.
4. Dillon, Nancy 'New York Lawmakers Introducing Bill to Limit Rap Lyrics as Evidence in Criminal Trials', *Rolling Stone* (2021). www.rollingstone.com/music/music-news/ny-state-senators-bill-legislation-rap-lyrics-evidence-criminal-trials-1258767/ [Accessed 29 March 2022].
5. The term 'Black' is used here to refer to cultural practices that are rooted in, evolve from and establish a dialogue with cultural traditions of the African diaspora. This is not meant to deny the term its coalitional meaning or potential in global anti-racist movements, but to apply it more narrowly to Afro-diasporic culture(s).
6. Khalil Gibran Muhammad *The Condemnation of Blackness: Race, Crime, and the Making of Modern Urban America* (Cambridge, MA: Harvard University Press, 2010).
7. Lambros Fatsis 'Policing the Union's Black: The Racial Politics of Law and Order in Contemporary Britain', in Gordon, Faith and Newman, Daniel (eds.) *Leading Works in Law and Social Justice* (London: Routledge, 2021a) pp. 137–150.
8. Lambros Fatsis 'Policing the Beats: The Criminalisation of UK Drill and Grime Music by the London Metropolitan Police' *The Sociological Review* 67/6 (2019a): 1300–1316; Lambros Fatsis 'Sounds Dangerous: Black Music Subcultures as Victims of State Regulation and Social Control' in Peršak, Nina and Di Ronco, Anna (eds.) *Harm and Disorder in the Urban Space: Social Control, Sense and Sensibility* (London: Routledge, 2021b): 30–51.
9. Angela Davis 'From the Prison of Slavery to the Slavery of Prison: Frederick Douglass and the Convict Lease System', in James, J. (ed.) *The Angela Davis Reader* (London: Blackwell, 1998): 74–95. See also Fatsis, Lambros 'Grime: Criminal Subculture or Public Counterculture? A Critical Investigation into the Criminalization of Black Musical Subcultures in the UK'. *Crime Media Culture*, 15/3 (2019b): 447–461.
10. 'Spitting' in the rap lexicon refers to rhyming, but the word is also used here to give a rap-focused spin on the idea and practice of speaking truth to power – as the mode through which public intellectuals raise their voice against social injustice. For a reformulation of this classic trope against the dominant Euromodern literature on public intellectuals and in the context of rap culture, see Fatsis 2019b: 452–456.

11. To avoid misleading generalisations about 'the public', it is important to stress the obvious point that there are publics that are *protected and not policed* (white, affluent, middle-class people) and there are publics that are *overpoliced and unprotected* (primarily Black people and other(wise) minoritised groups). For a book-length discussion on this, in the context of Covid-19, see Fatsis, Lambros and Lamb, Melayna *Policing the Pandemic: How Public Health Becomes Public Order* (Bristol: Policy Press, 2022).
12. Mararike, Shingi, Harper, Tom, & Gilligan, Andrew (2018) 'Drill, the "Demonic" Music Linked to Rise in Youth Murders'. *The Times*. Available from www.thetimes.co.uk/article/drill-the-demonic-music-linked-to-rise-in-youth-murders-0bkbh3csk [Accessed 29 March 2022].
13. John Simpson '"Drill" Music: A Nihilistic Genre Filled with Boasts of Death and Violence' *The Times* (2018) Available from: www.thetimes.co.uk/article/drill-music-a-nihilistic-genre-filled-with-boasts-of-death-and-violence-g7p736tcj [Accessed 29 March 2022].
14. The Sunday Times Magazine. 'The Knife Crime Rap: Everything You Should Know about Drill Music'. *The Sunday Times Magazine* (5 May 2019) p. 1.
15. Sam Knight 'The Soundtrack to London's Murders', *The New Yorker* (2018) www.newyorker.com/news/letter-from-the-uk/the-soundtrack-to-londons-murders [Accessed 29 March 2022].
16. Sian Boyle 'Soundtrack to Murder' *Daily Mail* (2021) www.dailymail.co.uk/news/article-9585461/Soundtrack-murder-time-gangland-drill-track-Number-One.html [Accessed 20 July 2021].
17. '808s' refers to the loud bass drum beats created by and composed with the 808 or TR-808 Rhythm Composer, an analogue drum machine that has been a staple ingredient in the making of 'phat'/fat/heavy hip-hop beats/rhythms. For a brilliant, original, imaginative and promising 'take' on '808s' as tools for knowledge production, see Katherine McKittrick and Alexander Weheliye '808s and Heartbreak', *Propter* 2/1 (2017): 13–42. For an overall defence of Black music(s) as 'Black method', or as epistemology in sound, see Katherine McKittrick *Dear Science and Other Stories* (Durham: Duke University Press, 2021). See also Fatsis 2021b and Lambros Fatsis 'Arresting Sounds: What UK Soundsystem Culture Teaches Us about Police Racism and Public Life' in Charles, Monique with Gani, Mary (Eds.), *Black Music in Britain in the 21st Century* (Liverpool: Liverpool University Press, 2023d).
18. Fatsis 2021b: p. 33; emphasis added; and Ilan, Jonathan 'Digital Street Culture Decoded: Why Criminalizing Drill Music Is Street Illiterate and Counterproductive', *British Journal of Criminology* 60 (2020): 994–1013.
19. See Amy Binder 'Constructing Racial Rhetoric: Media Depictions of Harm in Heavy Metal and Rap Music', *American Sociological Review* 58/6 (1993): 753–767; Carrie Fried 'Who's Afraid of Rap: Differential Reactions to Music Lyrics', *Journal of Applied Social Psychology* 29/4 (1999): 705–721; Carrie Fried 'Stereotypes of Music Fans: Are Rap and Heavy Metal Fans a Danger to

Themselves or Others?' *Journal of Media Psychology* 8 (2003): 2–27; Adam Dunbar, Charis Kubrin and Nicholas Scurich 'The Threatening Nature of "Rap" Music', *Psychology, Public Policy and Law* 22 (2016): 280–292; Adam Dunbar and Charis Kubrin 'Imagining Violent Criminals: An Experimental Investigation of Music Stereotypes and Character Judgments', *Journal of Experimental Criminology* 14/4 (2018): 507–528.
20. bell hooks *Outlaw Culture: Resisting Representations* (London: Routledge, 2006) pp. 134–144; Fatsis, 2023a.
21. Nielson and Dennis *Rap on Trial*, p. 114.
22. Forrest Stuart *Ballad of the Bullet: Gangs, Drill Music and the Power of Online Infamy* (Princeton: Princeton University Press, 2020); Jabari Evans '"We [Mostly] Carry Guns for the Internet": Visibility, Labour, Social Hacking and Chasing Digital Clout by Black Male Youth in Chicago's Drill Rap Scene', *Global Hip Hop Studies* 1/2 (2020): 227–247.
23. Ancillary orders, CBOs included, are imposed on offenders by the court in addition to an actual sentence. See CPS (2019) for more details.
24. See Fatsis 2019a: 1303–1305 and Tilman Schwarze and Lambros Fatsis 'Copping the Blame: the Role of YouTube Videos in the Criminalisation of UK Drill Music', *Popular Music* 41/4 (2022): 463–480.
25. London Assembly *Police and Crime Committee Meeting* (17 November 2021 at 10 am) Available from https://webcasts.london.gov.uk/Assembly/Event/Index/f546d1a1-66c0-452a-961e-d0d1b00ddebe?in=2021-11-17T11%3A58%3A13.788Z [Accessed 29 March 2022], timestamp: 02:15:18 – 02:19:40.
26. Quinn, E. 'Lost in Translation? Rap Music and Racial Bias in the Courtroom', Policy@Manchester Blogs. (2018) http://blog.policy.manchester.ac.uk/posts/2018/10/lost-in-translation-rap-music-and-racial-bias-in-the-courtroom/ [Accessed 29 March 2022]; Eithne Quinn, Joy White and John Street 'Introduction to Special Issue: Prosecuting and Policing Rap', *Popular Music* 41/4 (2022): 419–426. DOI: https://doi.org/10.1017/S0261143022000642; Fatsis, Lambros 'The Road, in Court: How UK Drill Music Became a Criminal Offence' in Jade Levell, Tara Young and Rod Earle (Eds.), *Exploring Urban Youth Culture Outside of the Gang Paradigm: Critical Questions of Youth, Gender and Race On-Road* (Bristol, UK: Policy Press, 2023b): 100–114.
27. Fatsis, 2019a; Ilan, 2020; Adam Lynes, Craig Kelly and Emma Kelly 'Thug Life: Drill Music as Periscope into Urban Violence in the Consumer Age', *British Journal of Criminology* 60/5 (2020): 1201–1219.
28. Sandra Paul *Tackling Racial Injustice: Children and the Youth Justice System: A Report by JUSTICE* (London: Justice, 2021).
29. Garden Court Chambers 'Drill music, gangs and prosecutions – challenging racist stereotypes in the criminal justice system' Webinar Series (2020). Available from www.gardencourtchambers.co.uk/events/drill-music-gangs-and-prosecutions-challenging-racist-stereotypes-in-the-criminal-justice-system [Accessed 22 March 2022].

30. Fried, 1999; Kubrin and Nielson, 2014; Nielson and Dennis, 2019; Fatsis, 2019a: esp. 1303; Erin Lutes, James Purdon and Henry Fradella 'When Music Takes the Stand: A Content Analysis of How Courts Use and Misuse Rap Lyrics in Criminal Cases', *American Journal of Criminal Law* 46/1 (2019): 77–132; Abenna Owusu-Bempah 'The Irrelevance of Rap', *Criminal Law Review* 2 (2022). ISSN 0011-135X.

31. For a comprehensive discussion on the (ab)use of 'gang discourses' as a criminalising tool in the UK, see Hannah Smithson, Rob Ralphs and Patrick Williams 'Used and Abused: The Problematic Usage of Gang Terminology in the United Kingdom and Its Implications for Ethnic Minority Youth', *The British Journal of Criminology* 53/1 (2013):113–128.

32. For a good critical discussion of joint enterprise law, see Becky Clarke and Patrick Williams '(Re)producing Guilt in Suspect Communities: The Centrality of Racialisation in Joint Enterprise Prosecutions', *International Journal for Crime, Justice and Social Democracy* 9 (2020): 116–129; Susie Hulley and Tara Young 'Silence, Joint Enterprise and the Legal Trap' *Criminology & Criminal Justice* 22/5 (2022):714–732, DOI: https://doi.org/10.1177/1748895821991622.

33. Fried, 1999; Dunbar and Kubrin, 2018; Nielson and Dennis, 2019; Nicholas Stoia, Kyle Adams and Kevin Drakulich 'Rap Lyrics as Evidence: What Can Music Theory Tell Us?' *Race and Justice* 8/4 (2018): 330–365.

34. Nielson and Dennis, 2019.

35. Owusu-Bempah, 2022.

36. Robert Ralphs, Juanjo Medina and Judith Aldridge 'Who Needs Enemies with Friends Like These? The Importance of Place for Young People Living in Known Gang Areas', *Journal of Youth Studies* 12/5 (2009): 483–500; Fatsis, 2021c.

37. Fatsis, 2021b: 38.

38. Fatsis, 2021b; Fatsis, 2023d; Lambros Fatsis 'From Overseer to Officer: A Brief History of British Policing through Afro-Diasporic Music Culture' in Cavalcanti, Roxana, Squires, Peter & Waseem, Zoha (Eds.), *Southern and Postcolonial Perspectives on Policing, Security and Social Order* (Bristol, UK: Policy Press, 2023c) pp. 45–61.

39. Murray Lee 'This Is Not a Drill: Towards a Sonic and Sensorial Musicriminology', *Crime Media Culture* 18/3 (2021): 446–465.

40. Ibid., 460.

41. Robin Kelley *Yo' Mama's Disfunktional: Fighting the Culture Wars in Urban America* (Boston: Beacon Press, 2008) p. 41.

42. Fatsis, 2021b: 37.

11 | Express Yourself

Education and Wellbeing in Australian Applied Hip-Hop Workshops

DIANNE RODGER

> [Hip-hop] has allowed me to express myself and to help others with their problems through my lyrics.

The preceding quote is from an interview with Jay 'Beats' Weston, an Australian MC and hip-hop mentor who now works in youth services. Beats was one of eight mentors interviewed for a pilot project exploring the benefits of hip-hop workshops for First Nations[1] young people in Kaurna Yerta[2] (Greater Adelaide) in the settler-colonial country now known as Australia. Beats had a long history of involvement in the Adelaide hip-hop scene, including running workshops in a juvenile detention centre. He explained that hip-hop had saved his life by helping him through times when he was 'suicidal and severely depressed'. While not all mentors interviewed for this project discussed issues related to mental health, they frequently described hip-hop as their emotional outlet or colloquially as a form of 'therapy'. This was also a central benefit that they identified when asked about the impacts of hip-hop workshops.[3] In this chapter, I explore this key project finding and provide an overview of academic studies that explore 'applied' hip-hop programs, a term I use to refer to any context where aspects of hip-hop culture including knowledges, aesthetics and embodied practices are employed to achieve intended practical outcomes. I review Australian scholarship, demonstrating the need for further studies that evaluate the impacts of applied hip-hop in diverse contexts across the country. Throughout this chapter, I use the term 'Australian hip-hop', but I note that what constitutes hip-hop in Australia is contested and diverse, with some people explicitly rejecting the term. I begin the chapter by providing a short summary of the applied hip-hop literature that sets up the analysis of Australian works that follows it.

Applied Hip-Hop: Multi-disciplinary Insights

The applied hip-hop literature has recently been mapped in two important works, a narrative synthesis[4] and a critical interpretive synthesis[5] that explore how hip-hop has been used to address student wellbeing in school settings. In their critical interpretative synthesis, Crooke, Moreno-Almeida and Comte identified two key strands in the literature that have developed in parallel: (1) 'Hip-hop based education' and (2) 'Hip-hop informed well-being strategies'.[6] Their synthesis traces the connections between these strands, demonstrating that disciplinary conventions shape applied hip-hop interventions in specific ways. This includes how authors position hip-hop and their methodological choices. For example, approaches in the field of education have typically been underpinned by critical and culturally responsive pedagogies[7] that share a social justice emphasis. While earlier works in this area focused on rap music lyrics, newer approaches incorporate other hip-hop elements, aesthetic forms, and worldviews.[8] This includes scholarship that defines hip-hop as pedagogy or curriculum *itself* rather than merely a supplement to existing curricula.[9] The origins of hip-hop mean that it has primarily been understood as a 'culturally relevant way to engage students of Colour in urban settings'.[10] Whilst recognising the significance of hip-hop to African-American and Afro-Latinx communities in inner-city neighbourhoods, Crooke, Moreno-Almeida and Comte encourage researchers to question 'whether Hip-hop is seen as only relevant for people of color and disadvantaged communities'.[11]

This question is indicative of broader trends across the applied hip-hop literature, whereby scholars are critically assessing the principles – and potential assumptions – that shape the design and delivery of hip-hop programs. These assessments consider how and why hip-hop is being utilised to achieve specific aims and identify factors that contribute to their effectiveness. Concerns about the exploitation or trivialisation of hip-hop culture in applied contexts have also been raised.[12] Researchers are considering what might be lost or gained[13] when hip-hop is employed in settings like schools that are 'traditionally oppressive to non-dominant populations and ultimately regulated by state forces'.[14] Such interventions may reduce hip-hop culture to a 'sweetner', an approach that could also be a form of cultural appropriation.[15] As studies of applied hip-hop increase in disciplines like education, music therapy,[16] and social work,[17] more studies based outside of North America are also emerging.[18] In the next section, I provide a targeted discussion of academic studies that examine applied Australian hip-hop programs.

Applied Australian Hip-Hop

Hip-hop workshops have been run in Australia since the 1980s and are important sites where hip-hop culture is shared and emerging artists are supported.[19] Jardwadjali hip-hop artist Munkimuk describes how he started practicing hip-hop in Redfern, Sydney in 1982[20] and shortly thereafter began leading workshops across Australia.[21] Munkimuk was also heavily involved in two well-documented applied events in the 1990s – 'Hip-Hopera' (1995) and 'Desert Rap' (1999). Hip-Hopera was a community theatre production held in Sydney that was directed by MC Morganics and run by several facilitators including Lebanese-Australian, Khaled Sabsabi.[22] Desert Rap was a three-week workshop run by Munkimuk, Murri hip-hop artist BrothaBlack and Morganics in Alice Springs.[23] Since the 1990s, hip-hop workshops have become commonplace across Australia, but there remains a lack of academic studies that document their histories and impacts.[24] Our project team identified seventeen academic sources that explored applied hip-hop interventions in Australian schools,[25] and in community or youth programs[26] including festivals.[27]

These sources were primarily located by Research Assistant Kynesha Temple who conducted an extensive literature search across four academic databases in 2018 to identify works that explored First Nations hip-hop workshops in Australia. In mid 2021, I expanded this search to locate other scholarly works that included in-depth accounts of applied Australian hip-hop. This search was less systematic and did not include PhD theses, except for the work of Grant Saunders. To keep within the chapter word count, when authors had published similar articles, (for example, the work of Tony Mitchell), I chose one representative source. The seventeen included sources were diverse, ranging from short mixed-method program evaluations to in-depth ethnographic accounts that included substantive discussions of workshops. All seventeen concentrated on young people, with thirteen focusing on the experiences of First Nations youth, especially in inner-city Sydney and remote communities. Only four included a sustained focus on hip-hop 'dance', and none discussed graffiti writing programs. To align with the scope of this edited collection, my subsequent discussion concentrates on studies of rap / hip-hop music, in particular rhyme-writing (fifteen sources).

Reflecting their influence, many sources discussed programs run by experienced hip-hop educators, Morganics (introduced earlier), and Gumbaynggirr hip-hop artist, Wire MC.[28] For example, Stavrias[29] attended a hip-hop performance that they delivered at a Sydney school and interviewed them at a nearby cafe. In the interview, Wire MC stated that hip-hop can affect people in both 'good' and 'bad' ways,[30] noting that in First Nations communities many Elders initially had concerns about the influence of 'gangsta rap'. However, he went on to say that these fears dissipated when Elders observed workshops first-hand. He stressed the need to consider why young First Nations men were attracted to hip-hop: 'young black loud men with a lot of money and telling the white man where to go and what to do [...] Man, that's some very attractive shit. Especially in a country like this'. Here, I believe he was referring to the ongoing impacts of colonisation and the 'violence of race and racism in Australia.'[31] Indeed, much of the literature about the benefits of applied Australian hip-hop programs focus on the empowerment of First Nations young people who face 'pervasive and systematic forms of oppression' every day on their own land.[32]

Amangu Yamaji academic Crystal McKinnon argues that surviving this oppression has involved the 'reclamation of and creation of social spaces through which an autonomous sense of Indigeneity can be created, continued and expressed.'[33] These spaces include hip-hop workshops and festivals, which can 'instill things such as pride and self-esteem amongst Indigenous youth.'[34] The use of hip-hop workshops to foster pride is also illustrated in Warren and Evitt's[35] study of the experiences of First Nations hip-hop artists living in remote and regional areas – the Torres Strait Islands and Nowra. Their research included semi-structured interviews with members of Torres Strait Islander group 'One Blood Hidden Image' (OBHI). One Blood Hidden Image provided informal recording advice to young people and encouraged them to be confident and get up on stage. They also ran formal workshops with positive outcomes: 'When they have a go at the workshop, rap to the beat [...] Like you can see it on their faces; Fuck we can do it.'[36] As in this example, several studies indicate that participation in workshops and hip-hop culture more broadly enable young First Nations peoples to articulate and celebrate their identities.[37]

These potentialities have made hip-hop an attractive medium for education scholars who are exploring how it can be incorporated into Australian curricula to dismantle racist 'deficit' discourses.[38] Dr. Faye Blanch is a Yidinij/Mbarbaram woman from the Atherton Tablelands, North Queensland,[39] who argues that a hip-hop curriculum can highlight the creativity, agency and determination of First Nations peoples.[40] Blanch's research with young male 'Nungas'[41] demonstrates that schools are spaces where Nunga bodies are surveilled and disciplined by the white hegemonic power of the state.[42] In this context, schools are sites of domination that fail to adequately 'include the narratives and discourses of Indigenous history and culture as well as contemporary cultural practice and reality, as understood by Nungas.'[43] In contrast, Blanch explores how a First Nations space in a South Australian secondary school – the 'Nunga room' – became a Nunga place where young people could rap, perform their identity, and freely express themselves 'often in ways not seen elsewhere in school.'[44] This distinction between hip-hop programs and 'mainstream' education was recurrent across the literature, both within and outside of school settings. Specifically, applied hip-hop programs were positioned as alternative sites of learning that were culturally relevant, participatory, and more flexible than formal education.

In an analysis of community workshops run across Australia from 2001 to 2009, Caines[45] notes that organisers Wire MC and Morganics employed informal pedagogies including improvised discussions and peer collaboration.[46] These strategies were central to engaging young people who were alienated from formal learning institutions. The use of informal pedagogies is also evident in a study of First Nations youth who participated in hip-hop workshops and performances in inner Sydney and Nowra.[47] In this ethnographic research, Morgan and Warren conclude that young Aboriginal men who 'resist formal education settings often thrive in informal settings' particularly those where they can participate with their peers.[48] They found that experienced First Nations mentors connected young people with community music-making programs[49] and provided ongoing 'performative and expressive guidance, motivation, education, support and encouragement.'[50] Mentors inspired First Nations youth 'not only in their hip-hop performances, but in their identification with Aboriginal culture.'[51] The essential contribution that mentors make to the success of hip-hop programs is further highlighted by Crooke and Almeida in an evaluation of an intensive two-day rap and beat-making program in a mainstream Melbourne school.[52] In this program, mentors were able to build rapport with students from diverse cultural backgrounds by using their hip-hop knowledge and casual demeanour to foster an informal, collaborative atmosphere. Mentors successfully differentiated the program from everyday classes and this 'change of scenery'[53] helped them to keep the interest of students who were defined by school staff as 'disengaged.'[54]

While most studies explored existing hip-hop programs, a small number examined interventions designed for research purposes. For example, a 'rap music' program intended to teach students about the 'use and misuse' of drugs and alcohol, through the production and performance of hip-hop songs at a Queensland high school.[55] The authors concluded that the intervention was successful, in part because hip-hop is a culturally relevant medium that can be used to make health promotion engaging. A similar rationale informed a youth sexual health awareness project conducted in four remote First Nations communities in the Torres Strait and Northern Queensland peninsula.[56] This project involved dance and hip-hop music workshops, with sixteen songs recorded and performed at a community event. A critical analysis of the project found that it achieved aims like raising awareness of sexual health messages, but its effectiveness could have been enhanced with additional measures like capacity assessments and post-workshop activities.[57]

This evaluation also highlights challenges that can arise when conducting hip-hop projects in partnership with First Nations peoples, a theme developed in recent studies that employ a decolonising approach.[58] Authors like Minestrelli and Dowsett have critically examined how uneven power relationships between First Nations and non-Indigenous stakeholders shape both program delivery and academic research into hip-hop in colonial Australia. They outline several problems raised by surface-level 'consultation' with Indigenous communities that is not truly collaborative, emphasising the need for First Nations hip-hop programs that support Indigenous sovereignty and incorporate Indigenous Knowledges.[59] The power of Indigenous-led research is exemplified by a recent documentary film and exegesis by Biripi man Grant Saunders titled *JustUS*. Through creative practice drawing on Indigenous auto-ethnographic reflections and interviews with hip-hop artists, Saunders explores the impacts of hip-hop workshops held at a Sydney Festival.[60] His work demonstrates the need for further research that examines how hip-hop–based education can be incorporated into Australian curricula[61] – a call that is repeated across the literature. There is a growing body of evidence documenting the benefits of applied hip-hop interventions for young people living in Australia, especially First Nations youth. However, additional research is required, particularly over longer time-periods.[62] In the concluding section of this chapter, I contribute to this burgeoning literature by describing an Adelaide-based hip-hop education pilot project. This example is not intended to address the gap identified earlier. Rather, it reiterates the need for further research in this area.

Case Study: Hip-Hop Workshops for First Nations Young People in Kaurna Yerta

While this chapter is sole-authored, it emerged from a team project including Dr. Margaret Becker, Dr. Paul Chambers, Kynesha Temple, and myself.[63] The research aimed to explore the design and delivery of hip-hop workshops for First Nations youth in Adelaide using ethnographic methods.[64] It began in late 2018 but the primary data collection period (2019–20) was disrupted by the COVID-19 pandemic. The research was conceptualised by myself and Dr. Becker (both White women), based on cultural advice from Kaurna Elders.[65] The University of Adelaide (UoA) funded a cadetship for Ngarrindjeri woman Kynesha Temple who worked on the project as a Research Assistant from 2018 to 2020. When Dr. Becker gained secure employment at another institution, Dr. Chambers joined the project. Our pilot project set out to examine workshops that incorporated any Element of hip-hop, but we were only able to conduct participant observation at two hip-hop music workshops. I interviewed nine people: eight mentors who ran workshops and one young workshop attendee. This means that research findings are predominantly based on mentors' perspectives. Interviews typically ran for one hour and were conducted face-to-face except for one email interview (Beats).

Mentors were all music artists, primarily MCs and producers, who had run hip-hop programs in diverse settings. They ranged in age from thirty-one to forty-six. Four mentors and one workshop attendee were First Nations peoples and four were non-Indigenous. Everyone self-identified as male and the failure to include female, trans, or non-binary mentors is a significant limitation of this research. As the project progressed, I also became concerned about leading research that focused on First Nations people's experiences. As a hip-hop fan who had previously conducted ethnographic research with Australian hip-hop practitioners, I began the project because I was passionate about hip-hop culture and wanted to use my research skills to benefit First Nations artists and workshop attendees. I sought to be reflexive and culturally sensitive but realised that I was taking up space that should be filled by First Nations voices. I raised this issue with participants, and seven people replied that they supported the publication of the research findings, including this chapter. I did not hear back from two participants, and I have de-identified them in all research outputs. Having now introduced the pilot research, the final section of the chapter sets out a key project finding.

Hip-Hop as Therapy

The therapeutic function of self-expression was a central benefit that mentors identified when asked about their own hip-hop practice and the impacts of workshops for First Nations young people. For example, 38-year-old Narungga man Col Darcy (formerly known as Caper) was a prolific MC and producer who had started an independent record label and brand called 'Lion Heart Nation'. When I asked how important hip-hop was to him, he passionately responded that it was '100% important' because it was 'an outlet as a way of expressing and it's therapy for me'. He described writing his album *Pursuit of Happiness* (2019) as a cathartic process that helped him to let go of his 'deepest pain' and 'grow to be a better person'. These insights informed his pedagogy, including a one-day activity that he ran at a primary school. He tried to create a comfortable space where children as young as five and up to 12–13 years old, could 'write whatever they want to write' and share it with their class. At the end of their sessions, all children enthusiastically shared their work with their peers. This included one child whose father had recently died: 'he never spoke to anyone about it. He wrote in his lyrics about his father passing, and how he was sad, and got up in front of everybody so confidently and told that story'. As in this poignant example, Col Darcy encouraged young people to tell their stories through rhymes, including sharing and releasing their emotions.

Similarly, thirty-three-year-old First Nations artist Jono 'Eskatology' Stier said that listening to hip-hop could shift his mood and that one of the reasons he began writing lyrics was to relieve stress:

Cause when I was younger I suffered a lot with my anxiety, so writing down lyrics that was therapeutic, and helped to [...] relieve a lot of those stresses, and occupy the mind so it's not stressing you. Put all those stresses out in the music.

He explained that even his artist name related back to anxiety: 'Eskatology means like the end of all things, the end of the world [...] And with anxiety, it's like, the feeling of things coming to an end.' Making hip-hop was one of the ways that Eskatology worked through these feelings. Hip-hop inspired him to 'keep going and to keep moving forward'. This was particularly important when he was younger and lived in a regional town where drug and alcohol abuse were prevalent. Eskatology explained that messages in hip-hop songs could encourage young people to see different futures for themselves:

Other people can hear it [hip-hop music] and they can see, oh that person's gone through that [...] they can sort of see what others are doing, and then, you know, maybe I can do this too. [...] I can kick out of here [regional town] and go and do other stuff.

In this example, hip-hop is understood as a resource that young people can draw on to imagine future possibilities for their lives and to cope with existing challenges.

This powerful resource was leveraged by mentors like forty-year-old Italian-Australian MC Social Change who said that hip-hop was an 'art form' that was designed for people 'to talk explicitly about how they're feeling'. Social Change was one of the first people to run hip-hop workshops in Adelaide in the 1990s[66] and had run numerous workshops locally and inter-state. He explained that he 'pitched' workshops to schools by using the label 'self-expression workshops' and emphasising the 'therapeutic value of music'. This enabled him to engage educators and students who were not interested in hip-hop: 'we're not all here to be rappers at the end; we're here to learn the value of self-expression and the value of learning about yourself'. Mentors like Social Change believed that participation in hip-hop workshops equipped young people with skills to work through emotions and life experiences in healthy ways. While more research needs to be conducted in this area, findings from this pilot project demonstrate that mentors identified writing lyrics, making beats, and simply listening to hip-hop as therapeutic outlets that were linked to well-being. These forms of self-expression were important for all young Australians, but perhaps more so for First Nations youth who had to confront racism and 'deficit' discourses in a colonial society. For example, an experienced First Nations mentor said that making hip-hop music could lift the spirits of young First Nations peoples, giving them a sense of achievement and boosting their confidence.

Conclusion: The Power of Hip-Hop

Because of the limitations of this pilot project, it would be problematic to generalise from these findings. I only interviewed one workshop attendee, a nineteen-year-old First Nations DJ and producer who did not define hip-hop as a medium of self-expression or therapy. He enjoyed the workshop that he attended because he learnt 'hard-skills', gained inspiration from experienced mentors, and formed friendships with peers. Further research should examine if 'self-expression' is a workshop outcome that young people value and if so, how it can best be achieved in settings where young people are supported. For example, if young people are encouraged to share their stories and personal struggles in workshops, then staff must be equipped to deal with any issues that emerge and avoid re-traumatising them.[67] While I am cautious about romanticising applied hip-hop or being too celebratory, in-depth accounts from mentors show that hip-hop has been an extremely valuable resource in their own lives and they are passionate about teaching a new generation about the power of hip-hop. Beyond this case study, the aim of this chapter has been to summarise studies of applied hip-hop with an Australian focus. Hip-hop practitioners and scholars must continue to explore and evaluate how hip-hop culture is being utilised in fields like education, health, and youth services.

Notes

1. Different terms are used in Australia to refer to First Nations peoples including 'Indigenous Australians' and 'Aboriginal and Torres Strait Islander Peoples'. I use the term 'First Nations peoples' because it was preferred by many people that I interviewed, but I stress the problematic nature of this collective term. See, for example, O'Sullivan, S. (2016) 'Translating Indigenous Reciprocity into University-Led Arts Practice and Assessment' B-L. Bartleet, D. Bennett, A. Power and N. Sunderland (eds.) *Engaging First Peoples in Arts-Based Service Learning: Towards Respectful and Mutually Beneficial Educational Practices*, Springer: New York: 20.
2. 'Kaurna Yerta' is Kaurna language for the Country of the Kaurna peoples who are the original people of Adelaide and the Adelaide plains.
3. More information about this project is provided in the final section of the chapter.
4. Crooke, A., Comte, R. and Moreno-Almeida, C. (2020) 'Hip-Hop as an Agent for Health and Wellbeing in Schools: A Narrative Synthesis of Existing Research' *Voices: A World Forum for Music Therapy*, 20(1): 1–24.
5. Crooke, A., Moreno-Almeida, C. and Comte, R. (2021) 'A Critical Interpretive Synthesis of Research Linking Hip Hop and Well-Being in Schools' *Journal of Hip Hop Studies*, 8(1): 127–160.
6. Crooke, Moreno-Alemeida and Comte 2021: 129.
7. Hill, M. L. and Petchauer, E. (2013) 'Introduction' in M. L. Hill and E. Petchauer (eds.) *Schooling Hip-Hop: Expanding Hip-Hop Based Education across the Curriculum*. Teachers College Press: New York, 1.
8. Hill and Petchauer 2013; Petchauer, E. (2015a) 'Back to the Lab with Hip-Hop Education: An Introduction' *Urban Education*, 50(1): 3–6; Petchauer, E. (2015b) 'Starting with Style: Toward a Second Wave of Hip-Hop Education Research and Practice' *Urban Education*, 50(1): 78–105.
9. Emdin, C. and Adjapong, E. (eds.) (2018) *#HipHopEd: The Compilation on Hip-Hop Education: Volume 1: Hip-Hop as Education, Philosophy, and Practice*, Brill:

Leiden; Baszile, D. T. (2009) 'Deal with It We Must: Education, Social Justice, and the Curriculum of Hip Hop Culture' *Equity & Excellence in Education*, 42(1): 10.
10. Crooke, Comte & Moreno-Almeida 2020: 19.
11. Crooke, Moreno-Almeida & Comte 2021: 139.
12. Baszile 2009; Gosa, T. and Fields, T. (2012) 'Is Hip-Hop Education Another Hustle? The (Ir)Responsible Use of Hip-Hop as Pedagogy'. B. J. Porfilio and M. J. Viola (eds.), *Hiphop(e): The Cultural Practice and Critical Pedagogy of International Hip-Hop*, Lang: New York, 195–201.
13. Baszile 2009.
14. Kelly, L. L. and Sawyer, D. C. III (2019) '"When Keeping it Real Goes Wrong": Enacting Critical Pedagogies of Hip-Hop in Mainstream Schools' in *IASPM Journal*, 9(2): 8.
15. Crooke, A. and Almeida, C. (2017) '"It's Good to Know Something Real and All That": Exploring the Benefits of a School-based Hip Hop Program' *Australian Journal of Music Education*, 51(1): 13–28.
16. Hadley, S., and Yancy, G. (2012) *Therapeutic Uses of Rap and Hip-Hop*. Routledge: New York.
17. Travis, R. (2016) *The Healing Power of Hip Hop*. ABC-CLIO: Santa Barbara.
18. See Pardue, D. (2004) 'Writing in the Margins': Brazilian Hip-Hop as an Educational Project' *Anthropology and Education Quarterly*, 35(4): 411–432; Ringsager, K. (2017) '"Featuring the System": Hip Hop Pedagogy and Danish Integration Policies' *Suomen Antropologi*, 42(2): 75–93; Wilson, E., Perez-y-Perez, M. and Evans, N. (2017) 'Editing Hip-Hop within Youth Work Activities: An Actor-Network Theory Analysis' *Journal of Youth Studies*, 20(10): 1396–1410.
19. Mitchell, T. (2008) 'Australian Hip Hop's Multicultural Literacies: A Subculture Emerges into the Light'. T. Mitchell and S. Homan (eds.) *Sounds of Then, Sounds of Now/Popular Music in Australia*, ACYS Publishing: Tasmania: 231–252.
20. Mitchell, T. (2006) 'The New Corroboree' *Meanjin*, 65(1): 20–28. Mitchell uses the spelling 'Munki Mark'.
21. Mitchell 2006: 21.
22. Mitchell 2006; Fernandes, S. (2011) *Close to the Edge: In Search of the Hip-Hop Generation*, Verso, Kindle Version; Dowsett, S. S. (2021) 'Sampling Ceremony: Hip-Hop Workshops and Intergenerational Cultural Production in the Central Australian Desert' *The Asia Pacific Journal of Anthropology*, 22(2–3): 184–202.
23. Mitchell 2006; Dowsett 2021.
24. Crooke, A. and Almeida, C. (2017) '"It's Good to Know Something Real and All That": Exploring the Benefits of a School-based Hip Hop Program' *Australian Journal of Music Education*, 51(1): 13–28; Dowsett 2021.
25. Stavrias, G. (2005) 'Droppin' Conscious Beats and Flows: Aboriginal Hip Hop and Youth Identity' *Australian Aboriginal Studies*, 2: 44–54; Blanch, F. R. and Worby, G. (2010) 'The Silences Waiting: Young Nunga Males, Curriculum and Rap' *Curriculum Perspectives*, 30(1): 1–13; Crouch, A., Robertson, H. and Fagan, P. (2011) 'Hip Hopping the Gap – Performing Arts Approaches to Sexual

Health Disadvantage in Young People in Remote Settings' *Australasian Psychiatry*, 19(1): S34–S37; Blanch, F. R. (2011) 'Young Nunga Males at Play and Playing Up: The Look and the Talk' *Discourse: Studies in the Cultural Politics of Education*, 32(1): 99–112; Harris, N., Wilks, L. and Stewart, D. (2012) 'HYPEd-up: Youth Dance Culture and Health' *Arts & Health*, 4(3): 239–248; McEwan, A., Crouch, A., Robertson, H. and Fagan, P. (2012) 'The Torres Indigenous Hip Hop Project: Evaluating the Use of Performing Arts as a Medium for Sexual Health Promotion' *Health Promotion Journal of Australia*, 24(2): 132–136; Paukste, E. and Harris, N. (2015) 'Using Rap Music to Promote Adolescent Health: Pilot Study of VoxBox' *Health Promotion Journal of Australia*, 26: 24–29; Blanch, F. R. (2017) 'Indigenous Australian Youth, Identity, Rap / Hip Hop: A Tool for Wellbeing and Ethical Care' P. T. Slee, G. Skrzypiec and C. Cefai (eds.) *Child and Adolescent Wellbeing and Violence Prevention in Schools*, New York: Routledge: 26–33; Crooke and Almeida 2017.

26. Mitchell 2006; Caines, R. (2010) 'Giving Back Time: Improvisation in Australian Hip-Hop Pedagogy and Performance' *Critical Studies in Improvisation*, 6(2): 1–19; Warren, A. and Evitt, R. (2010) 'Indigenous Hip-Hop: Overcoming Marginality, Encountering Constraints' *Australian Geographer*, 41(1): 141–158; Morgan, G. and Warren, A. (2011) 'Aboriginal Youth, Hip Hop and the Politics of Identification' *Ethnic and Racial Studies*, 34(6): 925–947; Minestrelli, C. (2017) *Australian Indigenous Hip Hop: The Politics of Culture, Identity and Spirituality*. Routledge: New York; Richards, J. and Gardner, S. (2019) 'Young People's Experiences in Hip-Hop Dance Participation' K. Bond (ed.) *Dance and the Quality of Life*, Switzerland: Springer: 459–474; Dowsett 2021.

27. McKinnon, C. (2010) 'Indigenous Music as a Space of Resistance' T. Banivanua-Mar and P. Edmonds (eds.) *Making Settler Colonial Space: Perspectives on Race, Place and Identity*, New York: Palgrave Macmillan 255–272; Saunders, G. (2020) *JustUS: What Hip-Hop Wants You to Know*, Doctor of Creative Arts, University of Technology, Sydney.

28. Stavrias 2005; Mitchell 2006; McKinnon 2010; Caines 2010; Morgan and Warren 2011; Dowsett 2021.

29. Stavrias 2005.

30. Stavrias: 49.

31. Watego, C., Singh, D. and Macoun, A. (2021) 'Partnership for Justice in Health: Scoping Paper on Race, Racism and the Australian Health System' Discussion Paper, *The Lowitja Institute*, Melbourne, DOI: https://doi.org/10.48455/sdrt-sb97: 28.

32. McKinnon 2010: 256.

33. McKinnon 2010: 256.

34. McKinnon: 267.

35. Warren and Evitt 2010.

36. Warren and Evitt: 152.

37. Stavrias 2005; Mitchell 2006; McKinnon 2010; Morgan and Warren 2011; Minestrelli 2017; Dowsett 2021.
38. Blanch and Worby 2010: 7, 11.
39. Self-description provided by Faye Blanch (personal communication 2022).
40. Blanch and Worby 2010: 7, 11.
41. Nunga is a term for Indigenous peoples that is 'used by sections of Indigenous community in South Australia' (Blanch and Worby 2010:2).
42. Blanch 2011: 210.
43. Blanch and Worby 2010: 4.
44. Blanch and Worby: 5.
45. Caines 2010.
46. Caines: 11.
47. Morgan and Warren 2011.
48. Morgan and Warren: 936.
49. Morgan and Warren: 935.
50. Morgan and Warren: 940.
51. Morgan and Warren: 941.
52. Crooke and Almeida 2017.
53. Crooke and Almeida: 21.
54. Crooke and Almeida: 16.
55. Paukste and Harris 2015: 24–25.
56. Crouch, Robertson and Fagan 2011; McEwan, Crouch, Robertson and Fagan 2015.
57. McEwan, Crouch, Robertson and Fagan 2015: 136.
58. Minestrelli 2017; Saunders 2020; Dowsett 2021.
59. Minestrelli 2017: 220–221; Dowsett 2021: 7–9.
60. Saunders 2020: 10.
61. Saunders: 126.
62. Crooke and Almeida 2017.
63. The project was funded by the Mountford bequest.
64. For an extended discussion of research aims, design, ethics and key findings, see the full project report: Rodger, D. (2022) 'Elevate the Spirit': Effective Hip-Hop Workshops for First Nations Young People in Kaurna Yerta (Kaurna Country – Greater Adelaide). Available at https://researchers.adelaide.edu.au/profile/dianne.rodger [Accessed 20 December 2022].
65. We also received cultural guidance from Noongar man Dr. Shane Hearn (then Pro-Vice Chancellor of Indigenous Research at UoA). We discussed the project with two Aboriginal Community Controlled Organisations and were advised by the Aboriginal Health Council of South Australia that our project did not require ethics clearance through them. The project was approved by the high-risk HREC at UoA.
66. With an MC named The Expressionist. Adrian Shepherd also ran DJ-ing workshops at this time.
67. Travis 2016; Crooke, Moreno-Almeida and Comte 2021.

12 | Rap to Skool

Hip-Hop in the Classroom

PATRICK TURNER

Introduction

Writings on hip-hop education typically treat hip-hop as an underutilised pedagogic resource for working with marginalised and racialised young people struggling to thrive within mainstream education. In this body of work, which often combines description and evaluation with advocacy, hip-hop education is portrayed as a means to align educational institutions, practices and spaces more closely with the vernacular identities and multicultural literacies of their students. Indeed, the enlargement of rap music's purview to include youth clubs, schools and universities is seen as the logical expression of rap's didactic and edutainment DNA. In this chapter I discuss the use of hip-hop culture in educational spaces, with a particular focus on rap lyricism. I begin with a discussion of the roots of hip-hop education in the 'hip-hop wars' of hip-hop's golden age and its aftermath.[1] I then examine some representative US studies from the first decade or so of hip-hop education (1996–) by scholars from disciplines that include education, anthropology, English and cultural studies. Here I attempt to show how the emergent field of hip-hop education articulates the hip-hop wars with the broader culture wars roiling the American educational system at the time. I then fast-forward to 2019 for a case study of a recent British hip-hop education programme, Roadworks. In my conclusion I address the thorny issue of how to judge the artistic and educational value of popular and youth subcultural expressions like rap music in a context of ongoing moral panic and wilful misunderstanding. I argue that hip-hop education arises from such longstanding cultural preoccupations and tensions and continues to embody them in novel form.

The Hip-Hop Roots of Hip-Hop Education

By the late 1980s hip-hop was, in Imani Perry's words, an 'ideological democracy'.[2] Comprised of ethically divergent strains of rap, it bore a complex relation to politics and commodification. Some believed that the lyrical content and tone of some of this rap and its promotional videos, not to mention the conduct of its creators, was a moral stain on the culture.[3] This ignited a heated public debate and, indeed, moral panic that pulled in critics, artists, fans and politicians, with blackness centre-stage.[4] These were the opening salvoes of the hip-hop wars.[5] The lyricism of golden-age rappers was, in dialectical fashion, vivified. In a doubling down on hip-hop's battle aesthetic of mockery and banter, a kind of cultural hypochondria of meta-commentary and intra-critique set in.[6] Three key aspects of these hip-hop wars gave impetus to the initial emergence of hip-hop education.

First, that hip-hop as a culture bore an organic relationship to education was due to the vernacular springs of its four aesthetic elements. In the hip-hop wars, a chief reason for decrying the commodification of rap music was that the resulting product was so detached from these cultural roots. Roots that, crucially, included the intrinsic didacticism of rap itself. To be clear, responsibility lay with the intrusion of commercial imperatives and the culture's misappropriation, not with the rap artist's braggadocio and compulsion to do battle. For, as golden-age rap lyricism amply demonstrated, that could be deployed in any number of ways, including educational admonishment. African-American sociolinguist Geneva Smitherman revealed some of the cultural mechanisms behind this. Inventorying the 'linguistic/stylistic machinery' of modern vernacular black poetry, she showed how forms like rap are continuous with an unbroken 'Black Oral tradition'.[7] Her account is replete with examples drawn from contemporary works of black American phonology, syntax, slang, musical rhythm, and use of folk narrative modes such as 'the dozens', 'signifying' and the 'toast'.[8] Hence, the form, content and context of black poetics may evolve – reggae toasting, rap and spoken-word poetry being just some recent incarnations. But their primary function – direct and efficacious communication through speech in the physical presence of others – is invariant. It is thus in the kinds of inter-subjective encounters produced in the rap emcee performance that we can best observe the essence of edutainment in action. And these functionally communicative currents run throughout the black oral arts continuum.[9] Richard Shusterman argued that hip-hop derives its edutainment aesthetic from the collision between antiphonic African culture and racialised American history.[10] Where rappers are concerned, he says, 'their role as artists and poets is inseparable from their role as insightful inquirers into reality and teachers of truth'.[11] As Baker Jr. observed, despite its 'self-aggrandizement and epic boasting', rap contains an 'insistent element of didacticism, polemical challenge, and ethical caution'.[12] Rap has always sought to alert and instruct in the ways and idioms of hip-hop culture, street lore, and black history. Hence, when commentators such as Michael-Eric Dyson and Geneva Smitherman declare that the modern-day rapper or emcee is an 'urban' or 'postmodern' *griot*, this is more description than figure of speech.[13]

Second, hip-hop education embodied reformist aspirations whose purist rhetoric, in keeping with the hip-hop wars, was both radically nostalgic and secessionist.[14] Those who clung to a countercultural positioning for hip-hop had set their face against its commercial expropriation and, sometimes, with a more essentialist inflection, its cultural appropriation. Partisans for a pro-social hip-hop thus sought to draw a kind of 38th parallel through the culture demarcating its positive and negative expressions.[15] From here it was but a short step to deduce a calling to educational outreach in the edifying lyricism of hip-hop's organic intellectuals and edutainers, its 'conscious' rappers.[16] In fact, by forcing it to mount a defence of its real and invariant Afrocentric ontology – and to talk up its constructive origins in social negativity – nihilistic rappers (ultimately the dupes of non-black expropriators) had actually done hip-hop a service.[17]

Third, the racial angst and hermeneutical ardour of golden-age hip-hoppers was often powered by a strong communitarianism.[18] Because rap music was seen as a vector for cultural transmission, artists should acknowledge that they have a responsibility to produce uplifting content and to act as positive role models, especially to young black people. The logical corollary was to follow through practically on critique and *give something back to the community*. Conscientious artists from the 'hip-hop generation' had a duty to go out into the places they were from and, as 'raptivists', minister to young people exposed to problematic rap content. Not only would this encourage the latter to be more critical of the anti-social and demoralising 'messages' and imagery that they consumed through rap music, it would provide opportunities to expose them to more elevated fare. And raptivists in turn, could improve the literary and intellectual quality of young people's own rap compositions, not to mention its ethical content.[19]

Hip-Hop Education: Liberating Multicultural Literacies through Critical Pedagogy

From the outset, hip-hop education joined the cultural politics of the 'hip-hop wars' to the 1990s 'culture wars' of progressivist educators in North America and elsewhere for multicultural modes of literacy.[20] The precise cultural coordinates and institutional affiliations of former and latter may have differed according to national and regional context, and the alliances they forged have been shifting and tactical. Yet all combatants were united in the conviction that mainstream educational and cultural organisations were complicit, past and present, in the marginalisation of black vernacular identities.[21] Hence, there was a common interest in agitating to have these groups fully included and represented, and one of its means would be the educational incorporation of hip-hop.[22] Thus, hip-hop education was the convergent point of social action during the 1990s on two civil society fronts. One, the communitarian and purist valorisations of hip-hoppers themselves as they fought the hip-hop wars. Two, the multiculturalist demands of mainstream progressive educators for a more inclusive allocation of cultural esteem and creative resources.

Multiculturalist criticisms of the ethnocentric biases and dominant epistemologies of mainstream educational institutions are well represented in writings on hip-hop education.[23] In an example of an early study, researchers Mahiri and Sablo directly took up these themes. Through ethnography and textual analysis, the latter explored what they saw as the disconnect between the rich and varied oral and written practices African-American youth voluntarily engage in outside the school setting and what is required of them in the classroom.[24] According to Mahiri and Sablo, one way to close this literacy gap would be to formally incorporate rap into the school curriculum: 'African American and youth culture can be used as a bridge to writing development.'[25] With hip-hop having sealed its cultural pact with spoken-word poetry, Jocson would aver: 'To improve learning and teaching practices in urban multicultural settings [...] We must consider how these cultural forms, as part of a larger hip hop culture, together shape student experiences in and out of school.'[26]

For these and similar studies into alternative youth literacy practices, hip-hop culture demonstrated conclusively what young people with little conventional schooling or cultural capital were able to achieve independently with oral poetic vernaculars.[27] Smitherman long ago insisted that black vernaculars are both a repository of subordinated cultural traditions and a site of resistance against cultural imperialism and erasure.[28] With such axioms in mind, Mahiri and Sablo claimed that their research findings offered compelling empirical evidence that the act of composing rap is one of the ways in which Black urban youth living amid poverty and violence can 'come to terms with [such] conditions'.[29] Thus, a fairly consistent claim in the literature was that bringing rap poetry into the classroom would foster a better awareness of the marginalised identities, speech communities and cultural practices of non-White, socially disadvantaged school and university students.[30] Hip-hop education would counter the ethnocentric libel that rap is – at best – a generically packaged 'outsider art', devoid of formal innovation, and offering little more than a spirited but primitive deviation from time-honoured grammatical and aesthetic rules.[31] If many students experience school and university curriculums as remote and arbitrarily imposed from above, hip-hop education would reverse this. In short, it would meet Houston Baker Jr.'s demand for a 'relational pedagogy', one responsive to the vernacular youth creativity that had invented rap music.[32]

Belle, for one, listed the strategic advantages to the urban educator of using popular examples of rap poetry in the classroom. The latter offered thematic relevance and accessibility to students over the denseness and obscurity of what she terms 'academic' forms of poetry.[33] In this vein, Green reported upon his own use of popular cultural texts such as rap in a pedagogy that sought to dissolve the borders between classroom and 'vernacular community'.[34] In this 'culturally situated' approach to the teaching of poetry, the educator attempted as far as possible to draw on the expressive modalities of each student's own cultural identity and biographical experience.[35] In an effort to connect socio-cultural 'outside' and 'inside' through rap, Morrell and Duncan-Andrade designed and taught a North American high school 'unit' that combined lit-crit with a sociological/cultural studies approach.[36] Students were encouraged to situate rap – as a 'post-industrial' poetics – on a historical continuum with earlier poetic genres and periods.[37] The aim was for students to engage in a comparative analysis of such canonical texts as T. S. Eliot's 'The Waste Land' and those regarded as vernacular and popular, such as Grandmaster Flash's 'The Message'. In this instance the thematic, historical and formal links traced and explored through a joint examination of these texts were related to modern and postmodern urban entropy and desolation.[38]

By the turn of the millennium, educators in North American urban schools and universities simply had to acknowledge hip-hop's prevalence and educative potential. According to Duncan-Andrade and Morrell, the alternative would be to wilfully ignore 'a critical literacy resource in their midst – urban youth engagement and familiarity with popular culture'.[39] 'Voluntary' out of school writing, claimed Mahiri and Sablo, assisted in the manifestation of agency with respect to a difficult situation not of young black people's making. This in turn, they maintained, supported the construction amongst their research informants of a more congruent biographical identity.[40] Rap in the classroom was a necessity because a significant number of socially marginalised affiliates of hip-hop culture were literally 'writing for their lives'.[41] Such interests – emancipatory, identitarian and therapeutic – propel hip-hop education (and its literature) to this day, and in the case-study that follows we shall see a contemporary UK-based iteration of this.[42]

Case-Study: *Roadworks*

I now turn to a case-study of a UK-based hip hop education project, *Roadworks*: 'a course set up to educate and engage young people through the medium of Drill music'.[43] It offers a course of workshops to secondary schools and pupil-referral units for young people adjudged to be 'at-risk' who create and consume the controversial Gen Z sub-genre of hip-hop, UK Drill.[44] *Roadworks* was launched in 2019 by journalist and youth worker Ciaran Thapar and UK rapper, hip-hop educator, and university educator Mehryar Golestani (emcee name Reveal) in partnership with UK youth musical charity, *Sound Connections*. One of its main aims is to use the cultural insider knowledge of its two creators (who jointly teach and mentor on the project) to counter the stigmatisation of UK Drill and to present a critically empathic alternative to denunciation and censorship. For this case-study discussion I draw on a short 2019 documentary film made about the project, *Beyond the Road* (Dir: Jake Jones), along with a couple of relevant online sources. The film features extracts of a six-day pilot run in Brixton, London, in 2019. The main purpose of my discussion is to highlight some salient features of *Roadworks* that I think are exemplary of the broader phenomenon of hip-hop education. The kind of egalitarian preoccupations with alternative literacies, critical pedagogy and the curative power of black vernacular just discussed are palpable in *Roadworks*.

In *Beyond the Road*, the half a dozen or so young black men participating in the pilot come from all over London and are by their own lights disaffected from mainstream schooling. *Roadworks* clearly attempts to meet the young men who make and consume UK Drill *where they are*, approaching any susceptibilities to negative social influence and expression with understanding rather than judgement. In an echo of the Brazilian radical educator Paulo Friere, the project is described as a 'non-hierarchical space'.[45] For Friere, if educational interventions are to be of critical and humanistic value 'the point of departure must always be with men and women in the "here and now", which constitutes the situation within which they are submerged, from which they emerge, and in which they intervene'.[46] Hence, whatever we may feel about UK Drill's disturbing content, 'that is literally', Thapar urges us to realise, 'just a reflection of the world that these young people are living in'.[47] And educators need to be prepared to enter it at least imaginatively and intellectually. As Thapar puts it: 'How can we use this undeniably organically popular type of music, and our understanding of that music, as a way of connecting with young people who otherwise are being lost to the system right now at unprecedented rates?'[48]

In keeping with the claim that rap is inherently didactic, one of *Roadwork's* key premises is that the spirit of rebellion and rule-breaking narrativised in UK Drill, and acted out in various ways by some of its young makers and listeners, should be understood as an incipient form of social science and philosophy.[49] We are told that the proper way of 'viewing Drill' is 'as a system of critical thought',[50] one that merely awaits its channelling, or in Freirean terms 'conscientization'. As a young man declares to camera in *Beyond the Road*, *Roadworks* provides a space in which makers of UK Drill can pause to consider 'how we actually get across our messages'. Another concludes that 'this workshop is gonna help us show that we are more conscious and we think a lot deeper about things'.[51] For the purposes of this project, then, the 'demonised' milieu that is UK Drill is not only a site of violence and social vulnerability but of organic intellect.[52] *Roadworks*, in this Ur hip-hop culture narrative, marks the creation of something positive from within the shell of the negative.

The classroom workshops involve a series of topically focused, facilitated discussions of specific examples of UK Drill/rap music, its lyricism and videos. Rap videos from across the decades are used for context, comparison, and genealogical analysis. For example, in *Beyond the Road*, we briefly witness a classroom screening of London Posse's track from 1990, 'How's Life in London'. The evident purpose of this is to highlight the continuous presence in UK rap over the course of the last thirty years of black vernacular–infused 'London twang' and video representations of gang menace and braggadocio. Golestani cites Golden-age hip-hop edutainment as his lodestar, formative of his artistic and pedagogic calling. The 'element of educating' in Golden-age hip-hop, Golestani maintains, was always prominent. As he puts it, 'There's the classic phrase, "Wu-Tang is for the children"'.[53] The facilitators weave in academic sociological, historical and philosophical perspectives to the group discussion and try to develop links between artistic, personal and political issues and practical careers and life skills. At one point in *Beyond the Road* we see what looks like an engaged and insightful classroom discussion on how Plato's Cave could be applied to UK Drill music. The facilitators display an illustration of Plato's Cave on the classroom AV screen. Golestani asks the participants how they would link 'the realities of life in the hood', 'the general public', 'drill music', and the 'actual artists' to the various elements of Plato's Cave. The extract of the discussion centres mostly on the significance of the cave's fire. One young man offers: 'I feel like the drill music's the fire because it's what's allowing the pictures to be made in the first place.' Another suggests: 'I'd say the fire is the experiences the drill artist go through, the stabbings, the shootings, people selling drugs.' Thapar rounds off the conversation with the observation that Plato's Cave is useful for offering a representation of the power enjoyed by 'different stakeholders' and, as evidenced by the preceding conversation, one that is fruitfully open to interpretation. Thapar and Golestani insist that this can enhance a young person's capacity for critical reflection in real-life situations, making them more likely to think before acting rashly: 'Do you retaliate to your friend getting robbed? Why is someone stereotyping me right now? Is it because they hate me? Or is it because they've been reading media reports that tell them they should hate me? [...]' They conclude that 'Those slightly more reflective decisions can be potentially lifesaving tools for young people'.[54] Moreover, for young people who have been exposed to high levels of trauma and social vulnerability there are also possible therapeutic benefits. Being able to share one's trauma and hear other people's testimonies may offer cathartic release.[55] The project does not (and cannot) claim it reduces the possibility of violent offending, but clearly amongst its many aims is the aspiration to road test interventions that may have something to contribute to this.[56]

The workshops involve bouts of critical reflection that are intended not only to develop the young people's consciousness but also the manner in which they conduct themselves individually and jointly as prospective artists and industry professionals. Each workshop consists of 50/50 academic and practical content, with 'industry leading professionals' invited in to lead sessions on 'things like management, marketing, distribution, videography'.[57] In an animated vox pop to the camera, one of the young men says: 'For something I can connect to like drill, it's nice to be in a space where you can learn about it, and use it in learning, and just help with my outlook on life an' that.'[58] Contributors to *Beyond the Road* attest to the 'life-changing' capacities of the project and how it can 'put hope' in young people. The participant's evaluative testimonies are, accordingly, studded with words like 'opportunity', 'accessibility', and 'platforms'. The workshop sessions are preparatory to the young men jointly creating and recording a UK Drill single at a professional recording studio used by many big names in UK hip-hop and Grime. Profits from the commercially streamed recording are split evenly between the young artists and *Roadworks*. After the single has been recorded, the group work with an industry-leading professional to make a video of it. In the successful aftermath to this, one young participant declares earnestly to the camera that 'we're trying to make a new wave in Drill. We're not just talking about all the cruddy stuff, we're bringing in things that could help other people, and to excel better in our lives'.[59] We hear something of this didactic and edifying aspiration in the lyricism of the finally recorded Drill song. The imperative to instruct, caution and challenge is on full display here: 'Like what them man know about street? You're either doing up jugg, time in pen, or doing up R.I.P./ Moving food like Deliveroo, doing drop offs like Uber Eats [..] But you can't blame them, that's just the environment that they came from/What you know about sitting in bandos, putting products in boxes like Avon?'[60]

Roadworks sets great store by treating the young people it works with as the *victims* rather than the source of the violence that they seem to be so inured to. For this reason, it is vital to the project that the content of UK Drill – lyrical and visual – be the start rather than the end of serious and nuanced conversation. Indeed, denunciation and moral grandstanding not only obfuscates, it is, the project's facilitators assure us, 'irresponsible', an abdication of our duty of care to those who, because of poverty, racism and limited options, have no choice but to live amid crime and violence.[61] Such moralising fails to grasp that whilst the normalisation of violence is, of course, bad for 'wider society', for some young people it may be a 'first step' to coping with biographical trauma.[62] It is easy to condemn an individual's insensibility to violence but what if that were a condition of their not being engulfed by fear, grief and guilt? At one point in *Beyond the Road*, Thapar refers the group of young people that are sat around the classroom table to a question on the AV screen: 'where did UK drill come from?' He then says, 'How would you answer that question?' A young participant replies flatly: 'Yeah. Gang beef, hatred'. Near the end of *Beyond the Road*, someone else from the same group acknowledges how difficult it might be for people remote from that reality to make sense of a UK Drill video. But, he contends, behind the scary media images of 'yutes in balaclavas talking madness' are 'stories'. We should not, he appears to be saying, assume that with UK Drill the idiom is just the message. Real life deprivations, existential torments and compensatory thrills flare in those sunless yet kinetic vernacular and media surfaces. The stories Drill rappers tell may be encased in a dense and malevolent subcultural code. And visually represented to accentuate this. But, like any other stories, they can be translated, deciphered, interpreted and explained. In short, despite appearances, these rap lyrics and videos are not, this young man implies, either devoid of content or so inscrutable that all efforts at interpretation must be in vain. Their opacity is only apparent. If non-Drillers genuinely wish to understand them, all they have to do is bracket their stereotyped preconceptions and make the requisite investment of time and imaginative effort. This, then, may begin to bridge gulfs of understanding and edge us a little closer to the reasons if not the ultimate causes of 'Gang beef, hatred'. As Thapar says, 'we can learn about the world through music'.[63]

Conclusion

At the conclusion to *Beyond the Road*, Thapar declares that all artforms – not just highbrow ones like 'literature or opera' – 'deserve equal respect'. But is this relativistic edict really germane to the underlying reasons for the incomprehension, incuriosity and bigotry that mark kneejerk responses to UK Drill? Such artforms, where the primary intended audience is fellow subculturalists, precisely seek to elicit discomfort in the uninitiated. We do not, however, need to like or enjoy an artistic expression to be able to (a) understand it, and (b) appreciate its significance or its potency. Nor do we need to value it aesthetically, let alone ethically or politically. It is enough that it grants us some access to things we dwell in degrees of ignorance of. And, that it *may* help us to appreciate why and how the 'stories' of, say, 'yutes in balaclavas talking madness' are in some way instructive. UK Drill's subcultural annals of delinquent menace and swank *should* be plumbed for what they can yield about the lives, places, identifications and vernacular cultures of disadvantaged urban teenagers in multicultural austerity Britain. We emphatically can 'learn about the world through music'.

Struggles over cultural, artistic and ethical value have been, as I hope my chapter has shown, a key driver of hip-hop education linked to hip-hop's origins in social and political 'devastation'. A good while after the first US hip-hop education projects, multicultural literacies – a battleground in the culture wars of thirty years ago – are evidently still a combat zone in the culture wars of today.[64] Now, as then, educators attempt to engage hard-to-reach and at-risk young people by mobilising the latter's 'voluntary' out-of-school writing and oral vernaculars. This may be for its instrumental value as a literacy 'bridge' into the mainstream academic curriculum; its cathartic and even therapeutic value to those 'writing for their lives'; or its critical pedagogic value in providing a common/shared entry point for historical, sociological and political reflection. Whether or not any of this depends, however, on a binding commitment to the proposition that all artistic forms 'deserve equal respect' is, in my view, questionable. Hip-hop practitioners, fans and critics alike continue, as they did in the hip-hop wars of yesteryear, to debate the relative artistic and ethical merit of innovations within the culture, such as UK Grime and Drill rap. *Roadworks* is exemplary of the hip-hop educational activism that has emerged out of this intra-cultural politicking. It offers, I would argue, compelling proof that these formative dynamics – with their artistic, cultural and social choke points – not only continue to supply hip-hop education with much of its impetus into the present day, but also its ideological inflections, topical concerns and pedagogic idiom.

Notes

1. Roughly late 1980s to early 2000s.
2. Imani Perry, *Prophets of the Hood: Politics and Poetics in Hip-Hop* (Durham: Duke University Press, 2004): p. 6.
3. Michael Eric Dyson, *Know What I Mean? Reflections on Hip Hop* (New York: Basic Civitas Books, 2007): p. 66; Manning Marable, *The Great Wells of Democracy: The Meaning of Race in American Life* (New York: Basic Civitas Books, 2003): pp. 259–260.
4. Perry, *Prophets of the Hood*, p. 50.
5. Tricia Rose, *The Hip Hop Wars: What We Talk about when We Talk about Hip Hop – and Why It Matters* (New York: Basic Books, 2008): pp. 221–228.
6. Patrick Turner, *Hip Hop versus Rap: The Politics of Droppin' Knowledge* (London: Routledge, 2017).
7. Geneva Smitherman, 'The Power of the Rap: The Black Idiom and the New Black Poetry', *Twentieth Century Literature*, 19/4 (1973): pp. 259–274, p. 272.
8. Ibid.
9. H. Samy Alim, *Roc the Mic Right: The Language of Hip Hop Culture* (London: Routledge, 2007): pp. 126–127.
10. Richard Shusterman, 'The Fine Art of Rap', *New Literary History*, 22/3 (Summer 1991): 613–632.
11. Ibid., p. 625.
12. Houston Baker Jr., 'Handling "Crisis": Great Books, Rap Music, and the End of Western Homogeneity (Reflections on the Humanities in America)', *Callaloo*, 13/2 (1990): 173–194, p. 183.
13. Dyson, *Know What I Mean?*; Geneva Smitherman, '"The Chain Remains the Same": Communicative Practices in the Hip-Hop Nation', *Journal of Black Studies*, 28/1 (1997): 3–25.

14. Molefi K. Asante Jr., *It's Bigger than Hip Hop: The Rise of the Post–Hip-Hop Generation* (New York: St Martin's Press, 2008).
15. Marable, *The Great Wells of Democracy*, pp. 259–260.
16. Bakari Kitwana, *The Hip Hop Generation: Young Blacks and the Crisis in African-American Culture* (New York: Basic Civitas Books, 2002): pp. 175–177.
17. Angela Ards, 'Organizing the Hip-Hop Generation', in Forman, M. and Anthony Neal, M. (Eds.), *That's the Joint! The Hip-Hop Studies Reader* (New York: Routledge, 2004): p. 316.
18. Errol A. Henderson, 'Black Nationalism and Rap Music', *Journal of Black Studies*, 26/3 (1996): 308–339.
19. Kitwana, *The Hip Hop Generation*, p. 213.
20. James A. Banks, 'Multicultural Education and Curriculum Transformation', *The Journal of Negro Education*, 64/4 (1995): 390–400.
21. On African-American Vernacular English (AAVE) and the US school curriculum, see Yolanda Sealey-Ruiz, 'Spoken Soul: The Language of Black Imagination and Reality', *Kappa Delta Pi's Educational Forum*, 69 (2005): 37–46.
22. Marc Lamont-Hill and Emery Petchauer, *Schooling Hip-Hop: Expanding Hip-Hop Based Education across the Curriculum* (New York: Teachers College Press, 2013): pp. 1–2.
23. In what now follows, I summarize some pedagogic nostrums and methodologies from the early literature on hip-hop education. See Jabari Mahari and Soraya Sablo, 'Writing for Their Lives: The Non-School Literacy of California's Urban African American Youth', *The Journal of Negro Education*, 65/2 (1996): 164–180; Ernest Morrell, and Jeffrey M. R. Duncan-Andrade, 'Promoting Academic Literacy with Urban Youth through Engaging Hip-Hop Culture', *English Journal*, 91/6 (2002): 88–92; Korina Jocson, '"Bob Dylan and Hip Hop": Intersecting Literacy Practices in Youth Poetry Communities', *Written Communication*, 23/3 (2006): 231–259.
24. Mahari and Sablo, 'Writing for their Lives', p. 176.
25. Ibid., p. 165.
26. Jocson, 'Bob Dylan and Hip Hop', p. 253.
27. David Yanofsky, Barry Van Driel, and James Kass, '"Spoken Word" and "Poetry Slams": The Voice of Youth Today', *European Journal of Intercultural Studies*, 10/3 (1999): 1–4.
28. Smitherman, 'The Power of the Rap'.
29. Mahari and Sablo, 'Writing for their Lives', p. 168.
30. Sealey-Ruiz, 'Spoken Soul', p. 38.
31. Alim, *Roc the Mic Right*.
32. Baker Jr., 'Handling "Crisis"', p. 176.
33. Belle, 'The Poem Performed', pp. 14–15.
34. Chris Green, 'Materializing the Sublime Reader: Cultural Studies, Reader Response, and Community Service in the Creative Writing Workshop', *College English*, 64/2 (2001): 153–174.

35. Green, 'Materializing the Sublime Reader', p. 167.
36. Morrell and Duncan-Andrade, 'Promoting Academic Literacy', p. 90.
37. Ibid., pp. 90–91.
38. Ibid., p. 91.
39. Ernest Morrell and Jeffrey J. M. R. Duncan-Andrade, 'Popular Culture and Critical Media Pedagogy in Secondary Literacy Classrooms', *The International Journal of Learning*, 12 (2005): 285.
40. Mahari and Sablo 'Writing for Their Lives', pp. 174–175.
41. Ibid., p. 168.
42. Darren Chetty and Patrick Turner, 'Towards a Hip Hop Pedagogy of Discomfort', *Journal of World Popular Music*, 5/1 (2018): 71–87; Richard Bramwell and James Butterworth, 'Beyond the Street: The Institutional Life of Rap', *Popular Music*, 39/2 (2020): 169–186.
43. See Sound Connections www.sound-connections.org.uk/news/drillosophy/ [Accessed 14 July 2023].
44. See Lambros Fatsis, 'Policing the Beats: The Criminalisation of UK Drill and Grime Music by the London Metropolitan Police', *The Sociological Review*, 67/6 (2019): 1–17, p. 2.
45. *Beyond the Road*.
46. Paulo Freire, *Pedagogy of the Oppressed* (London: Penguin, 1996) 66.
47. *Beyond the Road*.
48. Kameron Virk, 'Why Drill Music Is Being Used to Teach Philosophy', *Newsbeat* (BBC News: June 2020). www.bbc.co.uk/news/newsbeat-53025654 [Accessed 14 July 2023].
49. Ibid.
50. *Beyond the Road*.
51. Ibid.
52. Ibid.
53. Virk, 'Why Drill Music'.
54. Ibid.
55. Ibid.
56. Ibid.
57. *Beyond the Road*.
58. Ibid.
59. Ibid.
60. Ibid.
61. Virk, 'Why Drill Music'.
62. Ibid.
63. *Beyond the Road*.
64. Niall Reddy and Michael Nassen Smith, 'How Not to Change a Curriculum', *Africa Is a Country* (17 July 2019). https://africasacountry.com/2019/07/how-not-to-change-a-curriculum [Accessed on 12 November 2021].

PART IV

Contexts for Rap

13 | Honoring the Honorable

Tanzanian Hip-Hop Artists, Award Shows, and the Power of Popular Song

ALEX PERULLO

On a Thursday evening in February 2001, I sat in a crowded room at the Russian Cultural Center in Dar es Salaam, Tanzania at the country's first Grammy Awards.[1] Sponsored by the South African media conglomerate M-Net, the Awards brought together talent from throughout the country's diverse musical landscape. Around me were the most talented composers, musicians, producers, and radio personalities awaiting the announcement of winners in a variety of categories including best composer, radio personality, and television host. Most people, however, were anticipating the winners of two categories: the best female musician and the best male musician in the country.

As I had been doing research on Tanzania's music economy for three years, I sat among a group of prominent musicians: Remmy Ongala, a legendary local musician who found fame internationally by recording for the Real World label beginning in the late 1980s, sat in front of me. To my left were the most popular hip-hop artists and producers, including Mr. II (Joseph Mbilinyi), P Funk (Paul Matthysse), and Dola Soul (Ahmed Dola). On my right were artists in the Tanzanian genre *dansi*, a vibrant dance music with origins drawn from traditional Tanzanian rhythms, Latin American music, and American jazz. And, directly behind me were the esteemed singers of multiple taarab groups, a genre of sung Swahili poetry. To put the space into context, it would be as if you surrounded yourself with the fifty best musicians in your country's music scene, from the 1960s to the present, and waited for the announcement of who among them would be selected as the best in the country.

As the evening wore on, tensions grew in the room. Even though I had seen many of the musicians entertain thousands of people at live shows, most were visibly nervous in ways that I had not anticipated. As I thought about the meaning of these awards, however, I realized it was not just a trophy that these artists would receive. The winner would obtain publicity in local newspapers, on radio shows, and on television programs. They would be asked to perform at local events and, perhaps, work with promoters to tour the country. And, they would symbolically represent something about the state of music, since they would be the first winners of a prestigious award organized and presented by one of Africa's biggest media companies. Few events in Tanzania's history were as significant in selecting a single winner, male and female, from all the country's forms of popular music.

Two radio deejays, Seven of Clouds FM and Abubakari Liongo of Radio Uhuru, announced each of the awards. Their banter was slow – perhaps having been told to prolong the evening – and drew nervous laughter with each joke they made. After several hours, it came time to announce the last two awards. Throughout the evening I took notes on the event and recorded speeches on a portable recorder, but I have no information on the moment leading up to the announcement of the best female musician. I had been swept up in the ceremony and, like those around me, wondered who would win. Would it be one of the great taarab singers Khadija Kopa or Nasma Khamis Kidogo whose legend as the best singers in the country had kept them in the top taarab bands for over twenty years? Would it be Lwiza Mbuttu or Nytota Waziri, singers in two of the most successful dance bands in the country, African Stars and Kilimanjaro Band? Or would it be Judith Wambura, known as Lady Jaydee, an up-and-coming R&B artist who had just started her career in music? Five names were listed on the official Grammy Awards nomination list, and only one would be the 2001 winner.

After a long build up, the announcement came: the winner of the best female musician in Tanzania was Lady Jaydee. An audible gasp ran through the room. A twenty-one-year-old, new artist had just beat out the most significant musicians in popular music. Lady Jaydee rarely performed live and only had a few songs released at the time of the awards. People in the room started to speak to each other in low whispers about the results as Lady Jaydee made her way to the stage. In typical Tanzanian fashion, no one spoke out or complained about what appeared to be a great injustice, but their whispers carried great significance. I had interviewed all the women who were up for the award, including Lady Jaydee. I knew the positions that these artists took musically, socially, and politically. Mbuttu, for instance, had just given a speech an hour earlier on gender discrimination in music that drew applause and, later, widespread publicity. Kopa was a master at delivering biting verse in her lyrics that were avidly sung by audiences throughout the country. Lady Jaydee, by comparison, was a new artist in a new genre who had not tested her talents.

The last award for the evening was the best male musician. A similar group of five musicians were nominated including Ongala, two of the best popular dance band singers, the leader of a collective of artists, and the rapper Mr. II.² I was most nervous about this award since Ally Choky, one of the dance band singers, sat to my right, Mr. II to my left, and Ongala directly in front of me. These individuals had become friends of mine, and it was hard to know what I would say when all but one of them lost. Winning a prestigious award could do a great deal for their careers, and they each had a nervous energy about them. In my notes I wrote that one of the musicians bounced his leg up and down "like a jackhammer" as he wrestled with his anxiety over the impending announcement.

Finally, Liongo read the name of the winner of the 2001 M-Net Grammy Awards for best male musician. In an auditorium wrapped in silence he yelled out "Mr. II." Immediately Mr. II jumped out of his seat and yelled, "I knew it, I knew I would win." Applause came from a group of rappers in the room, but, like before, many people in the audience were stunned. How had two young artists in new genres prevailed over all other musicians in the country? I recorded Mr. II's speech, where he thanked his producer, fans, and others. Then he stated, "This award is for me and for all the street soldiers who battle for their lives without being helped. The war will continue. Thank you very much. "³ The powerful, political message demonstrated one reason that Mr. II had risen to become a top musician in the country. He was a voice for many young people struggling in a country that often treated poor youths as burdens on the state. The "war" symbolized the fight among young, impoverished youth to find a place in Tanzanian society.

The Genre of Tanzanian Hip-Hop

Tanzania is a country in East Africa with a population of nearly sixty-eight million people. Most individuals involved in the commercialization of popular music, including music producers, radio personalities, television hosts, videographers, and musicians, reside in Dar es Salaam, a sprawling coastal city of over eight million people. While many rap artists reside in Dar es Salaam, thousands of others live throughout the country in small villages and large towns. Considering the challenges of finding instruments or musical instruction in Tanzania, rap music offers an affordable and accessible means for people to both perform music and express themselves. In terms of active participation, more people in Tanzania are involved in hip-hop than any other artistic form.

As an anthropologist, I conduct fieldwork in different locations to study issues that would be difficult to comprehend from a distance. This requires living and participating in communities that are the focus of my research. While one could study topics, such as Tanzanian music, from afar, it is difficult to comprehend people's motivations, interests, and values without interacting with them. For instance, much of the content that circulates online regarding Tanzanian music is material from a particular vantage point: a means to promote artists and their music. Fieldwork necessitates talking with individuals, hearing their concerns, understanding power dynamics, and learning about individuals who never make it online or in spaces accessible outside of Tanzania. When I conduct interviews, I meet with a variety of individuals to better comprehend the state of the music economy. This includes musicians, agents, radio deejays, promoters, lawyers, politicians, and many others. The goal of this research is to develop a means to understand different social, political, and historical issues in order to answer specific research questions.

The M-Net Grammy Awards represented one fieldwork experience to learn about Tanzania's music economy. It gave a window into the popularity of certain genres and the way that awards shows could mold the sounds and ideas of music among those participating in the ceremony and the broader public. As other authors have noted, awards shows establish, normalize, and legitimize the sounds of specific musical genres.[4] By selecting R&B and rap artists with the highest honors, the Grammy Awards established these genres as significant in Tanzania's music economy and accurately predicted that these two genres would rise to become the most dominant in the country. Artists, producers, distributors, and others also recognized the symbolic success of these genres giving them an impetus to continue to expand these musical forms.

Since 2001, artists have transformed R&B into a pop-oriented genre called *bongo flava* that mixes foreign elements, including popular African and European musical forms, with local traditions. The term bongo flava derives from the words *bongo*, which is slang for brains or wisdom, and *flava*, the Swahilization of the word flavor. In terms of album sales, downloads, music video views, and audiences at live shows, bongo flava artists are the most successful and popular in the country.[5] Several artists, such as Ali Kiba, Harmonize (Rajab Abdul Kahali), and Diamond Platnumz (Nasibu Abdul Juma Issack) have found significant success across the African continent. They have elaborate videos and tour schedules, receive lucrative sponsorship deals, and win significant accolades. Diamond Platnumz, for instance, won six All Africa Music Awards, known as AFRIMA, between 2014 and 2016, including song of the year and best artist in African pop.[6]

Rap artists, by contrast, outnumber bongo flava artists but often encounter less commercial success. Part of the reason is audience interaction with these musical forms. Bongo flava tends to be a more danceable music that many people enjoy hearing at clubs, social halls, and in spaces where people gather. It is similar to American pop music in that it can occasionally address sensitive or social issues, but often has evergreen themes of love, romance, or personal relationships. Bongo flava artists also push themes related to working class and traditional aspects of African living, which resonates with a broad segment of listeners. Rap artists, by contrast, tend to focus on social issues or on themes of personal achievement. There are topics of wealth and status with artists performing in front of mansions or with sports cars. These themes and visuals connect with many urban listeners, particularly young people, but do not offer the same broad appeal as bongo flava.

Rap music in Tanzania is also dominated by male artists and audiences. The female rap artist Rosa Ree (Rosary Robert Iwole) commented "Gender discrimination has been my biggest challenge in the music industry and specifically the genre [rap] I am doing. Many people assume that women should not pursue rap or have the ambition to thrive in any male-dominated sector. It's as if you should either sing or go home and cook, maybe raise children."[7] Her comment about singing reflects the sense that female artists can sing but should not perform as rappers, instrumentalists, producers, or in other areas of the music economy. Female singers in bongo flava, including Zuchu (Zuhura Othman Soud) and Nandy (Faustina Charles Mfinanga), sell out large shows and generate millions of views for their music videos. Female rap artists, by contrast, often encounter challenges in terms of promotion, support from those in the music business, and negative social media commentary. Rosa Ree addresses many of these issues in the song, "I'm Not Sorry," where she raps, in English, about people on social media who comment about her: "You got a lot to say about me/ But I never met you/ Oh well, I am not sorry/ What gives you the power to say anything about what I do?" To not be sorry, in this case, means that Rosa Ree does not apologize for being a confrontational female rap artist.

The Politicization of Rap

Rap first emerged in Tanzania during the 1980s. In the early years, artists mimicked the sounds, dress, and dances of well-known American artists.

Live shows would sometimes feature competitions between performers who were judged on the closeness of their performance to that of the original recorded song. Beginning in mid-1990s, artists experimented with lyrics in Kiswahili, the most widely spoken language in the country. These same artists changed the lyrics to focus on issues that resonated with local communities, such as issues of poverty, marginalization, and urban living. The combination of Kiswahili lyrics and social commentary popularized Tanzanian rap music among young people throughout eastern Africa.

The politicization of rap became one the central elements of this musical form in Tanzania. Considering the history of censorship in the country, the risks that rap artists took to speak out should be recognized as a significant cultural transformation. Soon after independence in 1961, Tanzania's government created institutions and structures that censored the lyrics and content of popular music forms. Until 1995, only two recording studios existed in the country, both of which were controlled by state organizations. To record at these facilities, artists needed to submit lyrics, which were then edited to ensure that the content supported government policies and ideologies. The musicians would then be required to perform lyrics in the corrected form. Typically, artists knew the expectations of recording studios and live performance venues and, therefore, only composed songs that followed social and political standards established by the Tanzanian government or couched their lyrics in metaphors that censors would likely miss.

Beginning in 1999, rap artists pushed against these standards to speak openly about the issues they experienced. As the artist Fid Q noted, "what matters in music is that it has to reflect your community."[8] There were songs about police brutality, prostitution, and government mismanagement.[9] There were artists who addressed gender discrimination, human rights abuses, and the challenges of living with disabilities in urban Tanzania. Almost every artist who wanted to make a career in hip-hop had to have a song that addressed a social or political issue.

One of the most significant changes that rap artists brought to Tanzanian popular music was the directness of their messages. While previous composers would use metaphors or cleverly hide meanings in poetics phrases, rap artists often opted to speak directly to their audiences. In 2014, the rap artist Izzo Bizness released a song called "Riz One," meant as a critique of the fourth President of the country, Jakaya Kikwete. In a clever twist, Bizness aims the song at the son of the President, whose name is Ridhiwani Kikwete, nicknamed in the song as Riz One (Riz is a shortened form of Ridhiwani and One references him being the first son of the President). Bizness opens the song: "Let me start with Kikwete, the leader of my nation/ Our country is still fragile, this is my view/ He promised a better life for every Tanzanian/ The economy has slowed, suffering has increased."[10] Over three verses, Bizness then criticizes the leadership in the country on issues of electricity, healthcare, human rights, housing, drug use, and Parliamentary incompetence. Each verse ends with Bizness stating, "I'm talking to Riz One," a statement calling out the president's son for not using his influence to fight for causes significant to young people in the country. The biting commentary resonated with Tanzanians frustrated by the promises of the government and the continued lack of support for those in poverty.

Despite allowing more musical freedoms, the Tanzanian government did not welcome all lyrical directness. The government restricted the broadcasting or promotion of songs that contained foul language or overly sexualized content. This included a ban on songs that were seen as vulgar, violent, or against social norms. In several cases where songs were banned, artists rerecorded the lyrics in order to clear government restrictions.[11] Nonetheless, whereas Tanzania's government had censored artists in the past, the relative openness to speak about social and political issues created opportunities for artists to confront challenges that they viewed as significant. As a result, between 1999 and 2015, there were moments where freedom of speech was more widely practiced than in many other parts of the world since, even in developed countries, commercial radio often limits controversial content. In Tanzania, these songs became part of the dialogue occurring in the country and were regularly broadcast on local radio stations.

This popularity of political or socially pertinent lyrics led several rap artists to become politicians. The "army" mentioned at the M-Net Awards was a figurative representation of the many people who supported Mr. II due to the socially engaged messages in his lyrics. That army grew into a movement, which led to a career in politics as a Member of Parliament from 2010 to 2015. Professor Jay (Joseph Haule) also became a member of Parliament from 2015 to 2020, and Mwana Fa (Hamis Mwinjuma) won a Parliamentary seat in 2020. The transition from rapper to politician occurred among musicians in several African countries and demonstrated the influence of rap artists to speak to issues that concern populations in their countries. In Tanzania's case, the growth of hip-hop culture coincided with democratic movements away from a single party to multiparty elections (both Mr. II and Professor Jay represented the opposition party CHADEMA, while Mwana Fa represents the ruling party CCM).

In 2015, a new government led by President John Magufuli changed the course for Tanzanian music and society. In a series of draconian and stringent policies, some of which related to terrorism and crime, artists were no longer able to speak openly about the same issues. Political organizations silenced artists – by censoring their music or revoking visas to tour outside of Tanzania – and many of the most provocative artists left music as they could no longer speak openly about life in their communities. Many songs that could air in years past were no longer broadcast and several songs disappeared from the internet, most likely removed by the artists themselves as they wanted to continue to perform in music without being censored by the government. Mr. II was arrested for insulting the president on social media, and numerous artists were brought before the National Arts Council (BASATA) to promise that they would no longer compose controversial lyrics.[12] The government also found ways to silence people on social media, and several newspapers were forced to shut down – albeit for a short time – after publishing stories deemed counter or adverse to government initiatives.[13]

Despite the dramatic limits on free speech, rap artists continued to use music to speak on social issues. These issues, however, were ones deemed acceptable by the government. Kala Jeremiah's song "America" tells people about the challenges of getting a visa to travel to the United States. Released in May 2019, the song informs listeners of problems they will encounter in America: "I'm Black don't shoot me/ I have a dream don't kick me." Jeremiah then tells listeners about the beauties and joys of Tanzania: "I love Tanzania / I am proud of my country/ I am a patriot / I will return to greet you."[14] The pro-Tanzanian lyrics, which evade any conversation about the reasons many people attempt to attain foreign visas, were seen as positive for Tanzanian society and, therefore, acceptable under government policies.

As COVID-19 became an extensive problem globally, Magufuli argued that the disease was a hoax without scientific evidence to prove it existed.[15] He also refused to shut down churches as he noted, "Corona is the devil and it cannot survive in the body of Jesus."[16] People were afraid to speak out over social media about the situation in Tanzania, as they feared potential repercussions if someone found out their views. Although a few artists did compose and release political songs, they were couched in metaphor and never broadcast in the country. Magufuli, who became known as "the bulldozer" for the way he approached issues, increasingly pushed Tanzania into new areas of authoritarianism. Then, on 17 March 2021, Magufuli died of a heart ailment. Two days later, the Vice President, Samia Suluhu Hassan, became the country's sixth president.

When Magufuli went into the hospital, Tanzanians tested the opportunities of free speech. People wrote on social media about the president, COVID-19, and economic turmoil. Even before his death was announced, songs emerged that added social commentary about living in Tanzania, though none as strongly worded as those in the period before Magufuli took power. In addition, most of these songs used humor and storytelling to soften the politicization of the lyrics. In the rap duo Mabantu's song "Mwenye Nyumba (Landlord)," which was released a month before Magufuli died, a dialogue opens the song where a young man tells his landlord: "Excuse me, landlord. I will pay you your money. I took my mom to the hospital, she is sick." The landlord responds, "Don't compare my rent and your stupid things. Which is more important, your home or your mother? I want my rent. Eh, bwana, I want my rent."[17] The landlord becomes increasingly angry, scaring off the people who had gathered around him. The song then begins with the rap duo explaining what they must go through when they cannot pay their rent including selling off the stove and the radio. The song is comical for the severity and narrowmindedness of the landlord but also raises a significant point about economic turmoil and housing costs.

In the song "Liisa," released in June 2021, the rap artist Rapcha (Cosmas Paul Mfoy) uses a spoken-word style of delivery to tell the story of a girl who asks Rapcha for money and promises that she will meet up with him later. As days pass, Rapcha wonders why Liisa has not responded to his texts, and he goes to visit her. He enters her home to find her with another man. The man throws Rapcha out of the house and yells "thief." People come and beat Rapcha, believing that he is a thief. The last verse of the song is one of the most devastating in Tanzanian hip-hop, as Rapcha narrates being beaten and set afire by the mob. He laments, "I have a few seconds to inhale the good world that is full of so many bad people / Okay Lissa / I leave you in a state of happiness / The love I showed you decided to take my life / The promises we made are extinguished by your desires / I'm leaving, karma will get you."[18] The shocking lines about lost love and bad people marks a significant moment in Tanzanian music. This song, and the many others being composed by a new generation of artists, turn toward the anxieties and personal suffering involved with modern living. While neither "Mwenye Nyumba" nor "Liisa" are directly political, they raise concerns about social issues affecting Tanzanians. They also pull Tanzanian rap into a new direction of social consciousness where artists reflect on the meaning of modernization and their anxieties for the future.

Awarding the Masters

Given the thousands of young people attempting to make a career in rap, the competition to find success can be quite intense. Artists need to learn about performing, recording, promoting, and protecting their music. Learning to compose cogent lyrics and perform on stage requires practice and, as many people in Tanzania argue, an education in elements of poetry, language, stage performance, and dance. Local arts organizations, older musicians, and concert promoters in Tanzania provide basic coaching for stage performance including on the best techniques to hold a microphone. There are workshops, community gatherings, and even "camps," where artists gather to attain knowledge of the variety of skills needed to create, perform, record, and promote music. Considering that formal music education is nearly nonexistent in Tanzania, the informality of musical learning has become a standard practice throughout the country and is seen as an obligation of many senior artists who should pass their knowledge to younger musicians.

The challenges of making it as an artist in Tanzania mean that awards shows represent one of the key milestones in music. It is a recognition of an artist's achievements and their credibility as a successful and important musician. Even artists who have commercial success explained to me that awards shows represent an acknowledgement of the quality of their work and the importance of their contribution to Tanzanian society. As one artist told me, it is about "honoring the honorable (kumheshimu mheshimiwa)." Since the government-supported National Arts Council (BASATA) organizes the country's main awards show, the Tanzanian Music Awards (TMAs), winning also creates the sense of state acknowledgement of an artist and his/her achievements. One journalist noted, the TMAs are important for Tanzanians since "we [are] able to see how our government supports all the music genres that are produced in our country."[19]

Between 2002 and 2015, the TMAs featured anywhere from twenty to thirty-five categories including best singer, best entertainer, best song, best artist, as well as categories related to different genres, such as bongo flava, taarab, dansi, and hip-hop. Only twelve hip-hop artists have won awards during the fourteen years of the TMAs. Several artists, including Mwana Fa, Professor Jay, and Chidi Benzi, won awards in multiple years. Figure 13.1 lists the artists who won multiple awards over the course of

Mwana Fa	2004, 2006, 2007, 2008
Professor Jay	2002, 2003, 2004, 2006, 2015, 2022
Mangwea	2005, 2009
Fid Q	2006, 2008, 2011
AY	2007, 2008
Chidi Benzi	2007, 2008, 2009, 2010, 2011
Joh Makini	2010, 2011, 2015, 2015

Figure 13.1 Tanzanian rap artists who won TMAs in multiple years, 2002–2015, 2022.

the TMAs. Most of these artists have been in the music business for over twenty years, which has limited the opportunities for younger artists to compete or attain recognition. Interestingly, at the 2015 TMAs, the rapper Joh Makini spoke about the power of music for young people in his acceptance speech, "My talent started in the ghetto... And today we hope to inspire young people from the ghetto and let them know that music can lift you out of poverty and better the life of you and your family. It is important that the government looks after us. Music should not be managed because as you can see we are all there for music, right?"[20] The simultaneous point about not overly controlling music and allowing artists to attain commercial success in order to lift themselves out of poverty reflects the views of many who work in Tanzanian hip-hop.

One of the criticisms of the TMAs is that they tend to favor certain artists, particularly those who promote specific values, norms, and ideologies related to society. The more controversial artists or the ones who are most outspoken about government problems tend not to win or win less frequently. For instance, more provocative artists, such as Roma Mkatoliki, Gangwe Mobb, Dudubaya, and Wanaume Family have each only won a single award even though they have been nominated on multiple occasions and found significant commercial success during the years they were nominated. In 2012, even though he was nominated for several awards, Dully Sykes withdrew his name from the awards ceremony, commenting that the awards show was "full of lies" due to the biases inherent in the judging process. BASATA, which runs the TMAs, has responded to many of these criticisms and ushered in changes to the voting system. Nonetheless, the history of the awards demonstrates that a certain sound and style has been historically favored. Lady JayDee, who won the best female artist at the M-Net Grammy Awards in 2001, went on to win the TMAs eight times in fourteen years.

During the time of Magufuli's presidency (2015–2021), BASATA was not permitted to run the TMAs. In 2022, however, BASATA restarted the show and expanded the award categories. The show itself, which took place at the Julius Nyerere International Conference Center (JNICC) Theater in Dar es Salaam on April 2, was a tremendous spectacle with a light show, live bands, comedic banter by the announcers, and participation by a broad section of Tanzania's music economy. As in previous years, some of the same artists won awards: Professor Jay won best composer, Ali Kiba took home five other awards, and Harmonize, three. In the hip-hop categories, however, younger artists won for the first time, including Young Lunya, who won twice, and Chemical (Claudia Lubao), a female artist who is pushing against gender norms with her music and social media presence. The TMAs also featured new categories including emerging artist of the year, which was won by Rapcha. As an added benefit, the Minister of Culture, Arts and Sport, Mohamed Mchengerwa, announced that the government would provide health insurance, contributions to pension funds, and a special allowance to all winners of the TMAs.[21] Although I was unable to verify that the winners and their families received these benefits, the potential to be supported by the government in terms of health and pensions is significant.

Politics and Song Intertwined

On May 31, 2022, Joseph Mbilinyi (Mr. II) organized a concert about his life in music. He packed a room full of musicians and dignitaries, including the president of Tanzania and the American ambassador. The presence of President Samia signaled a significant transformation from the previous president who condemned or ridiculed local talent. After listening to a series of speeches and watching several hip-hop artists perform, President Samia went onstage to talk about her view of music, the arts, and politics. She spoke about the path that Mbilinyi took to become a musician, rap about politics, and then, using the votes of young people, become a Member of Parliament. She then thanked Mbilinyi and the other musicians who had worked to shape politics in the country. At one point she stated, "I recognize the contribution of the arts industry. Not only in providing entertainment but also in developing our country. Music is employment, music is the economy."[22] She then discussed the importance of artists, such as Mbilinyi, and argued that their talents were vital for the success of Tanzanian society. She mentioned that the struggles of rap artists in the early years, as hip-hop music was not widely accepted. "Even me," she lamented, "if I saw artists performing rap music,

I would ask myself 'what are they doing? Rappers are just hooligans.' But, it is not hooliganism... This music has brought tremendous respect to Tanzania." It is impossible to overstate the significance of President Samia's words, which were widely discussed in Tanzania. She attended a rap concert, albeit a formal one, and then spoke with knowledge and insight about the history of the genre in Tanzanian society. This close relationship between art and politics is striking. The president's words demonstrated a recognition by the government of the importance of rap music as a vehicle for social change and an icon of national identity, aspects of the music that were first acknowledged at the M-Net Awards show over twenty years earlier.

Notes

1. The name Grammy Awards was only used in 2001, as this was considered a violation of the trademark Grammy Awards, based in the United States. The M-Net Grammy Awards took place on February 22, 2001, and featured ten categories.
2. Mr. II has changed his name many times and is also known as Sugu, Jongwe, and Taita. His given name is Joseph Mbilinyi.
3. The original statement by Mr. II was in Kiswahili: "Zawadi hii ni ya kwangu mimi pamoja na wanajeshi wote wa mtaani ambao wapo kwenye mapambano ya maisha bila usaidizi. Vita itaendelea. Asante sana."
4. Mary R. Watson and N. Anand. "Award Ceremony as an Arbiter of Commerce and Canon in the Popular Music Industry." *Popular Music* 25/1 (2006): 41–56.
5. Many people use the term bongo flava to reference any newer style of popular music, including rap music. However, most musicians and members of the music community, as well as awards shows, make a distinction between bongo flava and other genres, including rap, zouk, reggae, taarab, mchiriku, singelii, and dansi.
6. All Africa Music Awards is an annual awards event. The awards event was established by the International Committee AFRIMA, in collaboration with the African Union to reward and celebrate musical works, talents and creativity around the African continent while promoting African cultural heritage.
7. Gesare, Tracy. "Why I Am a Goddess: Tanzanian Rapper Rosa Ree." *The Standard* (Kenya), published 2020 (www.standardmedia.co.ke).
8. Fid Q. Interview with author. May 13, 2022.
9. A. Perullo "Politics and Popular Song: Youth, Authority, and Popular Music in East Africa." *African Music* 9/1 (2011): 87–116.
10. The original Kiswahili of the verse by Izzo Bizness is as follows: "Acha nianze na Kikwete kiongozi wa taifa langu/ Nchi yetu bado tete, huu mtazamo wangu/ Aliahidi maisha bora kwa kila mTanzania/ Japo uchumi umedorora, mateso yametuzidia."

11. Perullo (2011). Many artists re-recorded cleaner versions of their songs after the songs were banned from the airwaves.
12. Ng'wankilala, Fumbuka. "Tanzanian Opposition MP Jailed for Five Months for Insulting President." *Reuters*, February 26, 2018.
13. See, for example, Ng'wankilala, Fumbuka. "Tanzania Shuts Down Newspaper for Two Years over Articles on Mining Row." *Reuters*, June 15, 2017.
14. The original Kiswahili in the verse by Kala Jeremiah is "Ninaipenda Tanzania/ Nchi yangu najivunia/ Mzalendo mwenye nia/ Nitarudi kusalimia."
15. Devermont J., and Harris M. *Implications of Tanzania's Bungled Response to COVID-19*. Center for Strategic and International Studies; Washington, DC: 2020. https://www.csis.org/analysis/implications-tanzanias-bungled-response-covid-19 [Accessed on January 28, 2021].
16. Harvie A. "Tanzania's Mild Response to COVID-19 and Its Implications for the 2020 Elections." Atlantic Council. March 27, 2020. www.atlanticcouncil.org/blogs/africasource/tanzanias-mild-response-to-covid-19-and-its-implications-for-the-2020-elections/ [Accessed on January 28, 2021].
17. The original Kiswahili of the song is as follows: "Samahani mwenye nyumba/ Hela yako nitakulipa/ Nimempeleka mama yangu hospitali, anaumwa/ Wewe usifananishe kodi yangu na vitu vya kijinga/ Kati ya nyumba yako na mama yako kipi muhimu?/ Nataka kodi yangu/ Ehh bwana, nataka kodi yangu."
18. The original Kiswahili of the verse from the song "Liisa" is as follows: "Nina sekunde chache za kuivuta pumzi ya dunia nzuri iliojaa binadamu wengi wabaya/ Sawa Lissa/ Ninakuacha ufurahi/ Mapenzi niliokuonyesha umeamua kunitoa uhai/ Ahadi tulizoweka zimezimwa na tamaa zako/ Mi nakwenda, karma itakulipa bye bye."
19. Ramadhani Ismail 2022. "Tanzanian Music Awards Return after Six-Year Hiatus." *The Citizen*. January 17. www.thecitizen.co.tz/tanzania/magazines/tanzania-music-awards-return-after-six-year-hiatus-3682432.
20. The original Kiswahili of Makini's speech is as follows: "Talanta uliyonipa ilianza ghetto . . . Na leo tunainspire vijana kibao kutoka kitaani kwamba muziki unaweza kukutoa maskani na kukuweka juu na kuendesha maisha yako na familia kwa ujumla. Kikubwa tu ni Serikali yetu ituangalie, Music usimamiwe kwasababu kama unavyoona watu wote tupo kwa ajili ya muziki, au siyo?"
21. Daily News Reporter. "The 2021 Winners to be Insured, Get Pension-Government." Published online on April 2, 2022. https://dailynews.co.tz/.
22. President Samia presented her speech in Kiswahili. Here are her original words: "Natambua mchango wa tasnia ya sanaa kwa ujumla. Sio tu katika kutoa burudani lakini pia katika maendeleo ya nchi yetu. Muziki ni ajira, muziki ni uchumi. . . . Hata mimi mwenyewe, nilikuwa nikiwaona wakifokafoka najiuliza 'hawa vijana vipi? Wanafokafoka hapa uhuni tu.' Lakini kumbe sio uhuni . . . muziki umeleta heshima Tanzania." (Author's translation).

14 | 'It Will Never Go Away'

Re-imagining Black German Identity in 'Ich bin Schwarz'

SINA A. NITZSCHE AND LAURA I. K. SPILKER

Torch. Samy Deluxe. Afrob. Black German rap artists have been actively taking part in hip-hop culture since its beginnings in Germany.[1] While there is a significant number of Black female German rappers today, only a few of them, including the rap pioneer Sabrina Setlur, the legendary rap trio Tic Tac Toe, or the mellow pop rap artist Namika, have had a similar commercial success as their non-Black colleagues. One of the most recent and most successful contemporary artists is Nura who started rapping as part of the duo SXTN in the mid 2010s. SXTN consisted of Nura who is of Eritrean and Saudi Arabian decent, and who migrated as a child to Germany, and Juju who was born in Germany to German and Moroccan parents. Before their split in 2018/19, SXTN became widely popular for their provocative lyrics, catchy party songs, and subversive performances centring on sexism, racism, and classism.

Our contribution will examine how race, class, and gender are represented in the song and music video 'Ich bin Schwarz' (I am Black).[2] Performed mainly by Nura, the song was released as part of the SXTN EP *Asozialisierungsprogramm* in 2016.[3] We argue that 'Schwarz' promotes a confident, self-empowered, and unapologetic Black female German identity by remixing the popular New German Wave song 'Ich will Spass', by subverting racist and sexist imaginations of Afrodiasporic womanhood, and by continuing hip-hop's political project of resistance against nationalism and right-wing extremism in Germany.

In our investigation of 'Schwarz', we combine transnational, intersectional, and feminist research.[4] We use discourse and media studies approaches to conduct a close reading of intertextual references, samples, lyrics, visuals, and signifying practices[5] as they are articulated and mediated in the audio, visual, and lyrical dimensions of the music video. We expand the existing research on rap music in Germany which has focused on questions of ethnicity and gender by emphasising how race, gender, as well as class and nationality intersect in 'Schwarz'. We hope to contribute to a growing body of work on racialised postcolonial identities in German rap music.[6]

We will first discuss how rap music in Germany resonates with global social justice issues before we analyse the music video's musical references, constructions of Black femininity, and political messages. In the next section, we start by exploring how hip-hop as an Afrodiasporic art form came to Germany and how Afrodiasporic artists and artists of colour have used it to express their complex realities in Germany.

Black Identities in German Rap Music: An Overview

Over the past forty years, rap music has grown into one of Germany's most commercially successful musical genres. Since its beginnings in the 1980s, African American soldiers, emcees, and their families participated in the formation of the genre.[7] Local Black and People of Colour (BPOC) youth were critical of the emergence of German-speaking rap music because they associated the German language strongly with the experience of discrimination, exclusion, and racism.[8] However, for Black German rappers who were from more sites of heritage, linguistic traditions, and family origins than, for instance, migrant rappers from Southern or South-Eastern Europe, German was also the only language they had in common.[9] Although racist and colonial terms are still tightly knit into the fabric of the German language, it nowadays is the predominant language in the German rap scene and widely used by white, BPOC, and migrant artists who mix it with words from Turkish, Arabic, and other languages, mirroring the diversity of the German rap scene.[10]

In Germany, as in the rest of Europe, rap music is considered first and foremost a Black American music.[11] Because German rap is a glocal cultural practice, it appropriates and reinterprets the narratives, discourses, and images that are circulating in global hip-hop culture.[12] This also applies to the negotiation of race: emcees employ mediatised images of US-American constructions of race and reinterpret them in their regional German contexts.[13] Rollefson's investigation of the Berlin rap scene, for instance, demonstrated that BPOC rappers, such as B-Tight and Tony D, feel connected to the experience of Black Americans and use hip-hop as a medium to bring attention to their own struggles in German society.[14] US-American assumptions of race continue to dominate Black transnationalism as they are obscuring other forms of international exchange.[15]

For Black artists and other *Bindestrich-Deutsche* (hyphenated Germans) in Germany, rap music is a powerful tool to voice their experiences of Othering in their daily lives.[16] Through their visible difference from white

Germans, they are treated as people who do not belong to larger German culture.[17] In 2021 the first-ever *Afrozensus 2020*, a ground-breaking statistical report about the realities, lives, and perspectives of Black people in Germany, showed that while Black German realities are incredibly diverse, the large majority of them experience racism and Othering.[18] About 80 per cent stated being sexualised and fetishised on dating apps, and 56 per cent experienced criminalisation through racial profiling and the assumption that they are dealing drugs.[19]

The gendered and racialised imaginations play into the construction of German identity in rap music. Mirroring US-American stereotypes of Black masculinity as associated with crime, one of Germany's traditional media representations of Blackness involves drug dealing, illegal migration, and violence.[20] This idea of Black masculinity fits well into ghettocentric hip-hop narratives as performances by Manuellsen and other commercially successful *Straßenrapper*[21] affirm. Complicating these imaginations, Kofi Yakpo, also known as Linguist, a German Ghanaian linguist and founding member of the legendary Heidelberg rap crew Advanced Chemistry, argues that rap artists also employ their lyrics to re-negotiate a sense of German belonging and continue to write Black German history through these performative acts.[22] One example for this practice is Advanced Chemistry's iconic song 'Fremd im eigenen Land',[23] in which Linguist and his fellow emcees Torch and Toni L address racism in Germany by positioning themselves against the racialised terror of the 1990s.[24] Black male rap artists employ their songs to create a distinctive German narrative and negotiate their place in German culture.

The social situation of Black female German rappers is a bit more complex since they face misogynoir.[25] Describing misogyny directed at Black women, misogynoir refers to an intersectional form of discrimination. BPOC women in Germany are affected by both structural racism and sexism due to the racist as well as patriarchal structures of German culture. They face specific cultural stereotypes, for example, about their portrayal in the media as 'Kriminelle, Putzkräfte oder als hilflose Opfer von Rassismus' ('criminals, cleaners or as helpless victims of racism').[26] Apart from the stereotype of being 'naturally' athletic, Black German women are also associated with other racist and sexist tropes that show similarities to the constructions of African American femininities such as hyper-sexualisation, fetishisation of their buttocks, or the images of the Jezebel or Strong Black women,[27] as our analysis of 'Schwarz' will show.

A New German Wave: Remixing German Popular Music

'Ich bin Schwarz' remixes one of Germany's most famous 1980s pop songs. The first bars of the track already showcase the most prominent cultural reference in the music video: the 1982 smash hit 'Ich will Spass' (I Want Fun) by Markus. 'Ich will Spass'[28] was one of the most popular songs of the Neue Deutsche Welle.[29] Characterised by bold lyrics, punk attitudes, Cold War influences, and provoking performances, the 'pop avant-garde genre'[30] NDW marked the rediscovery and successful commercialisation of the German language as a medium of (self-) expression in popular music in the 1980s.[31]

Markus' 'Spass' opens with a white male first-person speaker propagating driving around with his fast car and having fun on the streets:

Mein Maserati fährt 210	My Maserati drives 210
Schwupps, die Polizei hat's nicht gesehen	Swoosh, the police didn't see it
Das macht Spaß	It's fun
Ich geb' Gas	I'm stepping on the gas
ich geb' Gas	I'm stepping on the gas

'Spass' mocks one of (white middle- and upper-class) Germany's favourite and most hedonistic cultural pastimes, driving a car on the *Autobahn*. The juvenile speaker brags about driving his luxury Italian Maserati car too fast on a German street ('210' kilometres per hour/130 mph). He asserts that even the police do not realise that he is most likely exceeding the speed limit ('the police didn't see it'). The repetition of the line 'I'm stepping on the gas' not only exaggerates a cultural need for speed, but it also evokes comparisons to 1950s American street, youth, and motorcycle gangs who claim the public space as well.[32] The song's emphasis on a quintessential part of German culture, the use of the humorous hyperbole, and the pounding beat subversively comment on 1980s Kohl-era conservatism.[33]

SXTN's 'Schwarz' appropriates the subversive and transgressive humour of the synth pop NDW song. 'Schwarz' opens with a similar car reference as 'Spass', but the language between both songs differs. Nura raps:

Mein Bugatti fährt 410	My Bugatti drives 410
Schwupps, die scheiss Bullen ha'm mich nicht gesehen	Swoosh, the f*** [pigs/cops] didn't see me
Ich bin Schwarz	I'm Black
Ich bin Schwarz	I'm Black
ich bin Schwarz	I'm Black

SXTN's song overexaggerates German car culture by replacing Markus' Maserati reference with the even more expensive Bugatti. The Bugatti reference nods to a legendary pan-European car maker which has managed to reinvent itself in the past, pointing to the remixing of identity formulated in the rap song. In using the Bugatti as their mobility reference of choice, SXTN join famous US-American and German rappers, such as Ace Hood, Rick Ross, Olexesh, and Summer Cem,[34] who also celebrated the cult car in their songs.

Instead of the neutral term 'die Polizei' (the police), the first-person speaker in SXTN's lyrics uses the German derogatory term of 'die scheiss Bullen' (the f*** pigs/cops). The more aggressive use of police terminology indicates the different subject positions in the songs: while the privileged first-person speaker in Markus' lyrics is having fun on the streets without fearing the police, the first-person speaker's relationship to the police in 'Schwarz' appears to be more strained, possibly due to unwarranted police violence and racial profiling explained in the *Afrozenzus*.

Yet, the replacement of the lines 'It's fun/I'm stepping on the gas' with a triumphant 'I'm Black' highlights the fact that the speaker managed not only to bypass police force, but she also proudly claims her Black German identity. This is reinforced by the repetition and rephrasing of 'Ich bin Schwarz' beyond the chorus and throughout the entire song. The forty-three repetitions of the term *Schwarz* (Black) do not only underline the main theme of the song, but also form a confident affirmation of Nura's identity. She boldly proclaims her identity as a Black German woman and extends self-expressions previously formulated by the legendary 1990s rap trio Tic Tac Toe:[35] while Tic Tac Toe privileged gender identities in their songs, Nura privileges her racialised experience in 'Schwarz'.

The musical remix and the opening sequence already affirm that SXTN's traditions go beyond that of Markus. While they connect the song to one of Germany's most juvenile, humorous, and anarchic German pop music genres and claim to be their successors, they also introduce SXTN, and especially Nura, as representatives of a new movement in rap music which highlights their experiences as women of colour.

Tanning and Twerking: Deconstructing Hegemonic Imaginations of the Black Female Body

'Schwarz' critiques white (German) fascinations with the Black female body shaped by US-American popular culture. The song opens with a close-up shot of Nura rapping in a tanning bed. While positioned in the tanning bed, she is lying on her stomach. The whole setting is coloured in blue due to the tanning bed's lights that are striving straight towards the centre of the frame where Nura is positioned. This camera puts the focus entirely on the rapper and her upper body, her arms, hands, and face, which she uses to dance, gesture, and mimic along to the lyrics.

As is appropriate for the location, the rapper wears little clothing and shows a lot of skin which visually stresses the title 'Schwarz' and directs the attention to her Blackness. The only detail that stands out in the blue-toned setting is Nura's bikini bottom which has a neon orange colour. Due to the camera angle, it is not visible throughout a large portion of the first part. It only becomes the focus of attention for a second during the first refrain when Nura is shaking her buttocks along with the music and looking directly into the lens. Although it is only a moment, the colour and movement pull the audience's attention to Nura's buttocks and sexualise the rapper's body. This short take reveals an objectification of the rapper that caters to the general fetishisation of Black women and their buttocks in German culture mentioned in the *Afrozensus*. The opening therefore serves as an ironic commentary on the societal double-standard when it comes to race, gender, and colourism in Germany: while tanned skin is an ideal so desirable that white Germans frequent solariums and tanning beds to attain it, women of colour experience discrimination based on the colour of their skin.

'Schwarz' critiques a longer tradition of the objectification of Afrodiasporic womanhood in Germany rooted in European colonialism. During the nineteenth century, Black women, such as the Khoikhoi woman Sarah Baartman and other 'Hottentot Venuses',[36] were turned into a spectacle and put up for public display because of their big buttocks.[37] In the imaginations of many white Europeans, they portrayed the essence of Black femininity, a femininity that was highly sexualised and thus deviated from the constructed ideal of a virtuous white femininity.[38] This imagined Black hyper-sexual 'deviance' became the foundation for the construction of a white normality enforced through a colonial ideology of race and white supremacy.[39] Nowadays, the objectification of BPOC women in hip-hop music continues to be racialised because their sexualisation works as a symbolic protection of white women.[40]

This historically shaped white gaze onto the Black female body is subverted through the music video's verbal and visual language. In a party scene, the speaker raps 'Und du siehst mich twerken mit mei'm fetten Arsch [...] Ich hab Arsch, ich bin Schwarz' ('And you see me twerking with my fat ass [...] I have ass, I am Black'). The lyrics recall colonial stereotypes of the objectification of the female body and underline how having a 'fat ass' is equated with Black womanhood: whereas this statement is an obvious exaggeration, it emphasises how racial stereotypes become equivalent with (white German) imaginations of Blackness.

Yet, while Nura is dancing in a manner that includes moving her bottom during the first line, the shot only shows her upper body denying a voyeuristic gaze onto her body. This visualisation of the lyrics moves the focus away from the sexualisation of the female body and subverts twerking as a dominant German imagination of Black femininity inspired by Southern US-American dance traditions.[41] Faced with contradictory notions of Black womanhood, Nura 'flips the script' and re-appropriates misogynistic, sexualised, and racist images of Black femininity.[42] Instead of subjugating herself to those stereotypes, Nura is confidently appropriating the Jezebel figure, a stereotype originating from US-American slavery that imagined Black women as hypersexual temptresses,[43] in the tradition of American rap and pop music. In their songs, artists Beyoncé, Meghan Thee Stallion, Nicki Minaj,[44] and Cardi B[45] confidently appropriate the Jezebel. Nicki Minaj and Cardi B, for instance, use the legacy of the Jezebel figure to propagate and profit from a new beauty ideal that is centred around (artificially) big buttocks.[46] 'Schwarz' echoes those strategies of self-expression, sexual empowerment, and adopts self-presentation techniques of the digital age.[47] Thus, 'Schwarz' advocates for a broader understanding of Black womanhood inspired by US-American rap music role models and offers alternative constructions of Black German femininity. This also includes taking a firm stance against right-wing extremism.

Nazis raus: Fighting Nationalism and Right-Wing Extremism

Despite the rap song's overall ironic and sarcastic attitude, 'Schwarz' stands firmly against nationalism and right-wing extremism. The video situates itself in the contemporary German political context by opening with a disclaimer that ironically informs possible Nazi viewers and other sympathisers of right-wing populist parties, such as Pegida, the AfD party, or Neo Nazi groups, that the video will showcase a diverse Black crowd:

In den folgenden Szenen sind verschiedenste Schwarze Menschen zu sehen. Nazis und anderen Sympathisanten von rechtpopulistischen Parteien wird deshalb dringend davon abgeraten sich dieses Video anzuschauen.	In the following scenes, a wide variety of Black people can be seen. Nazis and other sympathisers of right-wing populist parties are therefore strongly advised not to watch this video.

The note plays with popular right-wing extremist prejudices about Blackness, such as crime, violence, and aggressiveness, and ironically frames its presence in the music video as upsetting or disturbing ('wird deshalb dringend davon abgeraten sich dieses Video anzuschauen', 'strongly advised not to watch this video'). However, instead of framing BPOC people as social threats, the disclaimer has the opposite effect and portrays anti-Black racism and right-wing populism as unreasonable, absurd, ridiculous, and dangerous. The note mimics xenophobic and racist sentiments in German culture after millions of migrants arrived in Germany from Middle Eastern and Northern African war and conflict zones in 2015.

The first-person speaker confidently addresses right-wing extremists' obsession about race by asking the rhetorical question: 'Was willst denn du mit deinem Rassenhass? / Ich bin lieber Schwarz als todesblass' ('What do you want with your racial hatred? / I'd rather be Black than pale as death'). The term *Rassenhass* (racial hatred) evokes associations with the racialised language and racial ideologies employed by the fascist Nazi regime that led to the Holocaust during World War II in which Jewish people, members of the Sinti and Roma communities, political dissidents, queer people, people with disabilities, as well as Black people were killed. The seldom-used adjective *todesblass* (pale as death) in the second line creates a semantic link between whiteness and the deathly consequences that constructions of race have had and still have for people of colour in Germany.

The lyrics return the white nationalist gaze onto the racialised subject. In the final part of 'Schwarz', the speaker addresses the double standard of Neo Nazis when she raps:

Nazis essen heimlich Döner	Nazis secretly eat kebab
Weil sie sich nicht trauen – Trauen!	Because they don't dare – Dare!
Schicken diese Hurensöhne immer ihre Frauen – Frauen!	These sons of b***s always send their wives – Wives!

The line 'Nazis essen heimlich Döner' (Nazis secretly eat kebab) is a humorous anti-Nazi protest slogan used by leftist political groups. The line ridicules Nazis by claiming that despite their racist beliefs they secretly indulge in ethnic cuisine, such as Döner Kebab, but send their wives to get it for them because they do not dare to do it themselves. These lines climax in an even harsher, provocative lyrical attack against racist ideologies:

Eure braune Scheisse riecht mies nach Dreck	Your brown shit smells badly like dirt
Ich bin Schwarz, ich bin Schwarz, es geht niemals weg	I'm Black, I'm Black, it will never go away

The tautology 'braune Scheisse' (brown shit) contains a double meaning: the adjective *braun* refers to the political ideology of the Third Reich since the colour is commonly associated with Nazism and the NS-Regime in Germany. The colloquial derogative *Scheisse* refers not only to Nazi ideology but also quite literally to their brown excreta. Thus, the lyrics strongly reinforce SXTN's rejection of racist Nazi ideologies and right-wing extremism.

Visually these rap lines are underlined by a scene during which Nura sits on a toilet and is obviously disgusted by the smell of her own faeces. While she raps 'Ich bin schwarz, Ich bin schwarz, es geht niemals weg' ('I'm Black, I'm Black, it will never go away'), the camera zooms in to how she disgustedly flushes the toilet while her excreta are in fact a *Weisswurst* sausage (white sausage), a traditional Southern German dish. The sausage symbolises the state of Bavaria, which often epitomises Germany to travellers and outsiders of German culture and is known for the state's politically conservative culture, nationalist tendencies, and historic exceptionalism.

This revelation creates an unexpected plot twist which is marked by a contradiction between the verbal and visual layers: whereas the lyrics talk about the Nazi's brown faeces, the camera shows Nura's white ones in the toilet. The *Weisswurst* becomes a symbol for the rejection of white supremacy, German national pride, and exclusive *Leitkultur* (leading culture). While this stereotypical symbol of a white nationalist *Leitkultur* that excludes BPOC and their contributions to the multicultural German society is disappearing in the toilet, the lyrics claim that Black, Afrodiasporic, and identities of colour will prevail in German culture, thus self-confidently proclaiming their position in a multicultural, multi-ethnic, and racially diverse German culture.

Nura's new take on contemporary German identity also becomes apparent in her personal statements and activism. In her 2020 published autobiography, she explains that she wanted to write a song that confidently messes around with racism instead of being sad about it.[48] Nura also performed the song at the 'Wir sind mehr' concert after nationalistic anti-immigrant protests erupted in the Eastern German city of Chemnitz in August 2018.[49] 'Schwarz' therefore continues hip-hop's tradition of protest, power, and resistance which started with US-American conscious rap music artists, such as Public Enemy, Queen Latifah and N.W.A. The video also reinforces the tradition of (male-dominated) political activism in German rap groups, as, for instance, Advanced Chemistry, Brothers Keepers, Megaloh, and Kraftklub, who have released songs and organised concerts in the wake of racialised violence and extremist attacks. Hence, Nura adopts a self-confident and assertive attitude to make a stand against racism, misogyny, hyper-sexualisation, extremism, and nationalism and positively affirm her identity as a Black German woman in contemporary German rap music and larger (popular) culture.

Conclusion

'Schwarz' uses a broad variety of cultural, musical, and political references from NDW songs to *Weisswurst* to negotiate Black identity in German culture. Through deconstructing dominant notions of Blackness and womanhood, remixing German popular music, and carrying on hip-hop's political project, the music video claims its rightful place in the German popular music canon. The video addresses the issue of Othering in German society with a humorous tone and rejects white-dominated notions of Germanness. Thus, 'Schwarz' positions itself against Nazis, racist ideologies, and nationalist tendencies, while empowering migrants, people of colour, and particularly Afrodiasporic Germans. Nura is part of a new generation of German rap music royalty, which includes artists such as BSMG, OG Keemo, and Leila Akinyi. They showcase a new self-esteem in demanding that larger German culture face its history of anti-Black racism rooted in its 'forgotten' colonial past and colour-evasive thinking. They call on white German culture to take action to abolish racial oppression, acknowledge the realities of a multicultural and multiracial Germany marked by immigration, and reflect on their manifold ties to the African diaspora.

Notes

1. Kofi Yakpo. '"Denn ich bin kein Einzelfall, sondern einer von vielen": Afro-deutsche Rapkünstler in der Hip-Hop-Gründerzeit'. *Bundeszentrale für politische Bildung* (10 August 2004), p. 2. www.bpb.de/gesellschaft/migration/afrikanische-diaspora/59580/afro-deutsche-rapkuenstler?p=all [Accessed 10 May 2020].

2. SXTN. 'SXTN – Ich bin schwarz (Official Video)', *YouTube*, uploaded by SXTN, 16 September 2016, www.youtube.com/watch?v=zU958I4Iqm4 [Accessed 26 March 2022]. From now on we will refer to the video as 'Schwarz'.
3. Anti-Socialization Program.
4. Kimberlé Crenshaw 'Das Zusammenwirken von *Race* und Gender ins Zentrum rücken' in Natasha A. Kelly (ed.), *Schwarzer Feminismus: Grundlagentexte* (Unrast, 2019): 145–186.
   Malte Friedrich and Gabriele Klein. *Is this real? Die Kultur des HipHop* (Suhrkamp, 2003).
   Sina A. Nitzsche and Walter Grünzweig, eds. *Hip-Hop in Europe: Cultural Identities and Transnational Flows* (Zürich, Lit, 2013).
   Heidi Süß *Eine Szene Im Wandel? Rap-Männlichkeiten zwischen Tradition und Transformation* (Frankfurt and New York: Campus, 2021).
   Heidi Süß (ed.) *Rap & Geschlecht: Inszenierungen von Geschlecht in Deutschlands beliebtester Musikkultur* (Weinheim: Beltz Juventa, 2021).
5. Justin Williams 'Intertextuality, Sampling, and Copyright' in Justin Williams (ed.) *The Cambridge Companion to Hip-Hop* (Cambridge University Press, 2015): 206–220.
6. David Chemeta 'HipHop und Postkolonialismus: Sprachgebrauch und "migrant rap"'. *Recherches germaniques* 48 (2018), http://journals.openedition.org/rg/476; DOI: https://doi.org/10.4000/rg.476 [Accessed 4 June 2019].
   Süß Heidi and Marc Dietrich *Rap & Rassismus Zur Aushandlung Von Rassismus in Musikvideos (Szene-) Medien und Social Media* (Weinheim: Beltz, 2023).
   Fatima El-Tayeb '"If You Can't Pronounce My Name, You Can Just Call Me Pride": Afro-German Activism, Gender and Hip Hop'. *Gender & History*, 15/3 (2003): 460–486.
   Ina Hagen-Jeske '*Zu weiß für die Schwarzen und zu schwarz für die Weißen': Der künstlerische Umgang mit Identität, Rassismus und Hybridität bei Samy Deluxe und B-Tight* (Marburg: Tectum, 2016).
   Sina A. Nitzsche '"besinne mich unserer Pflicht, geb' dir Geschichtsunterricht": Die Vermittlung postkolonialer Wissensdiskurse auf dem Rapalbum Platz an der Sonne (2017)' in Dominique Matthes and Hilke Pallesen (eds.), *Bilder von Lehrer*innenberuf und Schule: (Mediale) Entwürfe zwischen Produktion, Rezeption und Aneignung*. Studien zur Schul- und Bildungsforschung (Wiesbaden: Springer, 2022): 157–178. https://doi.org/10.1007/978-3-658-32564-0_8.
   J. Griffith Rollefson *Flip the Script: European Hip Hop and the Politics of Postcoloniality* (University of Chicago Press, 2017).
   Laura I. K. Spilker '*Wer hat Angst vor der Schwarzen Frau?' The Construction of Afro-German Femininity in Rap Videos*. (Dortmund: Technische Universität Dortmund, 2020) unpublished Bachelor's thesis.
7. Yakpo (2004): p. 2.

8. Ibid.
9. Ibid., p. 3.
10. Susan Arndt 'Kolonialismus, Rassismus und Sprache. Kritische Betrachtungen der deutschen Afrikaterminologie'. *Bundeszentrale für politische Bildung* (30 July 2004). www.bpb.de/gesellschaft/migration/afrikanische-diaspora/59407/afrikaterminologie?p=all. Accessed 10 May 2020, p. 4.
11. Rollefson (2017): p. 9.
12. Jannis Androutsopoulos (ed.) *HipHop: Globale Kultur – lokale Praktiken* (Bielefeld: Transcript, 2003); Heidi Süß 'Sex(ismus) ohne Grund? Zum Zusammenhang von Rap und Geschlecht'. *Bundeszentrale für politische Bildung* (23 February 2018): 1–12, p. 6. www.bpb.de/apuz/265104/zusammenhang-von-rap-und-geschlecht?p=all [Accessed 10 December 2019].
13. Sina A. Nitzsche and Laura I. K. Spilker '"Ich bin nicht so eine, doch genau so eine bin ich": Shirin David, sexpositives Selbstmarketing und die Aneignung der Jezebel-Ikonografie auf Instagram' in Heidi Süß (ed.) *Rap & Geschlecht: Inszenierungen von Geschlecht in Deutschlands beliebter Musikkultur* (Weinheim: Beltz Juventa, 2021) 26–45, p. 27.
14. Rollefson (2017): p. 57, Fn. 8.
15. Hutchinson, quoted in Nancy P. Nenno 'Reading the "Schwarz" in the "Schwarz-Rot-Gold": Black German Studies in the 21st Century'. *TRANSIT* 10/2 (2016): 1–8, p. 3.
16. May Ayim, Katharina Oguntoye, and Dagmar Schulz, eds. *Farbe bekennen: Afro-deutsche Frauen auf den Spuren ihrer Geschichte* (Berlin: Orlando-Frauenverlag, 1986) p. 135.
17. Ibid.
18. Muna AnNisa Aikins, Teresa Bremberger, Joshua Kwesi Aikins, Daniel Gyamerah, Deniz Yıldırım-Caliman *Afrozensus 2020: Perspektiven, Anti-Schwarze Rassismuserfahrungen und Engagement Schwarzer, afrikanischer und afrodiasporischer Menschen in Deutschland* (Berlin, 2021). The report also showed that, among Black people, those who are affected by multiple forms of marginalisation such as non-binary, inter and trans people, people with disabilities and people with two African or Afro-Diasporic parents were more likely to be affected by discrimination.
19. Aikins et al. (2021): pp. 214–216, 224.
20. Rollefson (2017): p. 68; Tyron Ricketts quoted in Mirjam Ratmann 'Is the German film racist?' *Fluter* (18 May 2020). www.fluter.de/rassismus-deutsche-filme-serien [Accessed 3 October 2023].
21. Street rappers/street rap, the German equivalent of gangsta rap.
22. Yakpo (2004): p. 4.
23. Foreign in One's Own Country, 1992; Advanced Chemistry. 'Fremd im eigenen Land'. *Advanced Chemistry*, MZEE Records, 1992.
24. Yakpo (2004): p. 3.

25. Moya Bailey *Misogynoir Transformed: Black Women's Digital Resistance* (New York: New York University Press, 2021).
26. Alice Hasters *Was Weiße Menschen nicht über Rassismus hören wollen aber wissen sollten* (Hanserblau, 2019) p. 104.
27. Hasters (2019): pp. 151, 140.
28. From now on we will refer to the video as 'Spass'.
29. New German Wave; in short, NDW.
30. Barbara Hornberger '"Ich will Spaß, ich geb Gas": German Pop between Fun and Subversion' in Mark Duffett and Beate Peter (eds.), *Popular Music and Automobiles* (London: Bloomsbury Academic, 2020): 111–118, p. 112 DOI: https://doi.org/10.5040/9781501352331.0012.
31. Schaal.
32. Hornberger (2020): p. 114.
33. Ibid., p. 118.
34. Ace Hood ft. Rick Ross and Future 'Bugatti' *Trials and Tribulations* (Cash Money Records, 2013); Lil Wayne ft. Boo 'Bugatti (Freestyle)' *Dedication 5* (Young Money, 2013); Olexesh 'Schwitze im Bugatti' *Masta* Universal URBAN (2015); Summer Cem 'Neue Bugatti' *Babas, Barbies & Bargeld* (Seven Days Music, 2013).
35. Dominik Djialeu 'Tic Tac Toe war eine der progressivsten und coolsten Bands' *Jetzt* (2 March 2021). www.jetzt.de/musik/tic-tac-toe-warum-die-band-noch-heute-aktuell-ist [Accessed 25 March 2022].
36. Margaret Hunter 'Shake It, Baby, Shake It: Consumption and the New Gender Relation in Hip Hop' *Sociological Perspectives* 54/1 (2011): 15–36, p. 18. https://doi.org/10.1525/sop.2011.54.1.15; Hasters (2019) p. 147.
37. Hasters (2019): pp. 146–147.
38. Ibid., p. 146.
39. Patricia Hill Collins *Black Sexual Politics* (New York and London: Routledge, 2004) p. 120.
40. Hunter (2011): p. 25.
41. Kyra D Gaunt '*YouTube*, Twerking & You: Context Collapse and the Handheld Co-Presence of Black Girls and Miley Cyrus'. *Journal of Popular Music Studies* 27/3 (2015): 244–273, p. 248.
42. Rana A. Emerson '"Where My Girls At?" Negotiating Black Womanhood in Music Videos'. *Gender and Society* 16/1 (2002): 115–135, p. 128.
43. Hasters (2019) p. 152; Stefanie K. Menrath and Clara Völker 'Rap-Models. Das schmückende Beiwerk' in Anjela Schischmanjan und Michaela Wuensch (eds.) *Female hiphop: Realness, Roots und Rap Models* (Ventil Verlag, 2007): 9–32, pp. 24–25.
44. Nicki Minaj 'Anaconda' *YouTube*, uploaded by Nicki Minaj, 19 August 2014, www.youtube.com/watch?v=LDZX4ooRsWs [Accessed 23 September 2023].

45. Cardi B. 'WAP – feat. Megan Thee Stallion [Official Music Video]', YouTube, uploaded by Cardi B, 7 August 2020, www.youtube.com/watch?v=hsm4po TWjMs [Accessed 23 September 2023].
46. Hasters (2019): pp. 152–153.
47. Gaunt (2015): p. 249.
48. Nura Habib Omer *Weißt du, was ich meine? Vom Asylheim in die Charts* (Ullstein, 2020) p. 166.
49. Omer (2020): p. 184.

15 | The Art of Capping

Exploring Digital Cloutchasing Strategy of Black Male Youth in Chicago's Drill Rap Scene

JABARI EVANS

Introduction

Prior literature has detailed the role social media has played in the popularity of the Drill music genre, a subgenre of gangsta rap that was born in Chicago's underground hip-hop scene in early 2010s. This work has highlighted how social media allowed gang-affiliated male youth in Chicago to both carefully manage their street reputations but also build sustainable music careers through their platformed creation. Though many scholars have generally theorized on the communication of Black youth in digital spaces, academic work on Drill has generally not sought artist perspectives about their relational labor. Using observation and interviews with Drill artists, their managers and other support workers, I examine relational practices of Black male youth on social media. I describe their work on social media toward acquiring "clout" – a digital form of influence self-described by emerging musicians as allowing them to leverage digital tools in building social and professional status, amplify authenticity, cultivate connections with fans, and connect to friends and other cultural producers. Particularly, I detail the practice of "capping" (strategic deception, exaggeration of toughness, desirability to women and financial wealth) as a relational strategy that respondents utilized to acquire clout. To conclude, I argue capping is an example of how race, class, gender, and geography influence the digital interactions of young people and how the social media practices of Drill rappers add significantly to the understanding of the counterpublics arising from globalizing social media.

Background

Social media is now critical to the promotional practices of musical artists, who must navigate how to construct artistic identity and communicate a personal brand as a part of their career path.[1] Logics of social media platforms (likes, followers, subscribers, and re-posts) are now vital to measuring a musician's popularity, as talent scouts and record label executives increasingly rely on social media metrics to identify the next stars.[2] Social media provide launching pads for burgeoning artists to speak directly to fans, building personal relationships with them, letting them share in their creative process, and aiding in their promotion and other business matters.[3] Though previous academic work has explored the digital practices of many kinds of influencers and creative workers, it has had less to say about the urban poor involved in hip-hop music, a unique context in which creators are innovators with digital tools but typically not viewed as digital experts. Focusing on male Drill rap musicians (Drillers) in the Chicago hip-hop scene, this chapter examines social media strategy from the perspective of people prominent in the scene. In seeking to understand the strategies Chicago's Drillers use to build their profiles, I address the following research questions. Firstly, what is the most popular visibility labor strategy used among Drillers? And secondly, how, if at all, are their strategies shaped by race, location, and technology?

In answering these questions, I utilized multiple qualitative methods to collect data. This data consisted of interviews and in-person fieldwork throughout Chicago, as well as observation of the social media profiles of key members of the Drill scene. Initially, I recruited interview participants through snowball sampling. Within months, I also began employing a virtual variation of this method: the first author used his Instagram and Twitter pages to offer brief information about this research and encouraged rappers to contact him to be interviewed for the project. I conducted fifteen in-depth interviews with musicians and artist managers self-identifying as part of the Drill scene. All participants have built massive audiences through social media, creating successful, sustainable, reasonably affluent careers akin to those of their peers affiliated with large music corporations. I recorded and transcribed interviews, before analyzing them. I compared identity performances across data types, comparing what I saw in person with what was on social media and what was said in interviews. Subjects who chose to speak entirely anonymously are marked with an asterisk by their names.

Throughout my findings, I argue that Drillers, Black male youth who are often understood as deprived, disadvantaged, or otherwise lacking, take advantage of the subcultural capital they do have with savvy social media engagement that allows them to amass urban cultural influence or "digital clout."[4] However, by capping, or exaggerating violent nature or material wealth for street credibility, visibility often came in ways that were dangerous to their well-being. This, in turn, creates ambivalence over their tactics for attention and fame. Ultimately, this chapter illuminates how Drillers use vernacular creativity[5] to articulate a sense of place and loyalty to that place's public reputation on their own terms and in their own words.

The Emergence of Chicago's Drill Rap Scene

For the last two decades, Chicago's hip-hop community has been remarkably successful by way of social media content and DIY digital music distribution tactics,[6] becoming a burgeoning Web 2.0 hip-hop mecca.[7] Simultaneously, the city has been in the national spotlight for street violence since 2012 when it was deemed the nation's "murder capital" based on FBI data.[8] This has created a scene where most of the hip-hop artists have historically been split between producing either gangsta rap or socially conscious music that speaks to the nuances of Black experiences in urban communities.[9] However, many of the more recent popular Chicago rap artists, like Lil' Durk, G Herbo, King Von, Polo G, and Chief Keef, are from some of the poorest, blighted, disinvested Black community areas of concentrated violence on Chicago's South Side and they have primarily used violent street-gang narratives about these neighborhoods to rise to prominent stature.

This group of artists along with many others formed what is known as "Drill Music," a subgenre of gangsta rap known for its grim, violent depictions of Chicago street life, especially the Englewood neighborhood.[10] The most popular Chicago Drill rappers and their local fans represent a newer form of music subculture initiated by Black youth who have experienced a lifetime of hyper-segregation, chronic poverty, poor education in overcrowded classrooms, and a regular loss of loved ones to both prison cells and gunshots.[11] Thus, Drill music functions as a way for poor Black youth to gain individual agency of their bodies, buck the authority of a racist and neoliberal capitalist society, and commodify the harsh and dangerous realities of their everyday lives, which are clearly at odds with the positive promotional images often advertised from the City of Chicago Mayor's office.[12]

Within Drill, a narrow range of hypermasculine cultural images (e.g. thugs, players of women), characterized by toughness, flamboyance, and sexual prowess, serves as a "standard" for authenticity. Forrest Stuart[13] argues that this standard practice has become more exaggerated for rappers because the capacities of social media disrupt the key impression management practices associated with the "code of the street," and confirming someone's authenticity now includes doing intensive cross-referencing of their digital footprint with the narratives in their music. Stuart has previously described digital efforts of Drillers as "hope labor,"[14] noting that the work they put in may echo the "aspirational labor" of Brooke Erin Duffy's beauty bloggers in its ambitions of fame and financial reward.[15] Duffy has written on how aspirational labor is the pursuit of creative activities that hold the promise of social and economic capital; yet the reward system for these aspirants is highly uneven.[16] For these Chicago youth, though, digital labor can also provide very real economic, social, and emotional benefits for their literal survival.

Findings: Capping for Clout

Previous research has shown that young people increasingly feel pressure to project a favorable version of themselves to their social media audiences.[17] This ideal self is something that these youth are continually re-negotiating, and often they reinvent themselves on the platforms they participate in. In the hip-hop music industry, rappers have historically used violence and misogyny as a marketing tool. They accomplish this in two ways: (1) publicly displaying extreme wealth, which symbolizes status and authority, and (2) an overwhelming display of womens' bodies as a requisite component of self-promotion.[18] In hip-hop studies, scholars have described this standard for authenticity as relating to demographic aspects including cultural Blackness, "being hard" heterosexual masculinity, hypersexual femininity, and coming from "the streets."[19]

Complemented by music and lyrics, hip-hop's visual images in creator culture provide a dynamic/immersive representation that is ubiquitous and cultivates a global youth culture which views the glorification of money and violence as necessary to gain respect in everyday life.[20] This was exemplified by the practice of self-staging that they called "capping." Importantly, capping usually amplified the seeds of authentic self-representation to make themselves seem as important and influential in this hard scene as they could. One of the most common ways to cap was to post pictures tagging places and @-replies[21] to people even when they weren't there/with them at that exact moment in order to reveal gang affiliations and/or residence in a neighborhood.

Beyond exaggerating relational ties to peers with more clout, respondents also often exaggerated their violent nature and material wealth on social media, posing for pictures holding large sums of cash or expensive champagne, sporting diamond necklaces, wearing monogram logo luxury brand clothing and brandishing guns, while often boasting about their crew, neighborhood, and gang affiliations in the captions of their posts. When asked why his artists often participated in this, artist manager Peeda Pan explained:

We spend time in Miami at places like Liv and though part of the mystique being there and walking to the front of the line while others can't get in, but other part of it is that brag about being there on Twitter, post a geotagged photo of all the women and bottles on Instagram, and go live on Snapchat from the section smoking a blunt. People have to see the tree fall or it never happened. We have an intern whose job is to make sure people see the tree fall.

Here, Peeda detailed the possession of power (business ownership), prowess (beautiful women), and paper (money) as the traits that earned bragging rights for his artists. In explaining the social media tactics of Chief Keef, a figure whose career notoriously blew up using social media, Peeda was describing what Rein et al. would call "sensation staging,"[22] or multi-layered communication with an audience through one piece of curated audiovisual content. Additionally, he hints here that the mystique of his artist's private life was made more intensified by the online content that they created. In explaining this rationale of capping, renowned driller King Louie's manager Big Homie Doe stated that most Drill artists originally saw themselves as "gaming" the public at large for clout on social media:

There's definitely a strategy to how we use social media. Real Drill was about doing stuff to others for money without getting caught. We never really let people know exactly where we were at while we are there. We might take photos with big ass guns and a wad of money in an alley but we wouldn't share our location ...

Artist Big Ballin[23] explained to me why he decided that he (and his clique) should exaggerate their gang involvement to gain more attention for their music:

Cappin' is a weird thing to me. I don't really be cappin but it is entertainment. I just emphasize a certain part of myself that will get the most attention. I used to have photo shoots in the alley with different outfits holding a big ass gun. If a young ass kid posts different pictures everyday, with a different gun, people gonna believe it's mine, right?

Shortly after this statement, Homie then showed me a screenshot of his newsfeed, where he was calling out "Opps" (rival gangs) online often in the caption, using a recycled photo of him holding his older cousin's semiautomatic weapon at a music video shoot. The photo had over 5,000 likes on Instagram. I asked him why he chose to post a photo holding a gun he did not own, and he spoke to me about how capping helped his perceived authenticity:

We gotta carry guns for the Internet. I did it for folks on the Southside to continue to respect me. (Social media and broadcasting) Stuff can be awkward because it can look like you're doing what you're doing for clout but in this era, if you don't show it, you lose.

In another example of capping, Marco Rackz[24] posted a picture on Facebook of himself at a video shoot with several local strippers that he paid to be in his music video. However, the caption of the picture gave the impression that the women were at his house hanging out in bikinis. In defending this strategy, Marko confided:

Big ass guns, lots of pretty chicks, money and tons of dope smoke. That's what you find on my page. That's how you show your clout. This is just part of what people assume your life is like as a rapper. I found the cutest strippers on Instagram and told them I'd pay them 700 bucks each to be in my music video. Drinks, weed and food included. More and more clout. Who cares how you get it? Once, you get that million dollar deal, no one cares if you was capping on IG (Instagram)! (laughs)

For respondents like Marco and Big Ballin, a financial investment in capping was worth doing because it solidified his digital reputation, maintained this street credibility, and amplified the narratives in that he wanted to drive home in his music. The chances of being called out as inauthentic seemed insignificant for Marko and he also didn't express much ambivalence about his usage of guns, drugs, and women's bodies being exaggerated to symbolize fearlessness, status, and authority. To that very point, rapper Young Benz described capping not as a way to be an exaggerated version of themselves but as an opportunity to, as he described, "spit in the world's face":

I started getting views and then I realized I should just go head and do this for real. Nobody is one thing 24 hours a day. Most days, I be just chilling in the studio or with my daughter, but that shit is boring. No one wants to see that. Like, if that means posing with money or going on live or the snap (Snapchat) when I'm smoking dope with females . . . I give them what they want to see.

In the music genre of hip-hop, self-aggrandizing and the usage of women's naked bodies as tools of status are germane to the marketing practices of the most popular male artists (Fitts, 2008). Though it garnered many drillers' hypervisibility online, the long-term cost of performing the role of the hyper-masculine, violent, materialistic, street infamous and/or sexually promiscuous rapper through capping is that the details of artists' content are hyper-analyzed and surveilled by rivals in ways that can set them up for negative offline encounters. DJ Onyx[25] spoke about recent shootings of many prominent Drill artists during our interview:

FBG Duck just got killed in downtown Chicago. That was partially because he was bragging and sharing his location to his enemies. (Lil) Reese got shot in his neck. King Louie was shot in the head. (Chief) Keef was almost killed outside the W hotel in New York. King Von got killed in Atlanta the same way. Posting money and jewelry with their location tagged and putting disrespectful captions in their posts. Bragging about having sex with another person's baby mama. Authenticity is one thing, self-sabotage is another. People get robbed and killed over posting too much.

In seeking to escape a life of poverty, the "street hustler" image can become a business-targeted persona when curated in tandem with an arguably authentic backstory. For many interviewees, the logic of capping was simple: sensationalism and conspicuous consumption boosted their followers, so they did it at all costs. At the same time this also meant strategically curating their social media stunts to appear authentic to their audiences. In using social media, respondents demonstrated a sophisticated form of self-efficacy rooted in a critique of racial capitalism, leveraging media interest in "Chiraq" to tell the story from their own deeper perspectives. One can read this story in two ways: the first emphasizes the affordances of the technology which enables marginalized Black youth to gain visibility through exploitation of stereotypes; the second emphasizes the social processes – the ways these marginalized Black teenagers in Chicago organized themselves around the shared purpose of representing their neighborhood, their crew, and their city – becoming political symbols of community in the context of a networked culture. Both readings add to existing work[26] on how local authenticity is broadcasted to global publics and how multi-national reputation is built and maintained by rappers seeking to forge careers in the music industry.

Overall, I found that though capping of these participants was an exercise that gave them local fame and clout, it also created ambivalence about how their work often required them to disregard their standards for attention. What I see in my observations of these youth, is that despite the attention provided by their self-presentation on social media they still felt like they had nothing to lose in exaggerating their street personas online. They talked incessantly about being highly surveilled, highly policed, highly judged, highly stereotyped, in addition to being denigrated, discriminated against, and, on many levels, dispossessed. Because of that, participants felt that at the very least, they could chase online visibility as a possible pathway into the music industry and mainstream celebrity.

Implications for Practice

The media teaches young black males that the patriarchal man is a predator, that only the strong and the violent survive. – bell hooks[27]

Using Chicago's hip-hop scene as a case study, this chapter identifies capping as a unique strategy of visibility and relational labor for Black male youth in Drill rap. What's specific to this case is a particular implication of race, technology, and geography within this practice that garnered the most clout for the participants. Artists who amassed the most clout mobilized (and exploited) explicitly the very dire social conditions they faced to forge their product. The ironies run deep: these artists turn the very social costs of urban poverty, violence, and social isolation into assets, and they place this enterprising "conversion narrative" at the heart of their imagery. Illustrating Robin Kelley's[28] suggestion that capitalism is both the greatest foe and greatest friend to young Black men facing deindustrialization, the personas of Drillers critique the options of dead-end service sector jobs and respectable middle-class upward mobility by staking out careers in gangsta rap through social media platforms. Additionally, respondents followed the trend of prior work on the gangsta rap music industry[29] that claims that artists turn the so-called deficiencies of their locales as assets to their storytelling, personal branding, and claims to authenticity. Likewise, if Black youth in Chicago also exist in a state of danger and are also considered to be disposable, subhuman menaces to society, then the chase for digital clout and careers related to social media influence becomes a way for them to regain ownership of their humanity. Ultimately, participants suggested that the detriment of capping didn't outweigh its potential for entrepreneurship, economic mobility, and sustained microcelebrity. Considering these findings in the global context, this is very much in line with what Malcolm James[30] found in his study of entrepreneurialism of Black male Drillers in East London and what Lee and colleagues found in their investigation of a popular Australian Drill rap group.[31]

However, I want to emphasize that I am not seeking to reinforce "new racism," in which Black Americans' inherent strength and will to overcome structural racism are re-framed in ways that glorify personal resilience and resourcefulness.[32] It is without a doubt that the practice of capping by Drillers is very much adding to the ways Black Americans and their communities are pathologized and stereotyped in negative ways. However, capping also is expanding and innovating on the types of digital participation and relational labor that musicians rely upon to further their careers. In beginning to understand the labor practices of these youth, I suggest that highlighting different types of digital participation and relational labor is as important as understanding how digital technologies have shaped the marketplace of attention.

As an essential source of Black cultural production, hip-hop culture innovates, disseminates, and commodifies experiences from the margins of Black society. As such, gaining the artist's perspectives on the nature of their work in digital spaces holds huge implications on the study of Black technoculture. For this and other reasons, theories of cultural production need to make the intertwined oppressions associated with race and ethnicity far more central than they have been until now – and these oppressions need somehow to be theorized in relation to power dynamics related to class, gender, and other factors.[33] Furthermore, as Hesmondhalgh and Saha also argue, practices of production are also significant in their own right. This study suggests that the practice of capping has unique insights into the ways Black youth seek to overcome marginalization and scarcity of resources. As new forms of racialization made possible by the Internet and social networking technologies formulates the digital street, Black artists/creators are forced to figure out how best to project an image of African-American identity to gain visibility. Future work will be necessary to explore how Black youth in urban America manage creating content for a mass media environment that has often rendered their lives disposable yet deemed their style aesthetics and cultural practices as a commodity spectacle. It is only this type of critical empirical work that will serve to show the kind of complexities in which power and inequality work for or against Black cultural producers seeking a place within modern creator culture.

Notes

1. Jo Haynes and Lee Marshall (2018). "Beats and tweets: Social media in the careers of independent musicians," *New Media & Society*, 20(5), 1973–1993; David Hesmondhalgh (2021). "Is music streaming bad for musicians? Problems of evidence and argument," *New Media & Society*, 23(12), 3593–3615.

2. Jean Burgess and Nancy K. Baym (2020). *Twitter: A Biography.* New York: New York University Press.
3. Nancy K. Baym (2018). *Playing to the Crowd: Musicians, Audiences, and the Intimate Work of Connection* (Vol. 14). New York: New York University Press.
4. Nancy K. Baym and Jabari M. Evans (2022). "The audacity of clout (chasing): Digital strategies of Black youth in Chicago DIY hip-hop," *International Journal of Communication*, 16, 2699–2687.
5. Jean Burgess Hearing ordinary voices: Cultural studies, vernacular creativity and digital storytelling. *Continuum*, 20(2), 201–214.
6. Ali Colleen Neff (2018). "Digital, underground: Black aesthetics, Hip-hop digitalities, and youth creativity the global south," in J. L. Oakes and J. D. Burton (eds.), *Oxford Handbook of Hip-Hop Studies*, New York: Oxford University Press, 1–28.
7. Geoff Harkness (2013). "Gangs and gangsta rap in Chicago: A microscenes perspective," *Poetics*, 41(2), 151–176; Natalie Y. Moore (2016) *The South Side: A Portrait of Chicago and American Segregation.* London: Macmillan; Forrest Stuart (2019). "Code of the tweet: Urban gang violence in the social media age," *Social Problems*, 67(2), 191–207.
8. Philip Sherwell (2013 September 13). "Chicago: The Murder Capital of America," *The Telegraph*, www.telegraph.co.uk/news/worldnews/northamerica/usa/10320186/Chicago-the-murder-capital-of-America.html [Accessed November 22, 2023].
9. Harkness, 2013.
10. Stuart, 2019.
11. Jabari Evans (2020). "Connecting Black youth to critical media literacy through hip hop making in the music classroom," *Journal of Popular Music Education*, 4(3), 277–293.
12. See Erin Harkey (2021). "Revitalizing our city's arts and culture scene is essential to our post-pandemic recovery," *Chicago Business*, www.chicagobusiness.com/forum-ideas-culture/city-chicago-will-invest-our-citys-creative-economy [Accessed November 22, 2023].
13. Forrest Stuart (2020). *Ballad of the Bullet: Gangs, Drill Music, and the Power of Online Infamy.* Princeton University Press.
14. Ibid.
15. Brooke E. Duffy (2017). *(Not) Getting Paid to Do What You Love: Gender, Social Media, and Aspirational Work.* Yale University Press.
16. Brooke E. Duffy (2015). "Gendering the labor of social media production," *Feminist Media Studies*, 15(4), 710–714.
17. Alice Marwick and danah boyd (2011). "To see and be seen: Celebrity practice on Twitter," *Convergence*, 17(2), 139–158.
18. Karisman Roberts-Douglass and Harriet Curtis-Boles (2013). "Exploring positive masculinity development in African American men: A retrospective study," *Psychology of Men & Masculinity*, 14(1), 7.

19. Low, B., Tan, E., and Celemencki, J. (2013). "The limits of 'keepin' it real': The challenges for critical Hip-Hop pedagogies of discourses of authenticity," in M. L. Hill and E. Petchauer (Eds.), *Schooling Hip-Hop: Expanding Hip-Hop Based Education across the Curriculum* (1st ed., pp. 118–136). New York: Teachers College Press.
20. Malcolm James (2015). "Nihilism and urban multiculture in outer East London," *The Sociological Review*, 63(3), 699–719.
21. @ Replying, commonly used on social media platforms like X, formerly Twitter, and Instagram, is a way to address or mention a specific user by using the "@" symbol followed by their username. It allows you to direct a message to someone, respond to their post, or engage in a conversation with them publicly. Geo-tagging involves adding location information, such as latitude and longitude coordinates or the name of a place, to a digital file, such as a photo or a social media post.
22. Rein, I., Kotler, P., Hamlin, M., & Stoller, M. (2006). *High Visibility: Transforming Your Personal and Professional Brand* (3rd ed.) McGraw-Hill, 70.
23. Name anonymized.
24. Name anonymized.
25. Name anonymized.
26. Geoff Harkness (2012). "True school: Situational authenticity in Chicago's hip-hop underground," *Cultural Sociology*, 6(3), 283–298; Anthony Kwame Harrison (2008), "Racial authenticity in rap music and hip hop," *Sociology Compass*, 2(6), 1783–1800; Kembrew McLeod (1999), "Authenticity within hip-hop and other cultures threatened with assimilation," *Journal of Communication*, 49(4), 134–150.
27. bell hooks (2004). *We Real Cool: Black Men and Masculinity*, Routledge: London, 26.
28. Robin D. Kelley (2017). "What did Cedric Robinson mean by racial capitalism?" *Boston Review*, 12.
29. Eithne Quinn (2004). *Nuthin' but a "G" thang: The Culture and Commerce of Gangsta Rap*. Columbia University Press.
30. James, 2015.
31. Murray Lee, Toby Martin, Jioji Ravulo, and Ricky Simandjuntak (2022). "[Dr]illing in the name of: The criminalisation of Sydney drill group ONEFOUR," *Current Issues in Criminal Justice*, 34(4), 339–359.
32. Patricia Hill Collins (2004). *Black Sexual Politics: African Americans, Gender, and the New Racism*, London: Routledge.
33. David Hesmondhalgh and Anamik Saha (2013). Race, ethnicity, and cultural production, *Popular Communication*, 11(3), 185.

16 | Drill as Cultural Form

Video-Music, Chromatism, War and the Alternative

MALCOLM JAMES

The Camera Catches Wiley's Eye

It's 2003, and at Deja Vu FM's[1] pirate radio studio Dizzee Rascal is on the mic in the company of Crazy Titch, Wiley, Maxwell D, Lady Fury, God's Gift, Demon, Tinchy Stryder, D Double E and Sharky Major heralding a scene which will come to be known as grime. The session, filmed by A-Plus, is the pirate's last stand. London's urban terrain is changing. The high-rise council blocks integral to transmission are being demolished. Labour Prime Minister Tony Blair has come to power, rescuing the inner city from decay, razing council estates and former industrial land for private developer profit. The roll call of pirate shoutouts to Clapton Park, Pembury, Packington, Holly Street and Stonebridge are debris in a capital flow. The record shops, bars, clubs and rave venues that comprised the mutual and also entrepreneurial arm of grime are being replaced with online possibilities, decoupling place from culture through networked content delivery.[2] But on Waterden Road that moment is far away. The poor-quality audio, all treble and mid, the attacking wordplay and close cypher, opens onto a different London moment. As the camera pans left to right, Wiley, screw-faced and staccato, crosses the frame. As it returns, the lens catches his eye. His performance falters, his interior surfaces. He is caught in the act.

A-Plus captures a moment of transition in which grime pirate radio is digested by video, and then consumed by YouTube.

Released on DVD, A-Plus's video is famous not so much for the congregation assembled, but for the fight that breaks out between Crazy Titch and Dizzee Rascal as the session concludes. That event gives the video its title 'Conflict' and helps ensure DVD sales in independent record shops. However, the 'Conflict' video only reaches wider celebrity after it has been uploaded to YouTube, and through that process Deja Vu's pirate radio sound culture, at odds with the dominant energies of the city, and a DVD culture linked to those energies through autonomous record stores is turned to the informatic temporalities and networked connectivities of

YouTube, which indeed becomes its media archive. From that moment on, grime artists growing up with YouTube come to see the economies, social practices and temporalities of their scene through the YouTube platform and equate 'doing the numbers' (number of views), not the first pirate radio slot or sound system appearance, as the benchmark of success.[3]

Grime's next generation do not launch their careers on pirate radios or in clubs – the police's campaign against grime nights is well documented[4] – but through mobile phones and YouTube. Stormzy recalls:

I know a lot of grime artists started off on pirate radio, but I missed that era, I was way too young. I was MCing in the playground, spitting lyrics over mobile phones – Sony Ericsson, Walkman W810s, the Teardrop Nokia phones, all of that. Vital equipment! I never even had a DJ set where a DJ's playing vinyl and I'm spitting.[5]

Over only a few years, black diasporic sound culture then shifted its twentieth century affinity for analogue sound technology to a twenty-first century compulsion for digital and networked music videos, enabled by mobile phones, increased data availability, and digital audio and video formats.

When YouTube was purchased by Google in November 2006, it quickly became the most popular music sharing platform for young people. The additional possibility of creating and uploading musical content using mobile phones, afforded grime artists the DIY expressivity formerly found in the make-do practices of sound systems and studios – now folded into the selfie-stick era. Grime's principal YouTube channels – SB.TV, Link Up TV and GRM Daily – emerge at this moment, and are followed by Mixtape Madness and PressPlay Media who, in addition to grime and rap, host the latest genre in the sound system continuum, drill. Drill takes YouTube music video culture to a new level, with videos regularly exceeding 10 million views, and associated tracks entering the Top 20 UK singles chart.

To date, academic discussion of UK drill has principally been criminological, owing partly to the urgency of defending drill artists and artistry against policing.[6] The shift to networked music videos, which affects K-pop as much as drill, has been addressed in scholarship on the cultural industries.[7] This chapter draws on these findings but returns to earlier preoccupations in Cultural Studies, centring its analytic focus on culture and cultural form. It argues, as writers of architecture and novels, reggae and jungle also did, that it is through the analysis of drill as cultural form that its political shifts are best evaluated. The cultural-political shifts of drill are contingently explored using the notion of the 'alternative'.

What Is the Alternative?

The 'alternative' derives from the analytic language of Raymond Williams, who sought, from a Marxist perspective, to understand how heterogenous forms of domination and residual revolution were lived in a post-revolutionary moment (the early 1970s), which is to say after the full onset (or so we then thought) of consumer capitalism. In his famous 1973 essay for *New Left Review*, 'Base and superstructure in Marxist cultural theory', he writes:

> That is why instead of speaking simply of "the hegemony", "a hegemony", I would propose a model which allows for this kind of variation and contradiction, its sets of *alternatives* and its processes of change ... [W]e have to recognize the *alternative* meanings and values, the *alternative* opinions and attitudes, even some *alternative* senses of the world, which can be accommodated and tolerated within a particular effective and dominant culture.[8]

Here, Williams breaks from Adorno's 'determinate negation' – the influential idea that, in the context of consumer capitalism, liberation can only come through a negative reaction to it. Instead, in Williams, we find 'contradiction' and change – what EP Thompson and Stuart Hall later refer to as 'ways of struggle', but also the appearance (or really a reappearance) of an alternative, which can be residual or emergent. The alternative is found in the contradictions of domination (sometimes as opposition), but it is not only formed as its negative reaction, but also has its own persistence and potential. While we are inclined today to speak in the neater binary language of oppression and resistance, celebration and condemnation, or symptom and critique, the alternative allows for a more contingent approach to culture, and therefore respects the contradictions inherent in drill music videos, in which oppression and resistance are entangled, and in which alternatives are discernible.

Against the grain, minor key, undercurrents, subterranean, the submarine, and the utopian impulse have all functioned as synonyms for this version of the 'alternative', and appear throughout humanist Marxist, cultural and postcolonial studies. These studies politically value the freighted humanisms found in Modernity. And on account of sound's alternative relation to dominant visual, textual and racial order, some also valorise its specific radical potential in black diasporic culture.[9] This makes the alternative condition of black diasporic sound culture politically significant for studies of Modernity, and it also implies that the contemporary estrangement of sound evident in drill YouTube music videos, should be of special interest.

Video-Music and Chromatism

Over the last forty years, popular music has seen a shift from sound to the visual, and to video in particular. This move has been told through the rise of MTV in the 1980s. MTV (and its related satellite and cable infrastructure) changed music promotion and consumption, making music videos for the first time an expected accompaniment to audio tracks. Music that was known through sound (that videos made strange) was consumed by video (that made audio strange). As humanities scholar Jody Berland explained, this was a form of 'cultural cannibalization', in which sound became 'digested lifetimes ago ... consumed by the image, which was singing'.[10]

While MTV was killing the radio star, the concurrent music genre jungle – a precursor to drill – was being pieced together from the sounds of hardcore, hip-hop and dub. Here, video was entirely secondary. Banned from mainstream broadcasts, on account of its alleged black and working-class profanity, its sonics provided the connective tissue for the intimate relations of a generation of early- to mid-1990s ravers, self-named 'the massive', who welcomed escape from the visual forms of racism that had conditioned their lives in the decade previous. In darkened raves, on radio sets and through vinyl records, the massive listened to – not visually verified – who could make the baddest basslines.

Jungle video culture, where it did exist, was make-do. The same generation of black box home electronic technologies that powered jungle pirate radio studios, and filled the bedrooms of its producers, were occasionally found in the rave, in the form of home video cameras. Those recordings, released on VHS packs and sold in independent record stores, were not essential viewing. Grime music videos followed that pattern, but with DVDs, and differently to jungle made inroads into cable TV broadcasts, populating Channel U in the early 2000s, and from there MTV Base.

Grime's embrace of YouTube, however, signaled a more fundamental change in the sound-video status quo. Over time video, and more specifically high-definition digital video hosted on social media platforms, became the conductor of the scene's feelings and relations. In UK grime and rap, that was announced by a new generation of YouTube video music stars. Adapting the street aesthetics of earlier YouTube videos (such as No Lay's 'Unorthodox Daughter' and Professor Green's 'Upper Clapton Stomp'), Lady Leshurr's 'Queen's Speech' series, and Nadia Rose's 'Skwod' pioneered a new affinity with the video camera. Their economy of intimate gestures, movements, humour and empathy, invisible in a darkened rave or radio broadcast, were now legible in microscopic detail to face-pressed screens.

Coming out of South London from 2012 onwards, UK Drill YouTube music videos from 150, 67, 410, Moscow 17 and latterly Harlem Spartans were also exemplars of the intensification of video music culture, as rappers donned balaclavas to provide camouflage from masculine interiority and state violence. These videos are highly performative, making use of genre-specific scripts (language, style, affect, symbols) to do artistic work.

The predominant genre for drill music videos is the street video, although freestyle videos are also common. The street drill music video is generally narrative based and follows the story of the estate-based rivalries of almost exclusively male rappers and their peers. Secondary attention is given to the rappers' relationships with the police, money and women. The housing estate is often central to the visual narrative, identified by its presence at the beginning of videos, either through bird's-eye-view drone footage (SL's 'Gentleman') or through head-on shots, with the rappers and their crew standing in front of the building or on stairways and balconies (C1's 'Hide N Seek'). If the estate isn't present, the local area is signified by local landmarks – roads, park names, and street signs. The narratives conveyed through the visuals are repeated in the word play which doesn't necessarily map onto the video sequence, but does reinforce the same message, providing descriptive detail.

Emotion is communicated through visuals and sounds with many videos adopting a restless energy that evokes excitement and unease. Tension is maintained by exploiting the disjuncture between slow and ominous instrumentals and video passages underlaid with exuberant and gritty sub-bass, *and* frenetic camera work, cuts, movements, lighting and postproduction effects, tense snares, high hats and haunting keys and strings.

The overall aesthetic is best described as chromatic. So, while drill music videos convey the agonistic 'fuck this, fuck everyone' of its precursor grime, they are not icy or 'from the ground'.[11] Rather, drill's chromatism communicates something different. Is it austere and opulent. It beats are sparse but rich, ominous, indulgent and decaying. It is unadorned black street uniforms, lavishing in blood – printed on trainers, jeans and jackets.[12] And, although the estate is central, it is produced less through its imitate relationship with place, and more through its imbrication in big data, global communication networks, screens, platforms, and mobile phones.

This shift in black diasporic sound culture from music-video to video-music is produced in this media ecology; in the interplay of Snapchat 'opps' videos (videos of a drill collectives' operations against rivals), Instagram promotional videos and YouTube music videos. These cross-platform interplays re-colour the properties of beats, instrumentals and lyrics, and move consumption from listening to watching. They generate music's feeling as the blue light of mobile phone screens stimulates adrenalin, raising resting heartbeats, inducing a chemical high that is addictive and compulsive. And they shape its rhythm as frenetic imagery is matched by the compulsive scanning of the algorithmically organized sidebar; peripheral visual cues loosely absorbed in the wider atmosphere of the track; before the drive to click takes over; the video is changed; and '[w]e are captured doing not what we want but what we must'.[13]

Nihilism, Narrative and Mediation

Aged 13, Deptford (SE London) drill rapper DigDat received a ten-year jail sentence for attempted murder. Upon release in 2018, having served five years of a ten-year stretch, he recorded the track 'Air Force', sporting the eponymous Nike shoe with blood splash design. The track accrued 34 million YouTube views, propelling him to number 20 in the UK singles charts.

The music video for 'Air Force' narrates DigDat's time in prison, his rivalries with neighbouring rappers, female conquest, and knife and gun play. Kaylum's visuals develop the chromatic aesthetic – austere-opulence or gritty-luxury. Shots of a prison fence, red brick railway arches, and broken glass shift to night-time images of DigDat and crew lit by the LED lights of high-end cars and the fluorescent tubes of an Esso filling station. Sharp metal provides a reflective surface for the harsh blue-green saturated images. The beats, by Dotty, are anxious and exuberant. Fast-paced snares and hats, haunting synths, and uneasy kick drums fold into rich and decaying sub-bass.

Read critically, 'Air Force', as with many drill music videos, is as an account of marginalization. Its presentation of imprisonment and policing is a response to UK penal society and to the Conservative government's austerity programme, which has presided over swingeing cuts to welfare, youth and mental health services; and has augmented levels of school exclusions, hardship, unemployment, and racist policing. Its narrative of peer-on-peer violence is likewise a commentary on the depoliticization of structural injustice; the individualisation of blame and shame; and the removal of potential pathways (real and imagined) to a productive and public life in capitalism. To take another example, 'No Fibz' by Nottingham drill artist SV, it doesn't take much imagination to see standing on a rubbish heap, rapping about violence and humiliation, as a critique of society's nihilistic condition.

However, drill music videos are not only critical documents of marginalisation and societal nihilism, for they also perform it in contradictory ways, and these contradictory performances are instructive for evaluating their cultural politics. 'Moscow March' by Moscow 17 (Kennington) against Zone 2 (Peckham) or any innumerable tracks by OFB (Broadwater Farm, Tottenham) against their Edmonton N9 or Wood Green rivals, perform narratives of inter-communal violence. If reggae culture was generally associated with an outer-national sensibility and jungle pirate radio with metropolitan reach, drill music videos' narratives of inter-communal violence reduce the commons to the estate, shrinking further the post-code area rivalries of the preceding grime culture.

In C1's video for 'Hide n Seek', JXYOXN's night-time imagery shows the estate, the face-covered crew, a car on ops, and images of the police. Over those images, C1 raps, 'We play hide and seek with the cops, Play it with the ops [rivals], It is what it is, put shanks [knives] in tops'. C1's metaphorical use of child's games goes on to detail a violent engagement with the ops, and a more contextual cat-and-mouse encounter with the police. The narrative breakdown of wider public constituencies is accompanied by the state's violent presence, and is instructive more broadly of societal shifts away from social-democratic perceptions of public good to a minimal state, authoritarianism and advanced economic stratification (evident also across Britain and Europe in the mainstreaming of clientelist politics – the next stage of capitalist expansion[14] – and the evaporation of the social-democratic consensus following the financial crash in 2008 and the Greek 'bailout').

Drill's groupist rivalries are narrated as war, and as 'unending war', which is to say war-as-life, and they often take the form of hunt and siege.[15] Loski's 'Hazard', and Skengdo x AM's 'Hunterz' both employ the metaphor of siege, with the estate and neighbouring streets constituting the space of siege, and also the location from which the hunt begins. Loski, 'we're putting two in the front, squash 4 n***** in the back seat, make man run like athlete'. Skengdo x AM, 'What you gonna do when the crashers summon? What's that smell in the air? Put it in gear and let's go hunting.'

Rivalries between young men, young men in music culture, and young men in working-class city culture are not new. They can be traced through football and music fandoms, park and pub punch ups; and in the intersecting history of black diasporic sound culture they are found in the dozens:

dance offs, rap battles and sound system clashes. These masculine competitions were on occasion fierce and sometimes used the language of war, or 'Conflict' as we have seen, but notably as far as music culture is concerned, they also foregrounded a horizontal vernacular dialogue. That is to say, they were systems of call-and-response, where the shout-out prefigured the reply. Drill's more military dialogue traces this history of call-and-response but does so on more asymmetrical and exceptional terms;[16] founded on a tighter communitarianism and a harder assignation of otherness, which extends to the degrading of humans to animals, for the hunt.

Drill narratives of inter-communal violence then cite those found in mass culture; wars against terror (Muslims) and woke (trans, BLM and cultural Marxism); the hunting of refugees; the siege of Fortress Europe; invocations of human migrants as plague or cockroaches; and the survivalist warlordism and end-of-time catastrophisations of Andrew Tate and Anders Breivik.[17] Drill music videos are then documents of advanced marginalisation and bellicose social policy under the latest stage of capitalism, and they also contradictorily employ its dominant cultural tropes to contribute publicly to a fascistic structure of feeling in which mutuality is displaced by normalised exceptional force, welfare by austerity or small state survival, and a horizon of humanist potential with end-of-time catastrophe.[18]

These narratives of groupism, authoritarianism and societal nihilism are tantalized by the affect- and symbol-driven economies of their social media platforms (Snapchat, Instagram and YouTube). Theoretically this implies that whereas reggae and jungle sound culture can be explained phenomenologically through theories of flow, trace, 'the changing same',[19] or 'roots and routes',[20] drill video-music narratives must be explained differently. They are better understood as glitch, pastiche or simulacra than as cultural flow. As with the contemporary mediation of narcissism, culture wars and grievance politics, they are out of time and place by necessity of the operating logic of social media capitalism. Crews, masculine and racialised somatic performance, and the chromatic aesthetic, function as open-coded affective hooks in which drill's hyper-local and hyper-violent invectives compete with similar global offerings for attention and views.[21] In this way too, drill music videos can exist simultaneously as local allegories of tangible violence, another global marginalisation, a generic fetish of dangerous white consumption, and merely a loved banger on a summer park playlist. Drill's hype is then the affective blip of incongruent codes momentarily fused, not a slow cancellation of the future, as Mark Fisher would say, but its disappearance; a horizon absolutely immanent and intensely empty.[22]

Pouring One Out: Humanism and the Sanctity of Life

In 2019, M24 x Stickz released 'We Don't Dance', a 41-million-view YouTube video which tells of how the drillers don't dance, except with gun fire. The video, directed by Pacmantv, was filmed in a Greater London industrial estate 'out East' and alternates extended shots of the rappers on and around empty shipping containers with scenes of pouring Hennessy and Wray and Nephew onto the ground. This act of libation symbolises a drink for the dead and celebrates the lives of those absent, connected to those present (the rappers and the viewers). It is through death, in the ritual, that life is then known, that the energy or psyche that constitutes life is rendered vital. Relatively commonplace in drill videos, libation thereby constitutes an incongruent humanism, an *alternative*, not reducible to the themes of war and nihilism with which it is also coterminous. A notable musical reference for libation is Tupac Shakur's 1994 track 'Pour out a little liquor', but the practice has wider historical resonance in black and African ceremonies, and indeed in the rites of many other world regions.

In bellicose societies, nostalgic repertories for the fallen serve to glorify war and propagate its continuation. They are mournful and melancholic affairs in which the pain of the nation always at war is interpreted though collective pathologies, which make sense of human sacrifice and undergird the desire for retribution and punishment against common enemies.[23] Drill's libation practices are to some degree consistent with this narrative of unending war. They function as a commemoration of the fallen, and as a marker of group affinity. At the same time, however, they are contradictory because they introduce a humanist presence, one that is collective and based on the thick materiality of life as temporal (lived) and shared (through death). Libation is not then a mournful ritual in the service of war and societal nihilism, although that is its context, but rather an affirmation of life lived with death, life understood through death. The living do not nostalgically serve the dead, but the dead the living.[24] In that sense libation creatively affirms human *being*, contradicting the glitch formation of groupism and difference. It opens possibilities for life when austerity and no-future shape the social horizon.

In 'We Don't Dance', the pouring of liquor moves to music, and develops through a more elaborate sequence of body rhythmatics, which given the video's theme of not dancing highlights the significance of the act; confirming a distinct political register from that otherwise communicated by not dancing – masculine somatic control in the context of racialised societal violence. It shows an intimate impulse to feel, feel-in-common, and to feel-in-public via the platformed music video. Here, the affective glitch, individual humiliation, groupist alterity and balaclava-ed interiority, is returned to the flow of human life. This is not a politics of the future, but of the now, and of a now out-of-time and out-of-keeping with (in alternative relation to) the dominant rhythms of its YouTube capitalist ecology.

Drill YouTube music videos are contradictory – nihilistic and collective, empty and humanizing, negatively assessing marginalization and societal nihilism, performing those scripts as a placebo for pain and humiliation, and also shaping popular culture in that image. That general dynamic should be expected of popular culture, as too should be the alternatives that persist therein. To that end, this chapter has explored YouTube music videos as cultural form, for what they tell us about the historical transformation of black diasporic sound culture, contemporary popular culture and its alternative cultural politics. Through an analysis of drill music videos it has identified a shift away from sound culture towards video-music, and therein a shift to the networked and platformed moving image, and to narrative. This requires a reevaluation of the role of sound in alternative cultural politics and in black diasporic popular culture, and asks that drill video-music be evaluated on its contingent cultural terms, not on the terms of other cultural and musical moments.

Drill video-music tells the networked-pastiche stories that dub and jungle could not. The negative accounts they provide of marginalised life might be thought (in negative hermeneutic terms) as the critical ground from which a politics of liberation is born, but drill music videos' convoluted critique of marginalisation also folds into the freighted static of popular nihilism, complicating that resolution. Understanding drill video music as alternative political culture, rather than determinate negation, is a more productive avenue of enquiry. As alternative cultural politics drill can be understood as contradiction and also as the persistent transmission of freedom's minor residues.

And this is where the analysis ends; in the act of pouring one out. In the contemporary context of social death, vernacular narratives of life through struggle, and life through death offer a powerful collective and universal alternative to the wider fascism of hostility and war in which the empty desire for killing has become otherwise trapped. Drill is not then to be denounced or crudely celebrated. It is not moral anathema to public good, nor the perspicacious corrective to domination. It might be a conjunctural bellweather, but with limited other avenues available, it might also be appreciated for its alternatives, understood on the terms in which it is produced, by which it *is* culture.

Notes

1. Dan Hancox, 'Pirates and Olympians: Deja Vu and the Copper Box Arena', in *Regeneration Songs: Sounds of Loss and Investment from East London*, edited by Alberto Duman et al. (London: Repeater, 2018).
2. Tom Cordell and Malcolm James, 'Mutualism, massive and the city to come: Jungle Pirate Radio in 1990s London', *Soundings*, no. 77 (2021).
3. Malcolm James, *Sonic intimacy: reggae sound systems, jungle pirate radio and grime YouTube music videos* (London: Bloomsbury, 2020).
4. 'The police vs grime music – a noisy film', Noisey, 2014, www.youtube.com/watch?v=eW_iujPQpys [Accessed 23 November 2018]; 'David Cameron is a donut', *Guardian*, 2006, www.theguardian.com/commentisfree/2006/jun/08/davidcameronisadonut [Accessed 20 January 2020].
5. Stormzy quoted in 'How British MCs found a voice of their own', *The Observer*, 2015, www.theguardian.com/music/2015/may/31/british-mcs-stormzy-jammz-little-simz-krept-konan-novelist [Accessed 5 October 2018].
6. Alex de Lacey, 'Live and direct? Censorship and racialised public morality in grime and drill music', *Popular Music* 41, no. 4 (2022); Lambros Fatsis, 'Policing the beats: the criminalisation of UK drill and grime music by the London Metropolitan Police', *The Sociological Review* 67, no. 6 (2019); Jonathan Ilan, 'Digital street culture decoded: why criminalizing drill music is street illiterate and counterproductive', *British Journal of Criminology* 60 (2020); Murray Lee, 'This is not a drill: towards a sonic and sensorial musicriminology', *Crime Media Culture* 18, no. 3 (2022); Tilman Schwarze and Lambros Fatsis, 'Copping the blame: the role of YouTube videos in the criminalisation of UK drill music', *Popular Music* 41, no. 4 (2022). See also Stuart's ethnography of Chicago Drill *Ballad of the bullet: gangs, drill music, and the power of online infamy* (Princeton: Princeton University Press, 2020).
7. Terje Colbjørnsen, 'The streaming network: conceptualizing distribution economy, technology, and power in streaming media services', *Convergence* 27, no. 5 (2021); David Hesmondhalgh, 'Streaming's effects on music culture: old anxieties and new simplifications', *Cultural Sociology* 16, no. 1 (2022); 'The impact of algorithmically driven recommendation systems on music consumption and production – a literature review', 2023, www.gov.uk/government/publications/research-into-the-impact-of-streaming-services-algorithms-on-music-consumption/the-impact-of-algorithmically-driven-recommendation-systems-on-music-consumption-and-production-a-literature-review [Accessed 23 May 2023].

8. Raymond Williams, 'Base and superstructure in Marxist cultural theory', in *Culture and materialism: selected essays*, edited by Raymond Williams (London: Verso, 2010), pp. 38–39 (author's emphasis).
9. 'Ghetto Thermodynamics', Cesura/Acceso, 2015, http://cesura-acceso.org/issues/ghetto-thermodynamics-dhanveer-singh-brar/ [Accessed 21 December 2016]; Paul Gilroy, *'There ain't no black in the Union Jack': the cultural politics of race and nation* (London: Hutchinson, 1987); Paul Gilroy, *The black Atlantic: modernity and double consciousness* (London: Verso, 1993); William Henry, *What the deejay said: a critique from the street!* (London: Nu-Beyond Ltd, 2006); Clyde Woods, 'Sittin' on top of the world', in *Black geographies and the politics of place*, edited by Katherine McKittrick and Clyde Woods (Cambridge, MA: South End Press, 2007); Richard Bramwell, *UK hip-hop, grime and the city: the aesthetics and ethics of London's rap scenes* (London: Routledge, 2015).
10. Jody Berland, 'Sound image and social space: music video and media reconstruction', in *Sound and vision: the music video reader*, ed. Simon Frith, Andrew Goodwin, and Lawrence Grossberg (London: Routledge, 1993), p. 31.
11. James, *Sonic intimacy*, pp. 92–6.
12. See Skengdo and AM's discussion of blood aesthetics for their Saatchi Gallery show ('Terms & conditions: a UK drill story', YouTube Originals, 2020, www.youtube.com/watch?v=kno5T4y5SBY, 1:04:00) [Accessed 27 July 2023].
13. Jodi Dean, 'Affective networks', *Media Tropes* 2, no. 2 (2010), p. 21.
14. Will Davies 'How "competitiveness" became one of the great unquestioned virtues of contemporary culture', LSE Blog, 2014, https://blogs.lse.ac.uk/politicsandpolicy/the-cult-of-competitiveness/ [Accessed 27 July 2023].
15. '"This war won't end": London gang murders on the rise', Sky News, 2019, https://news.sky.com/story/line-18-gang-warfare-is-killing-londons-young-black-men-11447089 [Accessed 27 July 2023].
16. Carl Schmitt historically develops the European juridical space of the state of siege to make an argument for dictatorship (Carl Schmitt, *Dictatorship: from the origin of the modern concept of sovereignty to proletarian class struggle* (Cambridge: Polity, 2014), pp. 148–179).
17. On catastrophisation as futurity, in relation to ecological crisis (John Urry, *What is the future?* (Cambridge: Polity, 2016), pp. 33–54). See also Stiegler's presentation of Florian (Bernard Stiegler, *The age of disruption: technology and madness in computational capitalism* (Cambridge: Polity, 2020), p. 9).
18. Antoine Bousquet, Jairus Grove, and Nisha Shah, 'Becoming war: towards a martial empiricism', *Security Dialogue* 51, no. 2–3 (2020); Henry A. Giroux, *Beyond the spectacle of terrorism: global uncertainty and the challenge of the new media* (Boulder, CO: Paradigm, 2006); 'Fascism in the age of hyperreality', Patreon, 2023, www.patreon.com/posts/fascism-in-age-84900683 [Accessed 27 July 2023]; Gavan Titley, *Racism and the media* (London: Sage, 2019). 'Theory in Crisis Seminar: Alberto Toscano, "Fascist Times"', University of

London Institute in Paris, 2020, www.youtube.com/watch?v=PmLUfG5h_no. [Accessed 18 January 2021]; Sivamohan Valluvan, *The clamour of nationalism: race and nation in twenty-first-century Britain* (Manchester: Manchester University Press, 2019).

19. Gilroy's version of citation or trace in Black Atlantic culture, building on the concept of Amiri Baraka (Gilroy, *There ain't no black in the Union Jack*).
20. Gilroy's conceptualisation of diasporic cultural space (Gilroy, *There ain't no black in the Union Jack*).
21. Stuart, *Ballad of the bullet*.
22. In comparison, dub is said to have moved out of capitalist time while jungle is said to have oxygenated an undefined future (James, *Sonic intimacy*); 'The slow cancellation of the future', 2014, www.youtube.com/watch?v=aCgkLICTskQ [Accessed 27 July 2023].
23. For discussion of melancholia, see Paul Gilroy, *After empire: melancholia or convivial culture?* (London: Routledge, 2004).
24. For discussion of life and death in Haitian Voudoun rituals, see (Maya Deren, *Divine horsemen: voodoo gods of Haiti* (London: Thames and Hudson, 1953), pp. 25–28).

17 | English Rap in India and the Fault Lines of Sociolinguistic Politics

ELLOIT CARDOZO AND JASPAL NAVEEL SINGH

Attitudes towards English in India usually fall somewhere on a dichotomic scale: at one end, English is seen as the language of social prestige and upward social mobility due to the sway it holds in the job market and its associations with globalised modernity; while on the other, the use of English is perceived as a colonial hangover that will and must be overcome as India progresses towards becoming a truly autonomous and self-sufficient superpower on the global stage. The present chapter attempts to problematise the reductionist nature of this dichotomy through an analysis of the sociolinguistic politics that inform Indian hip-hop artists' choices to use English to rap. This analysis allows us to understand how English in India is being nativised through artistic practices and taken from the cerebral domain (e.g. law, science, business) to the expressive domain of the proverbial street and how this reflects the changing role English occupies in India's complex language policies. We begin by historically situating English in India's multilingual environment and then move on to discuss why Indian rappers might choose to rap in English. We conclude by suggesting that rappers' negotiations of India's multilingual complexity are reflective of cultural and political fault lines and struggles.

English in India: The Intranational Politics of an International Language

As a former British colony, India's relationship with the English language is certainly strained. Housing one of the world's largest English-speaking populations, the forms, functions and perceptions of Indian Englishes are ever-changing and have been subject to heated political and cultural debate. English is a second language for many Indians, acquired mostly through formal schooling but also through media and transnational relationalities. It is estimated that Standard Indian English is used in an intelligible and regular manner by about 50 to 125 million people, making it the world's third largest variety of English after American and British English.[1] Having said that, it must also be pointed out that in a country of

1.4 billion people, the 'majority of realities and lives of people on the subcontinent are untouched by the presence of English'.[2]

The history of the English language in India stretches back to the early seventeenth century with the colonial establishment of the British East India Tea Company in the Gulf of Bengal and in Gujarat.[3] With the imperial consolidation of British administrative and political power in India in the eighteenth and nineteenth centuries, English became deeply entrenched in Indian society. By the nineteenth and early twentieth centuries, English-language education had been firmly established in the British Raj, mainly through Christian missionary schools, universities and newspapers. The need for more and more Indian civil servants required a widening of the educational efforts. At this point, English 'had begun to grow into a vehicle for personal communication among English-educated Indians and into a medium deemed appropriate for creative writing',[4] thus nativising English in the subcontinent.[5] When calls for independence rang louder in the late nineteenth and early twentieth centuries, this nativised English became the language of the Indian National Congress and the independence movement that operated across the subcontinent.

After India had finally gained her Independence in 1947, the colonial linguistic heritage of the British Raj prevailed. The Constitution, which came into effect in 1950, names both Hindi and English as official languages of the newly founded Republic. The Constitution includes a provision to eventually phase out English and make Hindi the sole official language after a fifteen-year transition period. Hindi is the largest language spoken and used in everyday interactions in the northern and most populous part of the country and it belongs to the Indo-Aryan language family. Indians who live in the southern part of the country mostly use Dravidian languages, such as Tamil, Kannada and Malayalam, which are mutually unintelligible with Hindi and other northern Indo-Aryan languages such as Gujarati, Punjabi, Marathi or Bengali. South Indians feared that the sole-official status of Hindi would linguistically discriminate against them. In 1963, when the fifteen-year cutoff date approached, widespread protests erupted in the south.[6] These protests, which often turned into riots, vehemently opposed the imposition of Hindi upon the southern states. It was eventually decided that English should be retained alongside Hindi as the official language for all pan-Indian communication, such as bureaucratic correspondence, national media, as well as educational provision.

Thus, English is sometimes conceptualised as a neutral language for the national politics of India; it is 'the language [that] helped in achieving national integration'.[7] Yet, sociolinguistically speaking, English is far from neutral. Some Indians, like Gandhi, think of English as 'a sign of the psychological conquest that the British have made over Indians'.[8] There are also those who think of English as an 'agent of decolonization that enables the urban poor to access the global economy',[9] owing to its position as a global lingua franca. English carries connotations of modernity and western liberalism. As such, English promises upward social mobility, especially since the early 1990s, when India liberalised its markets to attract foreign investment and enter the emerging neoliberal world order. Highet, for example, shows how English-language adult education promises young women in Delhi a better future for themselves and their families in the neoliberal and globalised marketplace. Yet, Highet also finds that English competence also complexifies these women's intra-caste marriage prospects. If a young upper-caste Brahmin woman's English is too good, she might be seen as less desirable on the Brahmin wedding marketplace, because it is believed that her high English competency would give her too much power over her would-be husband and thereby undermine caste-based gender morality.[10] Any form of sociolinguistic politics that portrays English in India as a monochrome of any one of these aspects is hence rife with fault lines where the other sociocultural aspects of the language rear their heads.

In what follows, we look at how hip-hop artists' choice to rap in English mirrors, as well as co-constructs, the sociolinguistic politics of English in India.

A Genealogy of English Rap in India

As rap goes global and begins to localise in different parts of the world, the English language seems to travel with it. As is well documented in the sociolinguistic literature on rap (see the further reading in the Notes section), for many youth from around the world, picking up the mic means spitting in English. Brodha V is a rapper from Bengaluru in the south of India who started off rapping in English and gradually shifted to incorporating more Kannada in his lyrics. In an interview with hip-hop journalist Raaj Jones, he ponders that this has to do with global hip-hop heads' listening practices and their preference for consuming English language rap music, presumably from the USA and perhaps other native-English countries, such as the UK: 'a lot of people start rapping in English because they listen to English rap a lot'.[11] Accordingly, the type of English used for rap in these early uptakes around the world could be described as a locally imagined variety of African-American English, which is infused with second and foreign language learner speech characteristics, and made locally relevant to some extent by incorporating local lexical items and word meanings.

In India, before the formation of local rap and hip-hop scenes, the earliest rappers in fact used local Indian languages as well as English. Baba Sehgal, who covered Vanilla Ice's 'Ice Ice Baby' with Hindi lyrics in his 1992 album *Thanda Thanda Paani* (Cold Cold Water), is sometimes credited with being India's first rapper.[12] The 1990s saw a rise in the consumption of American popular culture, spurred by India's economic liberalisation policies and the facilitation of the circulation of global cultural artefacts.[13] At that time, rap made appearances on the soundtracks of mainstream Indian films, for example 'Pettai Rap' (mainly in Tamil)[14] from the soundtrack for *Kadhalan* (1994) and 'Mumbhai' (in English and Bambaiyya Hindi) from the *Bombay Boys* (1998) soundtrack. Yet, the Indian public had a somewhat shallow understanding of hip-hop as a western trend and reduced it to 'elements of colloquialisms, body language, attitude, style, and fashion'.[15]

Around the millennium, a few rappers with Indian lineage who had grown up in the West, such as BlaaZe (who grew up in Zambia and studied in the UK and the USA), IshQ Bector from Canada and Hard Kaur from the UK, made fleeting appearances in the shoehorned peripheral positions that rap was afforded on the soundtracks of commercial films. While somewhat successful in the transnational Asian networks that exist between global cities like Chandigarh, Birmingham and San Francisco, these rappers had ultimately only limited reach in India. Their native Englishes, metropolitan colloquialisms and first-world accented pronunciations, it seems, felt inaccessible to many young Indians who started their experiments with hip-hop and formed underground scenes across urban India, in cities like Mumbai, Delhi, Chandigarh, Kolkata, Shillong, Bengaluru and Chennai.

A shift happened in the late 2000s, with the emergence of Pakistani American rapper Bohemia who raps in Punjabi, a language shared by Pakistan and India and understood to a certain extent also by speakers of Hindi/Urdu. Bohemia, and a five-piece underground rap crew inspired by him, Mafia Mundeer, authenticated Indian-language underground rap in India as well as in the wider South Asian diaspora. With Mafia Mundeer's breakup and the crew members, such as Yo Yo Honey Singh, Badshah, and Raftaar, gaining mainstream traction, the Indian masses eventually formed a conception of rap, and rap in Indian languages became a conceivable option. Problematically, Yo Yo Honey Singh's work developed a reputation for promoting misogyny and even earned him the moniker 'King of Rape Rap',[16] resulting in rap being vested with a reputation for promoting the ill-treatment of women in India.[17] This made rap twice-alienated for much of the Indian mass audience: first as a 'foreign' culture that promotes 'western' values in the language of the 'coloniser', then as a 'bad influence' rife with misogyny, leading to rappers being held almost solely responsible for propagating the mindset responsible for the safety issues surrounding women in India at the time.

A concurrent development in the mid 2000s saw the formation of 'underground' hip-hop scenes in India.[18] As Singh shows in his study of Delhi's emerging hip-hop scene in 2013, many hip-hop heads who would eventually grab the mic and rap had started off as b-boys and poppers and lockers. It was thus *dance*, not rap, that introduced many Delhi youth to hip-hop. Through dance they learnt to embody hip-hop's aesthetics, how to don its attire, how to move one's young masculine body and how to socialise with other young men invested in hip-hop. Hip-hop's forms of dance shaped Singh's participants 'bodily hexis; their ways of moving, standing, sitting, watching their friends and several other forms of their homosocial interaction'.[19] During that time, almost everybody in the Delhi hip-hop scene was male, and nobody was openly not heterosexual. Singh reports that only one b-girl and three female graffiti writers participated in the Delhi hip-hop scene at the time.[20] Soon, some of the b-boys began experimenting with writing and recording English rap lyrics in their bedroom studios and organising freestyle cyphers in their cities as well as online.[21] Orkut, an erstwhile social networking site, hosted many popular text-battling communities from India, which eventually played a role in the formation of numerous local hip-hop scenes in cities such as Bengaluru, Delhi and Mumbai.[22]

Many in this first generation of Delhi hip-hop heads have migration histories and so English might have played a part in their everyday interactions with their transnational families and friendship circles. Either they themselves or their families migrated from rural parts of the country to the massively expanding megacity that Delhi had become since the 1990s. Some of these early hip-hop practitioners also came from other countries in the Global South, for example Nepal, Afghanistan and Somalia.[23] At first, English played a central role in the formation of these rap scenes. For example, Singh shows how a group of Somalian refugees who grew up in Delhi, all fluent in several languages including English and Hindi, in their initial experiments with writing rap lyrics in 2013, gravitated towards English because they found it difficult to conceptualise rapping in Hindi on hip-hop beats.[24] They told Singh that they struggled with the aesthetic possibilities of Hindi rap, and so opted to write their lyrics in English, even though they also said that they were most comfortable with expressing their ideas through the medium of Hindi when speaking.

English played an important role in the development of these underground rap scenes across India. In Delhi, Slyck and Zan (collectively known as TwoShadez) as well as Kr$na and MicMaster Aeke were early rappers who used mainly English in their lyrics and later switched to Hindi and Hinglish. Substantial rap scenes developed in cities across India, including Mumbai (perhaps India's largest rap metropolis), Shillong, and Mizoram (in Northeast India), Chennai, Darjeeling, Kolkata, and various places in the state of Kerala. Most rappers, if not all, in these scenes started out rapping solely in English before either switching to regional Indian languages or turning markedly multilingual and actively code-switching and code-mixing between two or more languages (not always including English) in their rap lyrics.

Blend In or Stand Out: The Politics of Choosing to Rap in English

For almost a decade or so, a lot of the rap coming out of the local hip-hop scenes in India was somewhat imitational in nature: this meant that rappers dressed a certain way to 'look like a rapper' and also rapped in imagined versions of 'American' or 'African American' English to 'sound like a rapper'.[25] The mid-2010s saw a game-changing shift in the hip-hop culture in India. Rappers, new ones as well as many who had started out rapping in English, began rapping in local Indian languages. Even the few who continued rapping in English, such as Enkore from Mumbai, shed the imitational shades to their English and experimented with rapping in Indian varieties of English and extensively incorporated code-switching into their lyrics. This seemed to be a more authentic form of rap, given it now reflected the local culture, issues and concerns in a more linguistically genuine manner.[26] However, such an argument runs the risk of glossing over the fact that 'English is [...] becoming a home language for a considerable portion of the population in and around Mumbai',[27] due to the city's metropolitan nature with many South Indian, North Indian and international residents, as well as the perception of English as a language that offers good professional prospects down the line. Secondly, owing to its previously discussed sociolinguistic politics as the chosen alternative to the imposition of Hindi, English becomes the language of choice for a lot of speakers in multilingual settings within India, even if they do not identify it as their first language. Thirdly, owing to its status as a global language, English offers rappers the opportunity to reach out to a potentially larger audience not just within India, but outside it too.

For example, Singh discusses how the Indian rapper Manmeet Kaur, who was born in Kashmir, grew up in Punjab and Mumbai and now lives in Goa, uses mainly English for her raps to transcend her positionality as a woman in Indian hip-hop to instead position herself as pursuing international connections and garner recognition for her music beyond Indian hip-hop circles and across the Anglosphere.[28] Thus, while on the surface Manmeet's continued use of English for her rap music might be interpreted as a colonial hangover, a reading that takes into account her gendered positionality could lead us to understanding her use of English as a way to transcend locality and position herself as a cosmopolitan traveller who moves between places in India and in the world and thereby evades being held down by any one local patriarchal structure.

Despite English's appeal to reach global hip-hop heads across the world, rapping in local Indian languages became somewhat normalised in Indian rap music. An important paradigm shift was marked by Zoya Akhtar's 2019 Oscar-nominated Bollywood blockbuster *Gully Boy*, a film depicting Mumbai's underground rap scene, inspired by the lives of Mumbai-based rappers DIVINE and Naezy. DIVINE, who started out with rapping in English before switching mainly to Bambaiyya Hindi, first caught Sony Music India's attention with '*Yeh Mera* Bombay' (2013) [This is my Bombay] after which they signed him. He went on to release '*Mere Gully Mein*' (2015) [In my alleyway][29] featuring Naezy, under Sony Music. These two songs stood as the most significant markers of Divine's transformation from an English rapper, to one who raps in Bambaiyya, a Mumbai-based dialect of Hindi. '*Mere Gully Mein*' generated a buzz and Divine and Naezy were invited to numerous radio shows including an interview with RJ Malishka for Red FM India, and Bobby Friction's show *Friction* for BBC Asia. Hot on the buzz generated by the song, filmmaker Zoya Akhtar announced that she would be making a film on the underground rap scene in Mumbai, inspired by the lives of DIVINE and Naezy, with the US-American rapper Nas as an executive producer. While DIVINE and Naezy were part of a larger movement where rappers all around India started rapping in Indian languages, the announcement of *Gully Boy* saw many rappers from underground scenes all over the country feature more regularly on the soundtracks of commercial films as well as promotional advertising campaigns with the mainstream slowly beginning to assimilate to the aesthetics of underground hip-hop.[30] Suddenly, rapping in local

Indian languages became the 'cooler', and, importantly, the more marketable option. Rapping in Hindi opened avenues into the mainstream and became what distributors demanded from many rappers, including those who had been rapping exclusively in English for over a decade.

This meant that English rap started being seen as not just 'fake' and 'inauthentic' but also less sought after in the market (as opposed to Hindi rap). Now, even English rappers were often asked to rap in Hindi. Brodha V, an English and Kannada rapper, in his collaboration with Raftaar (by and large a Hindi rapper), rhymes in Hindi:

Haa, slow mera career,
Yahaan kaafi zyada language barrier,
Hindi mein mera haath thoda tight,
Warna pehle hi hota mai Bombay ki flight mein ...

Yeah, my career is slow,
Here's quite a large language barrier,
[Writing] in Hindi my hand is a little tight,
Or I would have been on a flight to Bombay long back ...[31]

Brodha V's use of the English word 'tight' in these lyrics can be seen as a double entendre. In one reading of the lyrics, he seems to be speaking about being bad at writing lyrics in Hindi. However, the fact that he chooses to use the English word 'tight' instead of an equivalent in Hindi, that too in a song which criticises the mass audience for their lack of understanding of the nuance of hip-hop, might be read as an allusion to the positive connotations the word has within global hip-hop cultures: tight bars are good bars. The lyrics, hence, can be read as him claiming to be able to write and spit 'tight' bars in Hindi despite not being fluent in the language. What he seems to be saying here is that his refusal to rap in Hindi all these years has denied him the fame and recognition that he is now getting (in being approached by producers and distributors and being flown out to Bombay/Mumbai).

It is clear that the sociolinguistic dynamics within rap are further complicated by multilingual rappers for whom English is just one of numerous languages in which they rap. Given the country's complex multilingual environment, Indian rappers are usually part of multiple linguistic groups. As Annamalai suggests, 'the composition of each linguistic group includes multiple group identities in terms of caste, class, religion, or region, which are more divisive and exclusionary than the linguistic identity'.[32] For example, anti-caste activist, rapper, and scholar Sumeet Samos chooses to rap in English, Hindi, and Odia with the simple aim of reaching out to a larger audience in order to raise awareness about caste-based atrocities. He points out that English gives him the verbal apparatus to think and speak about caste.[33] He also acknowledges the hostility that is sometimes directed towards the variety of English that he uses: 'People mock. They scorn at my pronunciation, my accent'.[34] Samos hence becomes the embodiment of Annamalai's argument that, despite the fact that the acquisition of English has led to the formation of a new Indian elite that often derides a lack of competency in the language, it still serves as a viable alternative to other local Indian languages that have been appropriated by the upper castes.[35] Samos' language choices interrogate the sociolinguistic fault lines of the nation-building narrative that surrounds the endorsement of installing Hindi as India's national language:

First thing I knew was my mother tongue, which is Dom. Neither do I speak Odia with fluency, nor do I speak Hindi with fluency, nor do I speak English with fluency. I also realised that this is my English ... And I'm like, 'okay, you know, this is my way of speaking English, this is my way of speaking Hindi. Maybe I don't have flamboyant words like you do, vocabularies like you do, or metaphors like you do. But there's a reality that I would like to present.' And I do it.[36]

Samos' predicament is indicative of how the sociolinguistic politics of India constantly relegates the linguistic minorities to the periphery, especially when using regional languages such as Hindi and Odia which end up hegemonising Dom: a minoritised language spoken by the Dom community in Odisha. In this sense, rapping in English offers Samos a sociopolitical slippage which he is not afforded by other local languages associated with higher-caste Hindus, such as Hindi or Odia. Especially in his choice to use a distinctly non-native variety of English that does not want to accord to the standardised Englishes associated with urban-bred Indians living in cosmopolitan cities, Samos' use of English can be seen as a means to wrest back narrative agency.

G'nie from Mizoram, just like several other rappers hailing from Northeast India, often raps about the racist discrimination he faces in India due to his appearance as an East-Asian or Chinese. In a feature track he spits:

I'm a ... a Chinese-looking Indian (hmm, what?),
Who raps like an American (hmm, what?),
A black white brown yellow man (what),
I'm a fucking chameleon (chameleon),
Blend in or stand out, I'm resilient,
Indian but a global citizen ...[37]

This opening to G'nie's verse in the track is significant for multiple reasons. In calling himself a 'Chinese-looking Indian' G'nie takes a swipe at the racist slander directed towards people with what Thongkholal Haokip terms 'mongoloid features'. Haokip points out how derogatory terms, such as 'chinkey' from the track's title, are used to otherise and question Northeast Indians' belongingness in mainland India.[38] G'nie's flexing of his linguistic prowess by associating himself with a native-like variety of English ('raps like an American') allows him to claim cultural capital within the global hip-hop nation. In further claiming to be a 'chameleon' or a 'black white brown yellow man' who can 'blend in or stand out' as he chooses, he employs raciolinguistic tactics that mark out his membership in the global hip-hop nation as well as subvert the racialisation to which he is subjected.

Conclusion

In the same way as the Constitution of India could not 'get rid' of English as a functional language in India's complex multilingual environment and globalised society, Indian rap music cannot get rid of English. In this sense, India is perhaps different from other countries in which rap music developed to fully embracing local languages. As rappers negotiate between using English and local and translocal Indian languages, such as Punjabi, Hindi, Kannada or Tamil, they construct a complex multilingual landscape for Indian rap, where cultural and political fault lines and struggles can be explored. English in Indian rap music is thus not simply a colonial hangover, blind imitation, or even simple nativisation of American pop culture; rather it allows Indian rappers to build transformative connections to the global hip-hop community and negotiate belonging to multiple identities within and outside of India.

Notes

1. J. Mukherjee and T. Bernaisch 'The development of the English language in India' in A. Kirkpatrick (ed.) *The Routledge Handbook of World Englishes*, 2nd ed. (Oxon: Routledge, 2021): 165–77, p. 165.
2. E. W. Schneider *Postcolonial English: Varieties around the World* (Cambridge: Cambridge University Press, 2007): p. 161.
3. J. Mukherjee 'The development of the English language in India' in A. Kirkpatrick (ed.) *The Routledge Handbook of World Englishes* (London: Routledge, 2010): 167–80, p. 168
4. A. Sedlatschek *Contemporary Indian English: Variation and Change* (Amsterdam: John Benjamins, 2009): p. 16.

5. E. Annamalai 'Nativization of English in India and its effect on multilingualism' *Journal of Language and Politics* 3/1 (2004): 151–62; Ravinder Gargesh 'On nativizing the Indian English poetic medium' *World Englishes* 25(3/4) (2006): 359–71; Schneider (2007).
6. S. S. Rao 'India's language debates and education of linguistic minorities' *Economic & Political Weekly* 43/36 (2008): 63–9; Mukherjee (2010): 171–72; S. Labade, C. Lange, and S. Leuckert 'English in India: Global aspirations, local identities at the grassroots' in S. Buschfeld and A. Kautzsch (eds.) *Modelling World Englishes: A Joint Approach to Postcolonial and Non-Postcolonial Varieties* (Edinburgh: Edinburgh University Press, 2020): 85–111.
7. Mukherjee (2010) p. 170.
8. Rao (2008) p. 65.
9. V. Vaish 'A peripherist view of English as a language of decolonization in post-colonial India' *Language Policy* 4 (2005): pp. 187–206, p. 187.
10. K. Highet '"She will control my son": Navigating womanhood, English and social mobility in India' *Journal of Sociolinguistics* 26/5 (2022): 648–65.
11. Brodha V. (2018). Brodha V – X-clusive & Rare Interview by Raaj Jones (Part 2). Interview with Raaj Jones: 5:34–5:38, *YouTube*. Available at www.youtube.com/watch?v=qImvPSsXl_0 [Accessed 12 May 2022].
12. H. Osumare 'Beat streets in the global hood: Connective marginalities of the hip hop globe' *Journal of American & Comparative Cultures* 24(1/2) (2001): 171–81, p. 174.
13. R. A. Lukose *Liberalization's Children: Gender, Youth, and Consumer Citizenship in Globalizing India* (Durham & London: Duke University Press, 2009); S. Mysore, E. Cardozo, and Y. Ingle 'India' *Hip Hop Atlas*, special issue of *Global Hip Hop Studies* 3(1/2) (2023): 73–79, p. 74.
14. There are three versions: one each for the Tamil ('Pettai Rap'), Hindi ('Patti Rap'), and Telugu ('Peta Rap') version of the film. All composed by A. R. Rahman. The original is in Tamil.
15. E. Cardozo 'Hip Hop goes to B-Town: Bollywood's assimilation of the underground aesthetic' *SRFTI Take One* 2/1 (2021): 26–43, p. 28.
16. K. Gabriel 'Sexuality, mediation, commodification: The business of representation' in R. Ramdev, S. D. Nambiar, & D. Bhattacharya (eds.) *Sentiment, Politics, Censorship: The State of Hurt* (New Delhi: SAGE, 2016): 207–23, p. 207.
17. L. G. Gomes and E. Cardozo 'Legal ambiguities and cultural power struggle: The moral and legal persecution of rap in India' in A. J. Nocella (ed.) *Beats Not Beatings: The Rise of Hip Hop Criminology* (New York: Peter Lang, 2024): 91–104, pp. 92–96.
18. J. N. Singh and E. Cardozo 'Narrating the Indian hip hop OG: Ethnography, epistemic-deontic stance and chronotope' in M. Haugh & R. M. Reiter (eds.) *Morality in Discourse* (New York: Oxford University Press, 2025): 97–116.
19. J. N. Singh *Transcultural Voices: Narrating Hip Hop Culture in Complex Delhi* (Bristol: Multilingual Matters, 2022): p. 192.
20. Ibid., p. 193.

21. E. G. Dattatreyan *The Globally Familiar: Digital Hip Hop, Masculinity, and Urban Spaces in Delhi* (Durham, NC: Duke University Press, 2020);
E. G. Dattatreyan and J. N. Singh 'Ciphers, 'hoods and digital DIY studios in India: Negotiating aspirational individuality and hip hop collectivity' *Global Hip Hop Studies* 1/1 (2020): 25–45.
22. S. Saxena 'Homeboys: A photo essay on Delhi's underground hip hop culture' in Q. Williams & J. N. Singh (eds.) *Global Hiphopography* (Palgrave Macmillan, 2023): 131–55, p. 132; Mysore, Cardozo, and Ingle (2023) p. 74.
23. E. G. Dattatreyan 'Waiting subjects: Social media inspired self-portraits as gallery exhibition in Delhi, India' *Visual Anthropology Review* 31/2 (2015): 134–46.
24. J. N. Singh 'Migration, hip hop and translation zones in Delhi' in T. K. Lee (ed.) *The Routledge Handbook of Translation and the City* (London: Routledge, 2021): 308–25.
25. Mysore, Cardozo, and Ingle (2023) p. 74.
26. C. M. Motley and G. R. Henderson 'The global hip-hop diaspora: Understanding the culture' *Journal of Business Research* 61/3 (2007): 243–53, pp. 251–252.
27. Labade, Lange, and Leuckert (2020) p. 106.
28. J. N. Singh 'Transcultural decoloniality, global hip hop and reflexive narrative analysis' in S. M. de Barros & V. Resende (eds.) *Coloniality in Discourse: A Radical Critique* (London: Routledge, 2023): 135–57.
29. Despite not necessarily meaning the exact same thing as street, '*gully*' has eventually become India's spiritual equivalent to the street ethos in global hip-hop culture.
30. For a detailed account of this phenomenon in Bollywood, see Cardozo (2021).
31. Brodha V 1:43–1:50 in Raftaar & Brodha V (2019). *Raftaar x Brodha V – Naachne Ka Shaunq*. [music video] YouTube. Available at: https://www.youtube.com/watch?v=QvswgfLDuPg [Accessed 20 Feb 2025].
32. E. Annamalai 'Reflections on a Language Policy for Multilingualism' *Language Policy* 2 (2003): 113–32, cited in Rao (2008) p. 64.
33. Samos 11:47–12:23 in Kappal, B. & Samos, S. (2018). *Sumeet Samos, Episode 9*. [podcast] Gully Se Gully Tak. Available at: https://www.audible.in/pd/Sumeet-Samos-Podcast/B08DCTV663?ref=a_pd_Gully-_c1_1Asin_1_0 [Accessed 26 May 2022].
34. Ibid., 26:22–26:30.
35. Annamalai (2004) pp. 153, 159.
36. Samos in Kappal and Samos (2018) 25:31–25:47; 26:06–26:22.
37. G'nie 2:17–2:33 in Rapper Big Deal & G'nie (2020). *Rapper Big Deal ft G'nie – I'm A Chinkey (Official Music Video) | Prod by Big Deal*. [music video] YouTube. Available at: https://www.youtube.com/watch?app=desktop&v=j65fOa_G7VE&t=0s [Accessed 26 May 2022].
38. T. Haokip 'From "Chinky" to "Coronavirus": Racism against Northeast Indians during the COVID-19 pandemic' *Asian Ethnicity* 22/2 (2021): 353–73, pp. 4, 16.

18 | Television and the Janus Face of Chinese Hip-Hop

Style, Ideology, and Precarious Syncretization in *The Rap of China*

SHENG ZOU

What is Chinese hip-hop? Is it crystallized in the energizing spectacles of hit talent shows like *The Rap of China*? Or is it represented by the burgeoning scenes of "underground" hip-hop music in Chinese metropolises, infused with dialects and regional pride? Is it both? Or neither? This question harks back to the fundamental problematics of global hip-hop – issues of authenticity, glocalization, and incorporation, which this chapter sets out to explore within the Chinese context. Instead of seeing Chinese hip-hop as a given cultural form, I conceptualize it as a precarious cultural formation suspended by competing claims to authenticity that contain the potential to cancel each other out. Whereas different parties may entertain their own ideas of what constitutes pure or "real" (Chinese) hip-hop, when Chinese hip-hop was thrown into the limelight, it was already multiply syncretized and overdetermined by divergent forces, such as the hip-hop communities, the state, record labels, media platforms, the mainstream market, and so forth.

The release of *The Rap of China* in 2017 was a decisive moment in the massification of hip-hop in China. The lingua franca of hip-hop (or *xiha* in Chinese) entered the everyday discourse of the Chinese audience, where terms such as "skr," "diss," "beef," and "freestyle" become popular catchphrases among young people. The show's phenomenal commercial success was, however, soon followed by tightening state censorship, which led to its rebranding and reformation. This chapter takes the show's development from 2017 through 2018 as a point of departure to examine hip-hop culture in mainstream Chinese media. It is essential to note that the aim of this chapter is not to provide a general overview of hip-hop's development in China but rather to focus specifically on its massification through the medium of online television. I will start by elaborating the cultural specificity of Chinese hip-hop and my construal of it as a precariously syncretized genre. Then I will use *The Rap of China* (Seasons 1 and 2) as a case to illuminate in more concrete ways how the shape of Chinese hip-hop was wrought by different forces to befit televisual representation.

Chinese Hip-Hop as Precarious Syncretization

This section briefly surveys key moments in the development of hip-hop, especially rap music, in China. It is not to be read as a complete genealogy of Chinese hip-hop; there is probably no easy way to construct one, since Chinese hip-hop did not spring out of a unitary root or follow a singular route. It is, to some degree, rhizomatic in that it has proliferated domestically through different nodes at different points in time. Originally an African-American subculture, hip-hop has circulated around the world through different routes, spawning the formation of a network of translocal style communities.[1] Rap music, as a key component of hip-hop culture, is localized in different societies to bear on locally relevant themes and sentiments. A central theme in the localization of hip-hop across the world is the overt politicization of the genre as a subversive cultural practice. Notable cases include the use of hip-hop as a means of political resistance in the social movements of North Africa and the Middle East,[2] and the influence of political rappers such as the Public Enemy, known for their slogan "Fight the Power!" This is unsurprising, considering that hip-hop emerged in African-American society to negotiate subaltern identities and experiences of marginalization.[3]

Yet a depoliticizing or mainstreaming tendency is equally noteworthy in global hip-hop, which deserves more scrutiny. Elham Golpushnezhad documents how hip-hop in Iran as an originally underground DIY culture has, over the past decade, become aligned with mainstream values and turned into a kind of mainstream popular music supported and funded indirectly by the Islamic state.[4] The officially legitimized hip-hop attempts to build a new youth culture with an Islamic identity that is considered appropriate for the young generations and the larger society. It creates a space for young artists to appreciate the progress that the Islamic state has made in technology, science, and politics. In Russia, the hip-hop scene is shared by pro-Kremlin, anti-establishment, and relatively moderate rappers, with the pro-Kremlin ones following the authoritarian ethos and pledging allegiance to the political leadership.[5] Similar trends could be observed in the increasingly mainstreamed Chinese hip-hop culture.

Hip-hop, particularly rap music, found its way into China in the early 1990s largely via *dakou* (literally "cut") tapes and CDs – excess stock from

Western record labels scrapped and shipped to China to be recycled, which ended up being traded on the Chinese black market.[6] Meanwhile, since the mid 1980s, some nightclubs and bars in Beijing and Shanghai started playing hip-hop music regularly; in the 1990s, they began to convene hip-hop nights.[7] Influenced by Western rap music as well as artists from Hong Kong and Taiwan, pioneering rap artists in mainland China emerged in the 1990s, such as D.D. Rhythm, Li Xiaolong, and Hi-Bomb (*hei bang*). At that time, Hi-Bomb was already mixing dialect (Shanghainese) with Mandarin and English in their rap; Li eventually got the opportunity to expose his music to a mainstream audience by rapping the theme song for the hit TV show, Loquacious Zhang Damin's Happy Life.[8]

In early 2000s, a couple of other rap groups influenced the development of hip-hop in Mainland China, such as CMBC (Chinese MC Brothers) and Yin T'sang. The former was established in 2000 in Beijing by several Chinese male rappers, and the latter was founded in the same year, consisting of four members, including Beijing b-boy MC Webber, Chinese-born Canadian Sbazzo, and two white Americans dubbed Lao Zheng XIV and Dirty Heff. Their records were produced by an independent label in Beijing named Scream Records (*Haojiao Changpian*). In 2002, Detroit-born Dana "Showtyme" Burton launched a rap battle series in Shanghai known as the Iron Mic, which provided a vital meeting space for underground rappers. Since the early 2000s, rap crews mushroomed in Chinese major metropolises such as Beijing, Shanghai, Guangzhou, Tianjin, Nanjing, Xi'an, Wuhan, Changsha, and Chengdu; such regional centers saw the blossoming of the underground hip-hop culture in China. In the 2010s, rap labels proliferated in numerous Chinese cities, some of which would later be popularized by *The Rap of China*, such as Monster Gang, NOUS, HHH, and GO$H. Although these labels claim to represent the ethos of underground rap in China, they bespeak the formation of a burgeoning commercial economy in the Chinese hip-hop scene.

The popularization of the Internet since the turn of the millennium has provided another venue for the production and circulation of localized rap music in China, enabling some rap songs to reach a wider audience. Some of these localized rap songs bear on a range of social issues in China, and "assert an oppositional, counterhegemonic voice against the Chinese educational system, high official culture, and mainstream discourse."[9]

In the 2010s, talent shows became another important venue through which rap music was brought to a wider audience. Since television in China is a heavily regulated space, the rap songs performed on television never stray too far from the officially endorsed ideology. In 2014, Fat Shady's performance of a Sichuanese rap song, "Not Going to Work Tomorrow," on the state-run network CCTV marked the legitimation of Chinese hip-hop in the new era. Since 2015, rap began to be incorporated in state-sponsored propaganda (co-)produced by Party organs and state-run outlets. The Sichuanese rap group CDC, who collaborated with the Communist Youth League on pro-state rap music videos, is a prime case in point. Yet it is not until the release of the hit show, *The Rap of China*, that a nationwide hip-hop craze was ignited.

The questions around authenticity always remain unresolved and continue to be contested till the present. It is also noteworthy that the mainstreaming and commercialization of hip-hop occurred long before *The Rap of China*. By the time hip-hop reached the mainstream audience via the show, it had already been multiply syncretized, blending artistic influences from the West, Hong Kong, and Taiwan while mixing Mandarin Chinese, English, local dialects, and sometimes elements of traditional musical and vocal arts. It has also been pushed and pulled – stabilized and destabilized – by multiple actors and forces, such as the grassroots, the corporate, and the state. Chinese hip-hop is thus a precarious cultural formation whose defining characteristics are constantly contested and reshaped.

The Rap of China: Battles for Authenticity

The Rap of China premiered on the Chinese popular video streaming platform IQiyi in 2017 and garnered 2.99 billion views before it ended.[10] The online TV show was intended to bring hip-hop from the underground to the mainstream. Artists from a number of rap crews and labels participated in the show, including GAI from Chongqing-based GO$H and PG One from Xi'an-based HHH, who would share the trophy in the end. These rap artists lay claims to authentic hip-hop and set themselves apart from those participants branded as "idols," who are trainees at entertainment companies catering to a mainstream market. Nonetheless, the entry of these underground rappers into this commercial spectacle, in effect, signifies the very incorporation of hip-hop into the mainstream culture.

Hebdige,[11] as well as Peterson and Anand,[12] examines the massification and commodification of subcultural forms, lending insights into the mainstreaming of hip-hop in China. Hebdige observes how a subculture is incorporated into mainstream culture at both commercial and ideological levels. At the commercial level, subcultural signs can be converted into mass cultural products. At the ideological level, a subversive cultural form can be redefined by the dominant groups; it can be trivialized, domesticated, or "transformed into meaningless exotica."[13] On a related note, Peterson and Anand point to the dialectical loop of resistance and appropriation: the subaltern enacts a resistant cultural style by appropriating popular cultural products; the authorities react to the resistant cultural groups, which attracts media attention and mass emulation; the industry then "denudes the resistance of any symbolic force" and mass-markets the sanitized symbols back to the consumers.[14] The televisual remediation of hip-hop in *The Rap of China* is characterized by sanitization, domestication, and commercialization, where the subcultural style is marketed to a mass audience as a symbolic commodity.

The hip-hop style is visually manifested in the contestants' baggy clothes, baseball caps, chains, tattoos, piercings, and braided hair. When one contestant Sun Bayi showed up in business casual clothes, he was initially teased for being out of place. The show utilizes a bold "R!CH" sign as its official logo and a golden chain as a symbol of recognition bestowed upon contestants moving to the next round of the competition. In terms of the format, the show combines open auditions, freestyle cypher battles, one-on-one rap battles, team performances, and so on. Lyrically, the rap songs on the show often contain English words commonly found in American hip-hop culture, such as "homie," "hater," and "gangsta." Among the common themes are "money," "girls," camaraderie, and braggadocio, which are not unfamiliar to fans of Western hip-hop.

Yet the localized rap songs also reflect distinct Chinese motifs, cultural frames, and social realities. Due to state censorship and industry-wide self-censorship, the rap songs performed on the show do not match up to the "Fight the Power" mantra as does Western politically conscious rap; nonetheless, it would be hasty to conclude that they do not contain any politics at all. In fact, many of them tackle the politics of everyday life, concerned with self-actualization and with the micropolitics of personal interests and life choices. Several rappers, who were born in the 1980s and 1990s, negotiate their experiences of growing up in the post-reform China marked by volatility, tensions, conflicts, and disparities, etc. They rap about personal striving, diligence, and the longing for a better material life.

Moreover, some rappers creatively incorporate elements of Chinese traditional musical style and literary/cultural references. The first season co-winner, GAI, is particularly known for his use of Sichuanese dialect and classic Chinese references in his trap and gansta rap, creating what is known as the "jianghu flow" – "jianghu" denoting a somewhat lawless and marginal space in Chinese literary imagination. The "jianghu" frame in

Chinese hip-hop serves as "a vehicle for themes like struggle, solidarity, and honor, and a metaphor for the Chinese 'underground' hip-hop community."[15] "Jianghu" is also an allegory of the street life in Chinese cities, especially the marginal experiences of young delinquents and hooligans.

The focus on the politics and struggles of everyday life is a major source of authenticity for underground Chinese hip-hop. However, the underground rappers' claim to authenticity is constantly contested by other parties and forces. In *The Rap of China*, a major fault line lies in the division among the celebrity judges, underground rappers, and the "idol" trainees. The "feud" between underground rappers and "idols" are shown not only in the two camps' reactions to each other's performances but also in their lyrics, where "fake rappers" are dissed. The underground rappers often cast doubt on the four celebrity judges' authority, as most of the judges are considered pop stars rather than respectable rappers. In fact, the show met with pushback and critique from the wider community of hip-hop artists and fans in China since the very beginning, with the onslaught of viral memes online mocking the celebrity judge Kris Wu, who would often confront contestants with the question, "Do you have freestyle?"[16]

Whereas the underground rappers see hip-hop as a spirit of being "real," the celebrity judges and idol trainees tend to approach it as a craft to be acquired and perfected through hard work and practice. The judges focus heavily on the technical aspects of rapping, such as rhythms, rhymes, and flows. When one rapper was eliminated during the open audition, he challenged Kris Wu, asking the latter for an explanation. Wu then pointed to issues with his rhythms, a reason that the rapper found unconvincing. Such technicalization of rap speaks to the depoliticizing tendency of the show, which separates style and ideology, form and meaning, techne and ethos. Not only do the judges regularly resort to musical jargons, but the show also utilizes on-screen visuals to count the contestants' verbal rhymes to popularize knowledge about the craft of rapping. The recourse to the technical is a vital means in which those unaffiliated with the underground community maintain their claims to authenticity.

Most importantly, the underground rappers' attempt to "keep it real" is counterbalanced by the political imperative to promote what is known as "positive energy" (*zheng nengliang*), namely dispositions and values aligned with the official ideology. For instance, a contestant named Huang Xu performed a song on the show called "Round 4," where he lambasted the kind of rap filled with vulgar language and references to drugs and alcohol while taking it upon himself to promote positive energy through hip-hop by emphasizing love and respect. This brand of "positive energy"-loaded rap became more salient in the second season of the show, which underwent a thorough reformation due to tightening state censorship.

From *xiha* to *shuochang*: The Return of Ideology

When I was researching the convergence of ideological governance and entertainment in China in 2018, I spoke to an editor from a state-run outlet about the use of rap in viral propaganda stunts. When I used the term *xiha*, a transliteration of hip-hop in Mandarin, he was quick to correct me, explaining that the word *xiha* was inappropriate and that the officially endorsed translation should be *shuochang*, literally "speak-and-sing." To the official media, *xiha* is suggestive of an unruly subculture, while *shuochang* appears more neutral. It was no coincidence that the Chinese name of *The Rap of China* was altered for the second season in 2018, with *shuochang* replacing *xiha*. This intentional word choice not only reflects what I have called the technicalization of hip-hop, but also reframes the foreign genre in relation to the Chinese vocal art tradition that combines singing and storytelling.

The renaming of the show was a result of tightening censorship after its first season gained mainstream popularity. Hip-hop in China, like other subcultural formations, faces a paradox between gaining visibility/viability on the one hand and retaining integrity/authenticity on the other. The more popular it becomes, the more susceptible it is to incorporation by the state and/or commercial forces. In early January, PG One was condemned by Chinese authorities for portraying womanizing and drug use in one of his songs. Meanwhile, GAI was abruptly removed from the line-up of a popular variety show *Singer*. Soon the authorities went further to put forth a ban on the representation of hip-hop culture on audiovisual programs. In January 2018, the State Administration of Press, Publication, Radio, Film and Television (SAPPRFT) of China mandated that audiovisual programs should not feature actors with tattoos or showcase hip-hop culture, non-mainstream culture, and dispirited culture.[17]

Under such pressure, the show underwent a thorough reformation, resulting in a heavier focus on "peace and love," a spirit more compatible with the promotion of "positive energy." The beefing between contestants and judges or among contestants themselves was significantly toned down, giving way to expressions of respect. The first episode of Season 2 included a couple of contestants who came from top universities, emphasizing their decent education background as well as their positive and affable images.

Another major characteristic of Season 2 is its salient nationalistic hue, particularly its promotion of a pan-Chinese identity. It recruited rappers not only from the Mainland cities, but also from Taiwan and overseas; it conspicuously features four artists from Xinjiang, who would be more widely known as the "Tianshan Four."[18] Two of them, LIL-EM and AIR, ended up competing for the trophy. Throughout the show, expressions of national pride and identification abound. In the opening cypher of the first episode, Kris Wu rapped, "I am from China, I represent this land," against the backdrop of Chinese-style stage props. In the season finale, he performed another song entitled "Chinese Soul," with a hook that repeats, "You see I am Chinese, you know I have a Chinese soul."

A number of contestants also proactively include statements of national loyalty in their performances. For instance, in "Erzi Wawa," Uyghur hip-hop artist LIL-EM rapped, "I'm from Xinjiang, and I'm made in China." AIR, another Uyghur rapper, had a similar line in his song "Hip Hop 101": "I come from a minority ethnic group but rap in Mandarin Chinese ... We Made it From China Westside." Likewise, Chinese-American rapper Al Rocco, expressed his cultural identification in a song called "Differences," with lines that said, "My dream is that Chinese culture goes global" "My skin is yellow, I'm really not different from you." Interestingly, Al Rocco also participated in Season 1 and got eliminated then due to his inability to rap in Chinese. Soon after his elimination from Season 1, he even released an English-language diss track online to lash out at the show. Yet when he came back to Season 2, he managed to rap fluently in Mandarin Chinese and became what he dubbed a "China representer." LIL-EM and Al Rocco also collaborated in another performance, "Rep that Culture," where the two rapped together, "We all made in China."

Rap thus becomes a cultural medium of propaganda reinfused with official ideology. The tenet of authenticity innate to hip-hop culture is seriously challenged. An important question to consider is the sincerity of the rapper's expressions. Is the nationalistic rap an expression of the musicians' deep-felt sense of identification, or simply a strategic response to censorship? From the outset, Season 2 of the show sought to strike a balance between artistic creativity, the aesthetic of authenticity, and the hegemonic ideological orientation – a balance that is difficult to maintain. As the rappers furnish their lyrics with Chinese references and cultural frames in a standardized manner (e.g., "descendants of the dragon," "yellow skin," "black hair"), such references and frames become formulaic and lose their vitality; they become a performative stylistic device serving the purpose of embellishment rather than signification. In this light, a latent paradox is at play, where the attempt to reimbue a subcultural style with official ideology eventually risks desensitizing the audience and reducing ideology itself into a vehicle of style.

In addition to nationalism, another important theme of the rap songs on the show is dedication to the family. In a sense, one's dedication to the family is consistent with one's loyalty to the nation-state, both being vital components of the hegemonic moral order. The rappers, predominantly male, often pay tribute to their mothers for raising them up and teaching them life lessons. Some male rappers also dedicate their songs to their wives and children. A notable example is LIL-EM's "Real Man," which discusses a (straight) man's responsibility as a son, a father, and a husband. The song defines a "real man," as one who works hard, protects his family, and maintains his moral integrity. Thus, the song promotes a type of hegemonic masculinity in line with the established ideology and moral order.

Not only does Season 2 of the show succumb to the dominant political ideology, but it also goes one step further in catering toward the mainstream market. Both seasons of the show are interspersed with catchy native ads, where popular contestants from the show rap for the sponsoring brands. Thanks to the show's prior success, Season 2 attracted more attention from advertisers and music streaming platforms. Moreover, commercial interests also started to play a more salient role in determining the value of the rappers' works. In one episode, executives from four Chinese music streaming platforms were invited as judges to select the semi-finalists. The major criterion they used was the degree to which a given contestant's music would appeal to the mainstream audience. Their decisions were contested by the celebrity judges who showed more sympathy to the rappers' musicality. The instance speaks to the contestation over authenticity and authority in localized Chinese hip-hop, an insoluble fault line that has been repeatedly turned into a spectacle throughout the show.

Conclusion

The Rap of China continued to be renewed for another two seasons and inspired other hip-hop talent shows such as *Rap for Youth, New Generation Hip-Hop Project*, and so forth. As the first show to experiment with the popularization of hip-hop, *The Rap of China* lent rich experience to the ensuing shows. The massification of hip-hop in China has been making headway, where a tried-and-true template is rehashed over and over again to tap a burgeoning market.

This chapter has shown how Chinese hip-hop took off amid the deepening process of cultural globalization and mushroomed rhizomatically via multiple nodes, venues, and media technologies. Chinese hip-hop, as we know it, is always already remediated and is to be understood as a precarious cultural formation, constantly evolving while overdetermined by divergent forces, including hip-hop communities, the state, and commercial forces. This conception challenges the idea that there exists any pure form of Chinese hip-hop or that "the underground" is the sole source of authentic hip-hop. It calls into question the line between "the underground" and the mainstream, showing instead the involvement of underground rappers in their own mainstreaming.

On the issue of authenticity, I concur with Pennycook that the concept should be understood "not so much as an individualist obsession with the self but rather as a dialogical engagement with community."[19] In the context of my analysis, the authenticity of Chinese hip-hop is subject to constant contestation and redefinition by different groups or communities, whose horizons differ from and negotiate with one other; they co-shape the unique trajectory of Chinese hip-hop, particularly what is visible, audible, and commendable.

In the syncretic cultural formation of Chinese hip-hop, the subcultural style and official ideology sit uneasily with one another. The endeavor to indoctrinate the dominant ideology through rap music is predicated on a precarious, if not untenable, balance between spontaneity and control, between authenticity and stratagem. Although the rappers may claim to be "real" when chanting nationalistic lines by way of expressing their cultural identification, the way in which their creativity is delimited and channeled fundamentally contradicts the ethics of authenticity. In response, the savvy audience may resort to oppositional readings to fend off the influence of the propagandistic rap. The battles for authenticity will continue to be fought on different fronts in and out of mainstream hip-hop shows. Despite the volatility of Chinese cultural policies and the uncertainty in the prospect of Chinese hip-hop, the issues discussed in this chapter will likely remain central to the development and dilemma of Chinese hip-hop in the years to come.

Notes

1. Alim, H. Samy, "Translocal Style Communities: Hip Hop Youth as Cultural Theorists of Style, Language, and Globalization." *Pragmatics*, 19, no. 1 (2009): 103–127.
2. Marcyliena Morgan and Dionne Bennett, "Hip-Hop & the Global Imprint of a Black Cultural Form." *Daedalus*, 140, no. 2 (2011): 176–196.
3. Tricia Rose, *Black Noise: Rap and Black Culture in Contemporary America* (Hanover, NH: Wesleyan University Press, 1994).
4. Elham Golpushnezhad, "Untold Stories of DIY/Underground Iranian Rap Culture: The Legitimization of Iranian Hip-Hop and the Loss of Radical Potential." *Cultural Sociology* 12, no. 2 (2008): 260–275.
5. Anastasia Denisova and Aliaksandr Herasimenka, "How Russian Rap on YouTube Advances Alternative Political Deliberation: Hegemony, Counter-hegemony, and Emerging Resistant Publics." *Social Media+ Society*, 5, no. 2 (2019): 1–11.
6. Nathanel Amar, "Do You Have Freestyle?: The Roots of Censorship in Chinese Hip-hop," *China Perspectives*, no. 1–2 (2018): 107–113; Jeroen de Kloet, *China With a Cut: Globalisation, Urban Youth and Popular Music*, (Amsterdam: Amsterdam University Press, 2010).
7. Wai-Chung Ho, *Popular Music, Cultural Politics and Music Education in China* (Abingdon: Routledge, 2016).
8. Shuhong Fan, "The History of Rap in China, Part 1: Early Roots and Iron Mics (1993–2009)." *RadiiChina* (February 1, 2019). https://radiichina.com/the-history-of-rap-in-china-part-1-early-roots-and-iron-mics-1993-2009/.
9. Jin Liu, "Alternative Voice and Local Youth Identity in Chinese Local-Language Rap Music." *Positions: East Asia Cultures Critique*, 22, no. 1 (2014): 266.
10. Mengyu Luo and Wei Ming, W, "From Underground to Mainstream and Then What? Empowerment and Censorship in China's Hip-Hop Music." *Critical Arts*, 34, no. 6 (2020): 1–12.
11. Dick Hebdige, *Subculture: The Meaning of Style* (London: Routledge, 1979).
12. Richard A. Peterson and N. Anand, "The Production of Culture Perspective." *Annual Review of Sociology*, 30, no. 1 (2004): 311–334.
13. Hebdige, 97.
14. Peterson and Anand, 325.
15. Jonathan Sullivan and Yupei Zhao, "Rappers as Knights-Errant: Classic Allusions in the Mainstreaming of Chinese Rap." *Popular Music and Society*, 44, no. 3 (2021): 274–291.
16. Alexander Zhang, "Keep It 'Skr': The Incorporation of Hip-Hop Subculture through Chinese Talent Shows and the Online Battle for Authenticity." *Georgetown Journal of Asian Affairs*, 5 (2019): 73–93.

17. Casey Quackenbush and Aria Chen, "'Tasteless, Vulgar and Obscene.' China Just Banned Hip-Hop Culture and Tattoos From Television." *Time* (January 22, 2018). https://time.com/5112061/china-hip-hop-ban-tattoos-television/
18. The Tianshan is a mountain range in Central Asia that stretches for thousands of miles across Xinjiang.
19. Alastair Pennycook, "Language, Localization, and the Real: Hip-Hop and the Global Spread of Authenticity." *Journal of Language, Identity, and Education*, 6, no. 2 (2007): 103.

Selected Bibliography

Agamben, Giorgio. *The End of the Poem* (Stanford: Stanford University Press, 1999).

Alim, H. Samy. *Roc the Mic Right: The Language of Hip Hop Culture* (London: Routledge, 2006).

Alim, H. Samy, Awad Ibrahim, and Alastair Pennycook (eds.), *Global Linguistic Flows: Hip Hop Cultures, Youth Identities, and the Politics of Language* (New York: Routledge, 2009).

Amar, Nathanel. "'Do You Freestyle?': The Roots of Censorship in Chinese Hip-Hop," *China Perspectives* 1/2 (2018): 107–113.

Androutsopoulos, Jannis (ed.). *HipHop: Globale Kultur – lokale Praktiken* (Bielefeld: Transcript, 2003).

Appert, Catherine M. "On Hybridity in African Popular Music: The Case of Senegalese Hip Hop," *Ethnomusicology* 60/2 (2016): 279–299.

Appert, Catherine M. *In Hip Hop Time: Music, Memory, and Social Change in Urban Senegal* (Oxford: Oxford University Press, 2018).

Augustyn, Heather. "Spinning Wheels: The Circular Evolution of Jive, Toasting, and Rap," *Caribbean Quarterly* 61/1 (2015): 60–74.

Ayim, May, Katharina Oguntoye, and Dagmar Schulz (eds.), *Farbe bekennen: Afro-deutsche Frauen auf den Spuren ihrer Geschichte* (Berlin: Orlando-Frauenverlag, 1986).

Bailey, Moya. *Misogynoir Transformed: Black Women's Digital Resistance* (New York: New York University Press, 2021).

Baym, Nancy K., and Jabari M. Evans. "The Audacity of Clout (Chasing): Digital Strategies of Black Youth in Chicago DIY Hip-Hop," *International Journal of Communication* 16 (2022): 2669–2687.

Blanch, Faye R., and Guthrie Worby. "The Silences Waiting: Young Nunga Males, Curriculum and Rap," *Curriculum Perspectives* 30/1 (2010): 1–13.

Boakye, Jeffrey. *Hold Tight: Black Masculinity, Millennials and the Meaning of Grime* (London: Influx Press, 2017).

Bradley, Adam. *Book of Rhymes: The Poetics of Hip-Hop* (New York: Basic Civitas, 2009).

Bramwell, Richard. *UK Hip-Hop, Grime and the City* (London: Routledge, 2015).

Bramwell, Richard, and James Butterworth. "Beyond the Street: The Institutional Life of Rap," *Popular Music* 39/2 (2020): 169–186.

Brennan, Tim. "Off the Gangsta Tip: A Rap Appreciation, or Forgetting about Los Angeles," *Critical Inquiry* 20/4 (1994): 663–693.

Burton, Justin Adams. *Posthuman Rap* (Oxford: Oxford University Press, 2017).

Caines, Rebecca. "Giving Back Time: Improvisation in Australian Hip-Hop Pedagogy and Performance," *Critical Studies in Improvisation* 6/2 (2010): 1–19.

Cardozo, Elloit. "Hip Hop Goes to B-Town: Bollywood's Assimilation of the Underground Aesthetic," *SRFTI Take One* 2/1 (2021): 26–43.

Chang, Jeff. *Can't Stop, Won't Stop: A History of the Hip Hop Generation* (London: Ebury Press, 2007).

Chetty, Darren, and Patrick Turner. "Towards a Hip Hop Pedagogy of Discomfort," *Journal of World Popular Music* 5/1 (June 2018): 71–87.

Clair, Isabelle. "'La racaille,' a Performed Figure in French Contemporary Youth," *Ethnography* 0/0 (2021).

Clark, Timothy. *The Poetics of Singularity* (Edinburgh: Edinburgh University Press, 2005).

Cordell, Tom, and Malcolm James. "Mutualism, Massive and the City to Come: Jungle Pirate Radio in 1990s London," *Soundings* 77 (2021): 109–120.

Cutler, Cecelia. *White Hip Hoppers, Language and Identity in Post-Modern America* (New York: Routledge, 2014).

Dattatreyan, Ethiraj G. *The Globally Familiar: Digital Hip Hop, Masculinity, and Urban Spaces in Delhi* (Durham: Duke University Press, 2020).

Dattatreyan, Ethiraj G., and Jaspal Singh. "Ciphers, 'hoods and Digital DIY Studios in India: Negotiating Aspirational Individuality and Hip Hop Collectivity," *Global Hip Hop Studies* 1/1 (2020): 25–45.

de Lacey, Alex. "Pirate Mentality: How London Radio Has Shaped Creative Practice in Grime Music," *Radio Journal International Studies in Broadcast & Audio Media* 19/1 (2021): 197–215.

de Lacey, Alex. "Live and Direct? Censorship and Racialised Public Morality in Grime and Drill Music," *Popular Music* 41/4 (2022): 495–510.

de Lacey, Alex. *Level Up: Live Performance and Creative Process in Grime Music* (London: Routledge, 2023).

Denisova, Anastasia, and Aliaksandr Herasimenka. "How Russian Rap on YouTube Advances Alternative Political Deliberation: Hegemony, Counter-Hegemony, and Emerging Resistant Publics," *Social Media + Society* 5/2 (2019): 1–11.

Derrida, Jacques. *Acts of Literature* (New York: Routledge, 1992).

Dowsett, Sudiipta Shamalii. "Sampling Ceremony: Hip-Hop Workshops and Intergenerational Cultural Production in the Central Australian Desert," *The Asia Pacific Journal of Anthropology* 22/2–3 (2021): 184–202.

Dunbar, Adam, and Charis Kubrin. "Imagining Violent Criminals: An Experimental Investigation of Music Stereotypes and Character Judgments," *Journal of Experimental Criminology* 14/4 (2018): 507–528.

Dunbar, Adam, Charis Kubrin, and Nicholas Scurich. "The Threatening Nature of 'Rap' Music," *Psychology, Public Policy and Law* 22 (2016): 280–292.

Durand, Alain-Philippe (ed.). *Hip Hop Français: An Exploration of Hip Hop Culture in the Francophone World* (London: Rowman & Littlefield, 2020).

Dyson, Michael Eric. *Know What I Mean? Reflections on Hip Hop* (New York: Basic Civitas Books, 2007).

Emerson, Rana A. "'Where My Girls At?' Negotiating Black Womanhood in Music Videos," *Gender and Society* 1/16 (2002): 115–135.

Evans, Jabari. "'We [Mostly] Carry Guns for the Internet': Visibility, Labour, Social Hacking and Chasing Digital Clout by Black Male Youth in Chicago's Drill Rap Scene," *Global Hip Hop Studies* 1/2 (2020): 227–247.

Exarchos, Michail. *Reimagining Sample-Based Hip Hop: Making Records within Records* (London: Routledge, 2024).

Fatsis, Lambros. "Policing the Beats: The Criminalisation of UK Drill and Grime Music by the London Metropolitan Police," *The Sociological Review* 67/6 (2019): 1300–1316.

Fatsis, Lambros. "Decriminalising Rap Beat by Beat Two Questions in Search of Answers," in Eleanor Peters (ed.). *Music in Crime, Resistance, and Identity* (London: Routledge, 2023) pp. 63–77.

Flew, Terry, Mark Ryan, and Chunmeizi Su. "Culture, Communication and Hybridity: The Case of *The Rap of China*," *Journal of Multicultural Discourses* 14/2 (2019): 93–106.

Ford, James Edward. "'The Unclean Break': Re-Imagining the Sound of Hip-Hop," *College Literature* 46 (2019): 269–274.

Gaetner, Thomas. *Hip-Hop: Le rap français des années 1990* (Paris: Editions Fetjaine, 2012).

Gana, Nouri. "Rap and Revolt in the Arab World," *Social Text* 30/4 (2012): 25–53.

Gaunt, Kyra D. "YouTube, Twerking & You: Context Collapse and the Handheld Co-presence of Black Girls and Miley Cyrus," *Journal of Popular Music Studies* 27/3 (2015): 244–273.

Gilbers, Steven. Ambitionz az a Ridah: 2Pac's Changing Accent and Flow in Light of Regional Variation in African-American English Speech and Hip-Hop Music. Doctoral dissertation. University of Groningen, 2021.

Gilroy, Paul. *There Ain't no Black in the Union Jack: The Cultural Politics of Race and Nation* (London: Routledge, 1987).

Gilroy, Paul. *The Black Atlantic: Modernity and Double Consciousness* (London: Verso, 1993).

Gladney, Marvin. "The Black Arts Movement and Hip-Hop," *African American Review* 29 (1995): 291–301.

Goldberg, David A. M. "Beats, Rhymes, and Life in the Ocean of Sound: An Object-Oriented Methodology for Encountering Rap Music," *Biography* 41 (2018): 587–606.

Golpushnezhad, Elham. "Untold Stories of DIY/Underground Iranian Rap Culture: The Legitimization of Iranian Hip-Hop and the Loss of Radical Potential," *Cultural Sociology* 12/2 (2008): 260–275.

Hadley, Susan, and George Yancy. *Therapeutic Uses of Rap and Hip-Hop* (New York: Routledge, 2012).

Hammou, Karim. "Mainstreaming French Rap Music," *Poetics* 59 (2016): 67–81.

Hammou, Karim. *Une histoire du rap en France* (Paris: La Découverte, 2014).

Hammou, Karim, and Marie Sonnette-Manouguian (eds.), *Quarante ans de musiques hip-hop en France* (Paris: Presses de sciences po, 2022).

Hancox, Dan. *Inner City Pressure* (London: William Collins, 2018).

Hancox, Dan. "Pirates and Olympians: DejaVu FM and the Copper Box Arena," in Alberto Duman, Dan Hancox, Malcolm James, and Anna Minton (eds.), *Regeneration Songs: Sounds of Investment and Loss from East London* (London: Repeater Books, 2018).

Harkness, Geoff. "Gangs and Gangsta Rap in Chicago: A Microscenes Perspective," *Poetics*, 41/2, (2013): 151–176.

Harrison, Anthony Kwame. "Racial Authenticity in Rap Music and Hip Hop," *Sociology Compass*, 2/6, (2008): 1783–1800.

Haynes, Jo, and Lee Marshall. "Beats and Tweets: Social Media in the Careers of Independent Musicians," *New Media & Society*, 20/5, (2018): 1973–1993.

Hebdige, Dick. *Cut 'N' Mix* (Abingdon and New York: Routledge, 1987).

Henriques, Julian. *Sonic Bodies: Reggae Sound Systems, Performance Techniques, and Ways of Knowing* (New York: Continuum, 2011).

Higgins, Paulo. "Femmes et Queers: des publics subalternes et cachés du rap français?" *Volume!* 17/2 (2020): 129–146.

Hill, Edwin C. *Black Soundscapes White Stages: The Meaning of Francophone Sound in the Black Atlantic* (Baltimore: Johns Hopkins University Press, 2013).

Hill Collins, Patricia. *Black Sexual Politics* (New York and London: Routledge, 2004).

Ho, Wai-Chung. *Popular Music, Cultural Politics and Music Education in China*, (Abingdon: Routledge, 2016).

Honkanen, Martti. "Tien estetiikka ja tietaide," in Arto Haapala, Martti Honkanen and Veijo Rantala (eds.), *Ympäristö, arkkitehtuuri, estetiikka* (Helsinki: Gaudeamus, 1995) pp. 51–57.

Hunter, Margaret. "Shake It, Baby, Shake It: Consumption and the New Gender Relation in Hip Hop," *Sociological Perspectives* 54/1 (2011): 15–36.

Ilan, Jonathan. "Digital Street Culture Decoded: Why Criminalizing Drill Music Is Street Illiterate and Counterproductive," *British Journal of Criminology* 60/4 (2020): 994–1013.

James, Malcolm. *Sonic Intimacy: Reggae Sound Systems, Jungle Pirate Radio and Grime YouTube Music Videos* (London: Bloomsbury, 2020).

Kajikawa, Loren. *Sounding Race in Rap Songs* (Berkeley: University of California Press, 2015).

Katz, Mark. *Groove Music: the Art and Culture of the Hip-Hop DJ* (New York: Oxford University Press, 2012).

Kehrer, Lauron. *Queer Voices in Hip Hop: Cultures, Communities, and Contemporary Performance* (Ann Arbor: University of Michigan Press, 2022).

Kelley, Robin. *Yo' Mama's Disfunktional: Fighting the Culture Wars in Urban America* (Boston: Beacon Press, 2008).

Keyes, Cheryl. *Rap Music and Street Consciousness* (Urbana: University of Illinois Press, 2002).

Kitwana, Bakari. *The Hip Hop Generation: Young Blacks and the Crisis in African-American Culture* (New York: Basic Civitas Books, 2002) 175–177.

Kochman, Thomas (ed.). *Rappin' and Stylin' Out: Communication in Urban America* (Urbana: University of Illinois Press, 1972).

Krims, Adam. *Rap Music and the Poetics of Identity* (Cambridge: Cambridge University Press, 2000).

Kubrin, Charis and Erik Nielson. "Rap on Trial," *Race and Justice* 4/3 (2014): 185–211.

Lee, Murray. "This Is Not a Drill: Towards a Sonic and Sensorial Musicriminology," *Crime Media Culture* 18/3 (2022): 446–465.

Lee, Murray, Toby Martin, Jioji Ravulo, and Ricky Simandjuntak. "[Dr]illing in the Name of: The Criminalisation of Sydney Drill Group ONEFOUR," *Current Issues in Criminal Justice*, 34/4 (2022): 339–359.

Leland, John, *Hip: The History* (New York: Harper Collins, 2004).

Liu, Siyuan, Chow, Ho Ming, Xu, Yisheng, Erkinnen, Michael G., Swett, Katherine E., Eagle, Michael W., Rizik-Baer, Daniel A., and Allen R. Braun "Neural Correlates of Lyrical Improvisation: An fMRI Study of Freestyle Rap," *Scientific Reports* 2 (2012): 834.

Luo, Mengyu, and Wei Ming, W. "From Underground to Mainstream and Then What? Empowerment and Censorship in China's Hip-Hop Music," *Critical Arts*, 34/6 (2020): 1–12.

Manabe, Noriko. "Representing Japan: 'national' Style among Japanese Hip-Hop DJs," *Popular Music* 32/1 (2013): 35–50.

McKinnon, Crystal. "Indigenous Music as a Space of Resistance," in T. Banivanua-Mar and P. Edmonds (eds.), *Making Settler Colonial Space: Perspectives on Race, Place and Identity* (New York: Palgrave Macmillan, 2010), 255–272.

Miszczyński, Miłosz, and Adriana Helbig (eds.), *Hip Hop at Europe's Edge: Music, Agency, and Social Change* (Bloomington, IN: Indiana University Press, 2017).

Molinero, Stéphanie. *Les publics du rap: Enquête sociologique* (Paris: L'Harmattan, 2009).

Morgan, Marcyliena, and Dionne Bennett. "Hip-Hop & the Global Imprint of a Black Cultural Form," *Daedalus*, 140/2 (2011): 176–196.

Morgan, George, and Andrew Warren. "Aboriginal Youth, Hip Hop and the Politics of Identification," *Ethnic and Racial Studies*, 34/6 (2011): 925–947.

Morrell, Ernest, and Jeffrey M. R. Duncan-Andrade, "Promoting Academic Literacy with Urban Youth through Engaging Hip-Hop Culture," *English Journal*, 91/6 (2002): 88–92.

Naukkarinen, Ossi. "Aesthetics of Popular Culture as Environmental Aesthetics," *Popular Inquiry* 1 (2017): 3–15.

Neff, Ali Colleen. "Digital, Underground: Black Aesthetics, Hip-Hop Digitalities, and Youth Creativity the Global South," in J. L. Oakes and J. D. Burton (eds.), *Oxford Handbook of Hip-Hop Studies* (New York: Oxford University Press, 2018), 1–28.

Negus, Keith. *Music Genres and Corporate Cultures* (London and New York: Routledge, 2013).

Niaah, Sonjah Stanley. *DanceHall: From Slave Ship to Ghetto*. Illustrated edition. (Ottawa: University of Ottawa Press, 2010).

Niederkrotenthaler, Thomas, Tran, Ulrich S., Gould, Madelyn, Sinyor, Mark, Sumner, Steven, Strauss, Markus J., Voracek, Martin, Till, Benedikt, Murphy, Sean, Gonzalez, Frances, Spittal, Matthew J., and Draper, John, "Association of Logic's Hip Hop Song '1-800-273-8255' with Lifeline Calls and Suicides in the United States: Interrupted Time Series Analysis," *British Medical Journal* 375 (2021): 8319.

Nielson, Erik, and Andrea Dennis. *Rap on Trial Race, Lyrics, and Guilt in America* (New York: New Press, 2019).

Nitzsche, Sina A., and Walter Grünzweig (eds.), *Hip-Hop in Europe: Cultural Identities and Transnational Flows* (Zürich, Lit Verlag, 2013).

Oddekalv, Kjell A. *What Makes the Shit Dope?* Doctoral dissertation, University of Oslo, 2022.

Ohriner, Mitchell. *Flow: The Rhythmic Voice in Rap Music* (New York: Oxford University Press, 2019).

Osumare, Halifu. "Beat Streets in the Global Hood: Connective Marginalities of the Hip Hop Globe," *Journal of American & Comparative Cultures* 24/1–2 (2001): 171–181.

Osumare, Halifu. *The Africanist Aesthetic in Global Hip-Hop: Power Moves* (New York: Palgrave MacMillan, 2007).

Pecqueux, Anthony. *Voix du rap. Essai de sociologie de l'action musicale* (Paris: L'Harmattan, 2007).

Perry, Imani. *Prophets of the Hood: Politics and Poetics in Hip Hop* (Durham, NC: Duke University Press, 2004).

Perullo, Alex. "Politics and Popular Song: Youth, Authority, and Popular Music in East Africa," *African Music* 9/1 (2011): 87–116.

Petchauer, Emery. "Starting with Style: Toward a Second Wave of Hip-Hop Education Research and Practice," *Urban Education* 50/1 (2015): 78–105.

Potter, Russell. *Spectacular Vernaculars: Hip-Hop and the Politics of Postmodernism* (Albany: State University of New York Press, 1995).

Powell, Elliot. *Sounds from the Other Side: Afro-South Asian Collaborations in Black Popular Music* (Minneapolis: University of Minnesota Press, 2020).

Quinn, Eithne. *Nuthin' but a "G" thang: The Culture and Commerce of Gangsta Rap* (New York: Columbia University Press, 2004).

Reynolds, Simon. "The Wire 300: Simon Reynolds on the Hardcore Continuum Series #6: Two-Step Garage (1999) – The Wire." *The Wire Magazine – Adventures in Modern Music*, www.thewire.co.uk/in-writing/essays/the-wire-300_simon-reynolds-on-the-hardcorecontinuum-series_6_two-step-garage_1999_.

Rivera, Raquel Z., Marshall, Wayne, and Deborah Pacini Hernandez. *Reggaeton* (Durham, NC: Duke University Press, 2009).

Rollefson, J. Griffith. *Flip the Script: European Hip Hop and the Politics of Postcoloniality* (Chicago: University of Chicago Press, 2017).

Rose, Tricia. *Black Noise: Rap Music and Black Culture in Contemporary America* (Hanover, NH: Wesleyan University Press, 1994).

Rose, Tricia. *The Hip Hop Wars: What We Talk about when We Talk about Hip Hop – and Why It Matters* (New York: Basic Books, 2008).

Ross, Andrew S., and Damian J. Rivers (eds.), *The Sociolinguistics of Hip-Hop as Critical Conscience: Dissatisfaction and Dissent* (Houndmills, UK: Palgrave Macmillan, 2018).

RSKY. 2008. *F**K Radio*. J Clarke Enterprise. DVD.

Ryynänen, Max. "Can the (Non-)Subaltern (Understand) Rap? Rap as Vernacular Critical Theory," *Journal of Asia-Pacific Pop Culture* 6/2 (2021): 213–229.

ya Salaam, Mtume. "The Aesthetics of Rap," *African American Review* 29/2 (1995): 303–315.

Santos, Jaqueline Lima. "Hip-Hop and the Reconfiguration of Blackness in Sao Paulo: The Influence of African American Political and Musical Movements in the Twentieth Century," *Social Identities* 22/2 (2016): 160–177.

Schischmanjan, Anjela, and Michaela Wuensch (eds.), *Female Hiphop: Realness, Roots and Rap Models* (Mainz: Ventil Verlag, 2007).

Schwarze, Tilman, and Lambros Fatsis. "Copping the Blame: The Role of YouTube Videos in the Criminalisation of UK Drill Music," *Popular Music* 41, no. 4 (2022).

Shusterman, Richard. *Pragmatist Aesthetics: Living Beauty, Rethinking Art* (London: Blackwell, 1992).

Shusterman, Richard. "Ghetto Music," *Journal of Rap* 2/1 (1992): 11–18.

Shusterman, Richard. "L'esthétique postmoderne du rap," *Rue Descartes* 5/6 (1992): 209–228.

Shusterman, Richard. "Rap Aesthetics: Violence and Keeping It Real," in Derrick Darby and Tommie Shelby (eds.), *Hip Hop and Philosophy* (Chicago: Open Court, 2008) pp. 53–64.

Smitherman, Geneva. "The Power of the Rap: The Black Idiom and the New Black Poetry," *Twentieth Century Literature*, 19/4 (Oct 1973): 259–274.

Singh, Jaspal Naveel. "Migration, Hip Hop and Translation Zones in Delhi," in Tong King Lee (ed.), *The Routledge Handbook of Translation and the City* (London: Routledge, 2021) pp. 308–25.

Singh, Jaspal Naveel. *Transcultural Voices: Narrating Hip Hop Culture in Complex Delhi* (Bristol: Multilingual Matters, 2022).

Singh, Jaspal Naveel. "Transcultural Decoloniality and the Study of Global Hip Hop Culture," in Solange Maria de Barros and Viviane Resende (eds.), *Latin*

American Thought in Discourse Studies: A Radical Critique of Coloniality (London: Routledge, 2023) pp. 136–154.

Sironen, Esa. "'Hip-hop don't stop': Katujen uutta kulttuuria," in Lauri Mehtonen and Esa Sironen (eds.), *Aistimellisuus, sivistys ja massakulttuuri: Fragmentteja eräästä projektista* (Jyväskylä: Jyväskylä University, 1987): 127–132.

Sonnette-Manouguian, Marie. "Des mises en scène du 'nous' contre le 'eux' dans le rap français," *Sociologie de l'Art* 1 (2015): 153–177.

Spady, James G., Alim, H. Samy, and Charles G. Lee. *Street Conscious Rap* (Philadelphia: Black History Museum Pub, 1999).

Sparks, Marvin. *Run the Riddim: The Untold Story of '90s Dancehall to the World* (London: No Long Stories, 2021).

Stuart, Forrest. *Ballad of the Bullet: Gangs, Drill Music and the Power of Online Infamy* (Princeton: Princeton University Press, 2020).

Sule, Akeem, and Becky Inkster. "Kendrick Lamar, Street Poet of Mental Health," *Lancet Psychiatry*, 2/6 (2015): 496–497.

Sule, Akeem, and Becky Inkster. "Eminem's Character, Stan: A Bio-Psycho-Social Autopsy," *Journal of Hip Hop Studies* 4/1 (2017): 43–49.

Sullivan, Jonathan, and Yupei Zhao. "Rappers as Knights-Errant: Classic Allusions in the Mainstreaming of Chinese Rap," *Popular Music and Society*, 44/3 (2021): 274–291.

Terkourafi, Marina. *The Languages of Global Hip Hop* (London: Continuum, 2010).

Toop, David. *The Rap Attack: African Jive to New York Hip Hop* (London: The Works, 1995).

Turner, Patrick. *Hip Hop versus Rap: The Politics of Droppin' Knowledge* (London: Routledge, 2017).

Viator, Felicia A. "West Coast Originals: A Case for Reassessing the 'Bronx West' Story of Black Youth Culture in 1980s Los Angeles," *American Studies* 58/3 (2019): 87–105.

Viega, Michael. "Exploring the Discourse in Hip Hop and Implications for Music Therapy Practice' Music Therapy Perspective," *Music Therapy Perspectives*, 34/2 (2015): 138–146.

Warren, Andrew, and Evitt, Rob. "Indigenous Hip-Hop: Overcoming Marginality, Encountering Constraints," *Australian Geographer*, 41/1 (2010): 141–158.

Watson, Mary R., and N. Anand. "Award Ceremony as an Arbiter of Commerce and Canon in the Popular Music Industry," *Popular Music* 25/1 (2006): 41–56.

Werner, Valentin. "Assessing Hip-Hop Discourse: Linguistic Realness and Styling," *Text & Talk*, 39/5 (2019): 671–698.

White, Joy. *Urban Music and Entrepreneurship: Beats, Rhymes and Young People's Enterprise* (London: Routledge, 2017).

Wiedemann, Felix. "The Local and the Global in Networks of Lebanese and Algerian Rappers," *Open Library of Humanities* 5/1 (2019): 1–40.

Williams, Justin (ed.). *The Cambridge Companion to Hip-Hop* (Cambridge University Press, 2015).

Wood, Brent. "Understanding Rap as Rhetorical Folk-Poetry," *Mosaic* 32/4 (1999): 129–146.

Zhang, Alexander. "Keep It 'Skr': The Incorporation of Hip-Hop Subculture through Chinese Talent Shows and the Online Battle for Authenticity," *Georgetown Journal of Asian Affairs*, 5 (2019): 73–93.

Zou, Sheng. "When Nationalism Meets Hip-Hop: Aestheticized Politics of Ideotainment in China," *Communication and Critical/Cultural Studies*, 16/3 (2019): 178–195.

Index

2Pac, 73, 78–82, 147, 153, 244
   'California love', 80
   'Death Around the Corner', 147
   'Pour out a little liquor', 244
   'To live & die in L.A.', 80
   Me against the world, 81
50 Cent, 1, 25, 43, 72
67, 572.1
9th Wonder, 65

A Tribe Called Quest, 51
   'Scenario', 39
   Beats, Rhymes and Life, 51
A.M.E.R.
   Pourquoi tant de haine?, 28
AAE. *See* African-American English
Ace Hood, 215
Aces International (sound system), 38
Advanced Chemistry, 213, 220
   'Fremd im eigenen Land', 213
   Linguist, 213
   Toni L, 213
   Torch, 213
aesthetics, 7, 8, 10, 31, 88–96, 100, 103, 107,
      115, 116, 117, 119, 122, 163, 253, 255, 274
   environmental, 96
   experience, 91
   material, 145
   phenomenology, 96
   violence, 95
African-American English, 72
Afrika Bambaataa, 17
AIR, 268
Al Rocco, 268
   'Differences', 268
Albania, 127
Algeria, 26, 31
Althea & Donna
   'Uptown Top Ranking', 43
Alton Ellis
   'I'm Still in Love', 43
Amiri Baraka, 89
Angel Haze, 150

'Cleaning Out My Closet', 150
Angola, 19
antiphony, 130, 182
Applied Hip Hop, 168–169
   Applied Australian hip hop, 173
   critical interpretive synthesis, 169
   narrative synthesis, 168
Arthur 'Duke' Reid, 35, 36
   Treasure Isle, 36
   Trojan, 35
aspirational labor, 228
   hope labor, 228
Assassin, 28
Australia
   Adelaide, 174
   Alice Springs, 170
   Queensland, 173
   Sydney, 170
Australian hip hop, 168
authenticity, 75, 79, 225–232, 261, 264, 270, 272

Baba Sehgal
   Thanda Thanda Paani (Cold Cold
      Water), 252
Bad Boy Records, 79
banlieue, 30, 33, 113, 114, 116, 120, 122
Barrington Levy, 136
   'Murderer', 136
   'Prison Oval Rock', 38
battle rap, 128, 182
BBC Asia, 255
b-boy, 253, 263
Beastie Boys, 22
beatboxing, 17, 50, 68
bedroom studio, 132, 253
Beenie Man, 129
Benin, 19
Bernard Zékri, 28
BET Awards, 1
Beyoncé, 217
Beyond the Road, 186, 188
b-girl, 253
Big Homie Doe, 229

Big L, 72
Biggie Smalls, 79, 136, *See* Notorious B.I.G
bio-politics, 53
BlaaZe, 252
Black Atlantic, 66, 110, 128, 248
Black Chiney (sound system), 45
Black Public Sphere, 128, 131
blackface, 22
Blondie, 23, 28
   'Rapture', 23, 24
Bob Marley, 36
Bobby Friction, 255
Bohemia, 252
bongo flava, 200, 201, 206, 209
Booba, 29
bounce
   New Orleans bounce, 129
Bounty Killer, 43
Brazil, 18, 19, 26
break, 18, 23, 37
breakbeats, 89, 91
breakdancing, 2, 17, 27, 153
British Council, 2
Brodha V, 251, 256
BrothaBlack, 170
Brothers Keepers, 220
Busta Rhymes, 1, 39, 128
   'Woo-Hah!!! Got You All In Check', 39

C1, 240
   'Hide n Seek', 242
caesura, 104, 105
California
   Bay Area, 79
   Los Angeles, 1, 12, 24, 79
   Oakland, 80
call and response, 57, *See* antiphony
calypso, 20
Campbell, Cindy, 18
Caper. *See* Col Darcy
capitalism, 24, 231, 232, 238, 241, 243
capping, 225
Cardi B, 217
Caribbean, 18, 19
censorship, 7, 10, 114, 128, 131, 132, 150, 186, 202, 203, 204, 261, 265, 267, 268
Chang, Jeff, 52
Charlie Chaplin, 40
chatting, 20, *See* toasting
Chemical (Claudia Lubao), 208
Chic
   'Good Times', 23, 43
Chicago, 159

Englewood, 227
Chief Keef, 227, 229, 231
China, 3, 11, 26, 273, 276
   Beijing, 262–263
   Chongqing, 264
   Hong Kong, 263, 264
   Shanghai, 263
   Xi'an, 264
   Xinjiang, 268
Chinese MC Brothers, 263
Chingy, 73
Chip, 135–136
Chipmunk. *See* Chip
Choice FM, 42
Christopher Small. *See* musicking
Chuck D, 88
Chunky Bizzle, 139
Ciaran Thapar, 186
cipher, 68, 136
citizens, 2, 114
citizenship, 119, 121
civil rights movement, 24
clash
   clashing, 34, 40, 42, 43, 128, 129
   indirecting, 135
   sends, 129
class, 9, 24, 35, 36, 96, 101, 102, 113, 114, 117, 118, 119, 120, 131, 165, 201, 211, 214, 225, 232, 233, 239, 242, 256
Clement 'Coxsone' Dodd, 35, 36
   Downbeat, 35, 36
   Studio One, 36
CMBC. *See* Chinese MC Brothers
code-switching, 254
Coke La Rock, 37
Col Darcy, 175
   Pursuit of Happiness, 175
Cold Crush Brothers, 37
colonial, 5, 8, 10, 92, 113, 162, 168, 173, 176, 212, 216, 220, 249, 250, 255, 258, 259
colonisation, 114, 171
Commander B, 42
commodification, 182, 264
coping, 189
cosmopolitan, 10, 255, 257
Count Machuki, 36, 37
Count Smith the Blues Blaster, 35
Count Suckle, 40
COVID-19, 174
Crazy Titch, 134, 236
criminalisation, 119, 120
   drill, 163
   rap as evidence, 161

cultural appropriation, 21, 22
cultural capital, 258

D Dark, 129
  'Lake Days', 129
D Double E, 132, 236
D.D Rhythm, 263
dakou, 262
Dana 'Showtyme' Burton, 263
dancehall, 1, 3, 4, 5, 6, 18, 35, 39, 41, 42, 44, 128, 129, 130, 131, 136, 141
dansi, 197, 206, 209
David Rodigan, 44
De La Soul, 55
  Stakes is High, 51
Death Row Records, 79
Debbie Harry, 23
decolonization, 251
Dee Nasty, DJ, 28
  Paname City Rappin, 28
deejay, 6, 18, 37, 38, 39, 40, 41, 43, 198, 200, 247
deejaying, 18, 36
Deja Vu FM, 134
denizens, 2
Destroy Man, 28
Devlin, 134, 138
Diam's, 29
diaspora, 26, 164, 220, 252
diasporic, 3, 20, 34, 89, 164, 237, 238, 240, 242, 245, 248
  Afrodiasporic, 128, 136, 211, 212, 216, 219, 220
DigDat, 241
  'Air Force', 241
digitalisation, 26
Dirty Heff, 263
disco, 18, 37, 43, 92, 93
discrimination, 30, 119, 121, 149, 198, 212, 213, 216
  gender, 201, 202
  racial, 21, 22, 257
Divine, 255
  'Mere Gully Mein' feat. Neazy, 255
  'Yeh Mera Bombay', 255
Dizzee Rascal, 4, 42, 134, 236
DJ Eastwood, 139
DJ Slimzee, 130
DJ Techniques, 138
  chopping, 138, 139
  cutting, 138
  punching, 139
DJ Unique, 133, 136–140
dJing, 2, 13, 17, 44, 60–61, 130, 138

Dola Soul, 197
dozens, the, 128, 182, 242
Dr Vades ft. Yxng Bane, Kojo Funds & Don Elito
  'Balenciaga', 44
Dr. Dre, 24, 44
Drake, 127
  More Life, 127
Drill music, 186, 188, 227, 243
  capping, 232, 233
  Chicago, 225–233
  code of the street, 227
  hyper-locality, 243
  hypermasculinity, 228
  UK Drill, 158, 186, 189, 190, 240–246
dubplate, 6, 41, 43, 132
Dudubaya, 207
Duke Reid, 40
Duke Vin, 40
Dully Sykes, 207
Dynamq, 44

Eastside Connect
  'Frisco Disco', 37
education, 206
  alternative literacies, 186
  colonial, 250
  edutainment, 181, 182
  hip hop, 181–191
  multicultural literacies, 183–186
  Roadworks, 186–190
edutainment, 187
electronic dance music, 45
Elephant Man, 129
emcee, 34, 72, 212, 213
emcee culture, 3, 6, 26, 34, 111
emceeing. *See* toasting
Eminem, 22, 72, 128, 147
  'Stan', 147
  'The way I am', 72
Emo-Rap, 150
enjambment, 102, 105
Enkore, 254
equality, 24, 30, 114, 119, 121
Eric B. & Rakim, 52
  Follow the Leader, 52
Eskimo Dance, 129

F**k Radio, 140
Fab Five Freddy, 23, 27, 28
Fab Five Freddy/ Beside
  'Change the Beat', 28
fascist, 218

Fat Shady, 263
  'Not Going to Work Tomorrow', 264
FBG Duck, 231
femininity, 215, 228
Fid Q, 202
First Nations hip hop, 170, 171, 173
Flinty Badman, 40
flow, 12, 52, 56, 57, 64, 75, 76, 77, 78, 80, 81, 82, 94, 96, 130, 135, 136, 140, 243, 266
  flow maps, 61, 63
  flow studies, 61, 62, 67
  jianghu flow, 265
flow studies, 60
Form 696, 131
France, 4, 6, 7, 10, 17, 22, 26, 27, 28, 29, 30, 31, 33, 113, 114, 115, 116, 117, 118, 119, 121
  François Grosdidier, 120
  Gérard Colomb, Minister of the Interior, 121
  Laurent Wauquiez, 121
  Marine Le Pen, 121
  Nicolas Sarkozy, 29
  Paris, 4, 27, 113
freedom of speech, 203, 204
freestyle cyphers, 253
freestyle rapping, 41, 151
French rap, 6, 28, 29, 30, 31, 113, 114, 115, 116, 118, 121
Fruity Loops, 132
Fugees, 41
  'Fu-Gee-La', 41
  'Killing Me Softly', 41
functional magnetic resonance imaging (fMRI), 151
funk, 18, 23, 37, 90, 93, 117

G Herbo, 227
G'nie, 257
GAI, 264, 267
galalas, 91
gangs, 25, 79, 113, 161, 187, 189, 214, 225, 229
  affiliation, 228
  association, 161
  experts, 161
  injunctions, 161
  narratives, 227
gangsta rap, 24, 25, 96, 161, 222, 278
Gangwe Mobb, 207
garage, 4, 26, 34, 41, 42, 129, 130, 131, 279
Gemini (sound system), 38
General Levy, 39
Genius
  Rap Genius, 74
George, Nelson, 52

Germany
  Bavaria, 219
  Chemnitz, 219
  Heidelberg, 213
Ghana, 19
Ghetto. *See* Ghetts
Ghetts, 128, 133, 134, 137, 138, 139, 140, 141
  Conflict of Interest, 141
  Ghetto Gospel, 134
Giggs, 44
  'Talking the Hardest', 44
Gil-Scott Heron, 89
globalisation, 20, 23, 26, 249, 251, 258
glocalization, 74, 261
GO$H, 264
graffiti, 2, 17, 23, 170, 253
Grammy Awards, 200, 209
Grandmaster Caz, 23
Grandmaster Flash, 37, 89, 185
Grandmaster Flash and the Furious Five, 24
  'The Message', 24, 185
Greg Tate, 50
grime, 4, 11, 13, 26, 34, 42, 43, 45, 111, 127, 189, 239, 274
  8-bar, 138
Griminal, 136, 137, 139, 140, 141
griot, 20, 21, 31, 33, 53, 61, 91, 144, 183
GRM Daily, 237
Gully Boy, 255

Hard Kaur, 252
hardcore continuum, 131
Harlem Renaissance, 94
Harlem Spartans, 240
healthcare, 203
Heartless Crew, 42, 130
  Bushkin, 42
Heavy D, 39, 40
hegemony, 89, 215, 257
HHNL. *See* Hip Hop Nation Language
Hi-Bomb, 263
Hip Hop Lives (I Come Back), 20
Hip Hop Nation Language, 13, 74, 82
  HHNL, 74
Hip Hop Psych, 146, 147, 151
  the biopsychosocial model, 146
hip-hop studies, 4, 12, 21, 49, 88, 89, 94, 96, 228
Hip-Hopera, 170
Hiphopographic. *See* hiphopography
hiphopography, 55
homophobia, 24, 25
housing, 203, 205
human rights, 202, 203

IAM
  De la planète Mars, 28
Ice T, 24
identification, 21, 101, 118, 172, 190, 268, 270
Incredible Bongo Band
  'Apache', 37
indentured labour, 19
India, 3
  Bengaluru, 251, 253
  Chennai, 254
  Darjeeling, 254
  Delhi, 251, 252, 253, 254, 259, 274, 279
  Goa, 255
  Kashmir, 255
  Kerala, 254
  Kolkata, 254
  Mizoram, 254, 257
  Mumbai, 253, 254, 255, 256
  Odisha, 257
  Punjab, 255
  Shillong, 254
indigeneity, 171
intermusical, 136, 138
intertextuality, 135
Iran, 262
I-Roy, 40
Isaac Hayes, 89
IshQ Bector, 252
Izzo Bizness, 202
  'Riz One', 202

J Dilla
  Dilla Time, 61
J Hus
  'Vacation', 44
Jamaica, 34, 35, 37–40, 129
  Kingston, 6, 18, 35, 36, 37, 38
James Brown, 37, 89
Jammer, 129
Jammz, 129
  'French Montana Riddim', 129
Japan, 60
Java (sound system), 40
Jay 'Beats' Weston, 168
Jay Z, 25
jazz, 19, 20, 35, 92, 93, 197
Jerry 'Wonda' Duplessis, 41
Jesse Bernard, 134
Jhony Go, 28
jive talking, 36
JME, 138
Joan Morgan, 50
Joh Makini, 207

John Holt, 36
Johnny Osbourne, 38
joint enterprise, 161
Jono 'Eskatology' Stier, 175
Josey Wales, 40
Juice WRLD, 150
jungle, 26, 39, 42, 129, 130, 237, 239, 242, 243, 245, 248

Kano, 129, 132
Kanye West, 153
  'Donda', 153
Kendrick Lamar, 146
  'Swimming Pools', 146
Keny Arkana, 29
Kery James, 29
Key Changes, 152
Kid Creole, 37
Kid Cudi, 149
King Edwards, 35
King Louie, 229
King Stitt, 36, 37
King Von, 227, 231
Kool Herc, 1, 6, 18, 23, 37, 40
  Herculords, 37
Kr$na, 254
Kraftklub, 220
KRS-One, 1, 20, 39, 145

La Rumeur, 29
Lady Leshurr, 239
Lao Zheng XIV, 263
Lauryn Hill, 25
Lee 'Scratch' Perry, 36
Li Xiaolong, 263
Lieutenant Stitchie, 39
Lil Nasty, 135, 136
Lil Peep, 150
Lil Uzi Vert, 150
Lil Wayne, 72
Lil' Durk, 227
LIL-EM, 268, 269
  'Real Man', 269
linguistic anthropology, 73
Link Up TV, 237
Lionel D, 28
Lisa 'Left Eye' Lopes, 67
Lloydie Coxsone
  Sir Coxsone Outernational Sound System, 38, 40
localisation, 20, 26, 251
Logan Sama, 132
Logic, 150

'1-800-273-8255', 150
London, 159
    Brixton, 186
    Newham, 137
London Posse, 39, 187
    How's Life in London, 187
Lord of the Mics, 129
Loski, 242
lyrical
    rap as component of hip hop, 17

M24, 244
    'We Don't Dance', 244
Mac Miller, 150
    'Self-Care', 150
Mafia Mundeer, 252
Maino, 148–149
Major Ace, 130
Major Lazer, 44
    'Lean On', 44
Manmeet Kaur, 255
Marcia Griffiths, 36
marginalisation, 27, 30, 118, 222
Markus
    'Ich will Spass', 214
Marshall, Wayne, 64
masculinity, 11, 213, 228, 234, 269
Mavado
    'Messiah', 44
Maxi Priest
    'Close to You', 39
Maxwell D, 130, 236
MC. *See* emcee
MC DET, 130
MC Morganics, 170
MC New York. *See* 2Pac
MC Social Change, 176
MC Solaar
    Qui sème le vent récolte le tempo, 28
MC Webber, 263
media ecologies, 240
Megaloh, 220
Meghan Thee Stallion, 217
Melle Mel, 24, 37
mental health, 107, 108, 144–154, 241, 280
    language disturbances, 152
Mercury Music Prize, 39
Merky Ace, 129
merry-go-round, 37
metre, 102
Mic Controller. *See* emcee
MicMaster Aeke, 254

Mighty Crown (sound system), 44
migration, 213, 222, 253
misogyny, 24, 159, 213, 220, 228, 253
Missy Elliott, 25, 96
M-Net Grammy Awards, 197, 209
modernity, 90, 122, 249, 251
moral panic, 114, 120, 181, 182
Morgan, Joan, 52
Morocco, 26
Moscow 17, 240
    'Moscow March', 242
Mr. II, 197, 199, 204, 208
multicultural, 17, 19, 21, 23, 181, 183, 184, 190, 219, 220
Munkimuk, 170
music economy, 197, 200, 208
music video, 2
musicking, 49, 131
Mwana Fa (Hamis Mwinjuma MP), 203
myth, 21

N.A.S.T.Y Crew, 132, 134
N.W.A., 24, 220
    'Fuck Tha Police', 24
    'Straight Outta Compton', 24
Nadia Rose, 239
Naezy, 255
Namika, 211
Nas, 25, 255
nationalism, 10, 211, 217, 220, 269
nationalist, 220
Nederhop, 75
neighbourhood nationalism, 137
Nelly, 73
neuroscience, 151–154
New Orleans, 91
New York, 23, 27
    Bronx, 18, 20, 89, 90, 144
    Harlem, 91
    Long Island, 24
    Manhattan, 79
    South Bronx, 54
New York City, 17
Nicki Minaj, 217
Nigeria, 19, 91
Ninja Man, 40
No Lay, 239
No Wave, 23
notation, 57–59
Notorious B.I.G., 25, 39
NTM
    Authenthik, 28

OGz. *See* P Money
Olexesh, 215
Olivier Cachin, 27
One Blood Hidden Image, 171
One Love (sound system), 44
ontology, 183
oral, 2, 3, 5, 7, 100, 102, 103, 111
   -poetic, 8, 100, 102, 111
   poetry, 90
orality
   black oral tradition, 182
Orelsan, 29
origins
   national (as proxy for race), 118
   of *dansi*, 197
   of grime, 128
   of hip hop, 2, 144, 169, 183, 190
   of hip hop therapy, 145
   of rap, 17
   of soundsystem, 18
othering, 114, 119, 212, 213, 220
otherness, 114, 243
Oxide and Neutrino
   'Bound 4 Da Reload', 41

P Funk (Paul Matthysse), 197
P Money, 129
Papa Levi
   'Mi God, Mi King', 39
Papa San, 39
Papageno effect. *See* Logic
Paragons
   'On the Beach', 43
patriarchal, 10, 213, 232, 255
Pay As U Go, 42, 130
   'Know We', 130
   Major Ace, 42
pedagogy
   critical, 183, 186
   hip hop, 169, 185
Peeda Pan, 229
People's Choice(sound system), 40
performative, 22, 158, 159, 213
persona, 25, 107, 108
Peter Kind, 130
Peter Metro, 39
PG One, 264, 267
phonology, 72, 73, 75, 77, 182
   West Coast -vs- East Coast, 73
Pigmeat Markham, 89
Pinchers, 39
pirate radio, 26, 41, 128, 131, 132, 237, 239, 242
   Deja Vu FM, 132, 236

Delight FM, 41
Rinse FM, 130, 132
Supreme FM, 41
pleasure, 100, 101, 107, 111
poetic, 100, 102, 105, 108
poetry, 7, 17, 100, 102, 104, 105, 106, 197, 206
Polo G, 227
popular music studies, 50, 56, 61
Post-Traumatic Stress Disorder, 147–148
postcolonial, 7, 30, 60, 115, 118, 211, 238
Prince Buster, 35, 36
   Voice of the People (sound system), 35, 36
Prince Jazzbo, 40
Professor Green, 239
Professor Jay (Joseph Haule MP), 203
Psy 4 de la Rime, 29
psychosis, 147
PTSD. *See* Post-Traumatic Stress Disorder
Public Enemy, 24, 53, 56–60, 88, 220, 262
   'Bring the Noise', 24
   'Fight the Power', 24, 57, 262
public health, 149–151

Queen Latifah, 25

racaille, 118, 120, 121, 274
racialisation, 113, 114, 117, 118, 120, 158, 258
racism, 6, 25, 30, 114, 119, 121, 211, 212, 213, 218, 219, 220
radio, 2, 6, 27, 28, 29, 34, 36, 37, 43, 115, 116, 123, 128, 132, 160, 197, 198, 199, 200, 203, 205, 239, 255
   BBC Radio 1Xtra, 40
   Channel M6, 28
   Clouds FM, 198
   Radio France, 27
   Radio Libre 7, 27
   Radio Nova, 29
   Radio Uhuru, 198
   Red FM, 255
   Skyrock, 29
Raftaar, 256
ragga, 114
raï, 31
Rakim, 17, 52
Rapattitude, 28, 113
Rapcha, 205, 208
raptivists. *See* edutainment
reality rap, 24
recording industry, 3, 10, 21, 23, 34, 43, 114–117
reggae, 5, 38, 39, 41, 42, 44, 130, 144, 182, 209, 237, 242, 243

reggaeton, 5, 45, 65, 114
relational labor, 225, 232, 233
resistance vernacular, 54
Reveal, 186
rhizome, 3
rhyme, 17, 20, 37, 52, 60, 61, 62, 63, 72, 91, 100, 104, 107, 108, 109, 130, 134, 158, 163, 170, 175, 256, 266
rhythm, 17, 18, 19, 27, 43, 58, 61, 62, 75, 76, 77, 86, 90, 92, 95, 96, 103, 110, 138, 139, 165, 182, 197, 241, 245, 266
rhythm & blues, 23, 35, 42, 114, 115, 198, 200
Rhythm Division, 131
Rick Ross, 215
Rico Rodriguez, 38
riddim, 6, 34, 38, 40, 41, 43–44
Risky Roadz, 133
RJ Malishka, 255
Roberta Flack, 41
Roll Deep, 42
Roma Mkatoliki, 207
Roots Manuva, 7, 39, 100–111
    'A Haunting', 107
    'A Haunting', 102, 103, 106, 110
    'Awfully Deep', 106
    'Colossal Insight', 109, 110
    Awfully Deep, 102, 106, 108, 109, 110
Rosa Ree (Rosary Robert Iwole), 201
rumba, 31
Rupie Edwards
    Yamaha Skank, 43
Russia, 262

Sabrina Setlur, 211
Salaam Remi, 41
Salt-N-Pepa, 25
Sanskrit, 89
Saxon Sound International, 38, 40
    Asher Senator, 39
    Dennis Rowe, 38
    Lloyd 'Musclehead' Francis, 38
    Maxi Priest, 39
    Papa Levi, 39
    Smiley Culture, 39
    Tippa Irie, 39
Sbazzo, 263
SBTV, 237
scat, 20
Schooly D, 24
Scientist, 131
Sean 'Puffy' Combs, 39
selector, 18, 38, 131

semantic, 102, 103, 104, 105, 106, 108, 218
semiotic, 102, 103, 104, 105, 106, 108
Senegal, 20, 56
sexism, 211, 213
sexualisation, 213, 216, 217, 220
Shabba D, 130
Sharky Major, 132, 236
Sha-Rock, 89
show and prove, 66
Sidney Duteil, 27
signifying, 91, 136, 182, 211
Sinik, 29
Skengdo x AM, 242
Skepta, 127, 129, 132
    'DTI', 132
    'Stageshow Riddim', 129
Skibadee, 39, 130
SL, 240
Smif-N-Wessun, 39
Smiley Culture, 130
    'Cockney Translation', 39
Sniper, 29
Snoop Dogg, 11, 25
So Solid Crew, 42, 130
    '21 Seconds', 130
    Asher D, 42
social conservatism, 20
social media, 2, 225
    digital clout, 225
Sociolinguistics, 73–75
Sophie Bramly, 28
SOS Racisme, 120
soul, 18, 90, 93, 117
Sound Connections, 186
sound studies, 50, 53, 54, 57, 68
sound system, 6, 18, 54, 128, 131, 237, 243
South Korea, 26
Spady, James G. *See* 'hiphopography'
Spoke, 151
Stat Quo
    'Here We Go', 44
Stereo Mars (sound system), 38
Stevie Hyper D, 130
stigma, 113, 120, 149, 151, 156
stigmatisation, 121, 186
Sting, 129
Stone Love (sound system), 41
Stormzy, 127, 237
Sugarhill Gang, 23
    'Rapper's Delight', 23, 43
Sumeet Samos, 256, 257
Summer Cem, 215

Super Cat, 39, 40
  'Dem No Worry We' (featuring Heavy D), 40
  'Dolly My Baby', 39
Suprême NTM, 120
Swahili, 197
Swarvo, 129
Sweetie Irie, 130
SXTN
  'Ich bin Schwarz', 211
  Asozialisierungsprogramm, 211
  Juju, 211
  Nura, 211

taarab, 197, 198, 206, 209
Taiwan, 263, 264
Tanzania, 3, 10, 127, 199
  Dar es Salaam, 197, 199, 208
  Mohamed Mchengerwa (Minister of Culture, Arts and Sport), 208
  President John Magufuli, 204, 205, 208
  President Samia Suluhu Hassan, 205, 208, 209
Tanzanian Music Awards, 206
Tate, Greg, 52
television, 2, 3, 11, 27, 28, 116, 197, 199, 261–262
  Channel U, 239
  H.I.P.-H.O.P., 27
  MTV, 24, 239
  MTV Base, 239
  online, 261
  Yo MTV Raps!, 11
terrorism, 121, 204, 247
The Movement, 134
  Tempo Specialists, 134
The Rap of China, 261–262
The Skatalites, 36, 38
The Whole Darn Band
  '7 Minutes of Funk', 37
therapy, 168, 176
  hip hop, 145, 146, 175
  music, 145, 152, 169
  rap therapy, 145
Third World
  'Now That We Found Love', 40
Tic Tac Toe, 211, 215
Timbaland, 129
Time Unit Box System (TUBS), 62
Timide Sans Complexe, 28
Tinchy Stryder, 129, 236
Tippa Irie, 39, 40, 130
toasting, 6, 20, 34, 37, 40, 89, 182

Togo, 19
Tokyo, 23
Tom 'the Great Sebastian' Wong, 35
Tones and Break Indexes (TOBI), 77
Tony Blair, 236
Toots and the Maytals, 36
Torres Strait Islander, 171
transatlantic slave trade, 18
translocal, 3, 258, 262
transnational, 3, 21, 31, 121, 211, 249, 252, 253
  hip-hop nation, 136
transnationalism, 212
Trinity
  'Three Piece Suit', 43
Troy 'A Plus' Miller
  Conflict DVD, 134, 236
Tupac Shakur, 25, *See* 2Pac
TwoShadez
  Slyck, 254
  Zan, 254

UK Drill, 11
Uniques
  'My Conversation', 43
  Jimmy Riley, 43
United Kingdom, 4, 6, 7, 8, 10, 26, 38–39, 40–43, 45, 100, 127, 130, 251, 252
United States, 1, 2, 3, 5, 6, 9, 10, 11, 18, 19, 20, 21, 22, 23, 26, 27, 31, 34, 37–38, 39, 73, 91, 100, 114, 115, 181, 204, 209, 217, 219, 251, 252
  constructions of race, 212
  popular culture, 215
Unity (sound system), 38, 40
U-Roy, 6, 36, 89
  'Rule the Nation', 36
  'Wake the Town', 36
  'Wear You to the Ball', 36
  Version Galore, 36
US State Department, 2
Uyghur rap, 268

value, 118, 190
  aesthetic, 100
  auditory experience, 52
  commercial, 269
  educational, 94
  evidential/probative, 162
  humanistic, 186
  instrumental, 190
  judgement, 181
  literary, 7, 101, 102, 105
  pedagogic, 190

political, 238
self-expression, 176
therapeutic, 176, 190
white racial frame, 59
values, 8, 11, 120, 200, 207, 209, 238, 253, 262, 266
Vanilla Ice, 22
'Ice Ice Baby', 22, 252
Vibe Magazine, 81
vinyl records, 36, 37, 42, 96, 140, 141, 237, 239
violence, 9, 12, 24, 25, 30, 113, 120, 145, 148, 159, 160, 163, 184, 187, 189, 213, 218, 227, 232, 241, 242, 243
   as marketing tool, 228
   crime, 158
   domestic, 4
   flashbacks, 148
   normalisation, 189
   police, 215
   racialised, 220
   racism, 171
   societal, 245
   state, 240
   threat, 159
Volcano (sound system), 38, 40
Vybz Kartel, 129
   'Touch a Button', 44

Wanaume Family, 207
Wassifa (sound system), 38
wellbeing, 168
Werther Effect, 150
West Coast -vs- East Coast, 76–78
white racial frame, 62
Wiley, 4, 42, 43, 130, 236
William S. Burroughs, 89
Wire MC, 170
World Health Organisation, 145
   WHO Advisory Group, 145
Wu-Tang Clan
   'Wu Gambinos', 62
Wyclef Jean, 41

xiha, 261, 267

Yellowman, 38, 39
Yin T'sang, 263
Yo Yo Honey Singh, 252
Young Lunya, 208
Youssoupha, 29

Zone 2, 242
Zoya Akhtar, 255

For EU product safety concerns, contact us at Calle de José Abascal, 56–1°, 28003 Madrid, Spain or eugpsr@cambridge.org.

www.ingramcontent.com/pod-product-compliance
Ingram Content Group UK Ltd.
Pitfield, Milton Keynes, MK11 3LW, UK
UKHW050108230326
469255UK00020B/448